THE ROUTLEDGE COMPANION
TO POSTMODERNISM

Third edition

Edited by
Stuart Sim

Routledge
Taylor & Francis Group

LONDON AND NEW YORK

First published in the United Kingdom 1998 by Icon Books Ltd
as *The Icon Critical Dictionary of Postmodern Thought*

First published in the United States of America 1999 by Routledge
as *The Critical Dictionary of Postmodern Thought*

Reissued 2001 by Routledge
as *The Routledge Companion to Postmodernism*

Second edition published 2005
by Routledge

Third edition published 2011
by Routledge
2 Park Square, Milton Park, Abingdon, Oxon OX14 4RN

Simultaneously published in the USA and Canada
by Routledge
711 Third Avenue, New York, NY 10017

Routledge is an imprint of the Taylor & Francis Group, an informa business

British Library Cataloguing in Publication Data
A catalogue record for this book is available from the British Library

Library of Congress Cataloging in Publication Data
The Routledge companion to postmodernism / edited by Stuart Sim.—3rd ed.
p. cm.—(Routledge companion series)
Includes bibliographical references and index.
Previous ed.: 2005.
1. Postmodernism. I. Sim, Stuart.
B831.2.R6795 2011
149'.97—dc22
2010052483

ISBN: 978–0–415–58330–5 (hbk)
ISBN: 978–0–415–58332–9 (pbk)
ISBN: 978–0–203–81320–1 (ebk)

Typeset in Times New Roman
by Book Now Ltd, London

MIX
Paper from
responsible sources
FSC
www.fsc.org   FSC® C004839

Printed and bound in Great Britain by
TJ International Ltd, Padstow, Cornwall

CONTENTS

CONTENTS

PREFACE TO THE
THIRD EDITION

THE MODERN, THE POSTMODERN
AND THE POST-POSTMODERN

It is a cliché by now to say that we live in a postmodern world, and indeed 'post-modern' has become one of the most used, and abused, words in the language. Yet it is striking that few people can say with any sense of assurance what that term 'postmodern' actually means or involves. Some theorists have suggested that it is as much a mood or attitude of mind as anything else, but they do seem to be agreed that it is widely in evidence – even if there is also a school of thought which claims that its moment has now passed. Such negative voices as Alan Kirby notwithstanding ('postmodernism ... is dead and buried'),[1] *The Routledge Companion to Postmodernism* is designed to outline what the phenomenon is, where to find it and why it is still culturally very significant.

In a general sense, postmodernism is to be regarded as a rejection of many, if not most, of the cultural certainties on which life in the West has been structured over the past couple of centuries. It has called into question our commitment to cultural 'progress' (that national economies must continue to grow, that the quality of life must keep improving indefinitely, etc.), as well as the political systems that have underpinned this belief. Postmodernists often refer to the 'Enlightenment project', meaning the liberal humanist ideology that has come to dominate Western culture since the eighteenth century: an ideology that has striven to bring about the emancipation of mankind from economic want and political oppression. In the view of postmodernists this project, laudable though it may have been at one time, has in its turn come to oppress humankind, and to force it into certain set ways of thought and action not always in its best interests. It is therefore to be resisted, and postmodernists are invariably critical of universalizing theories ('grand narratives' as the philosopher Jean-François Lyotard termed them),[2] as well as being anti-authoritarian in their outlook. To move from the modern to the postmodern is to embrace scepticism about what our culture stands for and strives for.

Since the first edition of this work was published in 1998, the cultural context in which postmodernism operates has changed quite dramatically. The events of 9/11 demonstrate that grand narratives can reinvent themselves, and the grand narrative of religious fundamentalism is now an acknowledged threat to global peace. One could argue that this is a phenomenon which undermines many of the claims of postmodernism, revealing these to be over-optimistic as to the extent of the cultural change that has occurred in recent times; equally, one could see it as evidence of why we need postmodernism to combat this essentially regressive tendency. The remainder of this introduction will look at postmodernism in a wider historical context, including recent challenges to its ethos, to argue that what postmodernism represents is still valuable and that it is more than just a brief historical episode of late twentieth-century culture that has now exhausted its cultural role. The postmodern is still with us in the twenty-first century: a positive aspect of our culture that deserves our support. We set out, therefore, to define and defend the postmodern.

A BRIEF HISTORY OF A CONCEPT

The first recorded use of the word 'postmodern' is back in the 1870s, and although it proceeds to crop up periodically over the next few decades, sometimes with positive, sometimes with negative connotations, it is only in the latter half of the twentieth century that it comes to take on the precise meaning of a reaction against modernism and modernity. We can run through some of those usages briefly to see how the concept arrives at its current form.

In the 1870s the English painter John Watkins Chapman suggested that any art going beyond Impressionism, the revolutionary new art style of the period, would be definable as 'postmodern painting'.[3] By 1917 'postmodern' was the term chosen by the author Rudolf Pannwitz to describe the new form of militaristic and anti-humanist culture developing in a Europe ravaged by war.[4] In the 1920s and 1930s the term had more positive overtones in the work of the American theologian Bernard Iddings Bell, for whom a postmodernist was someone who had turned his back on the secular modern world and embraced religious faith instead.[5] Bell is certainly anti-modernist, but not in the sense of the postmodernists of our own day. The eminent historian Arnold Toynbee returned to the pessimistic application, when in *A Study of History* he spoke of the period from 1875 onwards as the 'post-Modern Age of Western history';[6] an age marked by cultural decline as evidenced in its two 'world' wars. A postmodern world was an altogether less secure and inviting place to live in than the modern one (1475–1875) it had replaced. Eventually, 'postmodern' begins to take on the meaning of 'ultra-modern', with the architectural theorist Joseph Hudnut deploying it in that fashion to describe the new prefabricated buildings being produced in the aftermath of the Second World War.[7] Hudnut's postmodern man was unsentimental, and looked to science to improve the quality of his life.

It has proved to be in the discipline of architecture that postmodernism has taken root most firmly as a conceptual term. The architectural theorist Charles Jencks has done more than anyone to popularize postmodernism as a theoretical concept, particularly in the series of editions of his best-known book *The Language of Post-modern Architecture* (first edition, 1977). Jencks was highly critical of modern architecture, which he thought had lost touch with the general public. It was the so-called 'International Style', with its severe tower blocks constructed of concrete and glass, all straight lines and lacking in ornamentation, with which Jencks particularly took issue. As the name indicated, this had come to dominate architectural practice worldwide, with nearly all large cities featuring at least some buildings in that style. Jencks famously claimed that when one of the most representative examples of the style, the award-winning Pruitt-Igoe housing complex in St Louis, Missouri, was demolished in 1972, modern architecture died.[8] Pruitt-Igoe had proved a failure, declining into a vandalized shell of its former self in barely 20 years. For Jencks, that was a deeply symbolic history, the clear message being that the public had rejected the modernist creed encoded in a scheme like Pruitt-Igoe. Henceforth, architects were warned to come up with buildings in which the public would feel comfortable rather than alienated; in other words, buildings that could be described as 'double-coded':[9] able to appeal to both professional architects and the general public. The trend towards eclecticism in architecture, with old and new styles being freely mixed, was given its greatest boost by Jencks, and its products can now be found in most major cities (ironically enough, it has the makings of a new 'International Style' in this respect, if a less programmatic one than the previous).

Although architecture is arguably the area in which postmodernism first became a cause as such, the reaction to modernity and modernism has been widespread, expressing itself in a variety of ways. An ecology movement developed over the later twentieth century, concerned at the effect of technological progress on the environment. 'Green' political parties were formed in many Western European countries in consequence. Creative artists began to rebel against the strictures of the modernist style, which demanded, for example, abstraction in art and dissonant non-tonal composition in music. Many creative artists reverted to older styles that audiences felt more comfortable with, rather as Charles Jencks was calling on architects to do in their field. Philosophers and cultural theorists reacted against theories such as structuralism, which reduced the world to a series of interlinked systems with their own internal dynamic, or 'deep structure'. The workings of the entire world could, it was thought, be mapped out in terms of these deep structures, which dictated how all systems operated. One unfortunate consequence of the theory was that it seemed to deny the existence of free will; as Roland Barthes famously remarked of language, it spoke through human beings, suggesting that we were no more than channels for the actions of mysterious external forces.[10] Structuralism's dominance in mid-century intellectual enquiry (particularly in France) led to a reaction, collectively called poststructuralism, which increasingly came to challenge the assumptions on which structuralist analysis rested. Whereas structuralists emphasized similarity and inter-connectedness, poststructuralists emphasized difference and open-endedness. Structuralism was a universalizing theory, whereas poststructuralists spent their time demonstrating how such theories must always fail: the battle lines were drawn.

For our purposes here, postmodernism will be taken to encompass figures and debates within poststructuralism as well. Poststructuralism is a term that refers to a wide range of responses to the structuralist paradigm – responses such as the philosophically orientated 'deconstruction' of Jacques Derrida, the various 'archaeological' and 'genealogical' enquiries into cultural history of Michel Foucault, and the 'difference feminism' of such theorists as Luce Irigaray.[11] Poststructuralism has been an influential part of the cultural scene since the 1960s, but nowadays it can be seen to be part of a more general reaction to authoritarian ideologies and political systems that we define as postmodernism. We might say that postmodernism subsumes poststructuralism, and we shall proceed on that basis in this volume.

FROM POSTMODERNISM TO REACTION

Postmodernism is therefore a principled reaction to modernism and modernity, and what are regarded as their social and political failings, but since this book was first published it has become apparent that there can be large-scale reactions in turn against the postmodern ethos. Religious fundamentalism is only the most obvious example of a grand narrative reasserting itself in the face of what it considers to be unacceptable cultural trends, this time the drift towards moral relativism. A host of other grand narratives can also be instanced as in a process of reassertion: market fundamentalism, eco-fundamentalism, various kinds of political and nationalistic fundamentalism, to name the most prominent. I talk about these and others in my book *Fundamentalist World: The New Dark Age of Dogma*,[12] but it is worth running through some of them briefly here to discover what they can tell us about the current state of postmodernism as a cultural movement.

Postmodern theorists like to claim that we have crossed a watershed into a new world order where institutional authority no longer commands automatic respect, but it is clear that not just modernity but pre-modernity is fighting back and that grand narratives can still speak meaningfully to large sections of the world's population. Islamic fundamentalism is a very significant global force, seemingly able to claim the support, whether tacit or overt, of a majority of Muslim communities in its struggle against Western cultural imperialism. Several Islamic states, or in some cases provinces of these states, have reverted in recent years to shariah law, where the Q'ran is used as the foundation for the legal and political systems. Adherence to shariah law turns nation-states into theocracies, in which religious doctrine controls all aspects of human existence. Grand narrative in such cases is embraced with an enthusiasm which the postmodernist will find deeply disturbing. Institutional authority is once again accepted unquestioningly, obeyed blindly and allowed to direct the individual's life in the name of a larger cause. Faith, rather than reason or scepticism, becomes the basis of the cultural process. In its more extreme form – as with the Taliban regime in Afghanistan – Islamic fundamentalism is effectively a return to a pre-modern society, where almost all the modern world is rejected (with the significant exception of its weaponry).

Christian fundamentalism has been no less active of late, as witness the infiltration of the Republican Party in America by the Christian Right. Activists have led campaigns at local, state and national level to curb liberalizing legislation in areas such as sexual behaviour and abortion. Any move towards cultural relativism is bitterly opposed: conformity not difference is the ideal sought instead. Christian fundamentalism also has interesting, and more than somewhat bizarre, links with Zionist fundamentalism, since its theories of the Millennium demand a strong Jewish presence in the Holy Land (as was), in order for their conversion to be achieved – the conversion of the Jews being one of the critical signs of the imminence of the Second Coming. Zionist fundamentalists are happy to go along with this notion, as it fits in with their own desire to recreate Israel as it was in biblical times, the land of God's 'chosen people' (Palestinians excluded, of course). The close political links between America and Israel owe at least something to the successful lobbying by the Christian Right among high-ranking Republican politicians. The grand narrative of the Bible is held to provide all the information we need for the unfolding of human history. Cultural relativism is nowhere to be found on the agenda.

In the economic realm market fundamentalism is the current paradigm, and to its adherents it is a matter of blind faith, too. The term 'market fundamentalism' was coined by the international financier George Soros to describe the unrestricted, unregulated laissez-faire capitalism favoured by the International Monetary Fund (IMF) and the World Bank.[13] These institutions tend to impose this model on failing economies around the globe, sometimes, as in the case of Argentina, with quite disastrous results. Market fundamentalism demands the dismantling of the state sector (encouraging privatization programmes for all state-owned industries), low interest rates and an open market for capital. When Argentina followed such prescriptions in the 1990s, as directed, it led to the collapse of the currency and banking system; but to the IMF and the World Bank the needs of the market came first. Once more, faith was to be placed in the grand narrative at the expense of its impact on individuals. The market was to be regarded as an authority which could not be called into question. Even the recent credit crisis has not dented the faith placed by such institutions, and most Western governments, in the principles of the free market.

Political and nationalistic fundamentalism put their trust in grand narratives, of the political system or national identity, that assume an aura of total authority. For thinkers like Francis Fukuyama, Western liberal democracy is the only acceptable political system: the system that has unequivocally established its superiority over all others. We have reached the 'end of history', and it will only be a matter of time before everyone conforms to the Western model.[14] Even more insidiously, the Western states at the forefront of this cultural trend often espouse a nationalism which seeks to keep the relevant national identity as pure as possible and immigration from other poorer parts of the world at a minimum. Dissenting views are not tolerated, and indeed intolerance is a general feature of grand narratives. Postmodernism, with its commitment to dissent, pluralism, cultural difference and scepticism towards authority, finds itself in direct conflict with such systems, which substitute the authoritarian collective will for the individual. When eco-fundamentalists blow up ski resorts because of the threat they pose to local wildlife, or when pro-life advocates bomb abortion clinics, they do so in the name of grand narratives which are taken to represent universal truths overriding all opposition. In today's world, postmodernism confronts an array of such narratives, modern and pre-modern, that reject any challenge to their authority. The postmodern commitments just mentioned have a definite political edge.

DEFINING AND DEFENDING THE POSTMODERN

Postmodernism remains a notoriously diffuse cultural movement, but it does mean something – and does stand for something. This volume will show what that meaning is, in all its breadth and variety, and why so many thinkers and creative artists consider it to be worth defending. If the cultural context has altered in the past 13 years, the need to argue the case for the postmodern has not.

STRUCTURE AND SCOPE OF THE VOLUME

The Routledge Companion to Postmodernism is divided into two parts: (I) Essays, and (II) Dictionary entries. Part I consists of 19 extended essays tracing both the sources and the impact of postmodern thought, and includes such topics as 'Postmodernism and philosophy', 'Postmodernism and politics', 'Postmodernism and feminism' and 'Postmodernism and science and technology', as well as a series of essays dealing with postmodernism and the arts and media (architecture, literature, film, television, performance art and music, for example). The concluding essay, 'Postmodernism, modernity and the tradition of dissent', draws together the various strands of criticism of postmodernism, in order to demonstrate just how controversial the movement has turned out to be, and how much opposition it has managed to arouse even in such a relatively short time. Collectively these essays establish the breadth of postmodern thought that has transformed the cultural landscape of the late twentieth and early twenty-first centuries.

In Part II, the reader will find short dictionary-style entries, providing incisive definitions of key terms and critical concepts associated with postmodern thought. The object of the book overall is to provide accessible material on what can appear to be a forbiddingly complex and disparate area of discourse: a guide to 'who's who' and 'what's what' in postmodernism. It is a feature of this new edition that, as well as having been extensively revised, it includes much new material – namely, four extra essays (on 'Critical theory', 'Gender and sexuality', 'Organizations' and 'Performance' respectively), and a clutch of new dictionary entries on such topical subjects as 'Dark matter', 'M-theory' and 'Global warming'.

How to use this volume

To facilitate cross-reference, all the entries in Part II are picked out in bold when they appear elsewhere in the volume (for the first time in the particular context), and an index is also provided to enable readers to follow up the various appearances of specific figures and terms over the course of the Preface and essays in Part I. The two sections of the *Companion* are designed to interact, allowing more or less detailed information to be accessed, depending on the reader's requirements. You may merely want to refresh your memory as to the definition of a particular term, or go into more depth in, say, philosophy or popular culture. Alternatively, you may simply wish to range around the various networks of information the book offers, in order to build up your own particular picture of what postmodernism involves; 'Companions' provide just that creative possibility for each individual reader, and the choice is yours in this new, significantly expanded and revised edition.

Contributors

The contributors to this volume are drawn from a wide range of disciplines and are acknowledged experts in their particular areas. Their collective aim has been to map the postmodern such that its richness, diversity and cultural significance can be appreciated to the full by the general reader. Initials are given to identify A–Z entry writers in Part II. The contributors are, in alphabetical order:

Pamela Sue Anderson (Regents' Park College, Oxford) [PSA]
Adrian Baker [AB]
Eleanor Byrne (Manchester Metropolitan University)
Peter Dempsey (University of Sunderland) [PD]
Brian Dillon (University of Kent) [BD]
Angélique du Toit (University of Sunderland)
Antony Easthope (late Manchester Metropolitan University) [AE]
Sarah Gamble (Swansea University) [SG]
Peter Green (Abbots Bromley School for Girls) [PG]
Iain Hamilton Grant (University of the West of England) [IHG]
Chris Haywood (University of Newcastle)
Val Hill (University of Coventry)
Barry Lewis (University of Sunderland) [BL]
Karin Littau (University of Essex) [KL]
Mairtin Mac An Ghaill (University of Birmingham)
Anthony McGowan [AM]
Susan Melrose (Middlesex University)
Diane Morgan (University of Leeds)
Tony Purvis (University of Newcastle)
Derek B. Scott (University of Leeds)

Stuart Sim (Northumbria University) [SS]
Lloyd Spencer (Trinity & All Saints, Leeds) [LS]
John Storey (University of Sunderland) [JS]
John Strachan (University of Sunderland) [JStr]
Sue Thornham (University of Sussex)
Colin Trodd (University of Manchester) [CT]
Georges Van Den Abbeele (Northeastern University, Boston)
David Walker (Northumbria University) [DW]
Nigel Watson (University of Sunderland)
Brett Wilson (University of the West of England) [BW]
Alison Younger (University of Sunderland) [AY]

NOTES

1 Alan Kirby, 'The Death of Postmodernism and Beyond', *Philosophy Now*, 58 (November/December, 2006), pp. 34–7 (p. 34).

2 See Jean-François Lyotard, *The Postmodern Condition: A Report on Knowledge* [1979], trans. Geoff Bennington and Brian Massumi (Manchester: Manchester University Press, 1984).

3 See Dick Higgins, *A Dialectic of Centuries* (New York: Printed Editions, 1978), p. 7.

4 See Steven Best and Douglas Kellner, *Postmodern Theory: Critical Interrogations* (New York: Guilford Press, 1991), pp. 5–6.

5 See Bernard Iddings Bell, *Postmodernism and Other Essays* (Milwaukee, WI: Morehouse, 1926).

6 Arnold Toynbee, *A Study of History*, vol. IX (London: Oxford University Press, 1954), p. 235.

7 Joseph Hudnut, *Architecture and the Spirit of Man* (Cambridge, MA: Harvard University Press, 1949).

8 See Charles Jencks, *The Language of Post-Modern Architecture*, 6th edn (London: Academy Editions, 1991), p. 24.

9 Ibid., p. 12.

10 See Roland Barthes, *Image-Music-Text*, trans. and ed. Stephen Heath (London: Fontana, 1977).

11 See, for example, Jacques Derrida, *Of Grammatology* [1967], trans. Gayatri Chakravorty Spivak (Baltimore, MD: Johns Hopkins University Press, 1976); Michel Foucault, *Madness and Civilization: A History of Insanity in the Age of Reason* [1961], trans. Richard Howard (London: Tavistock, 1967); Luce Irigaray, *This Sex Which is Not One* [1985], trans. Catherine Porter (Ithaca, NY: Cornell University Press, 1985).

12 Stuart Sim, *Fundamentalist World: The New Dark Age of Dogma* (Cambridge: Icon Press, 2004).

13 See, for example, George Soros, *The Crisis of Global Capitalism: Open Society Endangered* (New York: BBS/Public Affairs, 1998).

14 Francis Fukuyama, *The End of History and the Last Man* (London: Hamish Hamilton, 1992).

Part I
Postmodernism:
Its History and
Cultural Context

1

POSTMODERNISM AND PHILOSOPHY

STUART SIM

Philosophy, particularly the recent French philosophical tradition, has been both a prime site for debate about **postmodernism** and a source of many of the theories of what constitutes postmodernism. Probably the leading figure to be cited is Jean-François Lyotard, whose book *The Postmodern Condition* is widely considered to be the most powerful theoretical expression of postmodernism.[1] Lyotard's plea that we should reject the '**grand narratives**' (that is, universal theories) of Western culture because they have now lost all their credibility, sums up the ethos of postmodernism, with its disdain for authority in all its many guises. There is no longer any point in engaging with, for example, Marxism, the argument goes; rather, we should ignore it as an irrelevance to our lives. Postmodern philosophy provides us with the arguments and techniques to make that gesture of dissent, as well as the means to make value judgements in the absence of such overall authorities.

One of the best ways of describing postmodernism as a philosophical movement would be as a form of scepticism – scepticism about authority, received wisdom, cultural and political norms and so on – and that places it in a long-running tradition in Western thought that stretches back to classical Greek philosophy. Scepticism is a primarily negative form of philosophy, which sets out to undermine other philosophical theories claiming to be in possession of ultimate truth, or of criteria for determining what counts as ultimate truth. The technical term to describe such a style of philosophy is '**anti-foundational**'. Anti-foundationalists dispute the validity of the foundations of **discourse**, asking such questions as 'What guarantees the truth of your foundation (that is, starting point)?' Postmodernism has drawn heavily on the example set by anti-foundationalist philosophers, perhaps most notably the iconoclastic nineteenth-century German philosopher Friedrich Nietzsche, whose call for a 'revaluation of all values' constitutes something of a battle-cry for the movement.[2]

Before considering postmodernism's sceptical credentials in greater detail, however, it would be helpful to say what, and who, can be regarded as falling under the heading of postmodern philosophy. It will be understood here to mean not just the inclusion of commentators on postmodernism itself like Lyotard, but also the various discourses, such as **deconstruction**, that go under the name of **poststructuralism**. Poststructuralism's rejection of the **structuralist** tradition of thought is yet another gesture of scepticism towards received authority, and can be treated as part of the postmodern intellectual landscape.

Although postmodern philosophy is a somewhat disparate area, we can note certain recurrent features, such as that gesture of scepticism, an anti-foundational bias, and an almost reflex dislike of authority, that make it reasonable to discuss it as a recognizable style of philosophy in its own right.

Poststructuralism is a broad cultural movement spanning various intellectual disciplines that has involved a rejection not just of structuralism and its methods, but also the ideological assumptions that lie behind them. It is to be regarded as both a philosophical and a political movement therefore, as is post-modernism in general. Poststructuralism called into question the cultural certainties that structuralism had been felt to embody: certainties such as the belief that the world was intrinsically knowable, and that structuralism gave us a methodological key to unlock the various systems that made up that world. Structuralism takes its cue from the theories of the Swiss linguist Ferdinand de Saussure, who revolutionized the study of linguistics in his posthumously published *Course in General Linguistics*.[3] Saussure's major point about language was that it was above all a system: a system with rules and regulations (or internal grammar) that governed how the various elements of language inter-acted. Language was made up of **signs**, and signs consisted of two parts, a signifier (word) and a signified (concept), which combined, in an act of mental understanding, to form the sign. Although there was no necessary connection between a word and the object it named (they were 'arbitrary', as Saussure admitted), the force of convention ensured that they did not change at anyone's whim. There was at the very least a *relative* stability to language and the production of meaning, and language was to be viewed as a system of signs which induced a predictable response on the part of the linguistic community.

The linguistic model set up by Saussure formed the basis of structuralist analysis, which applied it to systems in general, making the assumption that every system had an internal grammar that governed its operations. The point of structuralist analysis was to uncover that grammar, whether the system in question was tribal myth, the advertising industry or the world of literature or fashion. Ultimately, what poststructuralists object to is the overall tidiness of the structuralist enterprise, where there are no loose ends and everything falls neatly into place. Thus for a thinker like Claude Lévi-Strauss, or the early Roland Barthes, every detail of a **narrative** was significant in terms of the structure of the final product (there being no random elements), and narratives fell into specific genres, of which particular instances – say, a given tribal myth – were merely variations on a central theme.[4] From such a perspective one system (or narrative) comes to seem much like any other, and the analysis of its grammar turns into a fairly predictable exercise, almost as if one knew before-hand what one was going to find. One could even argue, and poststructuralists did, that the analytical techniques being used by the structuralist *determined* the results. What structuralism seems to allow little scope for is chance, creativity or the unexpected. For a poststructuralist these are much more important than all the similarities between systems, and there is what amounts to a commitment to locating, and dwelling on, dissimilarity, difference and the unpredictability of analysis among poststructuralist thinkers.

Jacques Derrida's deconstruction became one of the most powerful expressions of the poststructuralist ethos. Deconstruction was directed against the system-building side of structuralism, and took issue with the idea that all phenomena were reducible to the workings of systems, with its implication that we could come to have total control over our environment. Derrida was concerned to demonstrate the instability of language, and indeed of systems in general. Signs were not such predictable entities in his view, and there was never any perfect conjunction of signifier and signified to guarantee unproblematical communication. Some 'slippage' of meaning always occurred. For one thing, words always contained echoes and traces of other words, with their sound quality, for example, invariably putting one in mind of a range of similar-sounding words. Derrida provided evidence of this slippage in action by means of a concept called '**différance**', a neologism derived from the French word *différence* (meaning both difference and deferral).[5] One could not detect which of the two words was intended in speech (they are pronounced the same), only in writing. To Derrida, what was revealed at this point was the inherent indeterminacy of meaning.

Linguistic meaning was an unstable phenomenon: at all times, and all places, différance applied. (It is worth noting that Derrida denies that différance is a concept; for him it is merely the identification of a process embedded within language itself.) The fondness for pun and word-play within deconstructive writing – a recurrent feature of all its major practitioners – has as its goal the illustration of language's instability, as well as its endlessly creative capacity to generate new and unexpected meanings. Meaning is therefore a fleeting phenomenon that evaporates almost as soon as it occurs in spoken or written language (or keeps transforming itself into new meanings), rather than something fixed that holds over time for a series of different audiences. Derrida contends that all Western philosophy is based on the premise that the full meaning of a word is 'present' in the speaker's mind, such that it can be transmitted, without any significant slippage, to the listener. This belief is what he calls the '**metaphysics of presence**', and for Derrida it is an illusion:[6] différance always intrudes into communication to prevent the establishment of 'presence', or completeness, of meaning. The emphasis on difference, and on what fails to conform to the norm or to system-building, that we find in deconstruction is very characteristic of the postmodern philosophical ethos.

Michel Foucault is another thinker who turned against the system-building and difference-excluding tendencies of structuralist thought. Once again, it is the fact of difference that is emphasized. In Foucault's case, there is a particular interest in marginalized groups whose difference keeps them excluded from political **power**; groups such as the mentally ill, prisoners and homosexuals. Post-Renaissance culture has been committed to the marginalization, even demonization, of difference, by setting strict norms of behaviour. Foucault has written a series of case studies describing how these norms were implemented in seventeenth- and eighteenth-century Western Europe, such that a whole new range of regimented institutions – insane asylums, prisons, hospitals – came into being in order to deal with the 'different'.[7] For Foucault these institutions are expressions of political power, and of the way that a dominant faction in society can impose its will on others.

To demonstrate how sexual difference had been demonized in **modern** society, Foucault turned back to classical times in his three-volume study *The History of Sexuality* (1976–84) to investigate how homosexuality functioned in Greek and Roman culture.[8] Greek society was more tolerant of sexual difference than our own, although no less moral in its outlook. In Foucault's parlance, it had a different discourse of sexuality in which no one practice was privileged over others, but homosexuality and heterosexuality flourished side by side. Foucault contrasted this unfavourably to modern times, when heterosexuality was turned into a norm from which all other forms of sexual expression were treated as deviations. This insistence on the norm at the expense of the different is all part of the authoritarianism that thinkers like Foucault associate with modern culture.

Gilles Deleuze and Félix Guattari's *Anti-Oedipus* (1972) represented yet another poststructuralist attack on authoritarianism; in this case the authoritarianism embedded within psychoanalytic theory, which, through the mechanism of theories like the **Oedipus** complex, seeks to control the free expression of human desire. For Deleuze and Guattari individuals are '**desiring-machines**', who lack the sense of unity we generally associate with individual identity, but who find the opportunity to realize their desire being curbed by the socio-political authorities (with fascism as the most potent example of how the process works).[9] Psychoanalysis becomes for Deleuze and Guattari a symbol of how desire is suppressed, and in opposition to it they posit '**schizoanalysis**', based on the experience of the schizophrenic – who in their scheme becomes some kind of ideal model of human behaviour.[10] The political dimension to poststructuralist thought, often somewhat hidden under cloudy metaphysical discussions in deconstruction, is unmistakably foregrounded here.

Difference feminism can also be included under the heading of poststructuralism, in that it queries the supposed rigidity of gender categories. The argument is that gender identity, particularly female, is not fixed, but is instead a fluid process that cannot be reduced to any essence or norm of behaviour (in this instance a patriarchally derived norm of behaviour). Theorists such as Luce Irigaray have used this form of argument to challenge the assumptions of patriarchy, in particular the assumption of specifically male and female gender traits that lead to gender stereotypes that our society still largely adheres to, and uses as a basis for the suppression of women.[11]

The most influential voice of postmodern philosophy is Jean-François Lyotard, and there is a consistent thread of anti-authoritarianism running through his philosophical writings that we can now recognize as quintessentially postmodern. In his early career Lyotard can be described as a Marxist. He was a member of the group *Socialisme ou Barbarie* (Socialism or Barbarism), who were dedicated to subjecting Marxist theory to a searching critique from the inside, and he acted as the spokesperson on Algeria for the group's journal. Lyotard's writings on the Algerian war of liberation in the 1950s and 1960s reveal someone who is far from being an orthodox Marxist, and more than willing to call Marxist principles into question.[12] The major objection he registers is that Algeria was being treated by the Communist Party hierarchy as a classic case of proletarian revolution, when in reality it was a peasant society where Marxist categories had little practical value.

After the break-up of *Socialisme ou Barbarie* in the 1960s Lyotard self-consciously distanced himself from his Marxist past. Like many French intellectuals of his generation he was disenchanted by the pro-establishment position adopted by the French Communist Party in the 1968 Paris *événements*, and in works such as ***Libidinal Economy*** he vented the frustration he felt by then towards official Marxism.[13] *Libidinal Economy* claimed that Marxism was unable to encompass the various libidinal drives that all individuals experienced, since these drives lay beyond any theory's control (the argument is similar to the one expressed in *Anti-Oedipus*). What was precisely wrong with Marxism was that it tried to suppress these energies, and in so doing revealed its latent authoritarianism. Behind the book's vicious attack on Marxism lay a belief on Lyotard's part that neither human nature nor historical process was as predictable, and therefore controllable, as Marxist theory was insisting. Lyotard asked us to accept that libidinal energy (something like the complex of subconscious drives identified by Freud) demolished any claim that Marxism may have had to be able to direct events. The book can be seen as the beginning of the critique of 'grand narrative' that was to lie at the heart of Lyotard's most successful and influential work, *The Postmodern Condition*.

The Postmodern Condition argues that knowledge is now the world's most significant commodity, and that it may well become a source of conflict between nations. Whoever controls knowledge, Lyotard insists, now exerts political control, and he is keen to ensure that the dissemination of knowledge is kept as open as possible. His alternative to the centralized political control of knowledge is to make all data banks accessible to the general public. Knowledge is seen to be communicated by means of narrative, and Lyotard is critical of what he calls grand narratives: theories that claim to be able to explain everything, and to resist any attempt to change their form (or 'narrative'). Marxism, for example, has its own particular narrative of world history which it feels is true and thus beyond any criticism or need of revision. It is not a narrative to be reinterpreted constantly in the light of changing cultural events, but an impregnable theory that holds over time and whose authority is not to be doubted. To Lyotard, such an attitude is authoritarian, and he celebrates '**little narrative**' (*petit récit*) in its stead.[14] Little narratives are put together on a tactical basis by small groups of individuals to achieve some particular objective (such as the 'little narrative' combination of students and workers in the 1968 *événements*, calling for government reforms), and do not pretend to have the answers to all society's problems: ideally, they should last only as long as is necessary to achieve their specific short-term goals. Lyotard considers that little narratives are the most inventive way of disseminating, and creating, knowledge, and that they help to break down the monopoly traditionally exercised by grand narratives. In science, for example, they are now to be regarded as the primary means of enquiry. '**Postmodern science**', Lyotard informs us, is a search for paradoxes, instabilities and the unknown, rather than an attempt to construct yet another grand narrative that would apply over the entire scientific community.

Lyotard's objective is to demolish the authority wielded by grand narrative, which he takes to be repressive of individual creativity. 'We no longer have recourse to the grand narratives', he declares;[15] that is, we can no longer rely on them to guide our action, either at the public or private level. If we stop believing in grand narratives then it is to be assumed that they will simply wither away. Although this is a somewhat idealistic view of the political process, something like this withering away did occur a few years after the publication of *The Postmodern Condition*, when Eastern European communism collapsed – largely without violent clashes with the political authorities. In postmodern terms of reference, the populace stopped believing in the prevailing ideology, which then ceased to have any authority to enforce its will.

One of the problems we are left with when we dispense with grand narratives, or central authorities of any kind, is how to construct value judgements that others will accept as just and reasonable. Lyotard confronts this problem in *Just Gaming* when he argues that it is still possible to make value judgements, even if we have no grand narrative to back us up, on a 'case-by-case' basis (a form of pragmatism he adapts from Aristotle's political and ethical writings).[16] Operating in a case-by-case manner, where one is admitting the absence of any absolute criteria, is the condition Lyotard refers to as '**paganism**', and it becomes an ideal of how we ought to proceed in a postmodern world. There never will be such absolute criteria, or foundations of belief, to guide us; but that need not, Lyotard claims, entail a collapse into social disorder, as critics from the grand narrative side are wont to suggest. Lyotard is espousing anti-foundationalism: a rejection of the idea that there are foundations to our systems of thought, or belief, that lie beyond question, and that are necessary to the business of making value judgements. Postmodernist philosophy has proved to be resolutely anti-foundational in outlook, and unwilling to accept that this renders it dysfunctional as philosophy.

Lyotard's later philosophy is very much concerned with what he calls the '**event**', the concept of the '**differend**' and the **sublime**. The event is for Lyotard an occurrence that dramatically alters the way we view the world, and casts all our ideological assumptions into doubt in the process. Auschwitz is one such event, the *événements* another. The former in particular cannot be explained away by the application of grand narrative theory; in fact, it represents the point at which grand narrative theorizing breaks down. As for the latter, it is an explosion of libidinal energy the system cannot deal with either. To acknowledge that there are events which cannot be forecast or encompassed within any neat universal theory is to acknowledge not just the limitations of grand narrative but also the openness of the future. This openness becomes an article of faith to postmodernists: the future must not be considered as determined in advance such that all human effort is rendered meaningless.

Differends are conflicts of interest between parties which cannot be resolved, but must be acknowledged and kept in view at all times. Each party inhabits what Lyotard calls a different 'phrase regimen' (a development of the notion of **'language game'**) whose objectives are **incommensurable** with the other, and neither of which has any ethical right to make the other conform to its wishes.[17] What tends to happen in practice, particularly political practice, is that one party to the dispute enforces its view on the other, 'resolving' the dispute to its own advantage. In Lyotard's terms of reference, one phrase regimen exerts dominance over another – a classic instance of authoritarianism in action. As an example of this in the everyday world, Lyotard cites the case of an exploited employee who cannot gain any redress for her exploitation if she brings an action against her employer, since the court that hears her plea is set up on the principle that such exploitation is legal. The employer's phrase regimen is excluding hers from having a proper voice. It is the business of philosophers to help such suppressed phrase regimens find their voice, this being what Lyotard describes as a 'philosophical politics'.[18] Philosophical politics – the search for new, counter-cultural phrase regimens – can be considered the highest expression of postmodern philosophy.

Lyotard develops an obsession with the sublime, which comes to represent for him the fatal flaw in any totalizing philosophy. Immanuel Kant had wrestled with the notion of the sublime in his so-called 'Third Critique', since it appeared to create a gap in his theory of knowledge.[19] This theory required our concepts and our sense experience of the world to conform to each other. When we turned to the sublime, however, we were confronted with something infinite and absolute; that is, with the inconceivable, and thus a challenge to our claims to knowledge. While Kant was dismayed by this finding, Lyotard appropriated it for the cause of the postmodern as proof that no philosophical theory could provide a total picture of existence. The sublime always lay beyond our powers to represent or explain, and in consequence acquired immense symbolic importance for postmodern thought. All attempts to construct a grand narrative would be undermined by the fact of the sublime.

Towards the end of his career Lyotard is very much concerned with the way the forces of 'techno-science' (for which we can read the multinationals) are attempting to hijack the course of human history, by preparing for the end of life on Earth. Lyotard argues that techno-scientists are gradually eradicating humankind from the picture, by developing increasingly sophisticated computer technology with the ability to reproduce itself and to continue existing somewhere else in the universe when the Sun burns out (an event due in some 4.5 billion years or so). Techno-science's ultimate goal, Lyotard warns us in *The Inhuman*, is to make thought possible without a body, and this represents a threat to humanity and its values that should be strongly resisted, being 'inhuman' in spirit.[20] What techno-science wants is to reduce humanity to its assumed essence, that is, thought, and then to render this compliant in computer program form. Given thought without a body there are no longer events or differends to worry about of course, nor the openness of the future that post-modernists so prize. It is another case of excluding the different and the unpredictable in order to exert control. Conspicuously left out of the equation is the individual as well as the little narrative, neither of which has any place in the authoritarian scheme of things – and to wish to dehumanize humankind by reducing it to thought-process alone is an ultimate act of authoritarianism to Lyotard. Resistance at little narrative level becomes an ethical act on behalf of the cause of difference; and it is difference that must be protected at all costs in the postmodern world.

Jean Baudrillard's work is another important strand of postmodern philosophy. He too came to be very critical of Marxism and structuralism, eventually rejecting the notion that there were hidden structures behind all phenomena which it was the analyst's task to identify and explain. Baudrillard contended instead that the postmodern world was a world of **simulacra**, where we could no longer differentiate between reality and **simulation**.[21] Simulacra represented nothing but themselves: there was no other reality to which they referred. In consequence, Baudrillard could claim that Disneyland and television now constituted America's reality, and, even more provocatively, that the Gulf War of 1991 did not happen, but was merely a simulation (along the lines of a video game, it would seem). Not surprisingly, this latter view attracted a great deal of criticism for its apparent cynicism and lack of sensitivity to the human dimension involved.

Another argument of Baudrillard's that has inspired considerable controversy is that systems no longer need to be opposed, and that they can instead be 'seduced' – by which he means beguiled into submission.[22] Feminists have been extremely critical of what to them is the implicit sexism of the notion of seduction, and have accused Baudrillard of reinforcing sexual stereotypes by its use. While acknowledging the force of the feminist rejoinder, one might also regard seduction as yet another characteristically postmodern attempt to undermine systems by locating their weak spots. Postmodern philosophy in general sees no need for outright confrontation with systems of power, being more concerned to demonstrate how such systems (Marxism and communism being outstanding examples) can be made to implode.

The reaction against doctrinaire Marxism in the work of thinkers like Lyotard and Baudrillard is part of yet another cultural trend that is now known as **post-Marxism**. Post-Marxism has become an important theoretical position, and includes not just figures who wish to reject their Marxist beliefs, but also those who want to revise Marxism in terms of new theoretical and cultural developments. Ernesto Laclau and Chantal Mouffe gave voice to the latter constituency when they published their controversial book *Hegemony and Socialist Strategy* in 1985.[23] In this study they argued that Marxism ought to be aligning itself with the various new social movements that had been springing up (feminism, the **Greens**, ethnic and sexual minorities, for example); in other words, for Marxism to embrace political **pluralism** and drop its pretensions to be a body of received truth. Marxism also needed to take account of the various new theories that had been coming into prominence – theories such as deconstruction or postmodernism. Once again we can observe the characteristic postmodern distrust of grand narratives and their dogmatism coming to the fore. What is felt to be wrong with Marxism is that it has failed to move with the times, and to realize how pluralist society has become. Marxism is instead stuck at the level of trying to impose its theories on others, on the grounds that it alone possesses the truth. Viewed from this perspective Marxism is an authoritarian theory. Laclau and Mouffe, on the other hand, are putting the case for a more 'open' Marxism, able to adapt to changing cultural circumstances – and to attract new audiences in the process. Predictably enough, the Marxist establishment has been dismissive of Laclau and Mouffe's claims that Marxism requires drastic revision, or that it should aspire towards pluralism, holding on instead to Marxism's supposed truth and universality of application.

Another interesting line of post-Marxist thought can be found in the work of Slavoj Žižek, who put forward an interesting explanation of why grand theories like Marxism could exercise the hold they did, even when, as in the case of the Soviet Empire in its latter stages, it was plain that the theory was not delivering on its promises. Žižek 's argument was that those living under such a regime convinced themselves to believe in the theory's claims in some sense, even when, in the back of their mind, they knew these to be false. This was a condition he called 'enlightened false consciousness', and it was to be seen as a coping strategy.[24] To admit that the theory was completely wrong would be psychologically devastating, as one had no apparent way of escaping its controlling **power** in everyday life: 'they know that ... they are following an illusion, but still, they are doing it'.[25] Eventually, however, trust in the illusion faltered.

It is this distrust of grand theory, and its authoritarian bias, that can be considered the distinguishing feature of postmodern philosophy, which maintains a libertarian attitude throughout its various expressions. In the Anglo-American philosophical world, we can find such views being espoused by the American pragmatist philosopher Richard Rorty, a well-known champion of the recent **continental philosophical** tradition. Rorty also had no time for grand theory, and, in prototypically pragmatist fashion, was less concerned with whether theories were true or false than whether they were useful and interesting.[26] Philosophy, for Rorty, is no more than a form of conversation, and his own preference when it comes to identifying a source of ideas to guide our behaviour is for other subjects such as literature. Rorty's turn to '**post-**

philosophy', as it has been called, is characteristically postmodern in its rejection of the standard narrative associated with the Western philosophical tradition. Yet another authority is unceremoniously consigned to the historical dustbin.

Not everyone has been happy with postmodernism's frequent recourse to the historical dustbin. The American critic Fredric Jameson, for example, has dubbed postmodern theory 'the cultural logic of late capitalism', regarding it as being, unwittingly or otherwise, in collusion with the powers-that-be in helping to maintain the political status quo.[27] Postmodernists have consistently criticized the left's belief in the efficacy of ideological confrontation, and for a Marxist like Jameson that has the effect of serving the cause of the right, which has a vested interest in promoting apathy about the political process. Jürgen Habermas is another to find postmodernism ideologically suspect, defending modernity as being more in the public interest.[28] (For more on postmodernism's critics, see Chapter 19.)

Overall, postmodern philosophy is to be defined as an updated version of scepticism, more concerned with destabilizing other theories and their pretensions to truth than with setting up a positive theory of its own; although of course to be sceptical of the theoretical claims of others is to have a programme of one's own, if only by default. Postmodern philosophy, therefore, is a deployment of philosophy to undermine the authoritarian imperatives in our culture, at both the theoretical and the political level. Yet to some extent postmodernism has become its own grand narrative (there is a definite postmodernist line to most philosophical issues), and therefore vulnerable to attack in its turn. It is also possible to argue that postmodern philosophers have overstated the decline of grand narratives, and one highly pertinent objection to Lyotard's dismissal of their continuing significance has been that **religious fundamentalism** (a grand narrative if ever there was one) has manifestly been on the increase in recent decades. The growth of Islamic fundamentalism in particular seems to challenge the validity of Lyotard's judgement on this score, given that it is now a major factor in the political life of an increasing number of countries in the Middle East and Asia, making it a critical influence on the global political scene. Post-9/11 we must assume that postmodernism is in open conflict with fundamentalist trends in our world (we can include **market fundamentalism** in the equation as well).

Lyotard himself takes a cyclical view of cultural history, in which postmodernism and modernism succeed each other over time in unending sequence. Thus there have been postmodernisms in the past (figures like François Rabelais or Laurence Sterne qualifying as postmoderns for Lyotard), and there will be both modernisms and postmodernisms again in the future. It is just possible to argue that we are already into a **post-postmodernist** world, in which different cultural preoccupations – such as the reconstruction of grand narratives – are making their presence felt. Scepticism has gone in and out of fashion over the course of philosophical history, and it may well be that the current round has served its usual purpose in drawing attention to the weaknesses of certain philosophical positions and that a less negatively orientated philosophical programme can take its place for the immediate future. Already calls are being made in the realm of aesthetic theory to move past postmodernism with the hybrid of modernism and **postcolonialism** known as '**altermodernism**', which aims to transcend the restrictive world of 'isms' altogether and in the process create a new, more dynamic relationship between artists and their audience.[29] So be on the lookout for any similar 'post-postmodernist' initiatives: but be vigilant, also, for any drift back into intellectual authoritarianism.

NOTES

1 Jean-François Lyotard, *The Postmodern Condition: A Report on Knowledge* [1979], trans. Geoff Bennington and Brian Massumi (Manchester: Manchester University Press, 1984).

2 See Friedrich Nietzsche, *The Will to Power* [1901], trans. Walter Kaufmann and R. J. Hollingdale, ed. Walter Kaufmann (New York: Vintage, 1968), p. 3.

3 Ferdinand de Saussure, *Course in General Linguistics* [1916], eds C. Bally, A. Sechehaye and A. Reidlinger, trans. Wade Baskin (London: Peter Owen, 1960).

4 See, for example, Roland Barthes, *Image-Music-Text*, trans. and ed. Stephen Heath (London: Fontana, 1977), and Claude Lévi-Strauss, *Structural Anthropology*, vol. 1, trans. Claire Jacobson and Brooke Grundfest Shoepf (New York: Basic Books, 1963).

5 See Jacques Derrida, *Margins of Philosophy* [1972], trans. Alan Bass (Harvester: Brighton, 1982), p. 3.

6 See Jacques Derrida, *Writing and Difference* [1967], trans. Alan Bass (Chicago: University of Chicago Press, 1978), pp. 278–93.

7 See, for example, Michel Foucault, *Madness and Civilization: A History of Insanity in the Age of Reason* [1961], trans. Richard Howard (London: Tavistock, 1967).

8 See Michel Foucault, *The History of Sexuality*, vols I–III. Vol. I: *The History of Sexuality: An Introduction* [1976], trans. Robert Hurley (Harmondsworth: Penguin, 1981); vol. II: *The Use of Pleasure* [1984], trans. Robert Hurley (Harmondsworth: Penguin, 1987); vol. III: *The Care of the Self* [1984], trans. Robert Hurley (Harmondsworth: Penguin, 1988).

9 Gilles Deleuze and Félix Guattari, *Anti-Oedipus* [1972], trans. Robert Hurley, Mark Seem and Helen Lane (London: Athlone Press, 1984), p. 2.

10 See ibid., pp. 273–382.

11 See Luce Irigaray, *This Sex Which is Not One* [1985], trans. Catherine Porter (Ithaca, NY: Cornell University Press, 1985).

12 See Jean-François Lyotard, *Political Writings*, trans. Bill Readings and Kevin Paul Geiman (London: UCL Press, 1993), pp. 165–326.

13 Jean-François Lyotard, *Libidinal Economy* [1974], trans. Iain Hamilton Grant (London: Athlone Press, 1993).

14 Lyotard, *Postmodern Condition*, p. 60.

15 Ibid.

16 Jean-François Lyotard and Jean-Loup Thébaud, *Just Gaming* [1979], trans. Wlad Godzich (Manchester: Manchester University Press, 1985), p. 28.

17 Jean-François Lyotard, *The Differend: Phrases in Dispute* [1983], trans. Georges Van Den Abbeele (Manchester: Manchester University Press, 1988), p. 28.
18 Ibid., p. xiii.
19 Immanuel Kant, *Critique of the Power of Judgment* [1790], trans. Paul Guyer and Eric Matthews (Cambridge: Cambridge University Press, 2000).
20 Jean-François Lyotard, *The Inhuman: Reflections on Time* [1988], trans. Geoffrey Bennington and Rachel Bowlby (Oxford: Blackwell, 1991).
21 See Jean Baudrillard, *Simulations*, trans. Paul Foss, Paul Patton and Philip Beitchman (New York: Semiotext(e), 1983).
22 See particularly Jean Baudrillard, *Seduction* [1979], trans. Brian Singer (Basingstoke: Macmillan, 1990).
23 Ernesto Laclau and Chantal Mouffe, *Hegemony and Socialist Strategy: Towards a Radical Democratic Politics* (London: Verso, 1985).
24 Slavoj Žižek, *The Sublime Object of Ideology* (London: Verso, 1989), p. 29.
25 Ibid., p. 33.
26 See, for example, Richard Rorty, *Consequences of Pragmatism (Essays: 1972–1980)* (Brighton: Harvester, 1982).
27 See Fredric Jameson, *Postmodernism, or, The Cultural Logic of Late Capitalism* (London: Verso, 1991).
28 See, for example, Jürgen Habermas, 'Modernity versus Postmodernity', *New German Critique*, 22 (1981), pp. 3–14.
29 See Nicolas Bourriaud, 'Altermodern', in Nicolas Bouriaud, ed., *Altermodern: Tate Triennial* (London: Tate Publishing, 2009), pp. 11–24.

2

POSTMODERNISM AND CRITICAL THEORY

GEORGES VAN DEN ABBEELE

Postmodernism is most readily defined as the set of responses – cultural, political, intellectual – to the perceived failures of **modernism** both as a vanguard aesthetic movement and as a general ideology of human progress forged in the fires and bellows of the industrial age. Given the sheer diversity of modernism itself, though, the various postmodernist responses to it from the mid-1970s to early 1990s are themselves variable, even paradoxical and contradictory. The corresponding term, '**postmodernity**', applies to the socio-historical situation in which the discourses and practices of **modernity**, based in the ideals of the **Enlightenment**, are understood to have been superseded. And while this reputedly new epoch is best realized in a post-industrial America that also happens to be the primary locus for the cultural trends and intellectual debates associated with postmodernism, the theoretical inspirations for its analysis as *simultaneously* an aesthetic *and* a historical break – that is, as a fundamental change in social reality – are principally drawn from the writings of a number of French thinkers whose works are commonly grasped under the rubric **poststructuralism**, and more generally, that of critical theory. If the term poststructuralism, evokes the names of Jean-François Lyotard and Jean Baudrillard (the philosophers most identified with the name and concept of the postmodern), as well as Michel Foucault, Jacques Derrida, Guy Debord, Gilles Deleuze and Félix Guattari, the broader term, critical theory, hearkens back to an even earlier moment, that of the Frankfurt School for Social Research and the likes of Theodor Adorno, Max Horkheimer, Walter Benjamin and Herbert Marcuse. Interestingly, both of these intellectual movements evolved primarily *in reaction to* the perceived failures of preceding schools of thought. In the case of the Frankfurt School, critical theory thought to expand beyond the narrow economic determinism of traditional Marxism by uncovering and analysing the entire world of lived experience and culture, including aesthetics, which had previously been treated as a mere superstructural reflection of the economic infrastructure of modes and relations of production. In the case of poststructuralism, as the very name declares, the reaction was to the reputedly universalizing and scientist tendencies of classic **structuralism**. Where structuralism, as a theoretical approach inspired by linguistics and anthropology, insisted on finding commonalities, identities and recurring, self-replicating 'structures', poststructuralism emphasized disparities, irremediable **differences**, fragmentation and un-selfsame heterogeneities. But as movements that were themselves disparate in form and more readily defined negatively by what they were reacting to, both classic crit-ical theory and poststructuralism already contain the germs of postmodernism by their critical recycling of earlier ideas, just as postmodern art cites previous forms of visual or plastic expression. Indeed, postmodernism as both a trend and an object of analysis within the broadly defined field of critical theory draws much inspiration from contemporary developments in the arts. As for what we mean by critical theory writ large, that would encompass the wide array of theo-retical, interdisciplinary work in the humanities and social sciences based primarily in the contributions of the Frankfurt School and the various structur-alisms while drawing also and heavily upon the older legacy of Sigmund Freud, Karl Marx and Ferdinand de Saussure.

Although instances of the term 'postmodern' can be dated back as far as the nineteenth century (see 'Preface'), it came into prominence in the 1970s with the debates in American architecture over the limits of the International Style and its rejection by the likes of Robert Venturi, Paolo Portoghesi, Robert Krier and others.[1] Though the Centre Pompidou (Beaubourg) – completed in January 1977; designed by Richard Rogers and Renzo Piano – is considered by some to be a tribute to late modernism rather than a full-blown expression of post-modernism, it well illustrates key features and concerns of that architectural tendency. Rather than concealing its functional aspects (support girders, heating ducts, water pipes, etc.) under a geometrically clean design, Beaubourg overtly and colourfully flaunts them, exhibiting them to view in a kind of exoskeleton that likewise broadcasts the Centre's proclaimed reinvention of museum and library space. The cohabitation of an open-stack library (exceed-ingly rare in France), flexible exhibition spaces, cinematheque, coffee shop and so on were meant to make Beaubourg a truly congenial hub of cultural and social interaction. The colourful 'inside-out' design of the building also marks a ludic departure from the stark geometry and forbidding impersonality of high modernist functionalism. A carnivalesque celebration of the arts made public rather than a sombrely respectful and exclusivist cathedral in the eyes of its proponents, Beaubourg represents for its detractors a dangerous pandering to the pressures of mass cultural consumerism and a surrender to the increasing commodification of art in the late twentieth century. Interestingly, this very debate – revisited, for example, in the controversies over I. M. Pei's pyramid entrance to the Louvre built in 1989 – and an increasing unease with any sure distinction between high and low art, count among the harbingers of post-modernism.

In the arts more generally, postmodernism has come to designate the rejec-tion of high modernism and its paragon, abstract expressionism, by movements as diverse as Pop Art, Photorealism and **Trans-avant-gardism**. Inspired most dynamically by the example of Marcel Duchamp (a retrospective of whose work, incidentally, served as the Centre Pompidou's opening exhibit), the post-modern style typically features allusion, pastiche, humour, **irony**, a certain populism and kitsch as well as a resurgent classicism, even a distinct traditionalism; in other words, an eclecticism as shocking as its formulations remain unpredictable. What such gestures reject is the high seriousness of modernism, its universalist aspirations that deny local traditions and customs, and the elitism of the artist's vanguard status (as historically 'ahead' of the uncultured masses). In the literary realm, for example, one sees the esoteric *nouveau roman* with its experimentalist programme give way before the populist playfulness of a Georges Perec.

For the postmodern artist, there is no longer anything new about modernism's incessant quest for the 'new', merely the tired assertion of the contemporary as the sole defining gesture of the modern. Instead, postmodernism indulges in a volatile mix of the old with the new, what Charles Jencks has termed '**double-coding**', a concept able to describe an enormous variety of contemporary phenomena from neoclassical influences in the visual arts, to '**retro**' fashions, to the nostalgia film and the technique of 'sampling' in hip-hop music.[2] Rather than claiming absolute novelty as modernism did, postmodernism takes a special pride in manipulating the cliché, the citation, the allusion or the ready-made object, as the very material of its artistic production, as the occasion for its iconoclastic experiments in cultural recycling.

At the same time, this plethora of artistic and cultural responses to modernism has come in turn to be understood by many as a sign of some new socio-historical reality in the wake of a post-industrial world (such as theorized by Daniel Bell)[3] where the classic economic forces of production and industrialization have made way for a service, information and consumer-orientated economy. Postmodernity thus names a **paradigm shift** from the low-tech realm of smokestacks and locomotives to the high-tech world of silicon chips and digital communications. Whether this brave new world represents a break with capitalism or merely a new phase of it remains a source of tremendous discussion and dissension among critical theorists of the postmodern, who are eager to draw correlations between the artistic revolt of postmodernism and our possible entry into a new period of history and a new type of social organization. Postmodern critical theory thereby reopens the old debates about the status of the avant-garde, with various thinkers taking a variety of positions on the degree to which cultural postmodernism is either a reactionary effect of postmodernity, or a radical critique of it.

Within the specific context of critical theory, a frequent topic of debate was whether a given thinker, movement or set of ideas was to be understood as truly postmodern or merely modern. Innumerable academic conferences in the 1980s featured panel discussions or roundtables whose participants either championed or contested the attribution of postmodernism to the subject at hand. Perhaps the grandfather of such debates was the long-running intellectual feud between Lyotard and Jürgen Habermas, a debate which actually had nothing to do with picking sides in the modernist/postmodernist divide but with reassessing the political import of postmodernist theory itself. For Lyotard, the horrendous legacies of the twentieth century (world wars, concentration camps, genocide,

17

totalitarian regimes of various stripes) motivated an 'incredulity' about the utopian promises of modernism and its eschatological **grand narratives** (whether liberal or Marxist) and thus the need for a fundamental change of perspective along the lines of the postmodernity practised in the arts. Habermas vigorously rejected this viewpoint, arguing to the contrary that the horrors of modern times were not the fault of modernism as a system of thought based in Enlightenment ideology but the ongoing proof that these Enlightenment ideals have yet to be put into action or even given a chance. Thus, the divergence of thought between Lyotard and Habermas is as much an argument over the historical legacy of the Enlightenment as anything else. And it is perhaps not surprising that this clash between two intellectual titans drew mightily from their respective studies of the eighteenth century. For Lyotard, this meant his critical immersion in the works of Immanuel Kant as a kind of postmodernist precursor of post-Marxist political practices (cf. *Enthusiasm, Lessons on the Analytic of the Sublime*, various 'notices' in *The Differend*).[4] For Habermas, the response followed from his seminal historical study of the development of civil society in the eighteenth century (*The Structural Transformation of the Public Sphere: An Inquiry into a Category of Bourgeois Society*).[5] While both authors' works represent in their respective ways the culmination of the intellectual and theoretical trajectories each represents, both also point to a future of critical theory in the wake of the postmodernist debate, namely the movement away from high theory toward various forms of historicism, cultural study and identity-based political analysis.

Part of this post-theoretical tendency can already be perceived in the more pessimistic side of the modernity/postmodernity debate that emphasizes the inexorable commodification of artistic production within a media-driven society characterized by a consumerist fascination with images. This is the world Guy Debord has famously called the 'society of the spectacle', a society where reality itself comes to be 'derealized' through the virtualities of image production and circulation, epitomized by the ubiquity of the television screen and computer monitor.[6] What is meant by this derealization of social reality is that what were once the shared personal experiences of work, family or community have come increasingly to be supplanted by the virtual experience of commonly consumed images via television, cinema, **Internet** and so on. Under postmodern conditions (but as Walter Benjamin also foresaw, under modernism itself), the commodification of art dovetails with the aestheticization of commodities, that is their advertising appeal as well as occasional designation as works of art: Duchamp's urinal, Warhol's soup can. For thinkers steeped in Marxist theory, such as Lyotard or Fredric Jameson, this world where images take precedence over their reference in reality represents the final triumph of global capitalism, not merely because of the contemporaneous collapse of communism but, more profoundly, by the extension of marketplace logic from the strictly economic realm of manufacturing into the most intimate corners of cultural and psychical life. Everything can be commodified, bought and sold under postmodern conditions, including all forms of creative expression from emotions to signs to art, hence too the volatile transmutation of elitist and popular art forms into each other. In Jameson's well-known formulation, postmodernism is thus 'the *cultural* logic of late capitalism'.[7] Alternatively, there are those, such as Jean Baudrillard, who see the reformulation of contemporary society around the immateriality of endlessly self-referencing images or **'simulacra'**, not as a new phase of capitalism but as the utopian entry into some completely different world, not organized by production, but by some alternative, variously and rather obscurely theorized by him at different moments in his career as 'symbolic exchange', 'seduction' or the 'fatal strategy' of objects.[8]

Many of the terms and themes of postmodernist thought are readily familiar from poststructuralism: heterogeneity, free-floating subjectivity, difference, dispersal, pluralism, discontinuity, indeterminacy and so forth. But whereas poststructuralism developed such concepts by way of a critical interrogation into the conditions of possibility of identity formations, that is, by way of its **deconstruction** of Western forms of idealism, postmodernism translates poststructuralist ideas into both an intellectual *parti pris* – the ubiquitous celebration of difference for its own sake – *and* the elements putatively descriptive of the current historical state of post-industrial society.

Certainly, the most famous attempt to grasp together the aesthetically celebratory and historically descriptive sides of postmodernism is Lyotard's *The Postmodern Condition*, which is itself rather disingenuously presented as a 'report on knowledge' for the Quebec Ministry of Education. Eschewing the nicety of the distinction between cultural postmodern*ism* and socio-historical postmodern*ity*, Lyotard uses the single term 'postmodern' to refer to both as the specific 'condition' of our times.[9] In *The Postmodern Condition*, what is called the 'postmodern age' corresponds, on the one hand, to the advent of a specifically *post*-industrial society in Bell's sense *and*, on the other, to a generalized loss of faith in the 'grand narratives' of modernism that had seen the West through its heyday of industrialization, colonization and capital accumulation: whether Enlightenment rationality, liberal democracy, industrial progress or dialectical materialism. All these narratives, Lyotard argues, are modelled on the traditional Christian idea of redemption to the extent that they understand historical process in terms of an endpoint (the triumph of freedom and reason, a classless society, etc.) that will retroactively give meaning and legitimacy to all the toils we must undergo to get there. It is the organizational security of this overarching eschatology that has ceased to function within a postmodern world. The only remaining criterion of legitimacy in the state of globally triumphant capitalism is that of pure efficiency, or what Lyotard calls 'performance'. This rather pessimistic situation of contemporary humanity is what Lyotard terms the 'postmodern condition', and a phenomenon whose intellectual, aesthetic, pedagogical and socio-political consequences the philosopher takes as his or her task to elucidate.

Not that postmodernism constitutes itself therefore simply and self-righteously as a critique of the postmodern condition, for in a world where performance becomes the only criterion of **legitimation**, criticism, as Lyotard argues, becomes no longer an alternative but itself a part of the system to the extent that the latter solicits and recaptures criticism to bring about improvements in its own efficiency. The inspiration, then, for postmodernism is less frankly denunciatory than stragetically *dissimulative* in the Nietzschean sense, less accusatory than ironic, and Nietzsche is thus the philosophical figure who looms large over the postmodern enterprise. And, if anything marks the intellectual crisis of postmodernity – indeed what most saliently names the outrageousness of its dilemma – it is the disappearance of critique as the principal weapon in the intellectual's arsenal. For 'critique' remains inexorably ensnared in the sediment of the modernist grand narrative as the liberatory gesture Kant famously describes of enlightened thought freeing itself – and by extension all of humanity – from the shadows of superstition, fanaticism, repression or ideology. But if the end of criticism is merely to improve by reform the system it criticizes, to make it more 'efficient', to make it 'perform better', then the intellectual is no longer in the utopian position of the radical outsider but unmasked as a prime beneficiary and advocate of the system itself. In France, this particular crisis of the intellectual also dates back to the mid-1970s with the so-called *nouveaux philosophes* (such as André Glucksmann or Bernard-Henri Lévy) who sparked controversy less for the content of their ideas than their self-promotional skills as darlings of the media.

Part of the 'incredulity' towards grand narratives that defines the postmodern condition is also the loss of faith in the hermeneutics of depth associated with them that taught how to reveal the essence behind appearances, the timeless below the transitory, or the inside behind a deceptive exterior. For French thought still reeling from the *événements* of May 1968, this critique of 'critique' is specifically directed against the hermeneutics of Marxism and psychoanalysis, the suspicion being that the critical revelations of the psychoanalyst, far from liberating the analysand, merely enforce the straitjacket of normality (as argued most trenchantly by Deleuze and Guattari in *Anti-Oedipus*).[10] As for Marxian ideology critique, its analysis of the capitalist extraction of surplus value from human labour would produce not its overcoming but its mirror image, thus surreptitiously advancing the interests of capital even while offering an accurate 'descriptive theory' (Baudrillard's *Mirror of Production*).[11] At its best, the depth analysis that reveals what lies repressed below the social or psychical surface finds but another surface of repression, and beyond that never anything more than the dissimulations of the will to power. The 'incredulity' ascribed by Lyotard to those great narratives comes from the disabused recognition that there cannot be a final cure to repression any more than that a revolution can resolve all social inequities.[12] Indeed, the rejection of teleological modes of thinking is one of the hallmarks of postmodernism and a characteristic that distinguishes it from every modernism, which all share a common faith in the attainment of a project yet to be realized: if we all work hard enough, we can all be millionaires, or bring about a communist utopia or a true democracy and so on. Politics under postmodernism turns away from such projects for an ideal society (whatever the ideal might be) and espouses the resistance of refractory causes or identity groups: ecologists, feminists, gay rights activists, minority politics of all kinds, as well, it must also be said, as ultra-nationalists, neo-fascists and the like. For many, the decline of the traditional political parties and concomitant splintering of the electorate also mean the triumph of politics as spectacle and the pervasive sense that media and image manipulation determine success at the polls.

Where postmodernism and critical theory meet, the classic hermeneutics of depth have also given way to a concern with surfaces, inspired by semiotics' insistence on the externality of the signifier, and exemplified by the slippery play of citations that leaves the text unchanged but saying something very different from itself – the moment of deconstruction, where as Derrida himself states in *Of Grammatology*, there is always the risk that 'the ultra-transcendental text will so closely resemble the precritical text as to be indistinguishable from it'.[13] The deconstruction of identity is ascetically and methodically pursued throughout Derrida's corpus, as if to mourn, Rousseau-like, the loss of ideal identity in an era when such identities have reputedly ceased to function. In Deleuze, the Platonic hierarchy of model over copy that founds the Western ideality of identity and the 'corrupt double' that is representation is overturned by a non-hierarchical concept of mimesis understood as the serial repetition of simulacra without origin or end, that is, in Nietzschean terms, as the eternal return of the same as different. Instead of the rooted primacy of the model over its derived and implicitly deformed copies, the relations between simulacra are as multiple as they are transversal, **'rhizomatic'** rather than 'arboreal', to use Deleuze's vegetative metaphors. *A Thousand Plateaus*, with its complex, multi-layered network of cross-referencing sections, is explicitly presented by Deleuze and Guattari as an attempt to philosophize rhizomatically.[14] For the epistemological nihilist that is Baudrillard, the endless network of signs endlessly referring to other signs with no referent in sight is not just a philosophical conclusion but the postmodern actuality of a media-saturated society where any semblance of reality disappears into what he calls **'hyperreality'**.[15] Far from simply decrying this situation, the Baudrillardian intellectual can only ironically assume and affirm it. The philosophical question then turns around finding the most appropriate modes or genres with which to write, hence the experiments with theory written as fiction, travelogue or autobiography: Baudrillard's *America* and *Cool Memories*; Derrida's *The Post Card*; Lyotard's *Pacific Wall*, *The Postmodern Explained to Children* or *Postmodern Fables*.[16] And so the postmodern eclecticism of the arts, its ironic use of citation and allusion, the double-coded use of traditional forms, come to inform the very way critical theory itself is thought and written in the wake of postmodernity.

But this is to return then to the vexed relation between an aesthetic practice and a historical period. Do critical theorists and post-functionalist architects simply reflect different aspects of a common postmodern predicament? Are they both unconsciously bound by the cultural logic of late capitalism? Or, does post-modernism itself, in a typically postmodern gesture, turn around and bite the very concept of period which sustains theoretically its conceptualization? Is the postmodern turn a real historical break or just its simulation?

Not to take these questions seriously would indeed be to buy back into the familiar, disciplinary narrative of art history as the progressive development through the ages of a humanity whose historical periods are synonymous with aesthetic moments: Renaissance, Baroque, Rococo, Romanticism and so forth. And at the end of the line, modernism, which would be an aesthetic movement defined only by its *not* being whatever precedes it. But then, what would something coming after modernism be – a post-modernism – if not both like modernism and not like it, like it on account of its *not* being like it, not like it on account of its being like it?

The oddity is that the *absolute* historicization that defines modernism leaves us strangely unable to think in historical terms. Such is indeed how Jameson defines postmodernism in the famous first sentence of his *Postmodernism*, that is, 'as an attempt to think the present historically in an age that has forgotten how to think historically in the first place'.[17] Such assertions that postmodernity is a periodization that isn't, find uncanny echoes in Deleuze's longstanding meditation on the sense of Hamlet's pronouncement that 'the time is out of joint' – another instance where citation serves the purpose of postmodern thinking. For Lyotard, the postmodern is rejected as a period altogether, it being not the chronological sequel but the radicalization of the modern, in the root sense as its *condition* of possibility: 'A work can become modern only if it is first postmodern'.[18] Whichever version of this issue we take, periodicity would, thus, seem to be subject to an ineluctable recursiveness under postmodern conditions, such that the very concept of period is called into question at the same time that the widespread view that we have entered into some, new historical epoch must itself be acknowledged and explained at least as a societal phenomenon, if not as a historical reality.

Another approach to the question might be to return to our initial proposition, that postmodernism is itself the set of responses (not necessarily uniform or even compatible) to the perceived failure of modernism. That failure, if we again recall Lyotard, is the impossibility (or at least, our no longer believing in the possibility) of its following through on the promise of a universalizing end to history (call it progress, revolution, enlightenment or what have you) in which we would all find our place. Such grand narratives presuppose a single history, History with a capital H rather than different histories, rather than the chronological polyrhythms that actually scan and punctuate our own daily lives and that of our society, and that differentiate our lives from life elsewhere in that same society as well as in other societies. The failure of modernism, in this regard, would not necessarily be in forgetting this actuality but in actively seeking to repress it. Despite postmodernist theory's claim to the unrestrained proliferation of differences in our world, it can well be argued that the forces of

globalization, or late capitalism (to use Jameson's term, following Ernest Mandel)[19] are in fact making the world less and less different, imposing uniform standards and homogeneity worldwide – in a way not unlike that International Style of architecture Venturi and others so fervently rejected. In other words, is the increasing sense of temporal change and social diversification in a multi-lingual, multi-cultural, multi-ethnic world but the glitzy epiphenomenon of a globe increasingly brought under the reins of a single market? But, then, would this apparent triumph of capitalism worldwide not also grant a new urgency and possibility to cultural forms of resistance (in a post-communist context devoid of socio-economic alternatives), marking those allegedly superficial differences as the only possible site of contestation? And given the French intellectual contribution to defining postmodernism, there is little reason to be surprised that French resistances to the terms of the GATT agreements in 1994, for example, were all on the level of *cultural* resistance and preservation (i.e. protections for French cinema, music, etc.).

It may be that postmodernist critical theory needs to make more of a case for **difference** rather than merely assuming it, as Baudrillard so blithely appears to do, that it grasp the responses to postmodernity not as themselves theoretically uniform but as themselves different, reflective of the perhaps *pre-modern* differentiation between aesthetic trends and historical changes. That it face what ultimately still remains unthought, *malgré tout*, in the use of a category like postmodernism, namely that aesthetics and history, like time itself, may be radically 'out of joint'.

NOTES

1 See, for example, Robert Venturi, Steven Izenour and Denise Scott Brown, *Learning from Las Vegas: The Forgotten Symbolism of Architectural Form*, 2nd edn (Cambridge, MA: MIT Press, 1977).

2 Charles Jencks, *The Language of Post-Modern Architecture*, 6th edn (London: Academy Editions, 1991), p. 12.

3 See Daniel Bell, *The Coming of Post-Industrial Society: A Venture in Social Forecasting* (London: Heinemann, 1974).

4 Jean-François Lyotard, *Enthusiasm: The Kantian Critique of History* [1986], trans. Georges Van Den Abbeele (Stanford, CA: Stanford University Press, 2009); *Lessons on the Analytic of the Sublime* [1991], trans. Elizabeth Rottenberg (Berkeley, CA: Stanford University Press, 1994); and *The Differend: Phrases in Dispute* [1983], trans. Georges Van Den Abbeele (Manchester: Manchester University Press, 1988).

5 Jürgen Habermas, *The Structural Transformation of the Public Sphere: An Inquiry into a Category of Bourgeois Society* [1962], trans. Thomas Burger (Cambridge, MA: MIT Press, 1989).

6 See Guy Debord, *The Society of the Spectacle* [1967], trans. Donald Nicholson-Smith (New York: Zone Books, 1994).

7 See Fredric Jameson, *Postmodernism, or, The Cultural Logic of Late Capitalism* (London: Verso, 1991).

8 See Jean Baudrillard, *Simulations*, trans. Paul Foss, Paul Patton and Philip Beitchman (New York: Semiotext(e), 1983); *Symbolic Exchange and Death* [1976], trans. Iain Hamilton Grant (London: Sage, 1993); *Seduction* [1979], trans. Brian Singer (Basingstoke: Macmillan, 1990); and *Fatal Strategies* [1983], trans. Philip Bietchman and W. G. Niesluchowski (London: Pluto, 2008).

9 Jean-François Lyotard, *The Postmodern Condition: A Report on Knowledge* [1979], trans. Geoff Bennington and Brian Massumi (Manchester: Manchester University Press, 1984).

10 Gilles Deleuze and Félix Guattari, *Anti-Oedipus* [1972], trans. Robert Hurley, Mark Seem and Helen Lane (London: Athlone Press, 1984).

11 Jean Baudrillard, *The Mirror of Production* [1973], trans. Mark Poster (St. Louis, MO: Telos Press, 1975).

12 Lyotard, *Postmodern Condition*, p. xxiv.

13 Jacques Derrida, *Of Grammatology* [1967], trans. Gayatri Chakravorty Spivak (Baltimore, MD: Johns Hopkins University Press, 1976), p. 61.

14 Gilles Deleuze and Félix Guattari, *A Thousand Plateaus: Capitalism and Schizophrenia* [1980], trans. Brian Massumi (London: Athlone Press, 1988).

15 Baudrillard, *Simulations*, p. 2.

16 Jean Baudrillard, *America* [1986], trans. Chris Turner (London: Verso, 1988), and *Cool Memories* [1987], trans. Chris Turner (London: Verso, 1990); Jacques Derrida, *The Post Card: From Socrates to Freud and Beyond* [1980], trans. Alan Bass (Chicago: University of Chicago Press, 1987); Jean-François Lyotard, *Pacific Wall* [1975], trans. Bruce Boone (Venice, CA: Lapis Press, 1990), *The Postmodern Explained to Children: Correspondence 1982–1985*, trans. Don Barry *et al.*, eds Julian Pefanis and Morgan Thomas (Minneapolis, MN: University of Minnesota Press, 1992), and *Postmodern Fables* [1993], trans. Georges Van Den Abbeele (Minneapolis, MN: University of Minnesota Press, 1997).

17 Jameson, *Postmodernism*, p. ix.

18 Lyotard, *Postmodern Condition*, p. 79.

19 See Ernest Mandel, *Late Capitalism* (London: New Left Books, 1975).

3

POSTMODERNISM AND POLITICS

IAIN HAMILTON GRANT

Ever since **postmodernism** hit the cultural news-stand, it has been incessantly interrogated as to its politics. With its 'anything goes' **pluralism** and its delirious celebration of **difference**; with reality, according to Jean Baudrillard – to many, the 'high priest of postmodernism' – 'no longer what it used to be', what grounds remain for a politics necessary to counter the widespread and manifest injustices that remain in our postmodern world?[1] Surely any prospect of tackling endemic racism, the horrors of the military–industrial–entertainment complex, the invasion of Iraq, religious and political persecution or Chinese tanks crushing the bodies of protesting students, is given up in advance by any movement that, like postmodernism, renounces the **modern** ideals of universal freedom, equality and rights, without proposing any alternatives?

In many ways 'postmodern politics' is a problem peculiar to the history of postmodernism in the English-speaking world, where the term first arose in the world of art and architecture. Once postmodernism had reached a certain critical mass, it became irresistible to academic interests, and the path it then took shifted from the arts to politics and philosophy, from which something known loosely as 'postmodern theory' began to emerge. The various elements from which theoretical postmodernism emerged were almost exclusively, however, fragments of French philosophy. It is to some extent a consequence of this speculation or free trade in theories divorced from their historical, political and philosophical contexts that the question of postmodern politics has appeared to be so open and, therefore, to host an apparently endless range of debates.

Two questions may therefore be asked. First, what impact has postmodernism had on politics in what Richard Rorty called the North Atlantic bourgeois community, and second, what are the politics that inform the philosophy imported from France to this community in the guise of postmodern theory? The answers to both of these questions are linked through one of the very few **continental philosophers** to have directly addressed postmodernism. Jean-François Lyotard's *The Postmodern Condition* crops up in virtually every discussion of every aspect of these debates, so that his self-confessed extreme simplifications have assumed a definitive character with regard to postmodernism.[2] With this **text** comes an entire history and an entire politics – one that is generally replicated in all the European theorists who supply the resources for postmodern theory.

Before addressing this history directly, however, it is necessary, given the enormous credibility attaching to Lyotard's text, to consider some of its main points alongside critical reactions to them. While this may seem to over-restrict the full range of contributions to the theme of postmodern politics, it will get us to the core of many of the key debates in this area. Among the 'extreme simplifications' *The Postmodern Condition* announces, the one that has had perhaps the greatest impact concerns the status of what Lyotard calls '**meta-**' or '**grand narratives**'.[3] While grand narratives such as the **Enlightenment** narrative of infinite progress in knowledge and liberty, or the Marxist narrative of the progressive emancipation of labouring humanity from the shackles imposed upon it by industrial capitalism, have played a crucial role in anchoring knowledge and politics in modernity, **postmodernity** has entailed a crisis of confidence in them. One reason for this crisis is the rise of critical philosophy, begun, ironically, with the Enlightenment. While Immanuel Kant, who initiated critical philosophy at the end of the eighteenth century, had intended it to supply human reason with the means for self-government, rather than relying on some divine arbiter or other unknowable phenomena, reason was to subject itself to criticism in order to know itself and its limits. By the end of the nineteenth century, however, criticism was being directed at the hard-won gains of the Enlightenment itself, with Friedrich Nietzsche proclaiming that God is dead, and that truth, morality and knowledge itself were mere illusions. Karl Marx had also chipped away at the Enlightenment edifice, arguing that its politics had concentrated on ideals of progress at the expense of real progress in matters of human freedom, and that this idealism, rather than being a mistake, was a complex reflection of the ideals of the ruling classes. Meanwhile, Marxism has not yet brought about the freedom it promised, but has instead produced a series of anomalies, such as the crushing of popular protest against Soviet rule in Budapest in 1956 and the bloody terrors of Stalin's gulags.

Progressive conflict between the narratives has therefore weakened them all, so that, at the beginning of the twenty-first century, there seem to be no candidates to take over from them in tying all our knowledge and our actions to some coherent historical plan. All that is left is a field where the fragments left over from these grand narratives compete with one another and with new rivals. This field, however, is governed by a new alliance between technology and capitalism, constituting what some theorists have dubbed '**post-industrial** society'.[4] But what big story does capitalism have to tell? Whereas it used to tell the Enlightenment tale of increasing liberty being best guaranteed by a free market capitalism that maximizes choice and minimizes state intervention in the lives and careers of individuals, under alliance with technology, the efficiency gains of, for example, computing fall into line with the drive to profit, so that 'minimum in, maximum out' becomes the only rule governing commercial, social and political concerns alike. Moreover, as a rule, it is its own justification: when profit is made and efficiency gained, the rule is justified, short-circuiting any appeal to larger-scale **narratives** to '**legitimate**' it. Indeed, the other side of this coin is that governments and other regulatory bodies are misled if they suppose they can control, by the imposition of political ends, the 'free' move-ments of capital across national boundaries. Governments and their economic policies no longer tell stories that affect the real movements of money: consider the recent problems of Iceland, Greece and Ireland.

While 'late capitalism', to use political theorist Ernest Mandel's phrase, popularized by Fredric Jameson, is a major player in postmodern or post-indus-trial societies, as noted by many critics and theorists, its presence in Lyotard's text is often overlooked.[5] As we shall see later in this essay, it points to a very different evolutionary path for postmodernism than is often assumed by the celebrants of postmodern **difference**: the postmodern condition is a historical tale of the survival-of-the-fittest narrative. To return then to the matter of narra-tive, with capitalism ultimately triumphant in the conflict of the narratives, no single story is left to hold things together; as many stories are told as there are groups to tell them. None, however, has any cultural, historical, philosophical or political priority over any other. It is in this field that, by common consent, postmodern politics finds itself: where there was unity, so the story goes, now there are only differences. Where the political will of a people, a nation or a culture used to be harnessed to long-term general goals, now fragmented groups engage in short-term struggles. The spread of identity politics over the last few decades is testimony to this, with its emphasis on ethnicity, class, gender and sexuality replacing political credo.

Adherents of this state of affairs suggest that the celebration of the differ-ences between such groups and identities allows for a politics to develop that no longer needs, as did ideals of the 'general will' of the people, or the political ideal of cultural revolution, to subjugate its members' interests to an orthodoxy. Instead, micro-political alliances may unpredictably emerge that remain atten-tive to the differences between their constituent groups. Marxists, feminists, **Greens** and gays may thus find themselves in a loose coalition concerning one issue, but may equally find themselves at odds over another. Moreover, with the revolution off the agenda for the foreseeable future, direct action and issues-based politics assume a more urgent and realistic significance. Detractors, however, point to two main defects in such a view of the postmodern political condition. The first is, how can a culture organize itself around this liberal-pluralist, 'anything goes' ideology without the political muscle to back it up against those who, quite simply, are too different from ourselves, and who view Western liberalism in general, and the North Atlantic bourgeois community in particular, as pathologically weak and misguided? Consider, for example, the various **fundamentalisms** at work in the contemporary world. How does the North Atlantic bourgeois community respond when its basic rights are infringed, as happened when an ayatollah issued a fatwa against an author for blasphemy? If that community follows its liberal-democratic principles and continues to celebrate difference, how can it object to the death sentence? Such scenarios call for a basic commitment to enforcing certain laws and rights against those who are so different as to deny the value of difference. Second, by concentrating all its attention on 'micro-political' issues, or on short-term single-issue politics, the very real large-scale political structures that govern our everyday lives are disregarded and left uncontested to the enemy, which simply translates into covert support for, or actual complicity with, the status quo.

Meanwhile, of course, the champions of difference can point to a past riven with intolerance and the suppression of the majority of the world's population by a tiny minority of white, male, North Atlantic, well-educated and economically powerful individuals. Rather than celebrating difference, this regime has enacted a huge programme of colonization, political disenfranchisement and outright suppression. A postmodern world of differences opens up possibilities for the oppressed to find a voice with which to struggle against their oppression. Here, however, another aspect of postmodernism comes to the fore. Just as the Nation, the People or the Party are condemned for their totalizing aspirations, so too the ideal of a coherent and integrated self, such as promised by psychoanalysis, falls under suspicion. Once again, this is a problem that was initially opened up by Kant, who introduced an unbridgeable gulf between the knowable self and the knowing self, a gulf that was only provisionally held together by our ability to use the word 'I'. Nietzsche, seizing on the grammatical core of the Kantian **subject**, set about criticizing the belief in a coherent and integrated self as a product of a misplaced faith in grammar. Sigmund Freud put paid to this idea by drawing attention to conflicts between aspects of the self, and located diverse parts of our 'psychical personalities', the unconscious bulk of which remains permanently inaccessible to us. Finally canonized in postmodernism as multiple or schizophrenic selves, postmodern difference seems to give with one hand what it takes with the other: for difference to offer any liberatory potential, the corrosion of the self must come to an end so that there is some identity that can serve as the basis of an identity politics. Such dilemmas are keenly felt and hotly debated in many fields, notably feminism. On the one hand, postmodern feminists like Judith Butler argue that there is no core identity, no essential self, nor any essentialist category 'woman' that would serve to unify the aims of a political mass movement. Instead, the self and its gender are realized only as performances. Others, however, argue for the maintenance of the essentialist category 'woman', since without it what purpose could feminism conceivably serve? If we let go of the essential reality of women's oppression, we simultaneously take leave of our responsibilities to real women, making 'feminism' merely an academic ploy.

Apart from feminism's problematic alliance with postmodern theory, how do the main protagonists in the debates about postmodern politics line up? To develop this snapshot of the postmodern condition, I will continue to focus on positions that engage with Lyotard's version of postmodernism, since it has been one of the most influential and since a great deal more has, of course, been said about the themes of this essay than could be treated within it. As already noted, postmodernism came of intellectual age in the English-speaking world in the early 1980s. Hal Foster's collection *Postmodern Culture* (1985) marks this transition well. Originally titled *The Anti Aesthetic* (1983), the retitling of this collection of essays by academic heavyweights such as Jürgen Habermas, Edward Said, Fredric Jameson and Jean Baudrillard clearly signals postmodernism's shift away from the art world towards broader issues.[6] The early forays of two contributors in particular into this new territory have continued to focus debates ever since.

Habermas's essay in *Postmodern Culture*, 'Modernity – An Incomplete Project', clearly signals his rejection of 'postmodernism'. If, according to Lyotard and other recent French philosophers, whom Habermas collectively calls the 'young conservatives', none of modernity's narratives of emancipation and progress have borne fruit, this does not mean that they never will, but rather that they have *not yet* fully developed. [7] Diagnosing the problem faced in late modernity by the evolution, during modernity, of an increasing abstraction and specialization in the fields of knowledge (science), practical life (politics) and artistic practices, Habermas proposes to reinvigorate the Enlightenment project that directed all progress to the ideal benefit of the human race as a whole. Therefore, exponents of these rarefied practices ought to justify their abstractions to the life-world.

The means by which Habermas envisages this happening are found in the principles that govern communicative action: insofar as I speak to you, I give tacit assent to your speaking to me in return. Moreover, since speech replaces and modifies direct action (I do not just go ahead and change the world without asking), I also implicitly agree to be bound to seek agreement with you, rather than riding roughshod over your views. In other words, the aim of all rational communication is to reach agreement on what should be done. By not observing the rules implicit in all communicative action, I forfeit any right to engage in dialogue. Postmodernism, by insisting that this project is at an end, is simply not playing the game. That narratives are discredited and fragmented is no reason to assume that they need always be so. This merely poses us a problem that we must direct our efforts towards resolving.

Moreover, Lyotard, whose book *The Postmodern Condition* appeared in 1979 (Habermas's essay was first delivered in 1981), in relating a grand narrative about the end of grand narratives exposes a central contradiction in his account of postmodernism: if there is no longer any belief in grand narratives, then what grounds could there be for accepting Lyotard's own account? If we do accept this account, therefore, then paradoxically it must be wrong about the status of grand narratives. Moreover, in offering it, Lyotard must himself believe that it must have some credibility, so that even Lyotard himself believes his account to be false. Of course, in making these criticisms, Habermas effectively discredits Lyotard's extended analysis of *how it is* that this situation has indeed come about. We will return later to the roots of Lyotard's diagnosis of the condition of narrative under victorious capitalism. If Lyotard does not believe in the collapse of grand narratives, then, Habermas clearly does – certainly as regards Lyotard's narrative, at any rate! To the postmoderns, Habermas has too ideal a sense of what actually happens in communication: inevitably interested parties set agendas, so that agreement must be won even by threat and coercion: that is, by the exercise of **power**.

Habermas's own suggestions for healing the splits in the everyday life-world in which we all live and act are riven with effects of power to which they remain blind: either agree or shut up. To the postmoderns, this merely emphasizes the illegitimacy of consensus as an ideal outcome, since it is won at the cost of suppressing dissent. The solution offered by Lyotard is therefore not to suppress, but rather to emphasize and even experimentally to aggravate dissensus. Rather than accept norms and rules imposed top-down by circumstance or project, open-ended experimentation will create new rules from the ground up. (As we shall see in 'Postmodernism and Science and Technology' (Chapter 9), the scientific overtones in the language of experiment are crucial to understanding aspects of postmodernism that are often overlooked.)

While Habermas, following in the footsteps and the professorial chair of the Frankfurt School of Social Research, retains some of his forebears' commitment to the Marxist project along with his version of Kant's enlightened democracy, there are many other strands of the Marxist reaction to postmodernism. Ranging from Félix Guattari's neo-communist outright dismissal of postmodernism as something that 'does not merit the name of philosophy, for it is only a prevalent state of mind, a "condition" of public opinion that pulls its truths out of the air', to Ernesto Laclau and Chantal Mouffe's **post-Marxist** hybrid of Marxism and postmodernism, Marxist analyses have had, perhaps, the most to lose from the demise of the grand narrative of emancipated human labour and the postmodern disregard of large-scale political phenomena, such as the economy or the revolution.[8] It is at least curious, then, that the renowned Marxist critic and theorist Fredric Jameson seems so positive about it. Even more paradoxically, his contribution to Foster's collection and his *Postmodernism, or, the Cultural Logic of Late Capitalism* (1991)[9] – along with Laclau and Mouffe's *Hegemony and Socialist Strategy*, one of the most cited Marxist addresses to postmodernism[10] – seems to buck the trend represented by Foster's collection to have moved postmodernism from aesthetics to philosophy and politics, insofar as they resolutely remain within the realm of the aesthetic. This paradox is only apparent, however.

The title of Jameson's book, which refers to postmodernism as the cultural logic of late capitalism, repeats the orthodox Marxist distinction between the economic base of society and the cultural superstructure that reflects the conditions of this base. Art and philosophy are among the superstructural phenomena of a society, so that, as Marx put it regarding philosophy, '[t]he ideas of the ruling class are in every epoch the ruling ideas: i.e, the class which is the ruling *material* force of society, is at the same time its ruling *intellectual* force'.[11] By insisting that postmodernism has its roots in cultural phenomena, or, in other words, that it is located within this superstructural field, Jameson's book is a contribution to a long-running debate regarding the extent to which art and philosophy are to be regarded as simple expressions of fundamental economic shifts in society's base. A 'postmodern politics' would therefore be a misnomer, but the politics of postmodern culture can be revealed through the analysis of postmodern theoretical, philosophical and cultural artefacts. Rather than simply adopting the well-used strategy of criticizing it for its politics, Jameson is determined to gamble that, by conducting such analyses, postmodernism may be susceptible to treatment by Marxist theory, and to find a place within the persistence of the Marxist dialectic. Against Lyotard, then, Jameson argues that incredulity in grand narratives is not a final position on postmodernism, but rather that this incredulity has its roots within economic phenomena. One of the themes to which Jameson constantly returns is therefore the prevailing nostalgia for the exuberant confidence and economic security of North American society in the 1950s evident in so much contemporary film and literature. It is the collapse of this economic utopia under the regimen of late capitalism, then, that lies at the root of the distrust of large-scale political narratives and provokes what Daniel Bell called, in 1960, 'the end of ideology', finding expression in so much contemporary philosophy and theory, so that postmodernism's vaunted theories of fragmentation turn out to be expressions of this, or analyses of these expressions.[12]

Jameson does not, however, think that Marxism can survive these economic and cultural shifts without adapting its own theory to the new structures of the economic base effected by what sociologists such as Alain Touraine have referred to as 'post-industrial society'.[13] The analysis of postmodern culture will therefore have lessons for Marxism as well as postmodern political theorizing; for one thing, the strict separation of base and superstructure must be modified to take account of the dialectical effects on the base of cultural phenomena. After all, the idea that we can gain direct and unmediated access to economic reality by somehow sidestepping all theory and philosophy seems as untenable as the worst excesses of a 'just the facts, ma'am' scientism.

One of the holes in Jameson's book, which he explicitly and regretfully notes, is the absence of any discussion of recent **cyberpunk** fiction. As cyberpunk author Bruce Sterling notes, writing science fiction in today's technologically sophisticated world faces a new challenge: the readers of such works have themselves, owing to an ever-increasing rate of technological change, grown up in a science fictional world.[14] Now, disregarding for the moment the problems this presents to science-fiction writers and readers, cyberpunk fiction none the less reveals a concern with the singular phenomenon of runaway technological development. This is also one of the concerns that animates Lyotard's report on the postmodern condition. While the ins and outs of this development will be further discussed in 'Postmodernism and Science and Technology', it is important to note the extent to which Lyotard's account is an extension of the Marxist emphasis on the means of production to an analysis of changes in this sphere within post-industrial or computerized societies. That technology does not figure largely in Jameson's account demonstrates the possibility that the restriction of postmodernism to the field of culture and aesthetics is shaky, a shakiness compounded by his insistence that Lyotard's experimentalism is solely an advocacy of the avant-garde practices enshrined in aesthetic modernism.

To develop this point, however, it is finally necessary to return to what this essay promised at the start: the political roots of Lyotard's postmodernism. Far from being particular to Lyotard, however, the French philosophies that have been imported into the English-speaking world to form that hybrid creature, postmodern theory, have all been shaped, to varying degrees, by these same political histories and events. To understand why this is so, it is necessary to bear in mind the intellectual climate of post-war France. Between the two world wars, the names on everybody's contents pages were dominated by the 'three Hs': Hegel, Husserl and Heidegger. After the war, Jean-Paul Sartre, whose existentialist philosophy was the culminating French expression of this holy trinity, began to attempt to move towards an accommodation with Marxism, finally declaring the latter to be 'the one philosophy of our time which we cannot go beyond'.[15] This reflected the rise to intellectual prominence of the so-called 'masters of suspicion': Marx, Nietzsche and Freud. One reason for this, apart from much cultural soul-searching following the ghastly spectacle of France's collaboration with the Nazis under the reviled Vichy regime, were the Paris lectures of Alexandre Kojève on Hegel's philosophy. These lectures, which brought a particularly Marxist slant to the reading of Hegel, had a defining influence on the entire generation of thinkers who were to rise to the dizzy heights of canonization as 'postmoderns'. Marxism, then, became that narrative against which the **legitimacy** of all others must be measured. In consequence, it is for the collapse of this narrative in particular that we must account in order to understand the passage from a Paris saturated with Marxism to its collapse in postmodernism.

The *événements* in Paris of May 1968 saw students and workers barricading the streets of a modern, first-world economic power to such an extent that the government was on the brink of being overthrown. When the unions, the parties, the intellectuals and the good men of the left condemned the popular insurrection in the streets of Paris in May 1968, Marxism's promise of a revolutionary future redeemed from capitalist exploitation, and hence its legitimacy among the intellectual left in general, evaporated. Lyotard, for instance, scandalized by the French Communist Party's condemnation of the occupation of the Nanterre campus of the University of Paris by the radical student group led by Daniel Cohn-Bendit, the 22nd March Movement (commemorating the arrest of the student leaders of an anti-Vietnam protest organization), supported them against the Party, the unions, the press, the university authorities, the government and, ultimately, against the violent suppression of their occupation when Nanterre was stormed by the French riot police in early May. When the students reacted by taking to the streets in the company of the workers who, rejecting government pay policy, had staged a massively successful general strike, the failure of the Party and the unions to support the revolution, and their complicity with the state in helping to put it down in the name of a return to 'popular government', clearly demonstrated the left's betrayal of its revolutionary promise and its function as an organ of statist control. It is for this reason that Lyotard continued into the 1980s to regard May 1968 as a razor's edge severing the atrophied Marxist **metanarrative** from postmodernity. Hence, also, one of the slogans daubed on the walls of Paris during the *événements*: 'Comrades, humanity will never be happy until the last capitalist is hung on the guts of the last bureaucrat.'

Such a view had been vigorously championed by the **Situationist** International (SI), whose pamphlet of 1966, 'On the poverty of student life', written in collaboration with Strasbourg student activists enraged by the university's role as a training ground for the managers of the 'spectacle', forced the state to arrest, try and condemn the students[16] – and to recognize the threat posed to the everyday banality of life under capitalism by the SI. The Situationists themselves made much of their role in the *événements*, commenting that their strategies had been implemented as if taken from a Situationist textbook; even taking to the streets was a strategy the Situationists called 'drifting', a means of reappropriating the urban environment for the imagination: 'Beneath the paving stones, the beach!' Not only do elements of Situationist vocabularies and analyses find their way into Lyotard's texts from the late 1960s and early 1970s, it was also from this background that Jean Baudrillard's thesis of a society of simulated desire emerged, taking its cue from Guy Debord's *The Society of the Spectacle*, with its theses concerning the management and production of desire through what remained, in de Gaulle's France, a state-run media.[17] Whereas, however, the crux of Debord's analysis was that, under spectacular society, we either acquiesce as passive consumers of the spectacle of our own, alienated lives or, overthrowing the spectacle and its apparatus, we become active producers of revolution; for Baudrillard, a revolution against the spectacle can only take the form of a spectacle, since if it did not, it literally could not take place, and would not register within spectacular society.

The immediacy of the revolution for which the Situationists agitated, while it found equally immediate expression in the streets of Paris, ran directly counter both to the Marxian ideal of revolution as an organic development from capital itself, and to its Trotskyite variant, for which the proletariat had to be helped to see how unfortunate and miserable they were by an intellectual and political vanguard. Neither war nor economic hardship had produced a revolution; but the stifling banality of the affluent society had. The failures of both these programmes to deliver the revolution, and the increasing bureaucratization of international Marxism, had already prompted a large-scale re-evaluation of Marxism by groups such as *Socialisme ou Barbarie* ('Socialism or Barbarism'), to which both Debord and Lyotard belonged. Between 1956 and 1964, Lyotard, a tutor in Algeria at the time, contributed analyses of the popular struggle for Algerian independence and the lessons for Marxism it contained. The group's basic thesis was that the bureaucratization of international communism revealed the extent to which it had become an organ of bureaucratic capitalism. After the group began itself to become rigid and doctrinaire, Lyotard left to join *Pouvoir Ouvrier* ('Workers' Power'), where he remained until 1966, at which point, disillusioned, he became active in the emergent student politics and eventually joined the 22nd March Movement.

Although often enough at odds with each other, the Situationists, *Socialisme ou Barbarie* and the enraged students all shared the conviction that Marxism no longer held the blueprints of the revolution. In other words, Marxism was already a thing of the past, for Lyotard, by the time of the *événements*. What then prompted him to claim so decisive a position, vis-à-vis Marxism, for these events? Surely Marxism was already at an end? Not so. While the immediate revolution of May 1968 demonstrated the unviability of Marxism as a political programme, the collapse of the Marxist grand narrative, that was to reach its culminating *synthesis* in the great proletarian revolution arising out of capitalism itself, does not entail the rejection of Marxist *analysis*, merely a reorientation of its questions and a re-evaluation of its aims such as Lyotard had already been engaged in since 1956. Thus, if we look at the core questions asked in *The Postmodern Condition* – What form does capital take in postmodern society? How do the means of production in postmodernism differ from previous social formations? What form must a politics capable of responding to this situation take? – more rather than less continuity is revealed between the basic political orientation of Lyotard's thought on either side of the 'razor's edge' of May 1968.

What form, then, does postmodern capitalism take? As noted earlier, one crucial element of postmodern societies is the new alliance forged between capitalism and technology. It is this that provides the material basis for Lyotard's argument that capitalism emerges victorious from the conflict of the narratives: profit no longer need be legitimated by reference to a grand narrative of progressive realization of individual liberty through the market, since it is justified immediately by sharing its sole criterion of success with a technology that has become the means of production of knowledge, information and power. Thus the means of production that secure power in postmodern societies are informational rather than industrial. Every time a computer maximizes the output of information from the minimum of input, on every occasion when time or labour are saved by the implementation of a technology, capitalism immediately wins again. We cannot argue with capitalism, since within it there is no longer any role left for discursive reason. Nor does capitalism require propaganda: a self-confessed enemy of the state as much as of socialism, capital acts without loyalties, in accordance with its one rule of maximizing efficiency. The high ground of macro-political reality is not therefore merely 'left to the enemy', as so many critics of postmodern politics have suggested; rather, the postmodern condition results directly from these new social structures. What form, then, should a postmodern politics take? Lyotard's advocacy of experimentation, mentioned earlier, must be applied to the context of the material organization of post-modern societies. Such a situation requires experimentation not only at the aesthetic level, as Jameson argues Lyotard's experimentalism reduces to, nor solely at the level of narrative: it requires that the media of techno-capital in which knowledge, power and information are stored, be the object themselves of radical experimentation.

This, then, is the history of the postmodern condition: on the one hand, a history of the evolution of capitalism into techno-capital, on the other, a history of the demise of the Marxist grand narrative and a response to the void left by this most accomplished of critical repertoires. The free trade in theory characteristic of postmodernism in the English-speaking world has, generally speaking, sacrificed the political history of the French philosophy of postmodernism to a kind of short-term expediency, paradoxically derived in large part from theses propounded in such works. The rush for the new at the expense of its historical embeddedness remains, however, something of an experiment in forms of knowledge and political action, and the incursions made by postmodernism into fields such as law, political theory and feminism clearly demonstrate the stakes of this experiment: if theory is regarded as a kit to be assembled, not in accordance with some scholarly sense of its history, but variously according to the demands of the task at hand, then withdrawing it from the sterile catacombs of scholarly debate may yet have pragmatic benefit. Of course, ignorance of history, as is often remarked, condemns the ignorant to repeat it, but it is in the nature of an experiment to have an unknown outcome. Besides, if the tools of the past – Marxism, the Enlightenment project, market liberalism and so on – have been tried and found wanting, then experiment is demanded. As Lyotard says, the 'post' of 'postmodernism' does not signal that it comes at the end, but at the beginning of modernity. What new modernity might yet dawn from post-modern politics?

NOTES

1 See, for example, his discussion of 'hyperreality' in Jean Baudrillard, *Simulations*, trans. Paul Foss, Paul Patton and Philip Beitchman (New York: Semiotext(e), 1983).
2 Jean-François Lyotard, *The Postmodern Condition* [1979], trans. Geoff Bennington and Brian Massumi (Manchester: Manchester University Press, 1984).
3 Ibid., p. xxiii.
4 See, for example, Daniel Bell, *The Coming of Post-Industrial Society: A Venture in Social Forecasting* (London: Heinemann, 1974).
5 See Ernest Mandel, *Late Capitalism* (London: New Left Books, 1975).
6 Hal Foster, ed., *Postmodern Culture* (London: Pluto Press, 1985) (originally published as *The Anti-Aesthetic: Essays on Postmodern Culture* (Port Townsend, WA: Bay Press, 1983)).
7 Jürgen Habermas, 'Modernity – An Incomplete Project', in Foster, ed., *Postmodern Culture*, pp. 3–15 (p. 14).

8 Gary Genosko, ed., *The Guattari Reader* (Oxford: Blackwell, 1996), p. 112.

9 Fredric Jameson, *Postmodernism, or, The Cultural Logic of Late Capitalism* (Durham, NC: Duke University Press, 1991).

10 Ernesto Laclau and Chantal Mouffe, *Hegemony and Socialist Strategy: Towards a Radical Democratic Politics* (London: Verso, 1985).

11 Karl Marx and Frederick Engels, *The German Ideology* [1845] (London: Lawrence & Wishart, 1965), p. 61.

12 Daniel Bell, *The End of Ideology* (Cambridge, MA: Harvard University Press, 1960).

13 Alain Touraine, *The Post-Industrial Society. Tomorrow's Social History: Classes, Conflicts and Culture in a Programmed Society* [1969], trans. Leonard F. X. Mayhew (New York: Random House, 1971).

14 See Bruce Sterling, 'Cyberpunk in the Nineties', *Interzone*, 23 May 1998, lib.ru/ STERLINGB/interzone.txt (accessed 8 February 2011).

15 Jean-Paul Sartre, *Search for a Method* [1957], trans. Hazel E. Barnes (New York: Vintage Books, 1968), p. xxxiv.

16 UNEF Strasbourg, 'On the Poverty of Student Life' (AFGES: Strasbourg, 1966), library.nothingness.org/articles/SI/en/display/4p (accessed 8 February 2011).

17 Guy Debord, *The Society of the Spectacle* [1967], trans. Donald Nicholson-Smith (New York: Zone Books, 1994).

4

POSTMODERNISM AND FEMINISM

SUE THORNHAM

POLITICS AND THEORY

Feminism has its origins in a politics, aimed at changing existing **power** relations between women and men. Its starting point, as Maggie Humm points out, is 'the understanding that, in all societies which divide the sexes into different cultural, economic or political spheres, women are less valued than men'.[1] As a social and political movement, therefore, its *theoretical* developments have been bound up with demands for political change. The emergence of 'second wave' feminism, the term now usually used to describe the post-1968 Women's Liberation Movement, was marked by new political groupings and campaigns, organized around abortion legislation, demands for legal and financial equality, and against pornography and sexual violence against women. But it was also marked by the publication of ambitious theoretical works such as Kate Millett's *Sexual Politics* and Shulamith Firestone's *The Dialectic of Sex* (both 1970). Both works offered themselves as texts of revolution. Firestone insisted that what she called the 'pioneer Western feminist movement' of the nineteenth and early twentieth centuries should be seen as merely the first onslaught of 'the most important revolution in history'.[2] Millett heralded the emergence of 'a second wave of the sexual revolution'.[3] Both sought to re-claim a feminist history; both identified feminism as *theoretical* standpoint with the women's movement as *political practice*.

For feminism, politics and theory are interdependent. But, as the books by Firestone and Millett make clear, feminist politics have engaged as much with issues of culture and representation as in campaigns for social and economic change. Feminist theorists from Mary Wollstonecraft (1759–97) onwards have seen cultural constructions of femininity as a primary source of women's oppression. Women, writes Wollstonecraft, have been reduced to 'insignificant objects of desire'; the category 'woman' is constructed in opposition to that of 'human'.[4] From its beginnings, feminism has seen 'ideas, language and images as crucial in shaping women's (and men's) lives'.[5] It has been concerned both to analyse and intervene in the construction of knowledge, meanings and representations. It has also been engaged in the struggle to find a voice through which such knowledges might be expressed. For the development of an autonomous female subject, capable of speaking in her own voice within a culture which has persistently reduced her to the status of object, is also part of feminism's project.

As Rosalind Delmar describes it, feminism has sought to transform women's position from that of object of knowledge to knowing subject, from the state of subjection to subjecthood.[6]

AN ENLIGHTENMENT NARRATIVE?

All of this would seem to place feminism as an offshoot of the 'emancipatory **metanarratives**' of **Enlightenment modernism**, and this is indeed where many feminist theorists would position themselves. If, as Jean-François Lyotard suggests, two major forms of '**legitimation narrative**' have been used to justify the Enlightenment quest for knowledge and the importance of scientific research, both find their echo in feminist theory.[7] The first, the 'narrative of emancipation', in which knowledge is sought as a means to liberation, finds a clear echo in the concept of 'women's liberation'. As Sabina Lovibond writes, 'it is difficult to see how one could count oneself a feminist and remain indifferent to the modernist promise of social reconstruction'.[8] But Lyotard's second legitimation narrative, that of the speculative mind, in which knowledge is sought for its own sake, also finds its feminist echo – in the practice of 'consciousness raising'. Through consciousness raising, insight into the operations of male power (a feminist 'enlightenment') is achieved through communal self-analysis. The result is liberation from internalized patriarchal assumptions and ways of understanding (a patriarchal 'false consciousness'). Like Marxism, therefore, feminism's initial project ties theoretical analysis of oppression to a narrative of emancipation through social transformation.

Early feminism, then, had as its aim women's *equality*, through admission to those spheres from which they had been excluded, and this included the spheres of rational thought and intellectual discourse. If women have been *excluded* from political theory, from Marxism, philosophy, psychoanalysis and other dominant theoretical discourses, then women's inclusion could expand and perhaps transform those discourses, while at the same time their insights might be used to illuminate women's experience. Much feminist theory of the 1960s and early 1970s, therefore, set out to expand and transform existing theoretical models. But there are a number of problems with this approach. In the first place, it became clear that to expand such models to include women simply would not work, for women's exclusion is not an accidental omission but a fundamental structuring principle of all patriarchal thought. As Simone de Beauvoir pointed out in 1949, woman in Western thought has represented the **Other** that can confirm man's identity as Self, as rational thinking being. The concept of Self, she writes, can be produced only in opposition to that of not-self, so that the 'category of the *Other* is as primordial as consciousness itself'.[9] To constitute himself as Subject, man has constructed woman as Other: 'she is the incidental, the inessential as opposed to the essential. He is the Subject, he is the Absolute – she is the Other.'[10]

Second, even if women could be included within these discourses, it would be in terms only of *sameness* not difference; that is, within frameworks which could discuss women only in terms of a common, male-referenced humanity (what Luce Irigaray calls the 'hom(m)osexual economy' of men),[11] not specifically as *women*. As *subjects* of these knowledges, therefore – that is, as thinkers and writers – women could occupy only a range of pre-given positions. They could speak only from within a *masculine* logic, as surrogate men. Indeed, it became increasingly clear that the 'universal subject' of Enlightenment modernism, far from being ungendered and 'transcendent', was not only gendered but very specific: a Western, bourgeois, white and heterosexual man.

Once this theoretical step is taken, a further step is inevitable: if feminists seek to construct a universal, 'essential' *woman* as subject and/or object of their own thought, then that figure will be as partial, as historically contingent and as exclusionary as her male counterpart. Given her origins, she will simply be a Western, bourgeois, white and heterosexual *woman*. Feminist theory cannot *both* claim that knowledge and the self are constituted within history and culture *and* that feminist theory speaks on behalf of a universalised 'woman'. Rather, it must embrace differences between women and accept a position of partial knowledge(s). And once it occupies this position, feminist thought begins to move away from its Enlightenment origins, and to have much in common with **postmodernist** theory.

FEMINISM AND POSTMODERNISM

Craig Owens suggests a number of points of convergence between the two. Both feminism and postmodernism argue that the 'grand' or 'master' narratives of the Enlightenment have lost their legitimating power. Not only, they would both suggest, have claims put forward as universally applicable in fact proved to be valid only for men of a particular culture, class and race; the ideals which have underpinned these claims – of 'objectivity', 'reason' and the autonomous self – have been equally partial and contingent. Both argue that Western *representations* – whether in art or in theory – are the product of access not to Truth but to power. Women, as Owens points out, have been *represented* in countless images (and metaphors) throughout Western culture, often as symbol of something else – Nature, Truth, the Sublime, Sex – but have rarely seen their own representations accorded legitimacy. The representational systems of the West have, he argues, admitted only 'one vision – that of the constitutive male subject'.[12] Both present a critique of **binarism**, that is, thinking by means of oppositions, in which one term of the opposition must always be devalued. We have seen in the discussion of de Beauvoir's work how fundamental this critique has been to feminist thought. Both, instead, insist on '**difference** and **incommensurability**'.[13] Finally, both seek to heal the breach between theory and practice, between the subject of theory/knowledge and its object. Women, of course, are both the subjects and the objects of feminist theory, and women's sense of self, it has been argued, is far more 'relational' than that of men.[14]

In place of an essential, universal man or woman, both feminism and post-modernism offer, in Jane Flax's words, 'a profound skepticism regarding universal (or universalizing) claims about the existence, nature and powers of reason, progress, science, language and the subject/self'.[15] Yet the alliance thus formed has been an uneasy one. Feminism, as I have indicated, is itself a 'narra-tive (or series of narratives) of emancipation', and its political claims are made on behalf of women as *social* group(s) with an underlying community of interest, and of an *embodied female subject* whose identity and experiences (or 'truth-in-experience') are necessarily different from those of men. If we replace the concept of 'woman' with that of 'myriads of women living in elaborate historical complexes of class, race and culture', as some theorists propose[16] – if, in other words, we remove gender (or sexual difference) as a central organizing principle – how can a feminist *political practice* be any longer possible? If sexual difference becomes only *one* term of difference, and one which is not *fundamentally* consti-tutive of our identity, then how can it be privileged? Surely to privilege it would be to create, in Christine Di Stefano's words, 'just another ... totalizing fiction' which should in its turn be **deconstructed** and opposed in the name of differ-ence.[17]

In throwing in its lot with postmodernism, then, might not feminism be colluding in its own eradication, accepting the demise of 'metanarratives of emancipation' at a point when women's own emancipation is far from complete? Feminists have been understandably divided as to the answer to this question. Some, like Sabina Lovibond, have insisted that feminism must not be seduced by the attractions of postmodernism, for if feminism disowns 'the impulse to "enlighten"' it loses the possibility of all political and social action.[18] Others have taken a very different line, arguing that the critiques of Enlightenment beliefs which feminist theory has mounted *must* place it as 'a type of postmodern philosophy'.[19] Jane Flax, for example, argues that feminist theo-ries, 'like other forms of postmodernism, should encourage us to tolerate and interpret ambivalence, ambiguity, and multiplicity as well as to expose the roots of our needs for imposing order and structure no matter how arbitrary and oppressive these needs may be'.[20] In this argument, postmodernism becomes a sort of therapeutic corrective to feminism's universalizing tendency. In similar vein, Nancy Fraser and Linda Nicholson, while rejecting the philosophical pessimism of Lyotard, wish to adopt his critique of metanarratives for a feminist social criticism. Such a feminist theory, they argue, would eschew the analysis of grand causes of women's oppression, focusing instead on its historically and culturally specific manifestations. It would also replace unitary conceptions of 'woman' and female identity with 'plural and complexly structured conceptions of social identity, treating gender as one relevant strand among others, attending also to class, race, ethnicity, age, and sexual orientation'. In a thor-oughly feminising metaphor, they conclude that such a theory 'would look more like a tapestry composed of threads of many different hues than one woven in a single color'.[21]

This move towards a radical **anti-essentialism** has found its most powerful voice in the work of Judith Butler. Butler goes much further than Flax, or Fraser and Nicholson, in arguing that the very category of gender is a 'regulatory fiction' which functions to enforce compulsory heterosexuality (everyone is *either* male or female; opposites complement/attract). For Butler, gender is 'a kind of impersonation and approximation ... but ... *a kind of imitation for which there is no original*'. The appearance of 'naturalness' which accompanies heterosexual gender identity is simply the effect of a repeated imitative performance. What is being imitated, however, is 'a phantasmatic ideal of heterosexual identity'.[22] There is no essence of heterosexual masculinity or femininity which precedes our performance of these roles; we construct the ideal of that essence *through* our performances. And we construct it in the service of a regulatory heterosexual binarism. Gender, like other categories of knowledge, is the product not of Truth but of power expressed through **discourse**. Moreover, as a copy of a fantasized ideal, heterosexuality always *fails* to approximate its ideal. It is thus doomed to a kind of compulsive repetition, always threatened by failure and always liable to disruption from that which is excluded in the performance. Gender, in this view, is a performance which constructs that which it claims to explain. Rather than persisting in clinging to it as an explanatory category, therefore, feminists should celebrate its dissolution into 'convergences of gender identity and all manner of gender dissonance'.[23] Its abandonment promises the possibility of new and complex subject-positions and of 'coalitional politics which do not assume in advance what the content of "women" will be'.[24]

Other feminists, however, while not wishing to return to a unitary concept of 'woman', have been far more sceptical about the transformative possibilities of a feminism which embraces postmodernism. These theorists point to a number of major problems in this projected alliance. At the heart of all of these is the issue of power. Postmodernism, unlike feminism, as Linda Hutcheon reminds us, is not a politics:[25] it has no strategies of resistance and is not concerned with social and political change. A postmodernist feminism, in which sexual difference is no longer seen as a fundamental organizing category, but is replaced by the concept of multiple and shifting *differences*, threatens to make a feminist politics impossible. Such a politics must assume that women constitute specific – and specifically oppressed – constituencies. We can see these difficulties in the work of Judith Butler. Butler's early work proposed a strategy of 'gender parody', in which gender is self-consciously and parodically performed, in a masquerade which subverts because it draws attention to the non-identity of gender and sexuality, to the *multiple* sexualities which can be written on our bodies. Critics responded that this is not only an 'extremely individualistic solution to the problem of women's oppression';[26] it is also imbued with the political ambiguities of postmodernism. Parody, after all, depends on the stability of that which it imitates for its critical force, oscillating between complicity and critique. Butler's later work has wrestled with the need to reconcile on the one hand a continuing sense that gender norms can and must be 'exposed as non-natural and non-necessary' through forms of critical citation like drag, and on the other a recognition that 'norms are precisely what binds individuals together, forming the basis of their ethical and political claims'.[27]

Unease about the alliance of feminism and postmodernism has been even stronger when considering how easily this emphasis on self-conscious parody and play can be co-opted for a notion of '**post-feminism**'. Originating as a term in popular journalism of the 1980s, 'post-feminism' was seen as heralding a release from the narrow preoccupations of feminism, in a celebration of difference, personal liberation and play, performed primarily through processes of consumption. In more recent years it has been taken more seriously, proposed as both a continuation and a critique of 'second-wave' feminism, incorporating feminism's goal of equality while embracing the pluralism and diversity characteristic of postmodernism.[28] But as critics like Angela McRobbie have pointed out, in also embracing postmodernism's political ambivalence, it has in fact lent itself to the 'displacement of feminism as a political movement'.[29] When popular television series such as *Buffy the Vampire Slayer* (1997–2003), or *Sex and the City* (1998–2004) are described as post-feminist, for example, what is being referred to is their privileging of style and a notion of gender masquerade, but without any clear critical or subversive intent.

A NEW MASTER NARRATIVE?

Feminists, then, have criticized postmodernism's indifference to issues of power and politics. As Meaghan Morris points out, the diagnosis of crisis in modernism's 'legitimation narratives' offered by theorists of the postmodern will not necessarily benefit women, their designation as '*master* narratives' notwithstanding.[30] It might just as well mean the collapse of arguments for any kind of political intervention – since there are no longer grounds for deciding where, when or *as whom* to intervene. As Donna Haraway puts it:

> We unmasked the doctrines of objectivity because they threatened our budding sense of collective historical subjectivity and agency and our 'embodied' accounts of the truth, and we ended up with one more excuse for not learning any post-Newtonian physics and one more reason to drop the old feminist self-help practices of repairing our own cars. They're just **texts** anyway, so let the boys have them back.[31]

With no arguments for change, power is once again ceded to the powerful.

This last point takes us on to a further argument: that postmodernism may not simply be indifferent to questions of power. It may in fact seek to constitute itself as the new 'master discourse'. Craig Owens' concern at the absence of feminist voices within postmodernism, for example, offers to reinscribe feminism as 'an *instance* of postmodern thought'.[32] Postmodernism, that is, constitutes itself – where it considers feminism at all – as the *inclusive* category, of which feminism is merely one example. In so doing, it can be argued, it simultaneously moves to erase the specificity of the feminist critique and, in a repeat of modernism's self-constitution, to silence the voices of women.

That postmodernism has sought to deal with feminist critique by offering itself as a 'framing discourse' for feminism is a point made by a number of feminist theorists. They have pointed to the fact that postmodernism's debate with – or deconstruction of – modernism has been conducted pretty well exclusively within and by the same constituency as before: white, privileged men of the industrialized West. It is a constituency which, having already had its Enlightenment, is now happy to subject that legacy to critical scrutiny. In this debate the contribution of feminism, while acknowledged to be a key factor in destabilizing modernism's concept of a universal '**subject**', is of necessity (re) marginalized. The central protagonists are once again to be found elsewhere. Nancy Hartsock articulates feminist suspicions of this move. 'Why is it,' she asks, 'that just at the moment when so many of us who have been silenced begin to demand the right to name ourselves, to act as subjects rather than objects of history, that just then the concept of subjecthood becomes problematic?'[33] It is no accident, she argues, that at the moment when those who have been excluded begin both to theorize and to demand political change, there emerges uncertainty about whether the world *can* be theorized and about whether progress is possible or even, as a 'totalizing' ideal, desirable. For Hartsock, the intellectual moves of postmodernism constitute merely the latest accent of the voice of the 'master discourse', as it attempts to deal with the social changes and theoretical challenges of the late twentieth century.

Two further feminist suspicions are worth enumerating here. They concern the way in which postmodern 'gender-scepticism' permits an easy slide into what Susan Bordo calls the 'fantasy of *becoming* multiplicity – the dream of endless multiple embodiments, allowing one to dance from place to place and self to self'.[34] This has two aspects. The first is that being *everywhere* is pretty much the same as being nowhere; in other words, postmodernism offers to its male theorists simply another version of the disembodied detachment which characterized the Enlightenment speaking position. For postmodernist feminists to seek to occupy this position is to risk their own obliteration as distinctive voices. As Tania Modleski argues, only those who *have* a sense of identity can play with not having it.[35] The kind of disembodied, 'anti-essentialist' feminism which is produced from postmodernism's embrace is, she argues, at best a luxury open only to the most privileged of women. At worst, it is to collude in the masculine disavowal of female embodiment.

The second aspect of postmodernism's 'fantasy of becoming' which is worth noting is its tendency to become a fantasy of woman, even of 'becoming woman'. On the one hand, then, for some theorists of the postmodern the feminine remains, as it was in the narratives of modernity, a metaphor for that which is outside truth or meaning. For Jean Baudrillard in particular, the feminine is a constant metaphor for the postmodern.[36] It is woman's lack of subjectivity, her conflation of authenticity and artifice, that constitute both the horror and the seduction of the postmodern. For other theorists, most notably Gilles Deleuze And Félix Guattari, 'becoming-woman' is a way of deconstructing phallic identity, but ultimately with the aim of moving to a dispersed subjectivity 'beyond gender'.[37] Feminist critics have objected that such a move is possible in one direction only: as a *woman*, 'one cannot deconstruct a subjectivity one has never been fully granted control over'.[38] In both instances, one can argue, the use of femininity to represent the unrepresentable, the diffused or the fluid is yet another appropriation. The 'discourse of woman' is in reality the discourse of male philosophy. As Tania Modleski puts it, 'male power ... works to efface female subjectivity by occupying the site of femininity'.[39] Women, as embodied subjects, are once more erased.

'STANDPOINT' THEORIES

How, then, can feminist theory both hold on to a belief in 'woman' *and* insist on diversity and difference? Can we both accept the multiplicity and mobility of women's discourses and embodiments and argue for the centrality of sexual difference in the construction of subjectivity? Attempts to answer this question have produced some of the most exciting feminist thinking over the past few decades. One possible answer is provided by those who have been termed feminist 'standpoint' theorists. Borrowing from Marxism, these thinkers argue that the subjugated or marginalized not only produce *different* knowledges from those in positions of privilege; they also produce less distorted, less rationalizing, less falsely universalizing accounts. Nancy Hartsock, for example, argues that our task should be to develop an account of the world which treats these alternative perspectives not – as they are seen from the centre – as subjugated or disruptive knowledges, but instead as primary and as capable of constituting a *different* world.[40] This is an approach also embraced by black feminists like Patricia Hill Collins, who argues for what she terms a black women's or Afrocentric feminist epistemology.[41] Like other subordinate groups, argues Collins, African American women have not only developed distinctive interpretations of their own oppression, but have done so by constructing alternative forms of knowledge. The specific forms of black women's economic and political oppression and the nature of their collective resistance to this oppression mean, she argues, that African American women, as a group, experience a different world from those who are not black and female. The specificity of this experience in turn produces a distinctive black feminist *consciousness*, and a distinctive black feminist intellectual tradition. These 'engaged visions', in Hartsock's terms, can then produce the grounds for the recognition of commonalities, and 'the tools to begin to construct an account of the world sensitive to the realities of race and gender as well as class'.[42]

There are problems, however, with this rather literal interpretation of what a 'politics of location' might mean.[43] It can become over-simplified and reductive (*this* set of experiences inevitably produces *that* mode of consciousness). It is difficult to know *which* set of experiences is constitutive of a particular group and mode of knowledge-production. It places an emphasis on experience which should perhaps more properly be placed on particular ways of *interpreting* that experience. Finally, the appeal to a commonality of experience can elide both differences *between* and differences *within* women. Collins' work, for example, persistently assumes that all black women are *American*, insisting that '[l]iving life as an African American woman is a necessary prerequisite for producing black feminist thought', and that all African American women share a common position.[44] On the other hand, once we allow for the multiplicity of positionings *within* every 'standpoint', the concept of a commonality of experience within oppressed groups – and hence a distinctive standpoint – can become lost.

SITUATED KNOWLEDGE AND POLITICAL FICTIONS

The concept of 'situated knowledges' developed by theorists such as Rosi Braidotti and Donna Haraway is a more complex answer to the question of how, in Braidotti's words, to 'figure out how to respect cultural diversity without falling into relativism or political despair'.[45] The 'situatedness' envisaged here is no simple affair. It is in the first place a position which insists on the *embodied* and therefore sexually differentiated nature of the female subject. But embodiment does not, in this context, mean 'essentialism', where essentialism is defined as implying a fixed and monolithic essence to female identity which is beyond historical and cultural change. The embodied female subject envisaged here is, on the contrary, a '**nomadic**' subject, to use Braidotti's terminology. That is, she is 'the site of multiple, complex, and potentially contradictory sets of experiences, defined by overlapping variables such as class, race, age, lifestyle, sexual preference, and others'.[46] Haraway goes further: in the contemporary high-tech world, feminist embodiment is about 'nodes in fields, inflections in orientations, and responsibility for difference in material-semiotic fields of meaning'.[47] What both thinkers are trying to do in these rather complex formulations is to insist *both* that the female subject is embodied – that women's knowledge and thought cannot be separated from their lived experience – *and* that this insistence does not mean that feminism cannot recognize the differences both between women and *within* each woman. Within all of us, argues Braidotti, there is an interplay of differing levels of experience, so that our identities, while *situated*, are not fixed but 'nomadic'. It is such situated knowledges – 'partial, locatable, critical knowledges'[48] – which permit both a new definition of objectivity (objectivity as partial, situated knowledge) and the possibility of new political coalitions.

But this still leaves the difficulty of how, in Braidotti's words, to 'connect the "differences within" each woman to a political practice that requires mediation of the "differences among" women'.[49] For it is difficult – to say the least – to see how women could unite around the formulations quoted above. In answer, both

Braidotti and Haraway offer 'political fictions' (Braidotti) or 'foundational myths' (Haraway) as a way of framing understanding. These 'politically informed images', or 'figure[s] of hope and desire', are offered as a means of empowering both a shared sense of identity and the struggle against oppression.[50] Political fictions, argues Braidotti, may be more effective at this moment than theoretical systems. Both Luce Irigaray's image of woman as 'This Sex Which is Not One' and Judith Butler's description of a critically performative drag can be seen in these terms, as foundations for a feminism which will go beyond existing definitions of sexual difference. Braidotti's own image is the figure of the nomad, who is neither exile (homeless and rootless) nor migrant (displaced and suspended between the old and the new). Instead, 'situated' but mobile, the nomad employs a critical consciousness to cultivate 'the art of disloyalty to civilization', thus resisting incorporation by the host culture.[51] Haraway's 'political fiction' is more challenging. It is the figure of the **Cyborg**, a hybrid of body and machine, a 'kind of disassembled and reassembled, post-modern collective and personal self'.[52] As hybrid figure, the cyborg blurs the categories of human and machine, and with it those other Western dualisms: self/other, mind/body, nature/culture, male/female, civilized/primitive, reality/appearance, whole/part, agent/resource, maker/made, active/passive, right/wrong, truth/illusion, total/partial, God/man. It is embodied but not unified, and being a figure of blurred boundaries and regeneration rather than (re)birth, it cannot be explained by reference to conventional narratives of identity. It is locally specific but globally connected: Haraway reminds us that 'networking' is a feminist practice as well as a multinational corporate strategy, a way of surviving 'in diaspora'.[53]

It can be objected that theorists like Braidotti and Haraway are trying to have it both ways: to be both situated and multiple, within and outside postmodernism. They can also be accused of replacing a narrative of liberation directed at change in the real world with a utopian fantasy whose notions of 'embodiment' and 'situatedness' are slippery in the extreme. Susan Bordo, for example, criticizing Haraway's image of the Cyborg, protests:

> What sort of body is it that is free to change its shape and location at will, that can become anyone and travel anywhere? If the body is a metaphor for our locatedness in space and time and thus for the finitude of human perception and knowledge, then the postmodern body is no body at all.[54]

For Bordo, this kind of response to what Sandra Harding calls the contemporary 'instabilities' of feminism's analytical categories will leave feminist thought 'cut ... off from the source of feminism's transformative possibilities'.[55] A similar charge is made by Tania Modleski, who argues that it will leave us with a 'feminism without women'.[56] Nevertheless, the dilemma which all these theorists articulate is the same: in Modleski's words, how to 'hold on to the category of woman while recognizing ourselves to be in the *process* (an unending one) of *defining and constructing the category'.*[57] Since it is, as Haraway comments, 'hard to climb when you are holding on to both sides of a pole, simultaneously or alternately', the various 'political fictions' offered by feminist theorists can be seen as a way of finding new terms in which to theorize a way forward.[58] For the danger they recognize is also the same: that male postmodern theory will simply repeat the gesture of its modernist predecessors in appropriating 'femininity' as one of its multiple possible positions, at the same time as it erases and silences the work and lives of women. The task which is being addressed is, in the words of Meaghan Morris, 'to use feminist work to frame discussions of postmodernism, and not the other way around'.[59]

NOTES

1　Maggie Humm, *Feminisms: A Reader* (Hemel Hempstead: Harvester Wheatsheaf, 1992), p. 1.
2　Shulamith Firestone, *The Dialectic of Sex: The Case for Feminist Revolution* [1970] (London: The Women's Press, 1979), p. 23.
3　Kate Millett, *Sexual Politics* [1970] (London: Virago, 1977), p. 363.
4　Mary Wollstonecraft, *A Vindication of the Rights of Woman* [1792] (Harmondsworth: Penguin, 1992), pp. 83, 79.
5　Annette Kuhn, *The Power of the Image: Essays on Representation and Sexuality* (London: Routledge and Kegan Paul, 1985), p. 2.
6　Rosalind Delmar, 'What is Feminism?', in J. Mitchell and A. Oakley, eds, *What is Feminism?* (Oxford: Blackwell, 1986), pp. 8–33.
7　See Jean-François Lyotard, *The Postmodern Condition: A Report on Knowledge* [1979], trans. Geoff Bennington and Brian Massumi (Manchester: Manchester University Press, 1984).
8　Sabina Lovibond, 'Feminism and Postmodernism' [1990], in T. Docherty, ed., *Postmodernism: A Reader* (Hemel Hempstead: Harvester Wheatsheaf, 1993), pp. 390–414 (p. 395).
9　Simone de Beauvoir, *The Second Sex* [1949], trans. H. M. Pashley (London: Pan Books, 1988), p. 16.
10　Ibid.
11　Luce Irigaray, *This Sex Which is Not One* [1985], trans. Catherine Porter (Ithaca, NY: Cornell University Press, 1985), p. 171.
12　Craig Owens, 'The Discourse of Others: Feminists and Postmodernism' [1983], in Hal Foster, ed., *Postmodern Culture* (London: Pluto Press, 1985), pp. 57–82 (p. 58).
13　Ibid., pp. 61–2.
14　Nancy Chodorow, *The Reproduction of Mothering: Psychoanalysis and the Sociology of Gender* (Berkeley, CA: University of California Press, 1978); Carol Gilligan, *In a Different Voice: Psychological Theory and Women's Development* (Cambridge, MA: Harvard University Press, 1983).
15　Jane Flax, 'Gender as a Social Problem: In and for Feminist Theory', *Amerikastudien/American Studies*, 31 (1986), pp. 193–213 (p. 196).
16　Sandra Harding, 'The Instability of the Analytical Categories of Feminist Theory' [1986], in H. Crowley and S. Himmelweit, eds, *Knowing Women: Feminism and Knowledge* (Cambridge: Polity Press, 1992), pp. 338–54 (p. 339).

17 Christine Di Stefano, 'Dilemmas of Difference: Feminism, Modernity, and Postmodernism' [1988], in L. J. Nicholson, ed., *Feminism/Postmodernism* (London: Routledge, 1990), pp. 63–82 (p. 66).

18 Lovibond, 'Feminism and Postmodernism'.

19 Jane Flax, 'Postmodernism and Gender Relations in Feminist Theory', in Nicholson, *Feminism/Postmodernism*, pp. 39–62 (p. 40).

20 Ibid., p. 56.

21 Nancy Fraser and Linda J. Nicholson, 'Social Criticism without Philosophy: An Encounter between Feminism and Postmodernism' [1988], in Nicholson, *Feminism/Postmodernism*, pp. 19–38 (pp. 34–5).

22 Judith Butler, 'Imitation and Gender Insubordination', in D. Fuss, ed., *Inside/Out: Lesbian Theories, Gay Theories* (London: Routledge, 1991), pp. 13–31 (p. 21).

23 Judith Butler, 'Gender Trouble, Feminist Theory, and Psychoanalytic Discourse', in Nicholson, *Feminism/Postmodernism*, pp. 324–40 (p. 339).

24 Judith Butler, *Gender Trouble: Feminism and the Subversion of Identity* (New York: Routledge, 1990), p. 14.

25 See Linda Hutcheon, *The Politics of Postmodernism* (London: Routledge, 1989).

26 Tania Modleski, *Feminism without Women: Culture and Criticism in a 'Postfeminist' Age* (London: Routledge, 1991), p. 158.

27 Judith Butler, *Undoing Gender* (New York: Routledge, 2004), pp. 218–19.

28 Ann Brooks, *Post-Feminisms: Feminism, Cultural Theory and Cultural Forms* (London: Routledge, 1997).

29 Angela McRobbie, *The Aftermath of Feminism: Gender, Culture and Social Change* (London: Sage, 2009), p. 15.

30 Meaghan Morris, *The Pirate's Fiancée: Feminism, Reading, Postmodernism* (London: Verso, 1988), p. 223.

31 Donna Haraway, *Simians, Cyborgs, and Women* (London: Free Association Books, 1991), p. 186.

32 Owens, 'Discourse of Others', p. 62.

33 Nancy Hartsock, 'Foucault on Power: A Theory for Women' [1987], in Nicholson, *Feminism/Postmodernism*, pp. 157–75 (p. 163).

34 Susan Bordo, 'Feminism, Postmodernism, and Gender-Scepticism', in Nicholson, *Feminism/Postmodernism*, pp. 133–56 (p. 145).

35 See Modleski, *Feminism without Women*.

36 See Jean Baudrillard, *Seduction* [1979], trans. Brian Singer (Basingstoke: Macmillan, 1990).

37 See Gilles Deleuze and Félix Guattari, *A Thousand Plateaus: Capitalism and Schizophrenia*, trans. Brian Massumi (Minneapolis, MN: University of Minnesota Press, 1987).

38 Rosi Braidotti, *Metamorphoses: Towards a Materialist Theory of Becoming* (Cambridge: Polity Press, 2002), p. 82.

39 Modleski, *Feminism without Women*, p. 7.

40 Hartsock, 'Foucault on Power'.

41 See Patricia Hill Collins, 'The Social Construction of Black Feminist Thought' [1989], in B. Guy-Sheftall, ed., *Words of Fire: An Anthology of African-American Thought* (New York: New Press, 1995), pp. 338–57.

42 Hartsock, 'Foucault on Power', p. 172.

43 Adrienne Rich, 'Notes toward a Politics of Location', in *Blood, Bread, and Poetry: Selected Prose 1979–8* (New York: Norton, 1986), pp. 210–31.
44 Collins, 'Social Construction', p. 349.
45 Rosi Braidotti, *Nomadic Subjects: Embodiment and Sexual Difference in Contemporary Feminist Theory* (New York: Columbia University Press, 1994), p. 31.
46 Ibid., p. 4.
47 Haraway, *Simians, Cyborgs*, p. 195.
48 Ibid., p. 191.
49 Braidotti, *Nomadic Subjects*, p. 180.
50 Ibid., p. 4; Patricia Ticineto Clough, *Feminist Thought: Desire, Power and Academic Discourse* (Oxford: Blackwell, 1994), p. 89.
51 Braidotti, *Nomadic Subjects*, p. 30.
52 Donna Haraway, 'A Manifesto for Cyborgs: Science, Technology, and Socialist Feminism in the 1980s' [1985], in Nicholson, *Feminism/Postmodernism*, pp. 190–233 (p. 205).
53 Ibid., p. 212.
54 Bordo, 'Feminism, Postmodernism', p. 145.
55 Harding, 'Instability', p. 153.
56 Modleski, *Feminism without Women*.
57 Ibid., p. 20.
58 Haraway, *Simians, Cyborgs*, p. 188.
59 Morris, *Pirate's Fiancée*, p. 16.

5

POSTMODERNISM AND GENDER AND SEXUALITY

CHRIS HAYWOOD AND MAIRTIN MAC AN GHAILL

The emergence of female ejaculation, marriage to animals, pedal porn, male pregnancy as part of the cultural vernacular is beginning to exasperate the onto-logical certainties that are foundational to the **modern** gender and sexual order. Such an order can be traced back to the rise of industrialization in the eighteenth and nineteenth centuries and the subsequent state rationalization of relation-ships based on capital (re)productivity. Alongside this, the proliferation of **discourses** that naturalized gender and sexuality often located in physiology and biology, have contributed to the current Western hegemonic erotic configura-tion that prioritizes heterosexual marriage and monogamous fidelity. The fusion of gender and sexuality is built upon a common assumption that there is an ontological basis to sexuality premised on the existence of gendered sexual 'selves', 'natures' and 'being'. For Foucault sexuality is formed by a historical amalgam. The profusion and intensification of sexual discourses in the eigh-teenth century convened 'an artificial unity, anatomical elements, biological functions, conducts, sensations, and pleasures, and it enabled one to make use of this fictitious unity as a causal principle'.[1] An important dynamic in the consolidation of this unity was the predication embedded in medical, legal and educational doctrines that attitudes, behaviours and practices are reducible to gendered and sexual identities. Modernity's 'aspiration to reveal the essential truth of the world'[2] saw the emergence of nomenclatures, taxonomies and epi-demiologies that identify, categorize and explain gendered and sexual selves, natures and being. As a result, gender and sexuality are situated within a modern mimesis; what one does signifies what one is, and what one is signifies what one does.

However, a number of social, cultural and economic factors are challenging this hegemony. The changing emphasis from manufacturing to service modes of production has impacted upon the role of work and the material bases of iden-tity, family and community. A shift from working with the body, to working on the body has resulted in a reconfiguration of sociality from socio-economic loca-tion to an embodied aestheticism. Civil society has also witnessed a series of political changes. For example, Second Wave political activism had a pivotal role in questioning the link between female sexuality, reproduction and mother-hood. Lesbian and Gay activism has challenged the heterosexual exclusivity of marriage through forms of civil partnership. Also, technological developments have led to changes in how intimate relationships are practised. For instance, the emergence of online dating sites is redefining what constitutes private and public space. Alongside this, the **globalization** of capital relations is involved in the circulation of erotic goods, commodities and identities across a number of differentiated markets that are exchanged over a range of media platforms.[3] Baudrillard argues that a characteristic of modernity is 'an orgy of liberation'.[3] In this context new forms of social, economic and symbolic exchange are untethering gender and sexual identities from their social and cultural histories. Thus, with the dissipation of the modern gender/sexual order and the collapse of being and doing as mimetically connected, an erotic heterogeneity is emerging that is becoming increasingly difficult to situate. Commentators on **postmodernity** have suggested that such a unity is beginning to unravel, with the norms and values that circulate through and within gender and sexuality becoming destabilized. As traditions, formal and informal sanctions, habits, customs and mores are becoming increasingly disconnected from an (imagined) past there is an increasing intensification towards re-establishing the truth of gender and sexuality. This essay suggests a number of postmodern ideas and concepts that may be helpful in considering the changing nature of gender and sexuality. It begins by exploring the 'sexual' by not relying upon gender and sexuality identities to explain it.

THE SEXUAL WITHOUT SEXUALITIES

Within the gender order of modernity, sexuality is *the* reference point of the erotic and gendered sexualities such as heterosexuality, homosexuality, bisexuality have been pivotal in establishing the normative parameters of a sexual moral economy. These normative parameters enforced formally and informally through religious, political and legal sanctions have marginalized and **fetishized** other erotic possibilities. A sexuality identity template has been applied to a range of paraphilias including zoophiles, paedophiles and more obscure practices such as apotemnophilia (having amputation), formicophilia (being crawled on by insects) or dendrophilia (trees). It is argued that an increasing mutliplicity of sexualities continues the modernist pursuit of linking identities with practices. However, such linking can be understood as a modern phenomenon. Henry Abelove's account of the changing nature of sexual relationships in England between the 1680s and the 1830s provides an interesting case.[4] Examining the data from A. E. Wrigley's collection of mortality and fertility statistics, Abelove suggests that a population explosion occurred in the 1800s.[5] The drop in the average age of first marriage, the increase in the percentage of women marrying, the rise in illegitimacy and the increasing prevalence of pre-nuptial pregnancy contributed to a rise in fertility from 4.93 million to 13.28 million in 1831. As an explanation, Abelove argues that sexual intercourse *became* a popular form of erotic activity. It is suggested that with the increasing cultural emphasis on production (productive action as good/non-productive action as bad), activities deemed non-productive were put under 'extraordinary and ever-intensifying

negative pressure'.[6] He suggests that particular sexual habits, rituals and practices became marginalized by prioritizing the concept of productivity.
Furthermore, G. R. Quaife, highlighting the work of J. L. Flandarin, argues
that other forms of sexual activity were more prevalent than heterosexual
coition.[7] He argues that masturbation, oral and anal sex were highly popularized forms of sexual expression at the time. Abelove does not claim a causal relation between of the rise in capitalist production and sexual reproduction, but
explains it as a shift from cultural proclivity to industrial productivity. The
implication of this is that sexual cultures at other historical moments can
demonstrate the limitations of gender and sexuality through an identity
template as *the* explanatory framework.

The comparative power of history creates clarity when exploring how the
modern gender/sexual order is being transformed. A more recent challenge to
the modernist linking of practices to identity has been through '**queer theory**'.
Queer theory questions the categorical bases of identities and recognizes the
fluidity and creativity that may characterize erotic relations. Judith Butler
argues that sexuality is conceptually and affectively inadequate:

> Indeed, there are middle regions – hybrid regions of legitimacy and illegitimacy
> that have no clear names and where nomination itself falls into a crisis produced by
> the variable, sometimes violent boundaries of **legitimising** practices that come into
> uneasy and sometimes conflictual contact with one another.[8]

The claim of queer theory is that there is a fracturing occurring within conventional gender and sexual categories. For example, Phil Hubbard usefully
describes the emergence of scary heterosexualities 'such as fetishism, prostitu-
tion, pornography, masturbation, voyeurism and sado-masochism';[9] added to
that may be group sex, pre-pubertal sexualization, dogging or intergenerational
sex (the rise of the MILF/DILF phenomenon) and intersex. Alongside this,
there is also evidence that there are a range of pleasures, erotic practices and
alternative sexual mores that stand outside a heterogendered erotic economy.
Michel Foucault suggests that the erotic and the sexual could be considered
through the notion of a 'relational right'.[10] In contrast to a set of relations that
has sex-desire (gendered sexualities) at its centre, there could be a relation of
friendship through which the erotic would articulate itself. Another way of
disconnecting the erotic from sexuality is the possibility of framing the erotic
through something similar to adoption. For instance, he suggested that adoption could take place between two adults. A phenomenon that has become
increasingly visible across televisual and **Internet** media is the phenomenon of
adult babies. This involves adults, male and female, taking up *babylike* subjec-
tivities. Although Internet sites eroticize the disciplining or infantilism of the
experience, it is suggested that this erotic experience is premised on notions of
expressing and receiving love and care. Dressing up in nappies and playing with

toys, the adult baby disrupts conventional understandings of pleasure. Psychiatric interventions have named this as 'Adult Baby Syndrome', however web community dialogues tend to focus on the enjoyment of expressing and receiving love, support, security and care. Another under-researched area is that of an 'adult nursing relationship'. This is where a person (male or female) is physically or pharmaceutically induced to 'feed' breast milk to his or her partner. The practices may take place without sex and may involve forms of intimacy and tenderness that are not confined to the predominant conventional gendered sexual emotional literacy. As Foucault suggests: 'By taking the pleasure of sexual relations away from the area of sexual norms and its categories, and in so doing making the pleasure the crystallizing point of a new culture – I think that is an interesting approach'.[11]

Queer theory, conceptually and politically, identifies the possibilities of different economies of pleasure that question and challenge erotic templates configured by gender and sexual identities. Or, as Mary McIntosh reports: 'Queer means to fuck with gender'.[12] Of importance is that queer theory disrupts the epistemological foundation of all identities including gay, lesbian and bisexual identities. However, refusing to explain sexual practice and experience through a sexuality framework is not without its dangers. Judith Butler has criticized Foucault for this attempt at moving outside the regulatory regime of sexuality.[13] From her critique, Foucault requires the juxtaposition of gender/ sexuality [against] pleasure/bodies. In doing so, the oppositional force of the two positions generates an impossibility of an alternative to sexuality. This means, according to Butler, that in order to make sense of pleasure and bodies it has to be worked out against gendered sexualities. Thus the regulatory mechanism of sexuality – premised on gender – produces a notion of pleasure/bodies. Butler's concern about the absence of sexuality is about the attendant absence of desire: 'To deny the sphere of desire, or to call for its replacement, is precisely to eradicate the phenomenological ground of sexuality itself'.[14] Butler claims that this approach to sexuality is dangerous as the analytical purchase on the power circulating through gendered and sexual acts is obscured. There are also political ramifications as gender and sexuality have become important tools in understanding the dynamics of social (in)justice, such as heteronormativity. Thus a shift to an arrangement of bodies and pleasures:

> works in the service of maintaining a compulsory ignorance, and where the break between the past and the present keeps us from being able to see the trace of the past as it re-emerges in the very contours of an imagined future.[15]

With Foucault's emphasis on bodies and pleasures, there is a decentring of gender and sexuality as erotic templates. In doing so, the social and cultural inequalities that circulate through gender and sexuality become analytically more difficult to explain.

GENDER, SEXUALITY AND THE POSTMODERN CARNIVAL

If the first section suggests that a characteristic of the postmodern is the disconnection of the sexual from sexuality with gender, this section explores the idea of the sexual becoming increasingly disconnected from sex. This is somewhat confusing given the intensification of sexual messages across traditional and more recent digital platforms. In fact, it would appear that there is an increasing saturation of the sexual within everyday culture.[16] At the same time, access to such sexualization appears to be widening, with a range of social groups now able to access diverse sexual and erotic forms. Although there appears to be some agreement that the sexualization of culture is taking place, there is much debate about whether this involves the development of new genders and sexual forms, or whether it is a reinscription of existing structures of sexual and gender inequality. It is argued that the erosion of the modern gender/sexual order is contributing to what Simon refers to as pluralization of sexualities.[17] One of the consequences of this sexual saturation is that the normative boundaries that impel erotic charges are becoming less distinctive and leading to a postmodern erotic carnival. This means that the sexual is circulated through a wide array of cultural forms, being inserted into anything from ice cream adverts, to holiday destinations to children's clothing ranges. As a result, sex is beginning to lose its social and cultural ascriptions. Therefore postmodern gender and sexuality is more than simply the plurality of cultural forms, it is a process that is tied to the emptying of its signifiers. One of the ways to explain the changing nature of the sexual is through a notion of the 'carnivalesque'.

The concept of the carnivalesque draws upon the work on Mikhail Bakhtin and his research on medieval cultures of folk humour. One of the areas where folk culture emerged was through ritual spectacles such as the carnival. Importantly, this celebratory event was experienced outside the routine of the everyday. Of significance is that the carnival became a space where the official norms and values that supported the official hierarchy are temporarily suspended:

> laws, prohibitions, and restrictions that determine the structure and order of ordinary, that is non-carnival, life are suspended during carnival: what is suspended first of all is hierarchical structure and all the forms of terror, reverence, piety, and etiquette connected with it.[18]

According to Bakhtin, the carnival offers a space where those deemed marginal, aberrational and vulgar gain legitimacy and in effect challenge the formal rules of feudal society. Often taking place on or around religious festivals or periods of change (for example, historical or seasonal), the carnival often parodied 'serious' society, especially that of ecclesiasm. The significance of the carnivalesque is the inversion of an established order where the everyday norms are relaxed and where identities and behaviours become unfastened. Modern examples of this can be found when people go on holiday or manage relationships through mobile phones or use social media. It is argued that in these contexts the traditional rules surrounding the expression of the erotic become loosened. Other examples such as music festivals, the office Christmas 'do', hen/stag parties, 'nights out' are suggestive of carnivalesque space where the official gender/sexual rules become destabilized and at times 'turned inside out'.[19] One of the features of the carnival, according to Bakhtin, is that there is no audience, in the sense that those who participate in the carnival are both an object of and subject to the carnival episode.

An example of the carnivalesque nature of gender and sexuality is captured by the musical theatre production *The Rocky Horror Picture Show*. Based in 1950s America, the production tells the story of two teenagers (Brad and Janet) on the verge of getting married. On the way home from an evening date their car breaks down and in search of help they come across the home of Transvestite Transylvanians led by Dr Frank N. Furter. As the night progresses Frank N. Furter and his minions seduce Brad and Janet and they engage in a range of sexual practices. As much a parody of US popular romantic culture as it is science fiction and B-movies, the articulation of pleasure within the show is highly phallicized, in the sense that during the play the desire of the lead protagonist, until his murder by his second in command, penetrates and controls those around him. Although the story has a formal narrator, the modernist hierarchy of audience deference to the production is challenged as the audience become raconteurs. By shouting out inserts and insults, they reconstruct the flow of the theatre. Through parody, **irony** and transgression, the audience become entwined into the fabric of the show and through the raucous interludes, bawdiness and vulgarity come to the fore. Consequently, the narrator and the actors are disrupted in their performance and audience intervention becomes an expected part of the show. Furthermore, since the showing of the film version in the United States in the 1970s the audience often dress up and become part of the spectacle. This involves men erotically gender blending by wearing bras, basques, suspenders and stockings; and women adorned with hyper-sexual clothes, often leading to a theatre full of 'gender outlaws'.[20]

At the same time, *The Rocky Horror Picture Show* is characteristic of postmodern gender and sexuality as it is all about sex and nothing about it at all. There is a collapse of the central signifiers that should situate its normative boundaries such as straight/gay, private/public, masculinity/femininity. Bakhtin suggests that medieval cultures were bounded by:

> the *official* life, monolithically serious and gloomy, subjugated to a strict hierarchical order, full of terror, dogmatism, reverence, and piety; the other was the *life of the carnival square*, free and unrestricted, full of ambivalent laughter, blasphemy, the profanation of everything sacred, full of debasing and obscenities, familiar contact with everyone and everything.[21]

However, in a postmodern sense, this temporal and spatial dislocation is no longer split and there is an intensification of the carnivalesque moments within everyday practices. Baudrillard argues that capitalism has developed from a situation where the use value of products was indeterminable.[22] Part of this development involved the meaning of the sign and the product becoming more tenuous. As the relationship between capital and signs progresses, Baudrillard argues that the relationship between meaning and the product becomes discontinuous, resulting in confusion over what is real and what is false. Baudrillard uses the concept of **hyperreality**, where social and cultural forms not only simulate the 'real', the real itself is a **simulation**. However, at the point of a perceived loss of meaning there is a simultaneous intensified reassembling of the truth. Not only do practices trouble the modern order, they provoke the exaggeration and exacerbation of that order to a point where value reference points become increasingly difficult to identify. In other words, as the boundary between the sexual and the non-sexual becomes gradually more blurred there is a disruption of the normative parameters of the sexual. Therefore, the episodic sexual saturation destabilizes hierarchies through repetitive banality to the point where 'Sex is no longer located in sex itself, but elsewhere – everywhere else in fact'.[23] If the medieval carnival symbolized a form of liberation, postmodern sex is characterized as boring. The 'thrill', 'desire' and the *'jouissance'* of the sexual in postmodernity, is dulled by its increasingly routine presence in everyday lives. From Baudrillard's perspective, society is engaged in a recuperation of the 'specialness' of sex. The next section focuses specifically on this process of recuperation.

THE NECESSITY OF CULTURAL DISGUST

If the proliferation of carnivalesque moments is punctuating the veneer of the modern sexual/gender order, the social and moral compass that we use to navigate sexual and gender identities becomes increasingly difficult to follow. This section focuses specifically on the media and how through cultural representations, the sexual is reinserted back into sex; how sexual boundaries are recharged. Zygmunt Bauman's description of the postmodern highlights how media representations are creating social and cultural uncertainty. This means that the possibilities of knowing something for sure are continually being contested, in effect challenging the solidity and reliability of social relationships. Thus media reports tend to gain prominence when private acts disgrace or offend the idealized, dominant morality of a social community. The narrativization by the media produces a range of effects from 'ideological and cultural retrenchment to disruption and change'.[24] For Bauman: 'the main boundary line in society is a "rightful and secure position in society"',[25] where members of society have their own unquestioned space. Stories reported in the media, according to Bauman, are suggesting that identity is no longer solid and reliable. In the context of gender and sexuality, one of the areas that is constantly threatening the integrity of collective national identity is sex crimes against children.

Ulrich Beck, speaking in the context of fragmenting social roles and relationships, argues that the interest in childhood has intensified.[26] Children are now seen in some ways as dependable and permanent – in light of cultural and social transformations, childhood is constructed as enduring. Thus, although media accounts identify a collapse in moral boundaries, it is depicted as a collapse, precisely *because* of moral certainty. A depreciation of sexual morality is not generated through ambivalence or ambiguity – such a collapse is because right and wrong/good and bad are clearly defined.[27] According to Chris Jenks:

> To abuse the child today is to strike at the remaining, embodied vestige of the social bond and the consequent collective reaction is understandably, both resounding and vituperative. The shrill cry of 'abuse' is a cry of our own collective pain at the loss of our social identity.[28]

From a postmodern position, as gendered and sexual uncertainty intensifies, there is a corresponding fetish for the pure ideal child. Such an idealization can be traced through the rapid circulation of 'superconductive events'; events that emit a plethora of moral charges that nostalgically remodel the normal.[29] Currently, one of the most prevalent areas where the cultural imaginary is assembled is through media reports of the 'paedophile'. This mobilization of 'truth' has shifted from the depiction of the paedophile as a psychological invert based on an inadequate masculinity (the 'dirty old man'/'the flasher'),[30] to a 'mythological' or non-human creature often characterized by a monstrous or supernatural masculinity. Whereas fantasies recover that which is lost often in fairytale characteristics, the phantasy is an imaginary repudiation that in the media tends to work through contemporary **representations** of horror. The usefulness of the phantasy is that it is etymologically bound into the notion of the phantasm and its supernatural powers.

As phantasm, the paedophile is considered as possibly anywhere and anyone. This can be understood as the paedophile, a ghostly spectre that haunts cultural consciousness. The paedophile is always there, but its form remains unknowable. Therefore the truth of the 'paedophile' is one that cannot be known. Kevin Ohi points out:

> To sustain a stable picture of the paedophile, it is thus paradoxically necessary to assert that paedophilia cannot be detected, that a paedophile cannot be pictured at all. The same gesture that renders him locatable and quarantined makes him unlocatable, omnipresent, and dangerously at large: just the way we like him.[31]

Importantly, like ghosts they are virtually undetectable, only knowable through various traces. Thus, the paedophile is located as a different being – as something outside normal everyday society. The paedophile is reconstructed as subhuman, a beast, monster, a fiend existing in the shadows or the fringes of the social order. As meanings become disconnected from practice, there is an intensified anxiety to recalibrate uncertainty with an exaggerated abnormality and perfected normality. More specifically:

Imagination is the selecting out and re-arrangement of 'facts' in order to provide coherence, framework and unity between ideas and action or more precisely to provide a basis for the direction of social relationships and the social creation of categories.[32]

Thus particular gender and sexual practices become a staging ground for the negotiated representation of identities. Embedded in this imagination is a moral economy, a machinery for incitement that authorizes, elevates and **abjects** sexual being and doing.

While the boundaries between the paedophile and normal society are secured through hyperreality, newspaper reports also appear to be collapsing such a division. In other words, to mobilize the moral charge of a superconductive event, media reports create a cultural disgust that is both abhorrent and exciting. For example, in the following report, sexual abuse of 14-year-old girls by Geoffrey Davidson is eroticized in a number of ways: 'He treated his large comprehensive school near Leeds Yorkshire – we are forbidden to name it – as a personal meat market, feeding his odious appetite for sex slaves with a constant supply of wide-eyed virgins'.[33] Apart from the power of the insatiability, in this story children are metaphorically described as meat who are 'fed' – having no agency and no subjectivity. Furthermore, the notion of sex slaves invokes the invisibility of the child. The removal of the meanings of childhood, and a focus on the sex slave is continued with the description of 'wide-eyed virgins'. Deriving from the Q'ran, the term aligns Geoffrey Davidson with the martyrs who receive rewards in heaven. Furthermore, the children are discoursed into the phantasy through their subjection to Davidson's vampirism.

As Chris Greer suggests, the sexual stories in the media tend not to use explicit language to describe the nature of the abuse.[34] In Greer's perspective the most important aspects are the selection of the story and how it is told. Most importantly, the above report does not generate sympathy or compassion for the victims in the case; the power and voracious proclivity of the paedophile is often set against the impossibility of agency for a child. The implication is that the victims themselves are eroticized within the framework of the paedophile desire. It could be argued, therefore, that the paper actually metonymically re-enacts the sexual scene. One of the reasons for being seen and not being heard is the possible unambiguous juxtaposition of victim and predator. The narrative relies on uninterrupted **textual** sequences to activate an erotic **semiology** that makes the teacher fascinating and exciting. As a consequence, the account reconstructs the victims as sexual objects not simply to the abuser, but to the reader themselves.

CONCLUSION

Alan Bray argues that different historical periods have been witness to a range of sexual practices.[35] He considers the notion of transvestism, in London in the sixteenth and seventeenth centuries, as a legitimate male sexual pursuit. In the early sixteenth century men would participate in sexual relations with each other but were not defined as homosexual. Evidence suggests that such practices were explained through heterosexual terminology. For example, an interesting aspect of an erotic practice in the Molly House was that members took on characteristics of the wedded couple. The place where men participated in sexual relations was called the chapel, with sexual practices being termed the 'marrying' or 'wedding night'. He argues that as the century progressed such practices became associated with a particular kind of sexual culture. The difference according to Bray is that such older forms of sexual activity began to take on new meanings and were becoming comprehensible through a notion of gendered heteronormativity. This highlights a paradox faced by those working with postmodern theory to explain gender and sexual formations: we need to understand the erotic without recourse to the modern epistemologies of gender and sexuality. In other words the very concepts that we use to explore transgressions and transformations have their histories within a particular identity politics.

This chapter has suggested some initial steps in trying to engage with this paradox. Steven Best and Douglas Kellner suggest that the postmodern is a means through which to 'interpret a family of phenomena, artefacts, or practices' and we have used the postmodern to engage with gender and sexuality.[36] The first section identified how postmodern theory enables us to question the ontological certainties of gender and sexuality. In so doing, gender and sexuality are understood as an erotic architecture that provides the structure of modern unities of gender and sexuality. The second section suggested that given the rise of multiple platforms of communication and increasing access to those platforms, gender and sexuality are being articulated in a number of different ways. We have focused on the idea of the carnivalesque as a means of capturing how traditional certainties are beginning to unravel. In the third section we introduced the usefulness of the concept 'super-conductive event'. We suggested that the recent concern and reporting over paedophilia is part of a mobilization of a truth about gender and sexuality. The disgust and fascination embedded in the stabilization of truths is being produced through eroticization in media reporting.

NOTES

1 Michel Foucault, *The History of Sexuality: An Introduction* [1976], trans. Robert Hurley (Harmondsworth: Penguin, 1981), p. 154.
2 R. Boyne and A. Rattansi, 'The Theory and Politics of Postmodernism: By way of an Introduction', in R. Boyne and A. Rattansi, eds, *Postmodernism and Society* (London: Macmillan, 1990), p. 5.
3 Jean Baudrillard, *The Transparency of Evil: Essays on Extreme Phenomena* [1990], trans. J. Benedict (London: Verso, 1993).
4 Henry Abelove, 'Some Speculations on the History of "Sexual Intercourse" during

the "Long Eighteenth Century" in England', in Andrew Parker, Mary Russo, Doris Sommer and Patricia Yaeger, eds, *Nationalism & Sexualities* (London: Routledge, 1992), pp. 335–42.

5 E. A. Wrigley, 'Growth of Population in Eighteenth-Century England: A Conundrum Resolved,' *Past and Present*, 98 (1983), pp. 121–50.

6 Abelove, 'Some Speculations', p. 339

7 G. R. Quaife, *Wanton Wenches and Wayward Wives: Peasants and Illicit Sex in Early Seventeenth Century England* (London: Croom Helm, 1979); J. L. Flandrin, *Families in Former Times: Kinship, Household and Sexuality* (New York: Cambridge University Press, 1979).

8 Judith Butler, 'Is Kinship Always Already Heterosexual?', *Differences: A Journal of Feminist Cultural Studies*, 13:1 (2002), pp. 14–44 (p. 20).

9 Phil Hubbard, 'Sex Zones: Intimacy, Citizenship and Public Space', *Sexualities*, 4:1 (2001), pp. 51–71 (p. 57).

10 Michel Foucault, *Ethics: Subjectivity and Truth*, trans. Robert Hurley, ed. Paul Rabinow (New York: New Press, 1997).

11 David M. Halperin, *Saint Foucault: Towards a Gay Hagiography* (Oxford: Oxford University Press, 1997), p. 160.

12 Mary McIntosh, 'Queer Theory and the War of the Sexes', in Joseph Bristow and Angie Wilson, eds, *Activating Theory: Lesbian, Gay, Bisexual Politics* (London: Lawrence & Wishart, 1993), pp. 30–52 (p. 31).

13 Judith Butler, 'Revisiting Bodies and Pleasures', *Theory, Culture & Society*, 16:2 (1999), pp. 11–20.

14 Ibid., p. 19.

15 Ibid., p. 18.

16 Brian McNair, *Striptease Culture* (London: Routledge, 2002).

17 William Simon, *Postmodern Sexualities* (London: Routledge, 1996).

18 Mikhail Bakhtin, *Rabelais and His World* [1965], trans. Helen Iswolsky (Bloomington, IN: Indiana University Press, 1984), p. 251.

19 Ibid.

20 Kate Bornstein, *Gender Outlaw: On Men, Women, and the Rest of Us* (New York: Vintage, 1995).

21 Bakhtin, *Rabelais*, p. 256.

22 Baudrillard, *Transparency of Evil*.

23 Ibid., p. 8.

24 Zygmunt Bauman, *Intimations of Postmodernity* (London: Routledge, 1992), p. 3.

25 Ibid., p. 26.

26 Ulrich Beck, *Risk Society: Towards a New Modernity* (London: Sage, 1992).

27 James Lull and Stephen Hinerman, 'The Search for Scandal', in James Lull and Stephen Hinerman, eds, *Media Scandals: Morality and Desire in the Popular Culture Marketplace* (Cambridge: Polity Press, 1997), pp. 1–33.

28 Chris Jenks, *Childhood* (London: Routledge, 1996), p. 22.

29 Baudrillard, *Transparency of Evil*.

30 Malcolm Cowburn and Lena Dominelli, 'Masking Hegemonic Masculinity: Reconstructing the Paedophile as the Dangerous Stranger', *British Journal of Social Work*, 31:3 (2001), pp. 339–415.

31 Kevin Ohi, 'Molestation 101: Child Abuse, Homophobia, and The Boys of St. Vincent', *GLQ: A Journal of Lesbian and Gay Studies*, 6:2 (2000), pp. 195–248.
32 Marion O'Callaghan, 'Continuities in Imagination', in Jan P. Nederveen Pieterse and Bhikhu Parekh, eds, *The Decolonization of Imagination: Culture, Knowledge and Power* (London: Zed Books, 1995), pp. 22–42 (p. 22).
33 The *Sun*, 17 October 1999.
34 Chris Greer, *Sex Crime and the Media: Sex Offending and the Press in a Divided Society* (Cullompton: Willan, 2003).
35 Alan Bray, *Homosexuality in Renaissance England* (London: GMP, 1982).
36 Steven Best and Douglas Kellner, *The Postmodern Turn* (New York: Guilford Press, 1997), p. 24.

6

POSTMODERNISM AND LIFESTYLES

NIGEL WATSON

In looking at the linkages between postmodernism and lifestyles we will be considering some of the ways in which these ideas find their way into our everyday experiences. Lifestyle is a nebulous concept, but most writers agree that the discretionary choices which we make, especially consumer choices, contribute to the construction of our social identities. To a greater or lesser extent we are all defined in the eyes of **others** by what we buy. Our self- image is built upon the meanings associated with the objects which surround us and the activities which we follow.

It was during the late 1980s and early 1990s that **postmodernism** and its linkage to our everyday lifestyles first moved from the academic literature and into popular consciousness. At this time, it was impossible not to open a quality newspaper supplement or a high-end style or culture magazine, without discovering yet another article defining and exploring the characteristics of postmodernism. We were asked to consider the intricacies of the latest theory or to consider what might link, for example, Sarah Ferguson ('Fergie', the Duchess of York), Batman, Ross Perot (a former presidential candidate in the US elections), Vimto (a UK soft drink). or Mazda cars. All of these people and products represented the postmodern, because they were all said to share a self-consciousness about the past and they all only fully made sense if an **ironic** attitude of playfulness was acknowledged. The film *Batman*, for example, played upon references from comic books, while the Mazda MX5 was (and still is) a contemporary recreation of the English sports car of the 1960s. More recently Volkswagen, Fiat and Mini have all developed cars which resonate with models from their manufacturing past. This feature of postmodern styling and design has become best known as **retro** and a glance through catalogues of consumer goods will demonstrate the extent to which this trend has become part of everyday life, with telephones, radios, bathroom fittings and furniture all drawing upon our desire to recreate the mood of an imagined past.

The public images of 'Fergie' and Ross Perot made sense by referring to the past rather than the future: 'Fergie' because she drew upon a former age of royal decadence and Ross Perot because he appealed to the so-called lost values of a former America. The former Conservative prime minister, John Major, attempted a similar appeal in the United Kingdom by evoking an England of warm beer, cricket on village greens and spinsters cycling to church on balmy summer evenings. It has also been suggested that Ross Perot represented another feature of the postmodern in that he was a single-issue politician without roots in the traditions of party. The same was said of Sir James Goldsmith's Referendum Party in the 1997 UK general election, which had only one policy and which claimed that it would dissolve itself if its aim was achieved.

Postmodern politics are said to revolve around particular campaigning issues in which previously disparate groups coalesce and then dissolve again. This is exemplified by the so-called rainbow coalition of the 1980s and by the protests and campaigns against live animal exports in which elderly Tory women, liberal academics and New Age travellers united against the injustice of sending animals to their deaths thousands of miles away within the confined conditions of an animal transporter. At root this aspect of the postmodern condition is related to the dissolution of traditional class and status groupings. Values and allegiances are now transitional and no longer centred in the old alliances of production-based relationships and class-based political parties. Retro styling and the dissolution of tradition are only some of the features which characterize postmodernism and more of these will be explored later in this essay.

Newspapers also tended to ask celebrities and public figures if they could define the exact nature of postmodernism. Most were sceptical or dismissive, though some did hazard a guess that it might have something to do with being more flexible or challenging social hierarchies. Jean Baudrillard, however, one of the most quoted writers on postmodernism and culture, was entirely on the dismissive side: '[O]ne should ask whether postmodernism has a meaning. It doesn't as far as I am concerned. It's an expression, a word people use but which explains nothing. It's not even a concept. It's nothing at all.'[1]

In the early part of the twenty-first century there is still some confusion and controversy surrounding the concept, and for some philosophers, such as Christopher Norris, the term is little more than a lazy way of collecting together some of the features of contemporary culture and combining them with partly digested aspects of continental thought.[2] It is, they argue, only a transitory and relatively insignificant phase in our understanding of contemporary experience. Indeed at the time of writing, contemporary writers are identifying alternative definitions including **altermodernism** and **post-postmodernism** to define contemporary social experience. Alan Kirby has even gone so far as to say that post-modernism is dead.[3] It is true that the idea is less significant and falls into the background more now than in the 1990s; however, it cannot be denied that the concept has had a major impact across areas of thought ranging from geography to literary theory to cinema to architecture, and that for many writers it has provided a satisfactory way of explaining the significant changes in the nature of social experience over the past 50 years or so. This essay considers these changes in relation to consumer culture and in particular will reflect upon contemporary social identity. I try to answer the question whether the basis of everyday life can be said to have changed sufficiently to justify the claims of some writers that we are living in a new era or epoch – an era that can be called **'postmodernity'**.

POSTMODERNISM, IDENTITY AND LIFESTYLE

Although, for some, postmodernism remains a confused and vacuous term, it has been in use for long enough to have achieved at least a basic consistency of definition. Most commentators agree that there is a cluster of features which characterize contemporary culture and which when taken together can be called postmodern. Perhaps the most important of these for the purposes of this section is the suggestion that our experiences are now rooted in the processes of consumption rather than production. This can perhaps be illustrated by thinking of those regions of the United Kingdom which were once dominated by heavy industry. For most people in these largely working-class areas the future was one defined by a relationship with work and with, for example, the production of coal, or ships or cotton. The people were miners, shipbuilders or mill workers and the basis of social life was for these men and women their relationship with the process of production. Their personal, collective and cultural identities were rooted in the locality around the workplace and in the values of the industry for which they worked.

The past 50 years have seen a radical shift in the nature of this relationship. The land which used to house the factories and mines has now been developed for out-of-town shopping areas such as the MetroCentre in Gateshead or Meadowhall in Sheffield. The land by the rivers has been turned over to leisure marinas, theme parks and heritage museums and former cotton and wool mills converted for luxury living. In fact the heritage museums, such as the one at Beamish in the north-east of England, epitomize the postmodern process whereby a past is nostalgically recreated as a form of substitute reality. Ex-miners are employed to inform the rest of us about mining in a time in which they did not live, while the need for 'real' mining has disappeared. We pay our money and are entertained by consuming second-hand experiences which once formed the basis of everyday life. To a significant extent we have become tourists in our own cultures. Sunday no longer means a trip to church or chapel, but rather a visit to the cathedrals of consumerism. Shopping malls have become major sites of leisure activity; the pilgrimage is enough even without the act of buying.

We no longer conform to the traditions of the old occupational cultures and instead we choose a lifestyle. This term, not in itself a new one, was taken by the advertising and designer culture of the 1980s to stand for the individuality and self-expression that were the cornerstone of the free market revolution of that decade. The era of mass consumption, with its emphasis on conformity and similarity, has been replaced by an apparently endless choice and variety of consumer goods aimed at specific market segments. While it is important to remember that some people in developed societies and many throughout the world are excluded from this process, it is equally important to understand that the construction of identity through the acquisition of consumer goods is a voluntary one. Those of us who participate are not just fashion victims, we actively wish to join in and actively desire the opportunities for self-expression and display which are provided by the choices of the shopping malls. It is true that we may be targeted as part of grey **power**, owners of a pink pound or subscribers to consumption smoothing, but we like to identify with the style that best represents the way that we wish to be seen. Power has now come to be seen as the capacity to spend in order to find expression for an aspirational lifestyle.

Perhaps one of the most noticeable areas of growth in consumer markets has been in men's fashion and lifestyle accessories. The male body has been increasingly used in advertising, not simply in a functional capacity, as it would have been in the 1950s, but in a decorative one as well. Men are no longer just portrayed as the expert advisers to women on technical matters such as the choice of washing machine; they are also at the aspirational heart of advertising style. Older as well as young men now articulate their identity through a conscious and selective process of consumption involving clothes, hairstyles and body decoration. A casual glance at any newsagent's shelves shows a wide range of fashion and image magazines as well as those devoted to the latest electronic gadgets. Men are the focus of a shifting process of consumerization in which image overrides utility. This has developed through constructions like the 'new man' of the 1980s and 'lads' of the 1990s, leading to versions of male identity linked to self-conscious, playful and sexualized processes, unimaginable in the decades to which John Major so nostalgically referred.

The body is also a focus for identity construction in a more permanent and serious way. The opportunity for changing the shape and structure of our physical bodies through cosmetic surgery is widely advertised in fashion and style magazines. Noses can be reshaped, wrinkles removed, faces lifted, fat siphoned and breasts reduced or augmented. The body itself can be seen as a consumer commodity, and this is a process available and promoted to both men and women. In a competitive world it is not enough to be ordinary and we are all encouraged to approach more nearly the ideal of youthful bodily perfection in order to give ourselves added market value. We may even soon be able to design our children to correspond with our aspirations and pay a surrogate mother to grow the child in order to avoid disruption of career and lifestyle.

A massive, worldwide industry has developed devoted to assisting us in our responsibilities to maintain our bodies. The healthiness of the body has become associated with its appearance, and it is possible to buy into a bewildering array of products and services that trade upon the importance of the cultural values of youth and beauty. In this context youth and beauty are aligned with slenderness, muscularity and physical fitness, one extremity of which is represented by the increasing popularity of bodybuilding for both men and women. The corollary of this is that the ageing body has become a source of anxiety, and the non-exercised and overweight body a source of shame and ridicule. Although we are surrounded by health-promoting messages which encourage us to exercise and to eat the 'right' foods, the drive for us to achieve fitness is related as much to the desire for surface attractiveness as it is to the protective dimensions of health promotion.

It is not a coincidence that management of our lifestyles is at the heart of the health-promotion process. We are encouraged to believe that our leisure time should be devoted to activities which will enhance our potential for healthy longevity. It is as important to be able to demonstrate and display an association with the correct attitude as it is actually to participate. Owning a mountain bike and Lycra shorts immediately confers the desired surface appearance, provided of course those unsightly bulges can be hidden. Similarly, eating low-fat foods and the other acceptable commodities comprising a healthy diet gives an assurance of risk reduction and adequate body maintenance even if they are consumed in addition to, rather than instead of, proscribed foodstuffs. It is often the case that an emphasis on body maintenance is combined with the celebration of excess and indulgence. Postmodern fragmentation extends into dietary habits in which contradictory messages can be believed and simultaneously followed.

It can seem as if the efforts of the advertising industry are directed entirely towards the generation of false needs within us all, but one of the great strengths of the process of consumerism is that it is able to harness and direct our genuine needs, even if the goods and services on offer more often than not leave us frustrated and unfulfilled. Renata Salecl has identified how the multiplicity of choices in our everyday lives has led to the growth of deep anxiety.[4] Ironically the increase in unease has in turn led to the development of a range of caring and therapeutic services from which to choose. Humankind has almost certainly always desired better health, greater beauty, sexual fulfilment and longer life. The issue is, however, whether these are now sought at the expense of other more substantial aspects of life. It is also important to reflect what happens to the excluded in a world devoted to valuing the surface appearance. This will be returned to in the conclusion.

A FEW NECESSARY THEORETICAL POINTS

One of the features that emerges from the above discussion is that postmodernism emphasizes the importance of style and appearance over content. The construction of a personal lifestyle through the consumption of desirable consumer services has little to do with the usefulness of the goods and much to do with image and the way that people appear to others. This argument has also been applied to entertainment and to the arts. Many commentators have observed that the distinction between high art and popular culture has been lost because of the uncertainty which now surrounds establishing unequivocal criteria for judging the value of cultural forms. This is a difficult point, but essentially from a postmodern perspective it is not possible to assert that Shakespeare is better than *East Enders* or *Coronation Street*. Certainly there are writers for whom this would be an absurd statement because they continue to believe in the traditional standards by which literary merit is judged, and who would counter any assault on these standards with bitter and hostile academic debate.

There is an important link here with one of the fundamental characteristics of most postmodern thought. The key thinkers have all identified a common theme in the scepticism of the twentieth century towards the once great certainties of history and society. We no longer unquestioningly accept the universal claims to knowledge and truth of the **grand narratives** which have organized our culture. These include religion, the progress of **modernism**, the progress of science, and absolutist political theories like Marxism.

It is not always easy to grasp the significance of these abstract ideas for everyday life, but what is really in question is whether it is any longer possible to agree on absolute truth. We often hear on the television and radio about a breakdown in society because of the decline in shared values. Politicians of the main parties in the United Kingdom speak of the need to re-establish a common core of beliefs in order to bring society back together. From a postmodern perspective this does not make sense because the politicians are basing their claims on a mistaken belief in universal truths, or **metanarratives**, as postmodern thinkers would say. The supremacy of Western thinking has been challenged throughout the twentieth century and especially with the decline of colonial empires. The explicit assumption that their cultures and ideas represented the progress of civilization is one that is no longer universally accepted. It is now much more commonplace to assume that we cannot say that one society or culture is better than another.

Postmodern thinkers also point to the fragmentation of experience and a compression of time and space as defining features of the late twentieth century. It is now accepted that changes in the structure of multinational companies have led to the **globalization** of production. Cars, for example, may now be assembled in the United Kingdom using parts that have been manufactured at factories throughout the world. Communication and transport systems have developed to allow links between countries to occur with great rapidity. European financial institutions are able to transmit their data electronically to be processed overnight on the Indian subcontinent, ready for return for business the next day. The **Internet** allows us to view from home, and in real time, events on the other side of the world. When we telephone to a call centre, it may be located anywhere in the world. Whereas 40 years ago the family holiday might have been spent in Blackpool or Bournemouth, it is now unremarkable to travel to Florida, the Caribbean or the Far East. It is quite possible for the more adventurous to explore the Himalayas or the Arctic. A visit to any supermarket provides the opportunity to purchase food from every culture on the globe and which was growing on the other side of the world perhaps only two days previously. The average high street in the United Kingdom contains restaurants and takeaways offering cuisine from every continent. All of these practical changes in our opportunities to experience the world mean that our conscious appreciation of time and of physical space is compressed when compared with even the middle of the twentieth century. In the next section we will look at the implications of these ideas for our experience of leisure and entertainment, but before doing so we need briefly to consider the ideas of one particular theorist of the postmodern – Jean Baudrillard.

Baudrillard is associated, perhaps more than any other writer, with the cultural implications of postmodernism. His early writings provide a neo-Marxist critique of consumption in capitalist societies. However, he later comes to criticize any theories, like psychoanalysis, Marxism or **structuralism**, which depend upon looking beneath the surface appearance to an underlying truth or essence. Baudrillard is strongly influenced by a tradition in French philosophy called **semiology**. This leads him to look at the way that we understand signs and symbols in our culture, semiology being the science of **sign** systems which includes language, as well as visual and social codes.

The basis of this tradition is that we make sense of the world around us by associating signs and symbols with objects or ideas which are called referents. Baudrillard has outlined four stages in the way that the signs relate to their refer-ents and he has called this relationship **simulation**. It is possible to illustrate this in relation to the creation of images. While in medieval times the image was simply a direct reflection of reality, in the Renaissance period images were the individual and creative work of a single artist. The sign was emancipated and open to artistic interpretation; most importantly, it was unique and could not be reproduced in the same form: there is only one 'Mona Lisa'. He then points to the Industrial Revolution and the emergence of processes of production which allow for the manufacture of endless copies of the same artefact. In terms of images the camera provides the best example of this. There is no original of a photographic image, although it refers to an external reality. Finally he suggests that, with the start of postmodernism, we have entered the era of **hyperreality** in which the signs stand only for themselves. Signs are the reality, and the imagi-nary and the real have become confused. This can be illustrated in relation to the imagery of the pop video in which time and place are hard to identify and in which a blend of styles and references mix together, teasing, but not depending upon our knowledge of previous artists. These brief and fast-edited videos can then be watched in no particular order on digital music channels. Playful refer-ences to earlier musical styles are at the core of some successful bands, while others blend an eclectic mix of cultural and musical styles including Asian, European and Afro-Caribbean. Similarly, in our pursuit of a healthy identity, the fitness bike or the home rowing machine have come to have a place of their own. Such aids depend upon our understanding of the real processes of rowing or cycling, but their usage has evolved into independent activities with a reality of their own. At the core of this series of observations is a central tenet of post-modern thinking: images and cultural artefacts no longer refer to a single reality, but have instead become realities in their own right.

POSTMODERNISM, CITIES AND LEISURE

It was mentioned earlier that another of the features of postmodern analysis is the claim that there has been a breakdown in the distinction between elite art and popular culture. This is not a new observation and over 60 years ago the mass culture critics expressed concern that high culture would be undermined because of the commercial exploitation of mass taste. The major difference, though, between these early writers and the contemporary postmodern critics is that the latter are celebrating these developments. One of the central claims made by writers who are optimistic about postmodern changes is that the process is democratizing and potentially classless, and this is an issue that will form the basis of the concluding section. However, we are now going to look at the impact of postmodern change upon leisure and the urban spaces in which we live and work.

The starting point for much of the debate about postmodern issues in the twentieth century has been architecture. It has even been suggested that the transition from the modern to the era of the postmodern can be specified as 3.32 p.m. on 15 July 1972. This is the time when a prize-winning example of modern housing – the Pruitt-Igoe housing development in St. Louis – was blown up because it was considered unsuitable for human habitation even by those on a low income.[5] Modern architecture was characterized by the principles of architects such as Le Corbusier who was at his most influential in the 1920s, though his ideas are typified by the high-rise flats which came to dominate our cities in the 1960s.

The modernist architects – like modernist writers and painters in their respective fields – rejected all previous forms and insisted that both traditional and classical forms of architecture should be replaced by buildings based upon rational and universal principles. In practice this meant an emphasis on plain functional design, usually in concrete and glass. The building was decontextualized and universalized. The hearts of cities were flattened, to be replaced all over the world by buildings which looked the same. This was the metanarrative of modernism.

In contrast postmodern buildings and cityscapes are characterized by a sensitivity to context and self-conscious playfulness in which different styles and references to different historical periods are mixed together in an ironic and eclectic way. There is a characteristic focus on appearance over substance and purpose. It contains a deliberate mixing of vernacular and classical features as part of the process whereby popular and elite culture are given equal value. In many of our cities the cobbled streets ripped up in the 1960s are being replaced and embellished with fibreglass reproduction gas lamps, in an attempt to evoke the past.

In a related sense the MetroCentre in Gateshead (north-east England) had, when it opened, shopping areas that were themed to provide us with a pastiche experience. In the Mediterranean village it is possible to eat pasta in an Italian trattoria or calamares in a tapas bar on opposite sides of the mall with twinkling light bulbs designed to remind us of those longed-for sultry summer nights. If you are overcome by these feelings then travel agents are handily placed to complete the experience. Just around the corner we can enter a Dickensian world of cobbles, street-lamps and small-pane-windowed shops where we can eat cream teas or buy humbugs. Many writers, including Baudrillard, have pointed to theme parks, and especially Disneyland, as examples of postmodern entertainment space. However, we have to travel to them. In the themed shopping mall we have the playful creation of alternative realities brought to us as part of an everyday experience of shopping.

A unique feature of the twentieth century has been the expansion and proliferation of electronic means of communication which fill our world with a confusion of images and sounds unimaginable a hundred years ago. The very existence of so much competing information means that our attention span is shortened and that the potential for a continuous thoughtful **narrative** is undermined. Instead we mix and match styles and genres, creating an eclectic mix of short-lived experiences. This is exemplified by the choice of television channels on sattelite, all of which can be surfed by using the remote handset. The television becomes like a magazine in which we flick from page to page, mostly just looking at the pictures, sometimes taking in sections but rarely completing a programme or article from end to end. The development of BBC iplayer and other line ways of accessing programming have led to a shifting of linear time. This is a truly postmodern experience in which time and content are separated and narrative is controlled by the viewer and is always in the present.

There are examples of television programmes and films which have been said to reflect postmodern culture. One of the most often quoted examples is *Twin Peaks*. Like many of David Lynch's films for the cinema, this was characterized by disruptions of temporal and spatial relationships and by elements of parody and pastiche. *Twin Peaks* was notable for the fact that the entire series centred on a murder which occurred before the action began. It is referred to and elements of it are glimpsed in flashback, but the murder itself is never depicted. Lynch chose instead to make a film for cinema which disclosed the events upon which the television series was based, but only after the series had finished its run. It is a matter of controversy as to whether this film had a life of its own, or whether it depended for its sense and coherence upon knowledge of the television series. Certainly the sense of the television programmes was richest if the constant references to other television styles and series were appreciated. It has even been said that the programmes were as much about television as a medium as they were about the storyline, exemplifying the postmodern emphasis on surface and play.

It would be possible to give many other examples of the extent to which the characteristics of the postmodern can be seen in cinema, television and advertising. The films of Quentin Tarantino, especially *Pulp Fiction* (1994), and numerous television campaigns all contain the elements which have been discussed so far in this chapter. It is clear that there has been a major shift in the field of representation and in the way that signs and symbols are presented to us. In essence it is no longer possible to be naive in our understanding of culture. It is characterized more often than not by a knowing irony which clearly marks out the difference between the modern and the postmodern.

CONCLUSION

In summary, this essay has examined two central and related themes. First, the extent to which our activities as consumers define our identities in the contemporary world and, second, the impact of the postmodern upon our day-to-day lives. In particular the discussion has identified a shift from substance to style and has suggested that the certainties and the metanarratives of the modern era are no longer sustainable. If, as has been said, in the postmodern world the basic dictum is 'I shop therefore I am', we need to reflect on the question of what happens to those who cannot shop and are therefore excluded from the basis of social identity. This is of particular importance as the old principles of the welfare state are challenged by new values of consumerism. In this new world, pensions, healthcare and social support shift from the responsibility of the state to the responsibility of the individual. From a materialist perspective our capacity to consume these services constructs more than identity; it affects the physical basis of day-to-day life.

Critics of the postmodern perspective have pointed out that it can lead to an unprincipled emphasis upon personal and individual gratification at the expense of our responsibilities to others. For some writers this represents the capitalist market economy taken to its logical conclusion. For others, postmodern ideas are democratic, and it is argued that the dissolution of old class barriers and the strongholds of elite culture give all of us greater opportunities for full social participation.

I will finish with a quotation from the sociologist Zygmunt Bauman. In much of his writing he has explored the tension between acknowledging the reality of postmodern change and recognizing that it has led to the exclusion of many from a full and active part in society. This extract is taken from his book *Freedom*:

> [F]or most members of contemporary society individual freedom, if available, comes in the form of consumer freedom, with all its agreeable and not-so-palatable attributes. Once consumer freedom has taken care of individual concerns, of social integration and of systematic reproduction (and consumer freedom *does* take care of all three), the coercive pressure of political bureaucracy may be relieved, the past political explosiveness of ideas and cultural practices defused, and a plurality of opinions, life-styles, beliefs, moral values or aesthetic views may develop undisturbed. The paradox is, of course, that such freedom of expression in no way subjects the system, or its political organization, to control by those whose lives it

still determines though at a distance. Consumer and expressive freedoms are not interfered with politically, as long as they remain politically ineffective.[6]

NOTES

1 Jean Baudrillard, *Baudrillard Live: Selected Interviews*, ed. Mike Gane (London: Routledge, 1993), p. 21.
2 See Christopher Norris, *The Truth About Postmodernism* (Oxford: Blackwell, 1993).
3 See Alan Kirby, 'The Death of Postmodernism and Beyond', *Philosophy Now*, 58 (November/December, 2006), pp. 34–7.
4 See Renata Salecl, *Choice* (London: Profile, 2010).
5 See Charles Jencks, *The Language of Post-Modern Architecture* [1975], 6th edn (London: Academy Editions, 1991), p. 23.
6 Zygmunt Bauman, *Freedom* (Milton Keynes: Open University Press, 1988), p. 88.

7

POSTMODERNISM AND RELIGION

PAMELA SUE ANDERSON

The **postmodern** debates over religion have taken on various new dimensions and surprising directions – or, at least, awareness of postmodernism and/in religion has increased – since an earlier and shorter version of this chapter was written. A larger picture of the dimensions and directions of postmodernism clearly reveals significant disagreements between contemporary philosophers of religion, post-secular philosophers (i.e., 'radically orthodox' Christian theologians), **postcolonial** theorists on religion and post-post-secular philosophers; the latter include thinkers who write explicitly after the initial postcolonial critiques of philosophy of religion, but also *after the* 'religious' and theological' turns in **Continental** and Anglo-American philosophies, respectively.[1]

Today it is crucial to begin by assessing the very concept of religion, even before we turn to a greater understanding of postmodernism's relation to it. Despite twentieth-century postmodern critiques of religion as a western conception, twenty-first century critiques focus on what had been readily accepted as the opposite of the religious – the secular – by **modern** western Christians and by those who, in response to the postmodern, assumed a post-secular point of view. An **irony** emerges here for the (modern) concept of religion: post-secular perspectives on the secular, as well as on '*the* philosophy of religion', resemble ideas much closer to pre-modern thought – even to medieval Christianity – than to contemporary thinking in other fields of postmodern study of religious or other lived experiences.[2] Rigidity and restrictions in what counts as post-secular philosophy speak volumes about its distance from the fluidity and free play of the postmodern. It is for this reason that the present, revised chapter on 'Postmodernism and religion' takes into account what has emerged, so to speak, 'after the postmodern and the post-secular'.[3] Otherwise, the **post-postmodern** theologian who advocates post-secular philosophy, or 'a return of the sacred,'[4] will be out of step with contemporary theories of religion; that is, this post-secularity would be especially incompatible with both the pervasive postmodern scepticism about universal truth in religion or metaphysical theory and the global range of historical and cultural contexts of postmodern practices, whether the latter are described as 'religious', 'ritual' or 'embodied' actions.

During the past 15 years or more, the critique of the secular has led to lively philosophical debates about the post-secular in the sense of a turn to religion in European philosophy, especially but not only in phenomenology

and **poststructuralism**. Philosophical theologians influenced by French phenomenology, including John Caputo, Merold Westphal and Bruce Ellis Benson,
have come critically close to the post-secularity of the Radical Orthodox theologians John Milbank, Graham Ward and Stanley Hauerwas in their Continental
turn to religion. Radical Orthodoxy in theology became a highly vocal movement in the 1990s, but the seeds were planted already in the initial waves of postmodernism and religion.[5] Roughly, the western theologians and religious or
post-secular philosophers who developed critiques of the secular (as opposed to
the sacred or the religious) each appear to believe that the postmodern turn
rendered the secular redundant.

Yet the decisive question for those writers privileging radically orthodox
Christian theology as post-secular philosophy in support of the Continental
philosophers' turn to religion is: could postmodernism leave the western conception of religion in place, while doing away with the secular and the modern religion to which it was wed? In other words, it seems contradictory to think that
'the secular' could be undermined by the post-secular without its conceptual
opposite, 'the religious' being undermined by the postmodern. This pair of
modern concepts constitutes a highly specific set of relations within our western
conceptual scheme. Can we simply jettison one half of the pair of relations? If
so, where is the religious located, and to what does it relate?

In **modernity**, religion and secularity rise and fall together. Religion as a
modern concept for Christianity and its practices may have been opposed to
secular philosophy. However, without a dialectical relation to the secular can
the domain of religion be mapped out? A necessary conceptual pairing of religious, or sacred, and secular comes from their relational origins in philosophical
thought. But are these conceptual relations only part of modern thinking? Post-
secular philosophers may reasonably insist on a turn to 'theology', but not to
'religion' insofar as the meaning of religion rests on its **difference** from secularity. However the return to pre-modern Christian theology means reinstating
its singular, privileged form over and above other linguistically and socially
specific worlds of human lived experience. But with this privileging of Christian
authority we seem to have moved far away from postmodernism – or, have we?
Post-secular philosophers locate both the secular and the religious as embedded
in one historical stage of a larger Christian tradition which, as they see it, is left
behind by a 'post-postmodern agenda'.[6]

At this point, it is helpful to mention the postcolonial response to both post-
secular philosophy and modern philosophies of religion. In this context,
Richard King's postcolonial critique of philosophy of religion is a notable
example in raising two crucial questions. First, King asks about 'the appropriateness of the concept of "religion" as a useful cross-cultural category on the
grounds that it is the specific product of the cultural and political history of the
west'.[7] King has found support for arguing that 'religion' reflects 'the localized,
ideological imprints of western Christian and **Enlightenment** constructions of
the subject-matter'.[8]

Second, King questions the universality of religion:

> The category of 'religion', of course, has almost universal currency in the contemporary world. The universalization of the term almost renders transparent the translation process involved in its representation of diverse cultural forms and practices. It is important to realize, however, that to use the term 'religion' uncritically is already to re-present non-western traditions according to a culturally specific linguistic and conceptual scheme. The introduction of non-western traditions into the West as 'religions' interpellates them into a long-standing, fractious and, highly localized debate that frames the parameters of articulation before such traditions have a chance to speak.[9]

Insofar as postmodernism aims to subvert modern Enlightenment philosophy and western Christianity, especially in the universalized forms of modernity, postcolonial theorists would have to follow King in rejecting both the imposition of religion onto the practices in non-western cultural and political history and the articulation of non-western traditions in the universal terms of the west's conceptual scheme for religions.

Now, the significant and current philosophical challenge has been directed at Christian forms of theologizing, notably at twentieth-century forms of Continental and analytic philosophies of religion, but also at Radical Orthodox theology.[10] This challenge accompanies speculation for philosophy of religion which comes, according to Anthony Paul Smith and Daniel Whistler, *after* the post-secular and the postmodern critiques. The current philosophical critiques of postmodern theology and post-secular philosophy of religion take the form of two tasks. The first task is to find 'a way to perform a philosophical operation upon theological material, while retaining something properly philosophical'.[11] Smith and Whistler find support in turning philosophy 'outwards', that is, both as 'a critical operation on theology' and as 'a liberation of aspects of religion' from their own 'theological contamination'.[12] The second task for the contributors to *After the Postsecular and the Postmodern* is 'an aggressive alternative: a complementary philosophical contamination of theology'.[13] But, as Smith and Whistler admit, the latter task risks 'a disintegration of the philosophical body, in order to disturb theology's ideological and orthodox identity'.[14] Instead, the aim is to contaminate it. The stake here for postmodernism and religion lies at the heart of a field which has been and largely continues to be thoroughly Christianized, or theologizing. Liberation comes in this most recent stage after critiques of both the postmodern and the post-secular; but this is no longer a regressive turn. Instead it is open to new possibilities and energy without either jettisoning the modern or hanging on desperately to the old.

Smith and Whistler claim to follow 'in the footsteps of Pamela Sue Anderson, Clayton Crockett and Philip Goodchild (to name but three) who (in very different ways) have all already begun the process of liberating and/or mutating philosophy of religion'.[15] This means challenging the theological appropriations of recent Continental philosophy by following a range of contemporary European philosophers, including Dominique Janicaud, Alain Badiou and Michele Le Doeuff.[16] Smith and Whistler as a younger generation of philosophers have taken up a 'mantle of suspicion' towards the religious turn on the Continent by objecting, in particular, to the theologizing of contemporary philosophy of religion. With the help of their contributors, Smith and Whistler point out the **aporia** and shortcomings of that postmodern thinking. The core challenge is to think philosophy of religion otherwise than theologically; this becomes one of the most significant currents today for 'Postmodernism and religion'.

To regain health from this new, critical spirit after post-secularism religion must transmute the restrictive norms of a radically orthodox Christianity. Transformation of the western conceptual relations of religion and secularity opens postmodernism up to new channels for dialogue with postcolonial, or decolonized philosophy of religion. As already mentioned, King has argued for this shift away from the colonial preoccupations of religion as a Christian norm, and his writings on non-western religious practices are no longer on the wrong side of the border control of Christian philosophers and theologians. This also moves postmodern philosophy to a less simplistic or reductive understanding of the history of metaphysics, of immanent and transcendent reality, by emancipating speculative philosophy from the norms of a singular religion.

It is well worth quoting from the energetic, speculative project which aims to restore health to philosophies of religion:

> Once again (this time from within theology), philosophical thinking has been *theologised*, overrun by a theological virus whose intention is to obliterate the distinctiveness of philosophy of religion in the name of theology. Both the postmodern and the post-secular contamination are two sides of the same coin: a one-way injection of theology into philosophy until what is proper to philosophy becomes indiscernible. The deconstruction of the philosophy/theology binary has resulted, not in a true democracy of thought between philosophy and theology, but in the humiliation and debasement of philosophy before the Queen of the sciences, theology. To designate one of the solutions to this one-sided contamination 'the liberation of philosophy of religion' is therefore to call for a critique of such tendencies in the name of philosophy. Liberation is a two-stage operation: it shows up the normativity and partiality of recent contaminations, but it does so in order to free a practice of philosophy of religion from the constraints imposed on it by theological thinking.[17]

In this two-stage liberation of both the modern and the postmodern from the theologizing of post-secular Christian philosophers, Gilles Deleuze plays a highly influential role. Deleuze helps us to see how, first, 'God' enabled philosophy 'to free the object of creation in philosophy', liberating human creativity and, second, that the concept no longer necessary for the representation of things could take on new movements and lines never previously explored:

God and the theme of God offered the irreplaceable opportunity for philosophy to free the object of creation in philosophy (that is to say, concepts) from the constraints that had been imposed on them ... the simple representation of things. The concept is freed at the level of God because it no longer has the task of representing something. ... It takes on lines, colours, movements that it would never have had without this detour through God.[18]

In the version of this chapter in the second edition of the *Companion*, I characterized postmodernism in terms of a loss of modern belief in: (i) the moral progress of humankind in history, (ii) a conception of reason as ushering in universal agreement, or certainty, and (iii) a **grand narrative** account of being created human (assuming human sameness, not differences). This threefold loss provided a way to articulate the decisive impact which postmodernism had upon modern philosophy of religion at the end of the twentieth century. In retrospect we can understand the extreme fear which led certain Christians to follow the Radical Orthodox theologians and turn to the religion of post-secular philosophy. Both privileged and popular theologians found this threefold loss the ground for blaming the Enlightenment for misguided beliefs in moral progress, in certainty and in a grand narrative; an attractive alternative, then, became turning back to pre-modern ritual practices and religious ways of life which are less 'enlightened' by human reason alone.

At least initially, the postmodern displacement of modern beliefs aimed to shift western philosophy of religion away from the dominant, modern epistemological activity. An original task was to reject the rational justification of a core of commonly held beliefs, especially those beliefs which had bound religious persons together. It was not only the Radical Orthodox theologians who sought to undermine modern philosophical attempts to justify beliefs rationally as true, and so rejected justified true belief as a foundation for (universal) knowledge. In fact, generally an indication of the impact of postmodernism on philosophy was a turn away from the epistemic practice of justifying religious belief as true; and a move to creating a postmodern philosophy of religion which was 'beyond belief'.[19]

For examples, both feminist and postcolonial philosophers of religion were keen to debate the postmodern question, is religion a matter of belief? Or, is the practice of justifying religious belief strictly a modern, white male and western reduction of the culturally, racially, ethnically and sexually diverse embodied practices of men and women globally? The postmodern move 'beyond belief' was re-enforced by a post-colonial critique of the translation of the ritual practices of non-western cultures into 'other world religions'; the latter has been modelled upon the philosophy of western religion (Christianity) in the singular.

The danger in these initial waves of postmodern philosophy for 'religion' is a simplistic account of the relationship between postmodernism and Christianity – as two western conceptions – in direct opposition and discontinuity. Crudely, it was thought that whereas postmodernism undermines biological, cognitive and moral certainties, the Christian religion rests on them. A popular account of contemporary philosophy of religion and ethics confirms this simplicity:

> With the advent of Christianity, God was seen as providing ... a fixed point of meaning, truth and value in an unstable world. Postmodernism denies that there are any such rocks of certainty. It calls to human beings in the raging sea to abandon the search for rocks, to 'go with the flow' and simply to seek to understand where they are.[20]

This western picture may be true for a certain conception of religion, especially a **fundamentalist** view of Christian belief. The contemporary popularity of fundamentalism, despite more nuanced awareness of culturally and linguistically specific ritual practices, infiltrates not just Christianity and Islam, but Orthodox Judaism and the Oriental religions.[21]

Yet it has also been argued that fundamentalism in world religions took on westernized forms, especially when resisting a rational quest for knowledge. Arguably, then, religious fundamentalism could be read as an offshoot of postmodernism itself even while claiming to be in opposition to it. Fundamentalists who seek an unequivocal foundation for their beliefs have built their certainties point by point in a dependent, but oppositional relationship to postmodern uncertainties. Despite the ease with which an author could map out this oppositional relationship between postmodernism and fundamentalism in terms of arguments for and against specific uncertainties (e.g., that God exists), a straightforward separation of the two should be resisted. Instead an extreme form of fundamentalism is one of the defining features of the postmodern world: this fundamentalism attaches itself to postmodernism as its binary opposite, often claiming to be a remedy of a certain postmodern disease.

Another issue related to the opposition between postmodernism and religious fundamentalism is moral relativism. The flip side of asserting the absolute values of any fundamentalist position is a relativist view of another's claim to the opposite (held as absolute) values. Admittedly this relativism conceives religion in the positive terms of particular local narratives and practices, whether explicit universal claims are made or not. The nature and dangers of this relativism/absolutism bind is addressed elsewhere as one of the earliest indications of postmodernism.[22]

Yet any theoretical criticism of such reductive, binary thinking does not deny the fact that a global increase in fundamentalist religions runs parallel to a more widespread, postmodern celebration of differences of, in this case, religious perspectives. The range of fundamentalist movements in the world reflects not only academic shifts in thinking about belief but global, technological, economic and other cultural transformations. Human thinking, acting and feeling at the beginning of the twenty-first century are inevitably, if at times unwittingly, influenced by what are taken to be general characteristics of postmodernism: its fluidity, diversity, uncertainty and, ultimately, its lack of concern with truth (or, as explained earlier, with the belief in truth). Nevertheless, as discussed already, the orthodox Christian response to the relative/absolute choice of values is to advocate a radical form of post-secular philosophy; the attraction of the latter – at least initially – is a more nuanced, historically and intellectually sophisticated alternative.

The decisive issue for 'Postmodernism and religion' today is whether Christianity continues to determine the central and privileged norms in global debates about culturally specific ritual practices and highly local beliefs about suffering, life, death and immortality. Postmodernism has shifted much of both academic and popular concerns away from one dominant system of belief to culturally and historically nuanced practices which have bound individuals and groups together. Nevertheless, it is still common for westerners to think of other religions in terms derived from their own values and concepts within a Christian tradition; but the **other** also sees itself in relation to the dominant. Postmodern theorists continue to uncover and challenge the implicit westernized Christian values and concepts in religious and cultural studies. 'Belief' as the decisive, epistemological term for philosophy of 'religion' is a primary example of a modern, arguably western imposition on a field of study. The label 'Judaeo-Christian' is similarly an unwelcome imposition of Christianity as the rightful completion of Jewish tradition; as such this is another example of a westernizing process in European philosophy and theology.

The academic discipline of theology as a systematic study of the traditions and subject matter of the Christian religion faces the uncertainties of its own future. A fear persists that theology will be marginalized, and ultimately replaced, by the more wide-ranging and inclusive categories of religious or **cultural studies**. This changing scene is evident in the disruption of university departments of theology and of religion by the fluidity of postmodern thinking. The twofold phenomenon of change and of resistance to innovation in the studies of religion and of theology is an indication of the contemporary process constituting the postmodern transformation of 'religion', its definition and discipline.

It is interesting to consider further the contention of popular postmodern theorists on religion: that 'the philosophy of religion' should no longer be the study and justification of belief in a personal God (i.e., theism), but the critical engagement with religious 'practice'.[23] Here the postmodern critic claims that philosophy's obsessive concern with justification is also a product of modern philosophy's privileging of reason. Reason's role in the justification of theistic beliefs, reason's neutrality and universality are brought into question. Not only does the postmodern critic claim that belief is a western abstraction, but that reason as a faculty of the human mind, not the body, is criticized for being a particular western, male construction. In a well-known alternative to the modern, Talal Asad's postmodernism subverts modern philosophy of religion by engaging in genealogical studies of ritual action and bodily practices.[24] Instead of philosophical analysis of theological concepts, ritual action becomes the crucial form of signification for a genealogical study of religion. The post-modern critique of analytical reason poses a particular challenge to modern philosophy, as well as the equation of religion with belief. Insofar as successful, this critique became an initial step toward opening up the field of religion to issues of gender, sexuality, class, race and bodily practices.

To return to the postmodernism's impact upon theology, even at an early stage, consider David Brown's observations here:

> Christian theology has conventionally sought to provide ... an over-arching narra-tive, and indeed the term 'systematic theology' is often interpreted to mean just that, the attempt to systematize all of reality under a single Christian frame of reference.[25]

An over-arching narrative is precisely the target of Jean-Francois Lyotard's postmodern 'incredulity toward meta-narratives'.[26] Lyotard's critique of **meta-narratives** forced the conventional conception (as in Brown above) of Christian theology into a defensive position, if not undermining it completely. Yet Brown maintains that the matter is not so simple, and he documents five different theo-logical uses of postmodernism. One of these uses is especially worth exploring in this context: rather than opposing postmodernism, the Radical Orthodox theologians embrace it as a critique of a particular secular framework, that of universal reason.[27]

So, we can interpret the Radical Orthodox conception of postmodern theology as a response to the incredulity toward the master narrative of Enlightenment philosophy. In particular, it is a rejection of the optimistic view of historical progress, secular reason and 'man's' ability to find truth without God. Unlike the overly simplistic opposition between postmodernism and fundamentalist religions, the Radical Orthodox theologian seeks to create an alternative frame-work, which would be genuinely universal, since based upon the truth of Christianity under which all of reality fits.[28]

Radical Orthodox theologians assume that Christianity is more compatible with postmodern philosophy than with modern epistemology; but then, they slide from postmodern to post-secular philosophy. For these theologians, the postmodern claim to dethrone human reason opens a path for return to the faith of Christianity. Modern scepticism, for such theologians, rendered the faith, which had characterized Christianity, obsolete while scepticism also made it impossible to demonstrate the certainty of God's nature and existence. Postmodern fluidity and uncertainty could seem preferable to modern rigour and certainty; the former protects the faith of post-secular philosophers from the fixity of the certainties which were claimed by modern secular philosophy. However, neither all philosophers nor all theologians have been persuaded that this is a positive move.

Brown, himself a Christian theologian, is critical; and he points to the post-modern irony at the heart of the Radical Orthodox re-conception of theology as the new, truthful master narrative.[29] The decisive problem with this master narrative is the assumption of universality; but not everyone – not even every theist or Christian – would accept Radical Orthodox theology as a true account of reality, and, in particular, as an account of human and divine relations. Brown points to a similar problem with other exclusive master narratives in contemporary philosophy of religion; notably, Alvin Plantinga's warrant theory of belief which is produced as a ground of certainty for our postmodern world.

Plantinga raises a general epistemological question: is Christian belief acceptable for intelligent people living in a postmodern world? He answers by arguing that Christian beliefs are warranted to the extent that they are formed by properly functioning cognitive faculties. Plantinga's argument is that humans not only have natural cognitive faculties such as perception, memory and reasoning that allow us to know things, but we also have a natural cognitive faculty that enables us to form basic beliefs about God. Plantinga advocates his Reformed epistemology to demonstrate that *warrant* distinguishes knowledge from true belief. But problematically for postmodern open-mindedness, the master narrative of Plantinga's Reformed epistemology assumes the following: (i) that sin derives from the theology of John Calvin, applying to believers and non-believers; (ii) that the human natural cognitive faculty can be dulled or damaged by sin, and (iii) that those persons without Christian beliefs, or certainty, need to have faith 'repair' their damaged faculty; in the end, this will produce warranted Christian belief.[30]

Although Radical Orthodoxy and Reformed epistemology offer their respective master narratives as positive postmodern alternatives to either Enlightenment or fundamentalist forms of religion, there are serious worries with these two alternatives. The ambivalence between Enlightenment and postmodern conceptions of religion worries certain feminist philosophers of religion, especially when it comes to questions of women's identity, rationality and autonomy.[31] Doesn't postmodernism, especially but perhaps not only in its postsecular form, run the risk of undermining the many positive advances made for women in religion by the Enlightenment? Women may be loath to give up certain modern values. Steps taken as part of the Enlightenment in the eighteenth and nineteenth centuries to enable and protect women's self-identities as autonomous rational and moral agents within human communities remain hugely valuable and significant for overcoming various forms of oppression, including sexual, racial, social, material and economic oppression. The worry was and is that the creation of a postmodern Christian narrative whether of Radical Orthodoxy or of Reformed epistemology becomes essentially a return to pre-modern conceptions of religion, which were not only dogmatic, but oppressive to women and all those on the margins of socially and economically privileged theological circles. The choice of dogmatism rather than scepticism is not necessarily an attractive or forward-looking alternative for religion. Rather than being more inclusive, the conceptions of religion at the heart of master narrative forms of postmodernism exclude all but certain practitioners of

Christianity. A similar ambivalence toward postmodernism characterizes feminist debates more widely, in the context of cultural studies and other critical
social theories (see Chapter 4).

Further responses to postmodernism draw upon yet other aspects in the field
of studying the practices and/or beliefs of Jews, Moslems, Buddhists, Hindus,
Sikhs and Christians. Notably, there is the response to the postmodern threefold
loss of belief which focused upon religious experience understood as essentially
outside the limits of possible knowledge. In crude post-Kantian terms, postmodernism in religion became an exercise in finding new possibilities in experiencing
the impossible. Whereas modern philosophy of religion had been restricted by
the limits of human knowledge, postmodern religion placed itself outside the
possible, outside language, in the realm of mystery and, in what seems similar to
the more traditional idea of grace, 'gift'. A most significant example of this novel
conception is the give-and-take interchange of Jacques Derrida and Jean-Luc
Marion on the gift.[32]

Postmodern discussions of gift in particular aimed to demonstrate the way in
which the instability of gift as a concept results in experiencing the impossible.
As soon as a donor gives someone a gift the recipient is put into debt; this adds
to the donor, not to the recipient; but this is exactly the opposite of what the gift
is supposed to do. John Caputo brings together the postmodern philosophers
Derrida and Marion, as well as Richard Kearney, Mark C. Taylor and Edith
Wyschogrod, to debate the desire for experiencing the impossible, or for recognizing the inscrutable, as the defining element of postmodernism and as a new,
more inclusive – however mystical – conception of religion.

Added to this discourse concerning the gift is Lyotard's postmodern account
of the desire and possibility of experiencing the impossible in terms of the
Kantian **sublime**.[33] Roughly, the sublime is an experience of the absolute greatness, which cannot be capped by reason, understanding or imagination. In *A
Theology of the Sublime*, Clayton Crockett has advanced a post-Kantian
sublime in highly nuanced and generally more critical terms than found in more
orthodox theology; he engages critically with the post-secular philosophy of
Milbank and others.[34] In fact, for Lyotard, the sublime also always constitutes a
barrier to any search for totality. Postmodernism as conceived by Lyotard
himself is a movement against all totalizing accounts of ultimate reality. So, any
form of religion or (orthodox) theology, which seeks or offers a totalizing
project is doomed to failure.

Postmodern forms of religion shaped by the sublime, its greatness and inex-
pressibility have consistently aimed to avoid the problems with limiting religion
to the realm of the possible. But in doing so, they replace Kant's moral (rational)
religion with a mystically inclined, postmodern religion that seeks to avoid
conceiving God, or the divine, in anthropomorphic and gynaecological terms,
each of which are exclusive of an opposite sex. Some feminist theologians and
philosophers of religion have found this mystical alternative attractive for religion. Nevertheless, there remains the serious danger of illusion and mystifica-

tion: ironically, these are precisely the dangers which Kant's own modern philosophy of religion aimed to avoid.

To conclude, consideration of postmodernism's relation to religion opens up a whole array of significant questions. Is religion a western construction created by European Christian theologians? Or, is religion a modern conception distinguished by its difference from secular beliefs? The object of postmodern critiques includes the preoccupation of modern philosophy of religion with the justification of theistic belief. But has the postmodern shift of focus away from beliefs to bodily practices and ritual action achieved the goal of postmodern specificity, cultural and linguistic fluidity, and inclusivity, when it comes to religion? Or, has post-secular philosophy reinstated the privileged singularity, as well as the conceptual scheme, of western religion, thereby translating postmodern into pre-modern concepts and practices?

Alternatively, is the role of religion in the postmodern discourse concerning gift and sublimity part of a new narrative of negative theology? The postmodern critique of the metanarrative of secular reason may have initially sought an alternative to modern scepticism concerning the truth of theistic belief. But it has left unresolved the problem that not everyone assents to the narrative of give-and-take in Christian theology, or to a conceptual scheme reliant on the problematic 'universal particularism' of a mystical religion. To claim that any failure to assent to what is universal in particular experiences of the sublime and the gift results, crucially, from sin seems an inadequate response for a globally interconnected world of innovation and political interaction marred by religious violence and wars. Nevertheless, certain postmodern theologians continue to place their hope on religion in a postmodern world as a form of fluidity and uncertainty located in the gaps of reason, understanding and imagination.

The post-Kantian sublime as the heart of religion gives to some religious practitioners a strong mystical sense of inexpressible greatness in a generally shareable sense of the divine which was not available to modernity. And yet, even here a problem arises concerning the precise content of this (general) conception of religion for postmodernism: it suffers a loss of particularity due to the privileging of what is assumed to be universal. Religion without particularity simply fails to encompass the cultural and linguistic specificities of human embodiment and difference. Ultimately, in a postmodern, globally diverse world, religion remains in an unstable tension with the recognition of multiple concrete material and social differences. Perhaps the time is ripe for consideration of the new wave of speculative realism; the task would be to experiment with what philosophical speculation can still do concretely with and alongside the political reality of religion.

NOTES

1 For the Radical Orthodox presentation of post-secular philosophy, see John Milbank, Catherine Pickstock and Graham Ward, eds, *Radical Orthodoxy: A New*

Theology (London: Routledge, 1999). For the turn to 'religion' in European or Continental philosophy, see Philip Goodchild, 'Continental Philosophy of Religion: An Introduction', in Philip Goodchild, ed., *Rethinking Philosophy of Religion: Approaches from Continental Philosophy* (New York: Fordham University Press, 2002), pp. 8–16; also see Clayton Crockett, 'Gilles Deleuze and the Sublime Fold of Religion', in Goodchild, *Rethinking Philosophy of Religion*, pp. 267–80. For the turn to 'theology' in analytic philosophy, see William Wood, 'On the New Analytic Theology; or, the Road Less Traveled', *Journal of the American Academy of Religion*, 77:4 (December 2009), pp. 941–60. For what follows 'after' these turns to religion and to theology, see Anthony Paul Smith and Daniel Whistler, eds, *After the Postsecular and the Postmodern: New Essays in Continental Philosophy of Religion* (Newcastle upon Tyne: Cambridge Scholars Publishing, 2010), pp. 1–25; and Crockett, 'The Plasticity of Continental Philosophy of Religion,' in Smith and Whistler, *After the Postsecular*, pp. 299–315.

2 For key moments in the development of Radical Orthodox theology, or 'post-secular philosophy', see John Milbank, *Theology and Social Theory: Beyond Secular Reason* (Oxford: Blackwell, 1990), pp. 3–6, 390–92; and 'Problematizing the Secular: The Post- Postmodern Agenda', in Philippa Berry and Andrew Wernick, eds, *Shadow of Spirit: Postmodernism and Religion* (London: Routledge, 1992), pp. 30–44.

3 Here I recall the title of the collection of recent essays in Smith and Whistler, *After the Postsecular*.

4 Milbank, 'Problematizing the Secular', p. 30.

5 For example, see the essays of Part I 'Maps and Positions', in Berry and Wernick, *Shadow of Spirit*.

6 Milbank, 'Problematizing the Secular'.

7 Richard King, 'Philosophy of Religion as Border Control: Globalization and the Decolonization of "the Love of Wisdom"', in Purushottama Bilimoria and Andrew B. Irvine, eds, *Postcolonial Philosophy of Religion* (Dordrecht: Springer, 2009), pp. 35–53 (p. 44).

8 Ibid., p. 44, also pp. 41–47; cf. Richard King, *Orientalism and Religion: Postcolonial Theory, India and 'The Mystic East'* (London: Routledge, 1999).

9 King, 'Philosophy of Religion as Border Control', p. 44.

10 For one of the enduring critics in this area, see Crockett, 'Gilles Deleuze and the Sublime Fold', pp. 271–9; and Crockett, 'The Plasticity of Continental Philosophy', pp. 310–13.

11 Smith and Whistler, 'Editors' Introduction', *After the Postsecular*, p. 2.

12 Ibid.

13 Ibid.

14 Ibid.

15 Ibid., p. 4 n6. Cf. Pamela Sue Anderson, *A Feminist Philosophy of Religion: The Rationality and Myths of Religious Belief* (Oxford: Blackwell, 1998); Pamela Sue Anderson and Beverley Clack, eds, *Feminist Philosophy of Religion: Critical Readings* (London: Routledge, 2004); and Pamela Sue Anderson, ed., *New Topics in Feminist Philosophy of Religion: Contestations and Transcendence Incarnate* (London: Springer, 2010).

16 For relevant background, see Dominique Janicaud, 'The Theological Turn of French Phenomenology', in *Phenomenology and the 'Theological Turn': The French Debate*,

trans. Bernard G. Prusak (New York: Fordham University Press, 2000), pp. 3–103. Also see, Alain Badiou, *Saint Paul: The Foundation of Universalism*, trans. Ray Brassier (Stanford, CA: Stanford University Press, 2003); and Michèle Le Doeuff, *The Sex of Knowing*, trans. Kathryn Hamer and Lorraine Code (London: Routledge, 2003), especially pp. 27–68.

17 Smith and Whistler, 'Editors' Introduction', p. 3.

18 Gilles Deleuze, Seminar on Spinoza/Cours Vincennes 25/11/1980. www.webdeleuze. com/php/texte.php?cle=17&groupe=Spinoza&langue=2 (accessed 8 February 2011).

19 Ellen Armour 'Beyond Belief: Sexual Difference and Religion After Ontotheology', in John Caputo, ed., *The Religious* (Oxford: Blackwell, 2001), pp. 212–26; and Amy Hollywood, 'Practice, Belief and Feminist Philosophy of Religion', in Anderson and Clack, *Feminist Philosophy of Religion*, pp. 225–40.

20 Peter Vardy, *Being Human: Fulfilling Genetic and Spiritual Potential* (London: Darton, Longman and Todd, 2003), pp. 10–11.

21 Cf. King, *Orientalism and Religion*.

22 Cf. Ernest Gellner, *Postmodernism, Reason and Relativism* (London: Routledge, 1992).

23 Pierre Bourdieu, *Outline of a Theory of Practice* [1972], trans. Richard Nice (Cambridge: Cambridge University Press, 1977).

24 Talal Asad, *Genealogies of Religion: Discipline and Reasons of Power in Christianity and Islam* (Baltimore, MD: Johns Hopkins University Press, 1993).

25 David Brown, *Tradition and Imagination: Revelation and Change* (Oxford: Oxford University Press, 1999), p. 34.

26 Jean-François Lyotard, *The Postmodern Condition: A Report on Knowledge* [1979], trans. Geoffrey Bennington and Brian Massumi (Manchester: Manchester University Press, 1984).

27 Milbank, 'Problematizing the Secular', pp. 30–44.

28 Milbank, Pickstock and Ward, *Radical Orthodoxy*.

29 Brown, *Tradition and Imagination*, pp. 32–5.

30 Alvin Plantinga, *Warranted Christian Belief* (New York: Oxford University Press, 2000).

31 Anderson, *A Feminist Philosophy of Religion*; and Dorota Filipczak, 'Autonomy and Female Spirituality in a Polish Context: Divining a Self', in Anderson and Clack, *Feminist Philosophy of Religion*, pp. 198, 210–20.

32 For highly significant material in this area of debate, see 'Introduction: Apology for the Impossible: Religion and Postmodernism', in John D. Caputo and Michael J. Scanlon, eds, *God, The Gift and Postmodernism* (Bloomington, IN: Indiana University Press, 1999), pp. 1–19; also see 'On the Gift: A Discussion between Jacques Derrida and Jean-Luc Marion, Moderated by Richard Kearney', in Caputo and Scanlon, *God, the Gift*, pp. 54–78.

33 Jean-François Lyotard, *Lessons on the Analytic of the Sublime* [1991], trans. Elizabeth Rottenberg (Stanford, CA: Stanford University Press, 1994).

34 Clayton Crockett, *A Theology of the Sublime* (London: Routledge, 2001).

8

POSTMODERNISM AND THE POSTCOLONIAL WORLD

ELEANOR BYRNE

[I]f the interest in **postmodernism** is limited to a celebration of the fragmentation of the '**grand narratives**' of post**enlightenment** rationalism then, for all its intellectual excitement, it remains a profoundly parochial enterprise. The wider significance of the postmodern condition lies in the awareness that the epistemological 'limits' of those ethnocentric ideas are also the enunciative boundaries of a range of other dissonant, even dissident histories and voices – women, the colonized, minority groups, the bearers of policed sexualities.

(Homi K. Bhabha, *The Location of Culture*, 1994)

In recent years some of the most interesting interventions in discussions of **postmodernity** have come from a number of critics working on the borders of **postcolonial** and postmodern theory. In his above comment, in the introduction to his influential work *The Location of Culture*, the critic Homi K. Bhabha predominantly associates with postcolonial theory attempts to relocate the significance of postmodernism and the postmodern condition. He suggests that an effective understanding of the much fêted crisis of 'grand narratives', outlined by Jean-François Lyotard in *The Postmodern Condition*, involves a recognition that these seemingly overarching explanatory narratives might be ethnocentrically limited. That is to say, they are revealed as kinds of belief system and **narrative** that are attached to particular cultural histories of communities, cultures and elites.[1] He further suggests that even critics and theorists who enthusiastically theorize postmodernism might be guilty of a similar ethnocentrism, not recognizing that one of the critical forces that has destabilized so-called grand narratives is the impact of a range of dissident and dissonant voices, hailing from a range of minority positions. He locates them at the limits, a presence at the boundary, following Martin Heidegger's comments in his essay 'Building, Dwelling, Thinking' that the border is not only the limit or the end of a particular thing, but the place where the 'presencing' of something else begins.[2] For Bhabha this might be a useful formulation for the way in which minority voices could be envisaged.

Bhabha is clearly suggesting here that rather than seeing the experience of the postmodern condition as exclusively located in and experienced by the inhabitants of the so-called first world, that is to say largely Western or Westernized industrialized and capitalist countries or regions, the concerns of postmodernism might usefully be thought through the experiences of colonialism and postcolonial negotiations and struggles. In fact in another essay in the same collection, 'The Postcolonial and the Postmodern', he goes further:

> My growing conviction has been that the encounters and negotiations of differen-
> tial meanings and values within 'colonial' textuality, its governmental discourses
> and cultural practices, have anticipated, *avant la lettre*, many of the problematics
> of signification and judgement that have become current in contemporary theory –
> **aporia**, ambivalence, indeterminacy, the question of discursive closure, the threat
> to agency, the status of intentionality, the challenge to 'totalizing' concepts, to
> name but a few.[3]

Bhabha suggests that what are commonly viewed as characteristically post-modern concerns might easily be found in the context of colonial and anti-colonial narratives and histories from the postcolonial world. His proposals are based around the peculiar narratives and identities that colonialism produces both for colonizer and colonized. The experiences of both conditions are argu-ably highly differentiated and diverse depending upon the cultures involved, whether the colonies are settler or non-settler, and change historically through different periods of colonization. However, Bhabha's broad observations of the contradictions of colonial narratives: as a civilizing mission enforced by armed brutality; as a product of 'democratic' government which refuses to allow colo-nial democracy; as a system which asks its subjects to imitate or mimic its imposed culture, but never allows full membership of that culture – 'almost the same but not white' – suggest that the totalizing grand narratives of colonialism are perpetually in a state of crisis.

Ranajit Guha's writings on colonial power relations in India are suggestively illustrative of Bhabha's model:

> [T]he colonial state in South Asia was very unlike and indeed fundamentally
> different from the metropolitan bourgeois state which had sired it. The difference
> consisted in the fact that the metropolitan state was **hegemonic** in character with its
> claim to dominance based on a **power** relation in which the moment of persuasion
> outweighed that of coercion, whereas the colonial state was non-hegemonic with
> persuasion outweighed by coercion in its structure of dominance.[4]

Coming from a rather different angle, but equally concerned with the relation-ship between postmodernism and the postcolonial world, the Marxist critic Aijaz Ahmad is concerned in his book *In Theory* with the ways in which the cate-gory of third world is understood, and looks at both its origins and its prove-nance. Ahmad discusses the problems he finds in the work of a major theorist of postmodernism, Frederic Jameson, in his essay 'Third World Literature in the Age of Multinational Capitalism'.[5] Ahmad is concerned that Jameson sees all 'third-world' literature as having a single objective: that of producing 'national allegories'. He is disturbed that he as an Indian Marxist who also writes poetry in Urdu has in fact been '**Othered**' by a critic he has profoundly identified with and felt common cause with. He suggests that one of the causes for Jameson's homogenization and categorization of 'third-world literature' in this way is the mode in which he understands the term itself:

> I find it significant that First and Second Worlds are defined in terms of their production systems (capitalism and socialism, respectively), whereas the third category – the Third World – is defined purely in terms of an 'experience' of externally inserted phenomena. That which is constitutive of human history itself is present in the first two cases, absent in the third.[6]

Ahmad is sceptical about the various characterizations of the third world as either the reborn 'Orient' politically armed with a new confident nationalism, challenging Western imperialism and imperialist Bolshevism, as the critic Edward Said had suggested in his seminal **text *Orientalism***, or as a militarily non-aligned configuration of largely postcolonial nations that would be a force for peace.[7] Ahmad questions how the third world is understood in such a formulation, if it is understood to be neither capitalist nor socialist. He offers the example of contemporary India as a case that disturbs a homogenized view of the nations supposed to make up the third world and suggests that both India's industrialization and the growth of its multinational corporations bear comparison with the first world, and notes that its 'unbroken parliamentary rule of the bourgeoisie since Independence in 1947', is 'a record quite comparable to the length of Italy's modern record of unbroken bourgeois-democratic governance'.[8]

Ahmad's point is to unsettle any complacent labelling, and also to destabilize what he sees as a **binary opposition** created in Jameson's construction of a capitalist first world and 'a presumably pre- or non-capitalist Third World'.[9] Significantly he also turns the terms of the investigation on their heads, asking when the first world became the first. At the end of his discussion of Jameson he comments:

> [E]ven if I were to accept Jameson's division of the globe into three worlds, I would still have to insist … that there is right here, within the belly of the First World's global postmodernism, a veritable Third World, perhaps two or three of them.[10]

It is not entirely clear here whether Ahmad sees this 'third world' as participating in or distinct from the experience of postmodernism in the first world. He is certainly far more cautious than Bhabha about the figuring of minority experiences as postmodern. He comments scathingly on Bhabha's proposition that minority perspectives in dialogue with **poststructuralist** theory might effectively intervene in **discourses** of **modernity**:

> Bhabha, of course, lives in those material conditions of *post*modernity which presume the benefits of modernity as the very ground from which judgements on

that past of this *post-* may be delivered. In other words, it takes a very modern, very affluent, very uprooted kind of intellectual to debunk ... the idea of 'progress'[.] ... Those who live with the consequences of that 'long past' good and bad, and in places where a majority of the population has been denied access to such benefits of 'modernity' as hospitals or better health insurance or even basic literacy; can hardly afford the terms of such thought.[11]

Ahmad shares this scepticism about the possible convergence of postmodernism and postcolonial critical approaches with a number of important critics associated with postcolonial theory. In his review of Ian Adam and Helen Tiffin's *Past the Last Post: Theorizing Post-Colonialism and Post-Modernism*, Roger Berger cites Marxist postcolonial critic Benita Parry with approval. For Benita Parry postcolonial and postmodern methodologies should be recognized as distinct and unlikely to sustain a useful critical dialogue. A postcolonial approach, she suggests, should be understood as one which understands that cultural meanings are always finally political meanings, and that texts cannot be separated from the historical conditions in which they were produced and disseminated.[12] Postmodernism, Berger claims, wants to 'expand the territorial claims of the discursive infinitely, and therefore privilege textual stratagems as in and of themselves the location of gathering points for solidarity'.[13]

Berger's comments in his review point to a tendency within the featured debates on the relationship between postmodernism and postcolonialism to polarize around questions of textuality. Berger's particular re-use of Stuart Hall's formulation certainly does this when he characterizes a postmodern concern with textuality as operating in a neo-colonial mode; 'territorial expansion' suggests that postmodernism should be understood as complicit with late capitalism in the West and enacts a kind of 'western textual imperialism'.[14]

This is a critical paradigm through which a binary opposition is reinforced between a postmodern focus on 'text' and a postcolonial 'experience', but it does have some serious shortcomings. Berger comments that there is 'a fundamental incompatibility of post-modernist textuality and the lived realities of the post-colonial (or really neo-colonial) experience'.[15] Inevitably such a characterization of both camps is far too sweeping. While this approach seeks to align postmodernism with Western experiences and preoccupations, the erection of a binary between 'text' and 'experience' also risks performing a neo-colonial gesture where the colonial subject represents a 'good object' for colonial or neo-colonial knowledge and the 'truth' of colonized experiences enables the self-knowledge of the colonizer. It is arguably precisely this model that structured the Victorians' display of the possessions of indigenous peoples of the British Empire as artefacts in their museums.

This problematic had been discussed almost ten years earlier by one of the foremost and most influential postcolonial critics, Gayatri Chakravorty Spivak, in an interview in 1984 for the UK Channel 4 *Voices* series, *Knowledge in Crisis*. Asked to account for a poststructuralist assault on 'grands récits' (grand narratives) by Geoffrey Hawthorn, Spivak gives an answer that resonates with both postcolonial and postmodern concerns:

> I think of it myself as a radical acceptance of vulnerability. The grands récits are great narratives and the narrative has an end in view. It is a programme which tells how social justice is to be achieved. And I think the post-structuralists, if I understand them right, imagine again and again that when a narrative is constructed, something is left out. When an end is defined, other ends are rejected, and one might not know what those ends are. So I think what they are about is asking over and over again, What is it that is left out? Can we know what is left out?[16]

Spivak's description would seem to open both fields very productively onto one another. Further, she outlines comprehensively how a poststructuralist interest in 'text' should not be read as supporting a binary division between narrative and experience which goes almost uninterrogated in the *Past the Last Post* collection:

> Text in the way in which certainly Derrida and Lyotard understand it is not at all the verbal text. There are two ways once again perhaps of looking at this problem. When they read actual verbal objects that are political philosophy, philosophy of history or whatever, they like to show that those things are also produced in language – because there is a tendency to forget that they're produced in language. There you may say that the text is understood verbally. But when they talk about there is nothing but text, etc., they are talking about a network, a weave – you can put names on it – politico- psycho-sexual-socio, you name it. ... The moment you name it there's a network that's broader than that. And to an extent that notion that we are effects within a much larger text/tissue/weave of which the ends are not accessible to us is very different from saying that everything is language.[17]

It is perhaps the work of Jacques Derrida that has been most frequently cited as proving problematic to certain postcolonial perspectives, because of a perceived difference between poststructuralist questionings of foundational concepts in 'Western' philosophy and what is sometimes seen as an investment in some of those foundational concepts by some postcolonial critics. Primarily such polarization centres around questions of identity, where the 'decentring' of identity and the rejection of stable subjectivity are perceived to be a Western luxury contrasted to a need to adopt what Spivak calls 'strategic essentialism' on the part of those struggling against colonial and neo-colonial forces.[18] Such a strategy might involve uniting around particular categories of identity, ethnicity, gender or class positions. In recent years, however, a number of critics working in the postcolonial field have offered compelling arguments for a reconsideration of Derrida's work from postcolonial perspectives, as being, to use the overused term, 'always already' postcolonial.

In his essay '**Deconstruction** and the Postcolonial', Robert Young reflects upon his own changing apprehensions of the ways in which the emergence of poststructuralist modes of thinking need to be rethought.[19] His comments come from his opening remarks in his influential work *White Mythologies: Writing History and the West*:

> If so-called 'so-called poststructuralism' is the product of a single historical moment, then that moment is probably not May 1968 but rather the Algerian War of Independence – no doubt itself both a symptom and a product. In this respect it is significant that Sartre, Althusser, Derrida and Lyotard, among others, were all either born in Algeria or personally involved with the events of the war.[20]

Young argues there has been a characterization of poststructuralism (and we might usefully read postmodernism here too) as entirely in and of the West. He takes Aijaz Ahmad to task for assuming that 'anything that has come to be regarded as being of intellectual or political significance in the West could have nothing to do with the (so-called) third world'.[21] He continues:

> Those who reject contemporary postcolonial theory in the name of the 'third world' on the grounds of it being Western, however, are themselves negating the very input of the third world, starting with Derrida, disavowing therefore the very non-European work which their critique professes to advocate at the moment when they espouse it.[22]

Young argues that the references to this elsewhere, the decentred Algerian identity, have always been detectable in Derrida's work, but that in recent years he has increasingly come to be explicit about what he terms his Franco-Maghrebian identity. In *The Monolingualism of the Other or the Prosthesis of Origin* Derrida reflects on this trajectory in his thinking:

> Certainly, everything that has, say, interested me for a long time – on account of writing, the **trace**, the deconstruction of phallogocentrism and 'the' Western meta-physics ... all of that could *not* proceed from the strange reference to an 'elsewhere' of which the place and the language were unknown and prohibited even to myself, as if I were trying to *translate* into the only language and the only French Western culture that I have at my disposal, the culture into which I was thrown at birth, a possibility that is inaccessible to myself.[23]

Thus the two terms being discussed here, postmodernism and postcolonialism, find themselves intimately linked, co-dependent, rather than exploitative of one another. Interestingly, Derrida's own short article 'Et Cetera ...' in the collection *Deconstructions: A User's Guide* would just as readily apply to this volume, where the key term (in the latter case deconstruction and in this case postmod-ernism) is paired with a wide spectrum of topics.[24] He comments on the ways in which the pairing-up process depends upon the third term, the 'and', that appears insignificant but must produce a set of categorizations and orderings that actually contributes to delineating what can be added together, thought together or understood as belonging to the same series. That is to say that the 'and' can be seen as bringing two terms together, linking them in some way, but also asserting the lack of homogeneity between the two; otherwise there is no need for the 'and' in the first place. As we have already seen, some discussions of the postcolonial and the postmodern polarize around 'experience' and theory or text and reality. However, we might see in Derrida's intervention a truly postcolonial mode of addressing the imperative in this volume, this companion to postmodernism, to bring the categories of postmodernism and the postcolonial world into play. He comments on the diverse provenance of 'and': 'scansion, spacing, quasi-punctuation, respiration, exclamative opening, neutral addition, linking or following on, disjunction or simple scansion, upping the ante, objection, concession, etc'.[25]

Putting this kind of pressure on the third word, which we might have risked assuming had really only a subdued role in relation to the other two terms, opens up vastly different ways of reading. Consider: postmodernism 'therefore' the postcolonial world, postmodernism 'what's more' the postcolonial world, postmodernism 'against' the postcolonial world. Rather than seeing this as a retreat into textuality it might be critical that we are able to view with extreme caution our own investment in models of categorizing and knowing, surely an important strategy for any postcolonial activist and/or critic. In this respect, it is interesting to note the recent development of the concept of the **altermodern** by the art theorist Nicolas Bourriaud, which involves using postcolonialism as a way of transcending the category of the postmodern in the arts. Bourriaud feels that:

> we are on the verge of a leap, out of the postmodern period and the (essentialist) multicultural model from which it is indivisible, a leap that would give rise to a synthesis between modernism and post-colonialism. Let us then call this synthesis 'altermodernism'.[26]

Following on from Bourriaud, Okwui Enwezor argues that as the postcolonial world has never really experienced modernity in its full Western form, postmodernism is a concept of limited use to that world anyway. This raises the prospect of the postcolonial world 'against' postmodernism, offering us yet another perspective from which to think through the complexities of the relationship.[27]

NOTES

1 Jean-François Lyotard, *The Postmodern Condition* [1979], trans. Geoff Bennington and Brian Massumi (Manchester: Manchester University Press, 1984).

2 Martin Heidegger, 'Building, Dwelling, Thinking', in *Poetry, Language, Thought*, trans. Alan Hofstadter (New York: Harper & Row, 1971), pp. 143–59 (p. 152).

3 Homi K. Bhabha, *Location of Culture* (London: Routledge, 1994), p. 173.
4 Ranajit Guha, *Dominance without Hegemony: History and Power in Colonial India* (Cambridge, MA: Harvard University Press, 1997), p. xii.
5 Fredric Jameson, 'Third World Literature in the Age of Multinational Capitalism', *Social Text* (Fall, 1986), pp. 65–88.
6 Aijaz Ahmad, *In Theory* (London: Verso, 1992), pp. 99–100.
7 Edward Said, *Orientalism: Western Conceptions of the Orient*, 2nd edn (Harmondsworth: Penguin, 1995).
8 Ahmad, *In Theory*, p. 100.
9 Ibid., p. 101.
10 Ibid., p. 122.
11 Ibid., pp. 68–9.
12 See, for example, Benita Parry, 'Problems in Current Theories of Colonial Discourse', *Oxford Literary Review*, 9:1–2 (1987), pp. 27–58.
13 Roger Berger, 'Review of *Past the Last Post*' [Ian Adam and Helen Tiffin, *Past the Last Post: Theorizing Post-Colonialism and Post-Modernism* (Hemel Hempstead: Harvester Wheatsheaf, 1991)], *Postmodern Culture*, 2:2 (1992).
14 Ibid.
15 Ibid.
16 Gayatri Chakravorty Spivak, *The Post-Colonial Critic: Interviews, Strategies, Dialogues*, ed. Sara Harasym (London: Routledge, 1990), p. 19.
17 Ibid., p. 25.
18 Ibid., p. 51.
19 Robert Young, 'Deconstruction and the Postcolonial', in Nicholas Royle, ed., *Deconstructions: A User's Guide* (London: Macmillan, 2000), pp. 187–210.
20 Robert Young, *White Mythologies: Writing History and the West* (London: Routledge, 1990), p. 1.
21 Young, 'Deconstruction and the Postcolonial', p. 190.
22 Ibid.
23 Jacques Derrida, *The Monolingualism of the Other, or, The Prosthesis of Origin*, trans. Patrick Mensah (Stanford, CA: Stanford University Press, 1998), p. 71.
24 Jacques Derrida, 'Et Cetera ...', trans. Geoff Bennington, in Royle, *Deconstructions*, pp. 282–305.
25 Ibid., p. 290.
26 Nicolas Bourriaud, 'Altermodern', in Nicolas Bouriaud, ed., *Altermodern: Tate Triennial* (London: Tate Publishing, 2009), pp. 11–24 (pp. 12–13).
27 Okwui Enwezor, 'Modernity and Postcolonial Ambivalence', in Bourriaud, *Altermodern*, pp. 25–40.

9

POSTMODERNISM AND SCIENCE AND TECHNOLOGY

IAIN HAMILTON GRANT

Of all the worlds in which we might expect to discover signs of **postmodern** life, those of science and technology seem the least probable. Even those feedlines from science into culture that seem the most suited to **postmodernity**'s climate, such as the renowned uncertainties of **quantum physics**, stem not from **narratives**, but from nature. If postmodernism is simply, as Fredric Jameson has it, a cultural affair, then the sciences, reading only the book of nature, are surely unaffected by any postmodern 'loss of reality'[1]

– they never lost their way in the dead ends and labyrinths of the library of Babel. With postmodernism insisting, with Martin Heidegger (drawing on the words of the poet Stefan George), that 'where word breaks off, no thing may be'[2] – that beyond **signs** independent of speakers, beyond **text**, narrative or **discourse**, there is nothing – it remains difficult to consider tectonic plate movements and earthquakes as self-contained texts or discourses. So, with postmodern narrative in ruins, still reeling under the gravity of its collapse, could science simply step in to show, with mathematical precision, why stories have never been a substitute for formulae and experiment in the matter of the real? Moreover, with the postmodern 'empire of **signs**' leaving reality the victim of a crime so perfect, as Jean Baudrillard says, that even its corpse has disappeared, science and technology step onto the scene: what if this crime were a sideshow, and the real is elsewhere?[3]

With all these grounds for scepticism concerning the very idea of '**postmodern science**', it is surprising to find so much of science currently under the glare of postmodern scrutiny. Three aspects of science have in particular been singled out for postmodern interrogation: first, the study of science as a postmodern phenomenon; second, how postmodernism and science are negotiated within the scientific community; and finally, theories of postmodern science itself. Moreover, as will become increasingly apparent, technology, on which modern science has become almost entirely dependent, is also a crucial factor in this equation. Without compasses, printing presses, microscopes, computers and particle accelerators, whole chapters in the book of nature would remain illegible, or unwritten. Technology not only therefore emerges as what permits the study of nature, the changing forms and functions of technology in the postmodern world have become inseparable from even the forms contemporary science takes, prompting some historians to consider *Technological Innovation as an Evolutionary Process* (John M. Ziman),[4] and some scientists to leave organic life behind for the *Sciences of the Artificial* (Herbert Simon)[5] – **artificial intelligence** and **artificial life**. With these sciences, we are never far from science fictions, on the one hand, or from postmodern **simulation**, on the other. Given this unexpected convergence between the natural and the human sciences, technology, **ironically**, emerges as a vital component driving and shaping postmodern culture itself.

First, then, to the study of science as a postmodern phenomenon. Ever since Thomas Kuhn's *The Structure of Scientific Revolutions*, the world of the natural sciences has been opened up to study through the lenses of the social sciences.[6] Arguing that the history of the sciences shows a discontinuous series of breaks with, and radical departures from, past sciences (called '**paradigm shifts**' – a term that has enjoyed a certain celebrity in postmodern circles), rather than a progressive, linear accumulation of scientific knowledge, Kuhn effectively demystified science as the 'disinterested search for facts', and showed how scientific agendas were set by faculty squabbles, funding pressures and peer groups as much as by theoretical problems and experimental results. Science may or may not have been the study of nature, but it now became a culture to be studied like any other.

Of course, Kuhn's portrait of science-as-culture did not go unchallenged. Outraged scientists and philosophers lined up to knock holes in his theses. Some challenged the culturalist implications of Kuhn's ideas, insisting that just because science is inevitably practised within a culture, it would be absurd to say that this was all there was to it. Apart from this cultural dimension, there was also the thorny problem of nature itself, to which science had so successfully devoted its productive career. While from the armchair or the questionnaire science may look Kuhnian, laboratory work offered a very different, hands-on experience. Science could, therefore, be studied as a culture, but it would continue to study nature, regardless. Out of these disputes in the Anglo-American academy there emerged what came to be known as science studies. In the United Kingdom, for instance, groups devoted to the sociological study of science formed in the universities of Edinburgh and Bath, while in the mid-1970s the journal *Radical Science* began publication. These groups tended to examine the history and sociology of specific scientific and technological programmes, such as the development of missile-guidance systems or the politics of IQ testing, asking questions concerning the funding, ideology and politics of scientific knowledge. With scientific knowledge enjoying high status, and science studies being broadly Marxist in orientation, emphasis began to be placed on the role played by science in the social construction of broader questions. For example, while it is perhaps difficult to see 'life' as studied by biochemists as having any great social consequences, issues surrounding abortion make permanent appeal to scientific 'facts' about the age at which a foetus may be regarded as independently sentient, effectively defining the field in which these issues are contested and the roles of the contestants within it. Not only does the 'finished' science – science as a body of facts – therefore have enormous social implications, but so too does science in action, leading sociologists of science to consider 'laboratory life' (what do scientists actually do?) as centred around both the practical (which groups, in what circumstances and by what means, made what 'discovery'?) and ideological (how are class and gender positions implicated in scientific practice? What role does science play in constructing cultures?) construction of fact. If the first response to Kuhn had therefore been to 'naturalize' science, the second concentrated on science as a 'socialized' *power*, and set about exposing its class and gender biases.

Feminist science studies, indeed, have yielded some of the most pertinent work from the perspective of postmodernism, science and technology. The medicalization of childbirth, for example, provides an early example of the way in which medical science (obstetrics) and hospital technology (bed, stirrups, forceps) position women in childbirth as passive bodies on which medicine acts. Childbirth is therefore no longer exclusively a female act; women require medical intervention to deliver a child, and so must submit to the medical regime as the dominant or active partner in the act of childbirth. Issues such as the gender composition (how many doctors are women?) and distribution (how many nurses are men?) of the medical workforce begin to abut onto the complicity between medicine's **representations** of women and social representations of women: women are passive, while science and men are active, even in childbirth. The study of these situations is therefore crucial to understanding the relationship between science and the dominant social conceptions of femininity, as well as the social roles of women.

Such concerns eventually led to the question 'Whose science, whose knowledge?' What if science was not simply statistically male (dependent upon the proportions of men to women working in the field) but also *epistemologically* male: does the way in which scientific knowledge is produced reflect, far from the universal truths of nature, merely the results of a partial and therefore historically and culturally male experience of it? Following many studies of science and its impact on the lives and social roles of real women alongside its role in the social construction of femininity, feminist science studies, in the work of Sandra Harding, Ludmilla Jordanova and Donna Haraway, began to move to what became recognizably postmodern science studies.[7]

Suddenly, from being a practice and a body of unimpeachable fact inaccessible to study by the social sciences or by cultural criticism, science became first a socialized, ideological phenomenon susceptible to historical and sociological scrutiny and, second, a 'text', composed of representations that, regardless of their factual status, formed one set in a broader network of representations and discourses that themselves construct dominant images and concepts of women, animals and machines. It was insufficient to target local instances of the economic or lived reality of scientific intervention; rather, the discourses and representations produced by science, and even the discourses of science itself that perpetuate its immense power and prestige, must come under scrutiny. If this power was produced in a discourse of which the appeal to 'nature' or 'reality' was a component, critical science studies could not stop at demonstrating that nature is otherwise than science represents it.

The discourses that granted science its power and prestige had also to be challenged at the level of discourse itself. Not only therefore could scientific discourse be **deconstructed** to reveal its internal inconsistencies, other discourses could also be produced in which this challenge could be most powerfully mounted. Just as for early feminist studies in literary representations of women the twin images of the goddess on a pedestal, or the disease-ridden, whorish and inscrutable *femme fatale* bent on the destruction of men, created the social reality according to which women were classified, so too, for postmodern, feminist science studies, the myth is indissociable from the reality of science. Thus Haraway (building on Bruno Latour's 'actor-network-theory'[8]) in a famous essay entitled 'A Manifesto for **Cyborgs**', concluded that, always the passive objects to active, scientific subjects, animals, machines and women formed an unstable network of unrealized alliances between both human and non-human actors.[9]

Rather than stopping her critical labour at the very point of exposing the ideological, fictional and mythic structures inhabiting an allegedly purified scientific discourse (although this is precisely what she does in her epic study of the development of primatology in *Primate Visions*), Haraway accepted that science-as-mythology was a major component of its real situation and that science fiction formed a core resource for its expansion. Memorably noting, therefore, that 'fact' is simply the past tense of 'fiction', both deriving from the verb 'to make' or 'to fabricate', Haraway puts a slice of **cyberpunk** politics into the cybernetic ideal of biology and technology united under a single scientific paradigm. Accordingly, from the social and natural phenomena 'subjugated' by scientific mythology, she produces a '**hybrid**', cybernetic mythology where 'nature' is a trickster, a wily coyote, and where women and machines fuse, feminizing the cybernetic ideal from within the discourses of science themselves, while simultaneously refusing the feminist critique of technology that reduces it to a 'male thing'. Thus Haraway concludes the cyborg manifesto with the dazzling line, 'I would rather be a cyborg than a goddess'.[10]

Bizarre mixtures and cultural affinities aside, it may seem that the cyborg remains only an image: a cybernetic Minerva sprung fully formed from the head of a dreaming Zeus. Surely inventing such figures cannot of itself have any effects beyond the marginal realm of science-fiction fandom? As a 'non-human actor', however, a cyborg cannot merely be reduced to image; science and technology, indeed, are increasingly augmenting naturally occurring non-humans with artificial tones: nanomachines, robots, clones. While the postmodern reflex may be to respond in turn, 'Ah, but nothing, not even science, can escape this realm of signs. All cultural struggles are fought out there, in a world that is inescapably narrated rather than "natural", and science is a part of culture, after all', Haraway remains wary of claims to 'nature' being reducible to 'narrative', or science to signs. Rather, it is important to Haraway, and other postmodern science students, not to operate such a reduction, but rather to consider 'hybrids' as the points of connection between scientific, cultural and political issues without annexing reality to discourse. The hybrid and the network in which it is a node have become the crucial conceptual means of organizing science studies in postmodernity. Rather than '*either* narrative *or* nature; *either* real *or* simulated', postmodern science studies such as Haraway, Michel Serres or Bruno Latour are engaged in emphasize a 'hybrid' and inclusive approach to the networks of events, problems, inventions, technologies, fictions, simulations and ideas that most adequately characterize the social role of science.[11] Both the 'naturalizing' bent of early science studies and the 'narrativizing' bent of the more recent, deconstructive approaches, present bad, one-dimensional images of science. Haraway's cyborg therefore both combines the hybrid 'nature-culture' of the scientifically, technologically and critically sophisticated world, and the rise of 'non- human actors' within it.

The concepts of the hybrid and the network lend themselves to the post-modern imagination, not least because hybrid entities form an increasing element of contemporary *life*, in both the physical and the cultural sense. The human genome (part computer program, part chemical catalogue, all human) and cloning technologies; genetically modified plant and insect species; the rise of socio-biology and evolutionary psychology; the entire continuum of modified ecologies stretching from **global warming** and decreasing biodiversity to drawing-board protocols for terraforming (that is, engineering the atmospheres of currently uninhabitable planets) and the conservative idea of a genetic data-base; microchip palliatives for physiological incapacities and the re-engineering and patenting of organic forms as commercial entities: history has never witnessed such hybridizations as are now reported on a daily basis. Just as the mutability of bodies has *physically* eliminated the idea of biological essences, so culturally, without core identities or essences sustaining 'the self', we postmod-erns are hybrids of cultural influences, racial and sexual identities, histories and memories both real (my memories) and artificial (my memories of that movie). Further, Deleuze and Guattari's idea of two types of organizational structure, the one vertical, independent, top-down and 'arborescent' or 'tree-like', and the other horizontal, multiply connected, bottom-up and '**rhizomatic**', easily blends an apt image of postmodern conceptual relations where connections spread and multiply rather than being constrained by imposed and inflexible hierarchies, with methodologies being adopted in mathematics, physics and artificial intelli-gence research (in many ways, this coincidence of nature and culture is one of the most fascinating aspects of Deleuze and Guattari's work).[12] Going further still, and prompting the question 'Science fiction or social fact?', networks, according to Jean-François Lyotard, have even become one of the most impor-tant, even definitive, non-human actors in the production of the postmodern world, even suggesting that the 'post' of 'postmodernism' refers not to coming after **modernism**, but to the 'posts' at which subjects and objects are connected in computerized societies.

While we can now see how easily science studies becomes susceptible to 'post-modernization', it remains doubtful how far science itself could be regarded as postmodern. There are, perhaps, two ways of thinking about postmodern science. First, science displays some of the features commonly associated with postmodernism; and, second, there is science that *calls itself* postmodern. Much recent science invites description as 'postmodern' and, in *The Postmodern Condition*, Lyotard even canonizes René Thom and Benoit Mandelbrot as practitioners of postmodern science.[13] Thom, in particular, seems to be postmodern in his 'hybrid' researches into mathematics, science, anthropology and **semiotics**. We know we are on postmodern tracks when we read that 'scientists are sorcerers'! Mandelbrot's **fractals**, meanwhile, have become the icon of **chaos** that seems so aptly to sum up the endless fragmentations of postmodernity, with mathematics, since the mid-nineteenth century, dumping the strategy of approximating the ideal and unchanging forms of a Euclidean world for a geometry of endless change and differentiation. If under Mandelbrot, *geo-metry* goes back to the Earth, then it is only to prove that the Earth, once thought flat (pre-modern), then spherical (modern), is now fractal and infinite, thus demonstrably post-modern. It is not postmodern, however, because there is the possibility that this may be 'the truth' (although this is itself paradoxical); it is by virtue of the intensely paradoxical idea of a 'postmodern nature' as described by fractal geometries, along with the generalized pursuit of paradox by **complexity**, chaos or **catastrophe theory**, that its aims can be considered postmodern.

Even among scientists, however, there are advocates of a postmodern turn. Although Lyotard had coined the term in 1979, 'postmodern science' in this more 'hardline' context first appeared in the subtitle of cosmologist Stephen Toulmin's *The Return to Cosmology*.[14] What Toulmin refers to is, however, less recognizably postmodern than the work of Mandelbrot and Thom mentioned above. As we have already seen in our discussion of Haraway, modern science, its practitioners and its philosophers, had drawn a picture of the world subjugated to active **subjects** in pursuit of the knowledge of essentially passive objects. Moreover, nature was to be opened violently to the scientists' penetrating gaze, as can be seen from all the narratives of scientific heroism filling the pages of popular accounts of great scientific discoveries. Modern science, then, 'objectifies' nature, regarding it as something to be turned at will to the purposes of active subjects. With this bipolar split, science posed itself the insoluble problem of bridging the gulf between the subject's alleged knowledge and the actual constitution of the object in itself.

While such a characterization may seem excessively abstract and metaphysical, it comes into focus when we consider the debates about objectivity surrounding, for example, primatological field studies. Following Jane Goodall's well-publicized excursions into the field to study the great primates, a scandal broke out when it was revealed that she had solved the problem of making 'first contact' with a group of chimpanzees by laying out food for them. This, detractors argued, contaminated the evidence of her study since she had contaminated the habitat and intervened in an unacceptably overt manner to alter the conditions under which the chimps related to her, thus raising doubts as to the subsequent character of their behaviour, and in consequence invalidating Goodall's findings.

Others have, of course, confronted this problem. The philosopher Willard van Orman Quine posited the following situation, which he called 'radical translation':[15] suppose you are an anthropologist visiting a hitherto undiscovered culture. You want to understand their language, but since it has never been heard beyond that culture, you have nothing to go on. How do you set about assembling a dictionary? The anthropologist must, Quine responded, assume that the members of the visited culture organize their linguistic world no differently from the way we do ours. As a result of this assumption, which came to be known as the 'principle of interpretive charity', objectivity becomes meaningless. The culture under study is less an object than a group of subjects whose actions must be understood through the anthropologist's hands-on intervention. But what grounds do we have, other than sheer pragmatism, for making Quine's 'charitable' assumptions? The anthropologist Claude Lévi-Strauss, for example, perpetually asked how, when studying other cultures, it was possible to avoid contaminating the specimen with imported prejudices specific to the scientist's culture. Even the presence of the scientist significantly alters the situation, introducing **differences** where there were none, and forcing the culture to confront, and thus to renegotiate its relations to, a new outsider. Lévi-Strauss's solution was not to try to minimize contact or disguise his presence, nor to assume that the differences were negligible, but to attempt to be absorbed into that other culture.[16] Even the physical sciences face this problem: insofar, for example, as subatomic particles are to become available to observation, they must be 'produced' in a particle accelerator; to what extent, then, does the physicist observe natural or artificial phenomena? Just as there are those who argue the objectivist case that such particles could not be produced for observation if the situation in which they were so produced did not correspond in essential respects to the natural situation, so too there are 'instrumentalists' who insist that science is engaged in the manufacture and observation of artefacts that, as hybrid products of observation technologies and nature, could not otherwise be available.

If these scenarios problematize objectivity from an abstract point of view, primatologist Dian Fossey, following in Goodall's footsteps, brings the problem into a starkly moral focus. Fossey's objectivity was so shrouded in doubt that stories began to circulate about 'unnatural relationships' she may have been having with a gorilla. Things were exacerbated when hunters trapped and beheaded her favourite gorilla, prompting her to track the hunters in turn, only to become their next victim. In such circumstances, the question seems to be less one of how to maintain the proper scientific objectivity and detachment, than how pathological such detachment would be. Postmodern science, according to Toulmin, has learnt this lesson: nature is not an object – something that stands against us that we must subdue in order to know. Instead, postmodern science becomes part of 'man's new dialogue with nature', as complexity theorists Ilya Prigogine and Isabelle Stengers put it.[17]

The hermeneutic overtones in this version of postmodern science mark it out, however, as less postmodern than many a philosopher or critical theorist would recognize. Paradoxically, such postmodern science seems merely to have learnt the lessons of Martin Heidegger's hermeneutic critique of the 'essence of modern science', over-polarized between maniacally mathematizing subjects and indifferent, inactive objects, and insufficiently attentive to the being of nature, to how nature *is*. Modern science, Heidegger argued, has imposed an image upon nature that, rather than revealing or 'dis-covering' it, covered it over again, so that the 'age of the world-picture' dominates all the procedures and discoveries of modern science. Heidegger, however, while no modernist, is perhaps better characterized as anti- rather than post-modern. And, similarly, the 'discursive' turn to include nature as a partner in dialogue parallels Jürgen Habermas's advocacy of the 'unfinished project of modernity' against a post-modernist renunciation of its ideals.[18]

Once again, however, Heidegger's 'world-picture' brings us back to the issue of whether science studies nature or representations, substance or signs. Surprisingly, perhaps, it is along the lines of signs, representations and simulation that much of what is more recognizably postmodern in the sciences is currently leading. The sciences of the artificial have in effect mounted a two-pronged attack on modern science with its predilection for nature over representations, on the one hand, and analysis over synthesis, on the other. On the one hand, artificial intelligence (AI) research has become less concerned with programming the functions of understanding into a machine than with *simulating* intelligence. Thus the 'Turing test' for machine intelligence, named after its inventor, Alan Turing, placed a person into a divided room and asked them, by means of a typewriter, to engage the subject on the other side of the divider in conversation. The machine passed its intelligence test if the person was fooled into thinking that the machine was another person. Here the nature or essence of human intelligence is less important than its appearance: seeming or behaving intelligently is sufficient. As Lyotard says of postmodern knowledge in general, the goal is no longer truth but performance: we do not need to know what intelligence really is, just how to simulate it. Of course, AI therefore provokes questions which, ironically, have resulted in machines modelling human intelligence, rather than humans providing the 'program' for machine intelligence. Moreover, the manner in which machines 'learn' in contemporary AI research is, in Deleuze and Guattari's terms, more 'rhizomatic' than 'arborescent': learning makes connections between things rather than mining a thing for as much information about it as possible. In AI, this approach is therefore called 'connectionism', and the hardware that learns through such means is called a 'neural net', eradicating the difference between real and artificial neurones. Rather than the image of arborescent supercomputers such as HAL 9000 from the film *2001: A Space Odyssey* (1968), which must be programmed with intelligence before carrying out intelligent functions, neural nets form rhizomatic networks of computers that interact with each other and, through this interaction, resolve random input into emergent patterns (see **complexity theory** and **fuzzy logic** in Part II), thus actually learning. The 'cybernetic brains' of 1950s science fiction became, in the later years of the twentieth century, intelligent simulations of intelligence.

Perhaps the most obviously postmodern of all the sciences, however, is that of **artificial life** (Alife), otherwise known as 'synthetic biology'. Artificial life dispenses with nature altogether, studying instead the actions and simulated evolutions of pixel-creatures in computer environments. Surely, at last, science is studying signs and representations rather than nature? Once again, however, the difference between the real and the artificial is what is eradicated. Thus evolutionary biologist and Alife researcher Thomas S. Ray twists this paradoxical science still further, stating, at this new discipline's fourth international conference in 1994, that the life processes studied in Alife are not themselves artificial but natural; the resultant life-forms merely 'live' in an artificial environment.[19] Thus Alife naturalizes the artificial, making **simulacra** of life indistinguishable from their real-life counterparts. In a sense, Ray and other Alife researchers are quite right: what current definition of life – self-moving, feeding and excreting, growing and reproducing – can rule these artificial aliens out of the natural world of evolutionary biology, even if the life in question is silicon-rather than carbon-based? Synthetic biology, in the words of one of its avatars, is not so much the study of life as it is, but life as it could be.

If Alife represents a simulationist extreme of postmodern science, at the other, realist, extreme, the sciences in postmodernity make an important contribution to the rethinking of cultural phenomena in general. This was already explicit in Lyotard's *Postmodern Condition*, although it is often overlooked: grand narratives do not collapse due to the withering effects of the progressive nihilism Friedrich Nietzsche forecast, or merely because this is something 'in the air', but because of the *effects of computerization*. Computer-mediated communications replace language as the vehicle of reason with information measured according to its effects. In other words, the postmodern condition is effected by a technology that harnesses language for quantitative evaluation, so that it is no longer determined by universal ideals (truth, the just society, freedom, etc.), but rather by local imperatives ('re: figures – my desk, tomorrow'; divert resources from failing department, progress this project, etc.), subject only to the law of increased efficiency.

On the one hand, narratives, representations, metaphors; on the other, science, technology, determinisms; Lyotard's account gives equal weight to both poles of the postmodern condition. Ultimately, however, although he insists that the goals of postmodern epistemologies and sciences are species of 'local determinisms', his characterization of the condition as a whole is premised on the technological seizure of the means of communication. While technology does not do this in a vacuum, but acquires agency by the social premium placed by capitalism – or more precisely capitalist techno-science – on a performative efficiency that elevates information exchange above all other uses of language, the determination of language by technologically achievable imperatives (instant response, minimal transfer time between information and execution, everyone at their 'post' and so on) becomes a *universal determination of the social bond*; and it is this that finally puts paid to the great stories that sustained the modernist ideal of the rational co-determination of social goals by free participants. Although, therefore, the postmodern condition may appear to be – and has all too often been interpreted simply as – nothing but a play of discourses, a matter of narratives only, Lyotard's thesis is ultimately that technology has become finally determinant. This sits ill at ease with the 'something in the air' notion that postmodernity consists in what Baudrillard has called the 'perfect crime': the death of the real can neither be confirmed nor denied since the corpse has disappeared.[20]

The antithesis between this 'realist' understanding of postmodernity and the more common account given of it, satirized by the Sokal affair (when the physicist Alan Sokal had a spoof article accepted by the American academic journal *Social Text*),[21] as open-ended and non-foundational discursive power play (reality does not determine the fittest narrative, but is instead fixed by the dominant narratives, which therefore lack firm foundations, so that they are susceptible of deconstruction, reversal and replacement), is brought into sharp focus by a realism underlying the 'postmodern' sciences. Mandelbrot, for example, celebrated by Lyotard as an exemplar of postmodern science, insists on the paradoxically infinite measurements demanded by the *actual* coastline of, for example, Britain on the basis of the return of 'geometry' to the measurement of the real Earth.[22] Thom, similarly disposed to paradox in his modelling of unpredictable changes of state – catastrophes – in a system, is driven to this by a realist conception of mathematics in the morphology of living systems, following his mentor D'Arcy Thomson.[23]

Nor is this thesis proposed by Lyotard alone. The 1977 winner of the Nobel prize for chemistry Ilya Prigogine wrote, with chemist and philosopher Isabelle Stengers, of a 'new alliance' between the physical and the human sciences. The new alliance was premised on the discovery that time was not simply an abstract frame of reference, as Henri Bergson had complained against Einstein's conception of it when they debated the issue in Paris in 1922; nor was it, as Einstein in turn complained of Bergson's notion of it, merely a 'philosopher's time': rather, Prigogine's discovery of *non-linear* processes in the natural world established that time was integral to physical processes where there emerges 'order out of chaos', as the edited English language version of 1985 was titled. Significantly, one of the elements cut from the English edition was the author's discussion of Deleuze's work as an important contribution to rethinking non-linear processes. At the very moment, then, when the humanities were reeling under postmodernism's revelation that 'reality' was a matter of social or discursive construction, and that therefore 'scientific discourse' could be attacked for its 'unfounded' attempts to state the truth about nature, the sciences were promoting a critique of the conceptual conservatism of the sciences and a new realism therefore concerning not just the scientific, but also the philosophical, engagement with the world, its history, its ideas and its physics. Offering a non-reductive approach to scientific theory, the non-linear physics Prigogine and Stengers promote has been embraced by both commentators on postmodern thought, such as Ira Livingstone, and by those who embrace what such commentators would likely call 'scientism':[24] the uncritical adoption of the explanatory goals and methods of the physical by the social and human sciences. Non-linearity has not only, that is, been borrowed as a metaphor or narrative device, but has also been embraced as enabling an account of sociological and cultural processes by the same theories that are employed by the physical sciences. Whether overcome or repaired, the gulf between the physical sciences and the humanities, formalized by Wilhelm Dilthey in the nineteenth century, lies at the core of the issues foregrounded under the rubric of postmodernism and science.[25] Precisely where Michel Foucault famously sees only epistemic discontinuities, breaks, and ruptures in scientific practice and theory, the sciences invent the basis of a new continuity.[26]

This situation, however, has also led some who might be expected to have the most to gain from the postmodern turn to signs and constructions to reject it altogether. Thus sociologist of science Bruno Latour rejects the ideological criticism of science as practised by many of the originators of his field of study, but also, in response to the question of postmodernism, insists 'we have never been modern'.[27] In place of the simple segregation of the human world of thought and language from the physical one of things, Latour proposes the non-modern interconnection of concept and chemical, meaning and matter. In place of a world that restricts the capacity for action to rational beings, Latour draws our attention to the effects on that world of non-human agents. For example, viruses are discursively constructed, certainly (HIV as 'God's plague upon the sinner'; the immune system which HIV attacks as marking the limits of personal identity), but this is not all there is to them. They are also particular protein codes that can be isolated in laboratories, that have their own inscrutable genetic history, that have undeniably physical effects, and that spontaneously mutate and threaten populations. Similarly, technology is not simply an inert tool enabling human intervention in and control over the physical and social world; rather, it becomes an agent embroiled alongside human components in systems whose effects are greater than their constituents.

Perhaps the most powerful examples of such networks are provided by the emergent field of biotechnology: the ongoing genetic modification of natural organisms is neither natural nor discursive alone, although it combines both into a series of technologies with the aim of creating new specifications for natural objects. Such objects are not metaphorically, but literally hybridized, and not only in the specifically biological sense of the term: the effects of biotechnological networks can neither be contained under traditional scientific paradigms, nor under traditionally humanistic ones, since politics, economics and commerce are inextricably tied up with the particular functions newly engineered into real organisms. In place, therefore, of the sciences' rejection of the social, and of humanists' rejection of the physical, Latour's 'non-modernism' proposes a 'new constitution' that combines both the physical and the discursive, mountains, madness and machines, GM crops, global commerce, Frankenstein's monster and ecological politics as irreducible elements of one reality.

In one sense, then, the conjunction of postmodernism, technology and science yields new critical methods for the humanities' scrutiny of the sciences; in another, it occasions attempts to establish conceptual frameworks for a new connectivity between physical and discursive objects. While these are perennial concerns, and not specific to postmodernity alone, Lyotard, for example, argues precisely that postmodernity is what it is by virtue of the technological transformation of the paradigmatically humanist medium of language in general, subjecting it not merely to philosophical, literary and cultural study, but to engineering and physics. The net effect of this, Lyotard argues, is to spawn an urgent experimentation in modes of linguistic intervention, artistic practices and scientific theorizing alike. Concerning this latter, we have seen that there is experimentation aplenty, theoretical and practical. Unlike previous attempts to introduce theories stemming from the physical sciences into the social sciences – such as, for example, Auguste Comte's positivism, or Herbert Spencer's social Darwinism[28] – the attempts of the last 30 years or so do not seek simply to explain social and cultural phenomena in terms of physics, but rather pursue a larger philosophical agenda. Thus we find scientific theorists such as Roland Omnès arguing that the best guide to the overwhelmingly complicated ontology of quantum physics is not to be found among the back-catalogue of scientific heroism, nor in systematizing the current state of research, nor even from the sterile epistemological debates of the philosophy of science. Rather, Omnès claims, Heidegger's prolonged interrogations of Being, and the third-century neoplatonist philosopher Plotinus' complex meditations on the relation between language, logic and nature, will serve better to explicate the relations between *logos* and reality involved in the quantum world.[29] The agenda is quite simply a new metaphysics.

Three figures dominate postmodern science: the hybrid, the network and non-linearity. If the wave of experimentation affecting the arts, humanities and the sciences is what defines the postmodern condition, its outcome hinges on the simple antithesis brought to light by considering the interconnections between science, technology and postmodernism: are hybridity, networks and non-linearity *simply* figures, metaphors or 'manners of speaking', or are they the non-reductive articulators of a new metaphysical realism?

NOTES

1 See Fredric Jameson, *Postmodernism, Or, The Cultural Logic of Late Capitalism* (Durham, NC: Duke University Press, 1991).
2 Martin Heidegger, *On the Way to Language* [1959], trans. Peter D. Herz (New York: Harper & Row, 1971), p. 60.
3 See Jean Baudrillard, *The Perfect Crime* [1995], trans. Chris Turner (London: Verso, 1996).
4 John M. Ziman, ed., *Technological Innovation as an Evolutionary Process* (Cambridge: Cambridge University Press, 2000).
5 Herbert Simon, *Sciences of the Artificial*, 3rd edn (Cambridge, MA: MIT Press, 1996).
6 Thomas Kuhn, *The Structure of Scientific Revolutions* (Chicago: University of Chicago Press, 1962).
7 See, for example, Sandra Harding, *Science and Social Inequality: Feminist and Postcolonial Issues* (Champaign, IL: University of Illinois Press, 2006); Ludmilla Jordanova, *Images of Gender in Science and Medicine Between the Eighteenth and Twentieth Centuries* (Madison, WI: University of Wisconsin Press, 1989); Donna Haraway, *Primate Visions: Gender, Race and Nature in the World of Modern Science* (London: Routledge, 1989).
8 Bruno Latour, *Reassembling the Social: An Introduction to Actor-Network-Theory* (Oxford: Oxford University Press, 2005).
9 Donna Haraway, 'A Manifesto for Cyborgs: Science, Technology, and Socialist Feminism in the 1980s', in L. J. Nicholson, ed., *Feminism/Postmodernism* (London: Routledge, 1990), pp. 190–233.
10 Haraway, 'Manifesto', p. 233.
11 See, for example, Michel Serres and Bruno Latour, *Conversations on Science, Culture and Time* [1990], trans. Roxanne Lapidus (Ann Arbor, MI: University of Michigan Press, 1995).
12 See Gilles Deleuze and Félix Guattari, *A Thousand Plateaus: Capitalism and Schizophrenia* [1980], trans. Brian Massumi (London: Athlone Press, 1988).
13 Jean-François Lyotard, *The Postmodern Condition: A Report on Knowledge* [1979], trans. Geoff Bennington and Brian Massumi (Manchester: Manchester University Press, 1984).
14 Stephen Toulmin, *The Return to Cosmology: Postmodern Science and the Theology of Nature* (Berkeley, CA: University of California Press, 1982).
15 Willard van Orman Quine, *Word and Object* (Cambridge, MA: MIT Press, 1964).
16 See, for example, Claude Lévi-Strauss, *Structural Anthropology*, vol. 1, trans. Clair Jacobson and Brooke Grundfest Shoepf (New York: Basic Books, 1963).
17 Ilya Prigogine and Isabelle Stengers, *Order Out of Chaos: Man's New Dialogue with Nature* (London: Heinemann, 1984).
18 Jürgen Habermas, 'Modernity – An Incomplete Project', *New German Critique*, 22 (1981), pp. 3–14.
19 See Thomas S. Ray, 'An Evolutionary Approach to Synthetic Biology: Zen and the Art of Creating Life', *Artificial Life*, 1:1/2 (1994), pp. 195–226.
20 See Baudrillard, *Perfect Crime*.
21 Alan, Sokal, 'Transgressing the Boundaries: Towards a Transformative Hermeneutics of Quantum Gravity', *Social Text*, 46/47 (1996), pp. 217–52.

22 See Benoit Mandelbrot, *The Fractal Geometry of Nature* (New York: Freeman, 1977).

23 See René Thom, *Structural Stability and Morphogenesis: An Outline of a General Theory of Models* [1972], trans. D. H. Fowler (Reading, MA: W. A. Benjamin, 1975).

24 See, for example, Ira Livingstone, *Between Science and Literature: An Introduction to Autopoetics* (Champaign, IL: University of Illinois Press, 2005).

25 See, for example, Wilhelm Dilthey, *Selected Works, Volume I: Introduction to the Human Sciences*, eds Rudolf A. Makkreel and Frithjof Rodi (Princeton, NJ: Princeton University Press, 1991).

26 See, for example, Michel Foucault, *The Order of Things: An Archaeology of the Human Sciences* [1966], trans. Alan Sheridan-Smith (New York: Random House, 1970).

27 Bruno Latour, *We Have Never Been Modern* [1991], trans. Catherine Porter (Cambridge, MA: Harvard University Press, 1993).

28 Auguste Comte, *A General View of Positivism* [1848], trans. J. H. Bridges (London: George Routledge, 1908); Herbert Spencer, *The Man Versus the State* [1884], in *Political Writings*, ed. John Offer (Cambridge: Cambridge University Press, 1994), pp. 59–176.

29 Roland Omnès, *Quantum Philosophy: Understanding and Interpreting Contemporary Science* [1994], trans. Arturo Sangalli (Princeton, NJ: Princeton University Press, 1999).

10

POSTMODERNISM AND ORGANIZATIONS

ANGÉLIQUE DU TOIT

In order to determine the influence of **postmodernism** on the evolution of organizational theory and practice, certain aspects of postmodernism are selected for discussion. These will be applied critically for the purpose of challenging the traditional premises which underpin organizational **discourses**. In essence, postmodernism rejects the idea that an ultimate *truth* is possible and that the world as experienced is as a result of hidden structures. The attempt at discovering such an order is seen as both naïve and erroneous. However, the need for an organizational truth has had a significant influence on organizational theories, resulting in the creation of a fad industry of management and organizational gurus, promoting quick-fixes to organizational ills. A postmodern critique of organizational and management theories challenges the positivistic scientific approach and the need for prediction and control.

Postmodern theorists argue that organizational theories are dominated by a set of **hegemonic** discourses that require **deconstruction**.[1] Such theorists also challenge the focus of organizational analysis, namely that of organizational structures and substance, and instead propose an alternative framework founded on the relations within organizations. This framework is supported by the theories of constructionism and sensemaking as discussed below. **Modern** management and organizational theories were developed following industrialization and mass production which created a need for efficiency. The scientific idea of management with its focus on logic and reason was established by Frederick Taylor[2] and continues to influence much of the underlying assumptions of organizational theories and practice. Associated with such institutions the machine metaphor came to embody the drive for efficiency, with employees perceived as mere cogs in the wheels.

The philosophy of logic and rationality resulted in what has become known as the functionalist paradigm.[3] The assumptions associated with the functionalist paradigm perceive social science as natural science and therefore the existence of answers to organizational and management problems; it is merely a matter of finding them. Underlying the functionalist paradigm is a belief in man as rational and therefore the ability of management to make decisions in an unbiased manner and supported by perfect judgement and knowledge. The emphasis is on *man*, as industrialization resulted in the domination of men within positions of authority, which remains a significant feature of the contemporary organizational landscape. With postmodernism came a loss of confidence in the rationality which had dominated the practice and research of organizations. Individual rationality is replaced by communal negotiation and sensemaking which embraces a social constructionist view of reality. The purpose of postmodern education of aspiring managers is to instil within them the ability to be proactive creators of their organizational realities. It is therefore the responsibility of educators to create an environment where students become aware of how their ontological and epistemological assumptions will determine the organizations they will create.

With increased **globalization**, and the accompanying turbulent economic and political markets and technological advances, the reductionist approach of classical management and organizational theories has come under pressure from critical writers.[4] The myth of organizational rationality is challenged and management practices are perceived as permeated by political power battles and conflict. Instead, the theories of postmodernism are seen as being better equipped to deal with the paradoxes and ambiguity surrounding the constantly evolving organizational milieu and questioning the underlying assumptions of scientific management.[5] For example, Michel Foucault made a significant contribution through his writings in challenging the exercise of **power** and control over its members by institutions within society.[6] He also became a prominent figure in the evolution of organizational theory and was seen as the entry point for postmodernism into organizational studies in the 1990s. Institutions he referred to include organizations that have seen their power and domination grow in parallel with the growth of globalization. Global organizations are often richer and more powerful than many countries, resulting in exploitation of less powerful and emerging markets.

GRAND NARRATIVES

The work of Jean-François Lyotard is particularly relevant to organizations and the deconstruction of modernist principles which continue to have a significant influence on organizations. A central premise of the intellectual movement of postmodernism is its rejection of an ultimate truth or **grand narrative**. Grand narratives are perceived as embodying reality thereby resisting any attempts at questioning their authority. Lyotard, one of the key proponents of postmodernism, devoted his writings to challenging the monopoly of large-scale philosophies or **metanarratives**, as he defined them, which have dominated Western culture.[7] He goes on to argue that such metanarratives are incapable of containing the diversity of the many **little narratives** which represent society. Instead, the intellectual movement of postmodernism invites alternative and diverse epistemologies. Furthermore, postmodernism embraces the idea that the future is unpredictable and open to human influence, and rejects the assumption that metanarrative is capable of containing all knowledge and meaning. Postmodernism also rejects the notion of the existence of a social world which awaits discovery and argues that it is merely what society perceives it to be.

Postmodern thought has also given way to innovative ways of conceptualizing organizations, challenging some of the more traditional rigid modernist epistemologies which have underpinned organizational theories.

The earlier proponents of applying postmodernist thought to organizational theory argued that postmodernism enabled organizations to be understood not as natural phenomena, but as products of human attempts at creating order in an essentially irrational environment.[8] Organizations dominated by the ideologies of the modernist period are structured on a hierarchical, mechanistic, and command and control basis; whereas subscribing to postmodernism leads to differentiation, resulting in a more organic organizational design characterized by flexibility. Furthermore, job descriptions within a postmodernist organization are not subjected to clearly defined boundaries and definitions as the need of the job is continuously changing. The focus of the business is on the whole with the process fluid, driven by values and principles rather than logic and reason. While in the modernist organization, power is very much held at the top of the hierarchical structure and reserved for the privileged few; instead, power in the postmodernist organization is to be found and identified in an interconnected network of relationships. Such a network allows for the flexibility and balancing of paradoxes which are needed for new forms to evolve. Terms associated with modernity such as *true*, *real*, *rational* and *objective* serve a purpose and can be very useful, especially within organizations. The danger is when such terms assume the status of a metanarrative, leading to the subjugation of other perspectives and thereby suppressing creative thought. Postmodernism recognizes that organizations are dynamic and reality is continually being redefined and renegotiated, which encourages acceptance of ambiguity and creativity.

NARRATIVE AND STORYTELLING

As argued, postmodernism rejects the modernist perspective of a reality perceived through conventional scientific methods and focuses instead on the role of language in constituting reality. The interaction between interlocutors is seen as leading to action and to social practices, thus contributing to the production of social structure, for example the construction of organizations. The traditional view of language is that of a vehicle which reflects the world as it is. Language is therefore seen as conveying truth. However, language in itself does not represent any map or blueprint of reality. Instead, meaning is achieved through the use of language within human interactions. Sounds and symbols constituting language have no meaning *per se* other than the meaning assigned to them collectively within a particular culture or context. Language has inherent within it the interpretations and reflections of what constitutes meaning to a particular group of people.[9] Postmodernism argues that meaning is transitory and constantly evolving and therefore has no permanence or substance. The emphasis is on the joint authorship of meaning between the signifier and the signified. Meanings assigned to the words or symbols created by an author are suspended until the reader engages in the co-creative act of assigning meaning to those words. The **text**, therefore, has inherently a multiplicity of meaning. What is considered to be logic, knowledge or accepted wisdom, is the result of negotiated meaning.

Postmodernism suggests that the world can only be perceived through the forms created by a shared language. The **difference** in meaning from one language to another reflects a difference in a perception of the world. Shared meaning is an invisible substance that holds communities together, including organizational communities. Such communities have creative narratives specific to them, reflecting the meaning associated with certain words, such as globalization, strategy and competition. These words have a shared meaning within organizations which lead to shared action by its members. A challenge faced by postmodern organizations is the rapidly changing environment within which they operate and an equally rapid change in knowledge and information. This leads to a diversity of narratives and a denunciation of the *expert* within organizations, adopting instead the little narratives as put forward by Lyotard. Postmodernism challenges the beliefs which suggest that history, people and systems are sources of ultimate truths.[10] Jacques Derrida's arguments of deconstruction encourage people to free themselves from traditional authority and therefore a past which acts as a prison in both action and thought. His sentiments reflect the essence of postmodernism, namely to encourage a healthy scepticism of cultural ideals, including those of organizations. Postmodernism actively encourages the challenging of the old established ways of doing things and engagement in new conversations. The application of deconstruction allows organizations to challenge the dominant narrative associated with hierarchical structures and to invite the reconstruction of the organization through the little narratives referred to by Lyotard.

Postmodern analysis of organizations has resulted in storytelling as an approach through which organizations are able to contain a **plurality** of voices and realities. Storytelling is seen as a mechanism through which members of the organization make collective sense of their environment, creating an institutional memory.[11] Furthermore, organizational members are able to construct their individual roles through the scripts of their stories. The purposes of organizational storytelling are numerous. It provides a structure through which to make sense of the dynamics of corporate relationships and facilitates shared meaning-making which leads to the emergent organizational culture, reflecting the values and beliefs of the organization. Furthermore, storytelling is a powerful conduit for the transmission and sharing of knowledge within the organization. This is particularly relevant to the sharing of tacit knowledge. Because of its complexity, tacit knowledge is often difficult to transmit. The artful telling of stories is also a powerful mechanism through which to motivate organizational employees. Alternatively, from a critical perspective it could be argued that stories could equally be used as a tool of manipulation as they have the capacity to be used to exert power, manipulate and distort the perspectives of others.

Within the ever-changing landscape of organizations stories serve to provide certainty through a shared vision. Storytelling combines perceived facts with emotions, ideas, values and norms. It is through the telling of stories that organizations are able to organize and establish coherence. It makes the communication of abstract ideas and behaviours possible, creating shared expectations and interpretations. The narrative paradigm advocates that people come to know what they know by telling stories of personal experiences in different settings. In large organizations decision-making can be difficult and the qualitative nature of storytelling is often more powerful in reaching consensus and mobilizing commitment than the staid communication of factual data. The evidence of failed change management initiatives through a lack of commitment by employees is well documented. The sharing of stories provides employees with a mechanism for dealing with emotions which accompany change such as uncertainty, ambiguity and possible loss of identity. The telling of stories harnesses both the intellect and the emotions, which enables the organization to create a compelling future.

SOCIAL CONSTRUCTIONISM

Social constructionism views discourse about the world not as a map reflecting what is out there, but as the product of a communal interchange. Kenneth J. Gergen suggests that: 'Constructionism is one of the more challenging outcomes of postmodern thought.'[12] Truth and reality are products constructed between people within relationships. The objective of constructionism is to invite new forms of enquiry for the purpose of transcending metanarratives. Constructionism challenges the view that knowledge of the world is obtained through unbiased and objective observation. In keeping with a postmodern epistemology, social constructionism does not claim, nor does it offer, a replacement metanarrative and therefore does not remove or resist opposing views. On the contrary, 'constructionist views function as an invitation to a dance, a game, or a form of life'.[13] Social constructionism challenges the taken-for-granted beliefs about the world and the perception that knowledge about the world is acquired through observation. Instead it argues that experience is the result of active interchange between people engaged in reciprocal relationships. The emphasis is therefore on the interdependence of relationships.

Constructionism advocates the multiplicity of ways in which the world may be constructed and interpreted and rejects any attempt at establishing universal first principles. As advocated by storytelling, the cyclical nature of creation takes place through the application of language and the reciprocal and ongoing process of sensemaking. Norms and rules are created within cultures which determine the assumptions held by a particular society and which will lead to acceptable behaviour within the specific culture. Communities, whether they are located in a society or an organization, develop their own practices, rules and rituals. Rules are therefore culture specific and not universal and equally apply to the norms created within organizational communities. Similarly, organizational cultures influence the assumptions and truth associated with a particular organization or industry. Managing then becomes a dialogical activity in which managers create the organizational reality through the conversations they engage in with others. No matter how large an organization, it is socially constructed and is continually being re-constructed through the interaction of individuals, which means it is in a constant state of change. Organizations exist only through shared agreements of meaning and the pursuit of shared goals and objectives. The focus of constructionism is therefore on interactive relationships within a community and perceives language to give form to reality.

Social constructionism is also concerned with the practical aspect of knowledge. The interest is not what may be construed as truth, but instead what the implication for truth is for society and communities. The main tenet of constructionism is that knowledge, reason and morality do not reside within the mind of the individual, but within relationships.[14] According to constructionism, truth is an ever-changing landscape that taps into the rich interplay between experience, conceptualization and a communal understanding. What is then perceived as reality emerges as a result of such interaction. In conclusion, organizations are not defined by artefacts such as buildings, processes and policies but as social discourse relationally constructed within a specific context by social actors.

SENSEMAKING

Instead of seeking an external truth and organizational reality as advocated by traditional science, organizational members construct their organizations relationally by making sense of the constant stream of stimuli they deal with on a daily basis. Sensemaking supports the assumptions of postmodernism that there is no grand narrative and that collectively members of an organization create a sense of shared meanings. The traditional approach to organizational decision-making is through rationality and clarity, whereas the nature of sensemaking is about ambiguity, vagueness and confusion. In sensemaking parlance, rationality is best understood as in the eye of the beholder.[15] Furthermore, as defined by constructionism, sensemaking is achieved through ongoing conversations without beginning or end.[16] Sensemaking is perceived as the process through which people reduce the complexity of their environment to a level which makes sense to them. It is about being the author and the interpreter, creator as well as discoverer. Moreover, it is not a solitary activity, but takes place within a social environment which allows for interaction and the building of relationships. Continuing with the idea of sensemaking as a meaning-creating activity, it is perceived as the activity through which information, insight and ideas coalesce into something useful.[17] Sensemaking can be described as the reaction to the stimulation of the senses. The goal of sensemaking within an organization is for its members to share a common understanding of what defines the organization and its purpose. The longer term goal is to ensure that the organization develops the ability to adapt and ultimately to survive and thrive. However, organizations can only pursue their goals if there is a common understanding among their members which allows movement towards the goals through collective action. The underlying assumption of sensemaking resonates with that of constructionism and sees it as a communal activity. The prevailing sensemaking system within an organization will influence and direct interactions and activities among the members of the organization.

Thinking about sensemaking as an ongoing process is also to see reality as an ongoing and flowing activity. Furthermore, retrospection is an intimate part of the process of sensemaking. Comprehension is reflective by nature and a person only becomes aware of the sense made in retrospect. A significant element of sensemaking is that of variation. However, organizations go to great lengths to avoid diversity and subscribe to sameness and uniformity for the purpose of dealing with ambiguity and to gain a false sense of control. It is, however, diversity that allows for a multiplicity of realities and options. Through the process of organizational sensemaking, a shared understanding of values and assumptions emerges between the members of the organization. Organizational structures and practices may restrict the creativity and plurality created through the multiple interactions of its members. In extreme cases where face-to-face communication is severely hindered, organizations are likely to malfunction. The richness of the sensemaking process is dependent on the ability to embrace novelty and the expansion of vocabulary that will lead to an increased possibility of *realities* being perceived.

FEMINISM

Women remain conspicuous in their absence at senior and executive levels. Organizational theory and practice continues to marginalize women in favour of men and gender bias within organizations exists in the form of prejudice and discrimination against women. As discussed above, narratives implicitly frame meanings associated with both individual and organizational identities. Mainstream organizational theorists and writers have written from a rational and male-dominated perspective which has marginalized feminine ontology in numerous organizational discourses, for example leadership. Power is central to the archetypes of leadership which continues to be associated with men, and the right to rule is intrinsic to the paternalistic nature of society and organizations. Explanations for the under-representation of women in leadership positions vary. Mental attitudes continue to hold men and women captive in the straitjackets of traits associated with their respective genders. Women are stereotyped into 'caring' or 'people-orientated' roles, which are not traditionally associated with leadership but seen instead as a support to leaders, a role occupied by men.

Stereotyping of women portrays them as being less effective than men in leadership roles, mainly due to the fact that they are being measured against and compared to male values. Senior management positions are characterized in male terms, leading to discrimination against women and their stereotypical feminine characteristics. Such prejudice erroneously assumes therefore that men are better suited to leadership positions than women. The line management experience needed for senior positions in areas such as operations, manufacturing or marketing is often denied women. This contributes to the difficulties women face in reaching senior positions where such experiences are perceived as essential prerequisites for senior management positions.[18] In addition, the deeply held assumptions and beliefs of the male characteristics of senior management and those associated with women and related behaviours, add to the difficulties of women fitting into the role of senior management. Advancement within organizations goes beyond ability and competencies and includes conforming to social expectations and norms, which therefore leads to non-acceptance of women in positions of power.

The gender debate goes beyond the vocabulary dominating leadership issues to include deeply embedded values in society which reinforce the gender divide. Within the history of Western philosophy masculine and feminine have always been depicted as mutually exclusive with opposing traits. The core characteristics associated with masculinity are the traits assigned to leadership, which includes being objective, action-orientated, assertive and independent. However, as discussed under the heading of constructionism, traits are not fixed and are subject to culturally constructed meanings. The leadership style of women is perceived as participative and collaborative whereas the leadership style of men is seen as more transactional and directive. In addition to leadership differences there is also a perceived difference of communication styles between the genders and it is suggested that women have a preference for verbal communication and also give more emotional support than men. On the other hand men emphasize the dissemination of information and a demonstration of competence. Aspiring women leaders find themselves in a double bind. If they express leadership traits associated with men they are accused of being aggressive while men are seen as being assertive. On the other hand if they express a communal and inclusive style of leadership they are labelled as being weak and not able to demonstrate the requirements of leadership.

The lack of representation by women in senior management is also associated with organizational structures and vertical mobility within organizations. Furthermore, organizational boundaries between functions, divisions, professions and occupations correspond with the boundaries between what is perceived as 'male' and 'female' work. Such stereotypical segregation between femininity and masculinity has led to the myth of differences between men and women being 'natural'. This has led to hierarchization with men at the top and, by default, masculine values being ascribed as being superior to feminine ones. The low representation of women in senior leadership roles reflects missed opportunities for organizations to select from the best talent available, particularly as women represent more than half of the marketplace. Instead, organizational rhetoric continues to privilege a patriarchal worldview protecting the status quo and its bias against women.

SCEPTICISM

A postmodernist approach to knowledge also expects theorists to express the ability to be critical of the assumptions underpinning any discourse of knowledge. The purpose of critical theorists of organizations is to contest the positivist theories and their associated assumptions that have dominated the study and practice of organizations. Scepticism provides a framework through which to challenge organizational metanarratives and ideologies that have resulted in some of the business and market scandals of recent years. Organizations develop their own particular house metanarratives and these dictate a certain conformity of behaviour from its members – and in extreme cases attempts to silence critical voices whether they are internal or external to the organization. Organizational peer groups tend to develop shared norms and beliefs, leading to conformity of behaviour. Depending on the organizational culture, management often resists or rejects being opposed too strenuously on their decisions or strategies, expecting assent rather than dissent. Organizations are permeated by activities to create sameness, such as team-building exercises and training, which are all about serving the same cause, namely working towards a common objective, sublimating deviant voices.

Many organizations claim to support and celebrate a commitment to diversity, however the reality is that organizations are permeated by processes and procedures that lead to the practice of group-think. The concept of group-think is not a new phenomenon and was first suggested by Irving L. Janis in 1972.[19] One of the major symptoms of group-think is that of collusion and the reinforcing of certain group behaviours for the purpose of protecting the ideology of the group. One of the main motivations for group-think is the maintenance of group cohesiveness, as it engenders a sense of solidarity and positive feelings among the group members. On the other hand, it may lead to gross errors due to shared misjudgements, which may result in manipulation and the suppression of information as well as voices of dissent in order to present evidence to the contrary. Subtle constraints may also be imposed on group members to prevent individuals from exercising their critical powers and engaging in open challenge of the group norms. Group-think also leads to rejection of and isolation from outside critics who threaten to disrupt the status quo or the questioning of group norms. One way of preventing this phenomenon is through critical thinking, which provides healthy scepticism and is one of the most appropriate ways to ensure that an open mind is exercised and assumptions challenged and scrutinized.

Social constructionism, as discussed above, also offers a further theory by way of explanation for the phenomenon of group-think. The relationships within any community, including those of an organizational community, are fundamental to constructionism. The central premise of social constructionism is that knowledge is a product of this relatedness and constructed between individuals. Conformity can have disastrous consequences for organizations resulting in the silencing of new ideas or critical voices which may mean survival of individual organizations or industries as a whole. Asking awkward questions about the assumptions of organizational policies and ideologies is what scepticism encourages and it may pay dividends for the organization in the longer term. Scepticism can be perceived as negative in its approach and therefore met with resistance; however the benefit is a rejection of the status quo, fostering an enquiring mind at all times. Organizations that do become trapped within their metanarratives rarely prosper and neither do their employees. An organization which is open to new and different narratives is more likely to thrive during good times and survive the bad times. Postmodernism provides the theoretical tools by which both theorists and practitioners are able to construct this position, which ultimately leads to more transparency within the organization and acts as an antidote to the abuse of metanarratives, thus giving little narratives the opportunity to flourish.

CONCLUSION

The exploration of postmodernism for the study of management and organizations has had its critics, and some have advocated 'soft' or 'sceptical' postmodernism, encouraging a critical approach to metanarratives while at the same time honouring academic boundaries and critical thinking. This is evident in some of the top tier academic journals of management and organizational studies which have failed to publish any or only a cursory attempt at a dialogue and debate with postmodern theories as they apply to the study of organizations. The contribution of postmodernism to the study of organizations can be summarized as providing a critical voice for challenging organizational metanarratives. It also provides a framework for both theorists and practitioners of organizations to understand the practices that are less susceptible to concrete measurement such as costs, bottom-line and profits, yet which provide the very essence of what defines an organization – namely the relations which both create and sustain the existence of the organization.

NOTES

1 David M. Boje, Robert P. Gephart Jr. and Tojo J. Thtachenkery, eds, *Postmodern Management and Organization Theory* (London: Sage, 1996).
2 Frederick Taylor, *Principles of Scientific Management* (New York: Harper, 1911).
3 Gibson Burrell and Gareth Morgan, *Sociological Paradigms and Organisational Analysis* (London: Heinemann, 1979).
4 Vincenzo Dispenza, 'Encountering Management', in David Golding and David

Currie, eds, *Thinking About Management: A Reflective Practice Approach* (London: Routledge, 2000), pp. 17–33.

5 Angélique du Toit, *Corporate Strategy: A Feminist Perspective* (London: Routledge, 2006).

6 Michel Foucault, 'Power and Strategies', in *Power/Knowledge: Selected Interviews and other Writings, 1972–1977*, ed. Colin Gordon (New York: Pantheon Books, 1980).

7 See Jean-François Lyotard, *The Postmodern Condition: A Report on Knowledge*, trans. Geoff Bennington and Brian Massumi (Manchester: Manchester University Press, 1984).

8 Robert Cooper and Gibson Burrell, 'Modernism, Postmodernism and Organizational Analysis: An Introduction', *Organization Studies*, 9:1 (1988), pp. 91–112; Kenneth J. Gergen, 'Organization Theory in the Postmodern Era', in Mike Reed and Michael D. Hughes, eds, *Rethinking Organization: New Directions in Organization Theory and Analysis* (London: Sage, 1992), pp. 207–26; Martin Parker and John Hassard, *Postmodernism and Organizations* (London: Sage, 1993).

9 Kenneth J. Gergen, *Social Construction in Context* (London: Sage, 2001).

10 Stuart Sim, *Irony and Crisis: A Critical History of Postmodern Culture* (Cambridge: Icon Press, 2002).

11 David M. Boje, *Storytelling Organizations* (London: Sage, 2008).

12 Kenneth J. Gergen, *Toward Transformation in Social Knowledge*, 2nd edn (London: Sage, 1994), p. 242.

13 Ibid., p. 79.

14 Kenneth J. Gergen and Mary M. Gergen, 'Social Construction and Research as Action', in P. Reason and H. Bradbury, eds, *The SAGE Handbook of Action Research: Participative Inquiry and Practice*, 2nd edn (London: Sage, 2008).

15 Karl E. Weick, *Sensemaking in Organizations* (London: Sage, 1995).

16 See ibid.

17 Deborah J. Dougherty, Leslie Borrelli, Kamal Munir and Allan O'Sullivan, 'Systems of Organizational Sensemaking for Sustained Product Innovation', *Journal of Engineering and Technology Management,* 17 (2000), pp. 321–55.

18 Judith G. Oakley, 'Gender-Based Barriers to Senior Management Positions: Understanding the Scarcity of Female CEOs', *Journal of Business Ethics,* 27 (2000), pp. 321–34.

19 See Irving L. Janis, *Victims of Groupthink* (Boston, MA: Houghton Mifflin, 1972).

11

POSTMODERNISM AND ARCHITECTURE

DIANE MORGAN

While motoring across the Californian desert, a young woman encounters a young male student who had been engaged in the militant activities of May 1968. He is later shot by the police. Thanks to this encounter, her eyes are opened to the capitalist materialism surrounding her; the prevalence of consumer culture; social inequality and the shady dealings of big business. She arrives at her destination in the middle of the desert, and enters her boss's house – a splendid **modernist** oasis, consisting of a cantilevered steel frame with strip windows, which perches on the edge of an arid rocky outcrop. She can now see through its refined design to its impure preconditions: its slick form, cleverly unobtrusive, as it parasitically clings to the natural surroundings, sums up the exploitation rife in society at large. She exchanges knowing looks with the native American servants in the house and appears to sense what natural values might be as she gives herself up to a waterfall in the grounds of the house. For her boss, by contrast, value is not something intrinsic in things or people but rather a product of commercial speculation. He reminds his business contact, hesitant about signing a deal with him for the development of a shoreside site, that 'the price of anything is neither high nor low except in relation to its potential use'. Value is only to be assessed in terms of what can be extracted financially. Water is not to be treasured for its natural properties but for the business opportunities it opens up: in this case, the construction of a marina, pier and airstrip and perhaps hotel complexes so as to turn the place into a marketable resort. Having understood the full significance of the house and its residents, the woman imagines it being blown up, dramatically ripped apart by an explosive rejection. As the highly aesthetic modernist house bursts into flames, it is followed up by further iconoclastic demonstrations: fridges, clothes, all sorts of commodities are blasted into the air. These emblems of a materialistic culture epitomize a society gone astray: an instrumentalized world which 1960s
youth refuses in the name of fundamental rights and natural values.

What I have just described is Michelangelo Antonioni's film *Zabriskie Point* (1969) and it provides a good starting point for a discussion of **postmodern** architecture. In this film, modernist architecture is no longer associated with the innovations of the avant-garde – as it was in the 1920s and 1930s – but with the establishment, the well-heeled, the older generation. Its pure, transparent style, the regime of living it offers to its residents, is equated with the arrogance of wealth and **power**. The sweeping away of its **traces** in the film marks the possibility of a radically new departure which is also a return to, or retrieval of, all too neglected values. This reinscription of the past conjoined with an enthusiasm for the variety of the contemporary could serve as a positive definition of postmodernism as understood by Charles Jencks, its most vocal of exponents on things architectural.

Jencks suggests that postmodern architecture at once continues the traditions of modernism and transcends them – his term for this process is **'double-coding'**.[1] Anxious to defend postmodernism against allegations that it is just an irresponsible free-for-all, whose lack of political commitment plays straight into the hands of those who want to maintain the status quo at any price, Jencks stakes out nobler aims. Postmodernism, he claims, aims at a realization of 'the great promise of a **plural** culture with its many freedoms'.[2] Whereas modernism was a 'univalent formal system' which suffocated dissenting voices in an attempt to impose general principles of minimalist taste, Jencks associates postmodern architecture with eclecticism and openness. For us to understand the stakes of this debate between postmodernist and modernist architecture, it is necessary to trace the latter's passage from the exciting and dynamic world of Bauhaus and Le Corbusier in the earlier twentieth century through to the 1960s and 1970s where what used to be the avant-garde is now perceived as the enemy of change.

One of the most telling images of a modernist architect is given to us by Ayn Rand. In her best-selling novel, *The Fountainhead*, the uncompromising architect Howard Roark declares: 'I set my own standards. I inherit nothing. I stand at the end of no tradition. I may, perhaps, stand at the beginning of one.'[3] Here, modernist architecture is represented by one who is unwilling to adapt his projects to the tastes of his public. Ahead of his time, he will not pander to the retrograde mass demands for mock-classical buildings with their tacked-on pilasters, scrolls and leaves. His constructions are absolute in their demand for recognition: harsh, rigid glass skyscrapers and standardized mass housing which does away with individualized nooks and crannies, the idiosyncrasies of clutter, in the name of purity and clarity. Democracy, the negotiation of **differences**, is regarded by him as a levelling of genial creativity.

Le Corbusier also announces a rejection of past standards. He kicks away the props and supports of conventional taste, castigating old-fashioned, artisanal values as redundant in the age of the machine aesthetic: 'Handicraft. Cult of "failures". Excuse for daubs. Slack hour of imprecision. Triumph of weak egoism. Delight of the free will, regard for the individual. Refusal of control.'[4] Handed-down assumptions must be put to the test, not just absorbed unquestioningly. The architect is a virile superman, an affirmative nihilist boldly overturning today's conventional values in an attempt to think and construct the future: 'Culture is the flowering of the effort to select. Selection means rejection, pruning, cleansing, the clear and naked emergence of the Essential.'[5]

This tough selection process, this jettisoning of all that is presumed to be superfluous, weak and impure in the name of discipline and hygiene, coupled with Le Corbusier's personal admiration for technocrats and strong, if not totalitarian states, brings together most of the worrying aspects of modernist architecture. A movement which started off with utopian visions of serving the masses, introducing standardization so as to set higher standards of living for all – not just the already privileged – seems to end up dictating to those same masses.

The same disquieting tendency can be detected with the Bauhaus. As essays by Grete Lihotzky and Bruno Taut included in *The Weimar Republic Sourcebook* made clear, this highly influential school of thought and practice saw in mass mechanical reproduction a solution to social injustice and gender inequality. Cheaply manufactured mass housing, rationalized into compact housing units, would not only reduce the difference between rich and poor by setting minimal standards for all, but would also emancipate the woman from household slavery by systematizing the 'best and simplest way' to keep the house in running order.[6] Such Taylorist efficiency would mean that household chores would become so self-evident and easy to accomplish that even husbands and children could contribute to 'making the beds, cleaning the washstand, etc., as necessary'![7] The final result would mean that the woman would save time and be freed up for other activities – intellectual pursuits or leisure activities as she wished.

This liberating aspect of Bauhaus's ethos has to be read alongside the other, more sinister, side of systematized rationalization. Consider this extract from Rudolf Arnheim's 'The Bauhaus in Dessau' (also in *Sourcebook*):

> In a room hung with diagonal curtains, in which a sofa sits obliquely to the corner and ten different, fully loaded little tables are set up every which way, there is hardly any reason why a new floor lamp should be placed here rather than there. But the position of everything in a Bauhaus room can be decided with nearly lawlike precision. One will soon learn to understand theoretically that it is not a question here of subjective taste, but that such feelings are a very secure and generally valid psychological phenomenon that leads to very similar results from different people. That is why one can speak even in the case of such problems as those of 'objectively determined solutions'.[8]

Here more manipulative overtones creep in. Instead of standardization promoting individuation, a general programmatization of taste is fantasized. In a Bauhaus flat there would only be one destination for your newly acquired lamp. Your flat would be designed in such a way that that particular item would belong to it *there* as if it were conforming to some ineluctable natural law. Emancipation tips over into dictatorial prescription; egalitarian standardization becomes totalitarian uniformity; the iconoclastic break with the past cashes out as a smashing of people's sense of place and rootedness; a disrespect for the all too human fondness for familiar localities.

For Jencks, the alienation felt by residents forced to fit into idealistic, overzealous modernist building schemes marks the failure of that movement (and the beginning of a more modest, *post*modernist reorientation). He describes how grand 'utopian' housing schemes gradually fell into disrepair, being progressively vandalized as the inhabitants tried to register their sense of despair at being abandoned to soulless, concrete jungles:

> Modern Architecture died in St Louis, Missouri on July 15, 1972 at 3.32pm (or thereabouts) when the infamous Pruitt-Igoe scheme, or rather several of its slab blocks, were given the final *coup de grâce* by dynamite. ... Pruitt-Igoe was constructed according to the most progressive ideals of CIAM (the Congress of International Modern Architects) and it won an award from the American Institute of Architects when it was designed in 1951. It consisted of elegant slab blocks fourteen storeys high with rational 'streets in the air' (which were safe from cars, but as it turned out, not safe from crime); 'sun, space and greenery', which Le Corbusier called the 'three essential joys of urbanism' (instead of conventional streets, gardens and semi-private space, which he banished). It had a separation of pedestrian and vehicular traffic, the provision of play space, and local amenities such as laundries, crèches and gossip centres – all rational substitutes for traditional patterns. Moreover, its Purist style, its clean, salubrious hospital metaphor, was meant to instil, by good example, corresponding virtues in the inhabitants.[9]

Modernist architecture is regarded as having brutalized people in its attempt to rationalize, to impose a strict and systematic order on, their ways of living. Unfortunately for the idealist, humans are not entirely rational, ordered or disciplined. Their tastes are variable and mostly non-justifiable, and they are prone to fits of folly. For these reasons postmodern architecture, with its proclivity for crazy pastiche, its wacky blending of styles, its disrespect for monastic regularity and tolerance for historical referentiality is deemed more human than the rigours of modernist purism. As Jencks explains in *What is Postmodernism?* modernist architects were characteristically unsympathetic to human foibles: 'Ornament, polychromy, metaphor, humour, symbolism and convention were put on the Index and all forms of decoration and historical reference were declared taboo.'[10]

Postmodern architecture is also more cautious about the uses technology can be put to and more sceptical about the merits of industrialization. Whereas mechanization was jubilantly celebrated by the modernists for its exactitude (see Le Corbusier's tirade against imperfect artisanal goods, cited above), its ability to dispel the stuffy **aura** of the past and to launch a fresh, disenchanted modern world, postmodernists are less optimistic. The world post-Auschwitz, post-Hiroshima, knows too much about the terrors of abstraction and instrumentalization. A dislocated, disembodied relation to the world results in people becoming figures to be 'processed' or materials to be 'recycled'. (Alain Resnais' documentary film, *Night and Fog* (1956), on the Nazi concentration camps, contains some of the most graphic evidence of the results of such abstraction. People are reduced to spare parts – divided up, sorted into piles: hair for stuffing cushions, skin for soap and lampshades.) Science should not be allowed to 'progress' according to its own self-generating laws, without due concern to its long-term impact on the world and its inhabitants. As a consequence, Jencks wants to suggest that postmodernist architecture draws on some of the ethical and ecological lessons the past has inadvertently taught us. As in *Zabriskie Point*, Jencks suggests that once having rejected the arrogant assumptions of the modernist elite, one rediscovers the rights of the environment:

> Perhaps in the future with the environmental crises and the increasing globalisation of the economy, communications and virtually every specialisation, we will be encouraged – even forced – to emphasise the things which interact, the connections between a growing economy, an ideology of constant change and waste. They who don't realize the world is a whole are doomed to pollute it.[11]

Reacting against the modernist disdain for personalized space and thereby reconsidering the artisanal respect for the local and the traditional, postmodern architecture reinscribes place while meeting the challenge of present-day **globalization**. It is this double articulation, the negotiation of place and that which threatens to erode it, the placelessness of global communication networks, which is a central concern for postmodern architects.

As architecture is the most down-to-earth art form, the most fixed in space, it has an intimate relation to questions of **presence**, origin, rootedness and dwelling. All these concepts have taken a battering from postmodern thought. The virtual world of the **Internet** is one development which poses a serious challenge to architects used to concretizing projects in the here and now. If liberation is now to be equated with exhilarating surfing forays on the Net, which seems to promise another, virtual world, not tied down to earthly restrictions or prejudices, how is the architect supposed to carry on constructing the future? As we have seen, in the past the architect felt it was incumbent on him, as heroic demiurge, to take upon his shoulders the burden of responsibility for building the right, improving context for society. In the postmodern world, the restrictions of a particular place appear to have been circumvented. One might not have or know any neighbours, but instead be in regular, even intimate, contact with people all over the globe whom one has never met *as such*, according to traditional notions of encounter.

Faced with such developments in information technology, there can be no nostalgic return to an antiquated idea of place, despite the lamentable attempts of architects such as Quinlan Terry to return to a bygone age. Indeed any such hankering after precise geographical fixity and any such celebration of rooted, supposedly unproblematic identity is regarded as reactionary by this ever emerging mobile global culture which espouses decontextualized **hybridity** and the intersplicing of cultural differences. Architectural theorists have reacted to such challenges to their profession in different ways.

Kenneth Frampton, who is no friend of Jencks and his version of postmodernism ('postmodern architects are merely feeding the media-society with gratu-itous, quietistic images'),[12] nevertheless agrees that the modernist project is at an end and that what comes after is to be radically rethought. He accepts the fact that modernization can no longer be celebrated, as it was by his modernist predecessors, as the key to progress. Such a blind faith in the power of tech-nology, as well as a nostalgic return to a pre-industrial past, cannot be sustained. Frampton recognizes the dangers inherent in an avant-garde movement which has an overbearing sense of its own importance and truth, yet he is not prepared to lapse into apolitical quietism. He is still searching for a critical purchase on society and advocates that this stance is best achieved by an 'arrière-garde', not tempted by the **grand narratives** of modernism, which is still invested in resisting dominant forms of ideology.

Frampton's form of postmodernism focuses on architecture which can mediate between the 'ubiquitous placelessness of our modern environment' and a particular site.[13] His stance can best be understood by juxtaposing him with what he is reacting against: consider this ecstatic celebration of the American city – that antithesis of the well-integrated environment, that enemy of the urban project – by the guru of postmodern euphoria, Jean Baudrillard:

> No, architecture should not be humanized. Anti-architecture, the true sort (not the kind you find in Arcosanti, Arizona, which gathers together all the 'soft' technolo-gies in the heart of the desert), the wild, inhuman type that is beyond the measure of man was made here – made itself here – in New York, without considerations of setting, well-being, or ideal ecology. It opted for hard technologies, exaggerated all dimensions, gambled on heaven and hell. ... Eco-architecture, eco-society ... this is the gentle hell of the Roman Empire in its decline.[14]

Baudrillard disdains a 'soft' consideration for human scale and local setting. Postmodernism, with its exciting new technologies, is not to be shackled by the dead weight of the human with his or her pedestrian concerns. Instead he extols the intricacies of the freeways and that antithesis of the European urban experi-ence, Los Angeles:

> No elevator or subway in Los Angeles. No verticality or underground, no intimacy or collectivity, no streets or facades, no centre or monuments: a fantastic space, a spectral and discontinuous succession of all the various functions, of all signs with no hierarchical ordering – an extravaganza of indifference, extravaganza of undifferentiated surfaces – the power of pure open space, the kind you find in the deserts.[15]

Frampton exactly pitches himself against this uncritical acceptance of the decline of the urban project. He seeks to puncture this rhetoric of **simulation** and the **hyperreal** with buildings which, interacting with the singularity of their sites, resonate with a certain 'density' of experience. Subverting the otherwise unques-tioned superiority of the eye over the remaining senses, Frampton calls on architecture to appeal to the tactile: 'The tactile resilience of the place-form and the capacity of the body to read the environment in terms other than those of sight alone suggest a potential strategy for resisting the domination of universal technology'.[16] Touch, smell, the 'whole range of complementary sensory perceptions which are registered by the labile body' are evoked by Frampton as a way of reinscribing the human into an *experience* of place.[17] Rejecting apocalyptic cries by the likes of Stelarc announcing the obsolescence of the body in this '**post-human**' age,[18] Frampton sees his variety of postmodernism as permitting the resurgence of what Jean- François Lyotard would call '**little narratives**' or 'local **legitimacies**'.[19]

Another theorist who, like Frampton, takes a stand against the prevailing placelessness of postmodernist architecture, is Fredric Jameson. In 'Postmodernism and Consumer Society' he too recognizes the ossifying institutionalization of modernism against which postmodernism reacts.[20] He is also trying to reinvent artistic experimentation – a sign of oppositional, critical art which rudely disrupts conventionalized ways of seeing – while not falling into the trap of modernism, which all too quickly became equated with elitism because of its uncompromising difficulty. For Jameson, the summation of postmodern despair, the total abandonment of any attempt to contribute positively to the urban environment, is encapsulated by the Bonaventura Hotel in Los Angeles. This building frustrates the experience of place. Whereas the nineteenth-century city, the home of the **nomadic** *flâneur*, provided a forum for enriching, if brief, encounters, this hotel pre-empts exploration. It discourages independent mobility, obliging the unsuspecting visitors passively to give themselves up to its 'transportation machines' which conduct them from one isolated point to another. Instead of the rich 'density of its objecthood' sought by Frampton, this hotel thins out space by disallowing any appreciation of volume.[21] No general impression of the building can be snatched, no transitory vantage point can be seized from which to gather some sense of place. However, this is not to say that, by contrast, modernist space provided the visitor with static, solid viewing platforms with nicely set up perspectival privileges from which to dominate the surroundings. Far from it: the modernists delighted in spaces which were dynamic, even vertiginous, but which could be *experienced* as such. Indeed Sigfried Giedion's book *Buildings in France: Building in Iron, Building in Ferro-Concrete* is packed full of exhilarating descriptions of buildings such as the Eiffel Tower and the Transporter Bridge in Marseilles, the precursors of modernist architecture, which orchestrate dizzy and destabilizing – yet enriching – experiences of space.[22] By contrast, it is the paucity of the 'postmodern' experience which is lamented by Jameson. (Or to reframe this debate yet further using Walter Benjamin's distinctions in 'Experience and Poverty', one could contrast the stark, 'barbaric poverty' of modernist architecture, which violently breaks with the past in order to begin afresh, with the opulent paucity of postmodernism which marks a compromise with the status quo.)[23]. The Bonaventura Hotel, with its opaque reflecting surfaces, is therefore seen to be repelling the fractured city outside, refusing any communication with it, and thereby to have self-destructively turned in on itself. It cannot generate any meaning from within itself and the result is a 'milling confusion'.[24]

Jencks begs to differ from critics such as Jameson. In *What is Post-modernism?* he reads postmodernism not as a destructive emptying out of, or as a sceptical rejection of, value, but rather as a paradoxical 'relative absolutism, or fragmental holism', a challenge to attempts to categorize postmodernism as any one thing.[25] Robert Venturi, the other architectural theorist most associated with the fate of postmodernism, also equates it with a medley of different styles and approaches:

> Architects can no longer afford to be intimidated by the puritanically moral language of orthodox Modern architecture. I like elements which are hybrid rather than 'pure', compromising rather than 'clean', distorted rather than 'straightfor-ward', ambiguous rather than 'articulated', perverse as well as impersonal, boring as well as 'interesting'. ... I am for messy vitality over obvious unity. I include the non sequitur and proclaim the duality.[26]

Mocking the rigid and minimalist purity of modernist architects such as Mies van der Rohe, who had proclaimed earlier on in the century that 'less is more' – Venturi saucily retorts 'less is a bore' – he celebrates the 'messy vitality' of places like Las Vegas.[27] The casinos, diners, hotels and bars of Las Vegas are often mainly composed of enormous signs designed to catch the eye of touring motor-ists prowling The Strip for somewhere ostentatiously to squander their money. As Venturi remarks in *Learning from Las Vegas*: 'The sign is more important than the architecture. ... The sign at the front is a vulgar extravaganza, the building at the back, a modest necessity'.[28] The signs are not just words but pictures, shapes and figures illustrating the enticing nature of the place: one of Venturi's examples is a 'duck store in the shape of a duck, called "The Long Island Duckling"'.[29] Venturi goes on to explain how Las Vegas would be blas-phemous for modernist architects who strictly adhere to the biblical injunction against 'graven images' in the name of pure spatial expression:

> During the last 40 years, theorists of Modernist architecture ... have focused on space as the essential ingredient that separates architecture from painting, sculp-ture and literature. Their definitions glory in the uniqueness of the medium; although sculpture and painting may sometimes be allowed spatial characteristics, sculptural or pictorial architecture is unacceptable – because Space is sacred.[30]

The example Venturi uses to illustrate his argument is a most convincing one: Mies van der Rohe's German Pavilion in Barcelona, described by Henry-Russell Hitchcock as 'perhaps the supreme example of architectural design of the decade of the twenties'.[31] Mies' 'universal grammar of steel I-beams' filled in with glass and brick is interrupted, but by no means disrupted, by the inclusion of a single statue, the Kolbe sculpture of a naked woman. As Venturi points out:

Objects of art were used to reinforce architectural space at the expense of their own content. The Kolbe in the Barcelona Pavilion was a foil to the directed spaces: The Message was mainly architectural.[32]

Rather like the Bauhaus lamp mentioned above, the Kolbe statue is fitted into an overall design, not for its own sake but as the ornament which is required to adorn the building at that point, in that previously determined and circumscribed place. Far from producing a dissonant note which upsets the harmony of the building, the statue actually effaces itself, symbolically communicating nothing boldly. By contrast, by celebrating the garish language of signs, Venturi is praising the merits of 'an architecture of bold communication' over 'one of subtle expression'.[33] However, the question can be raised: how boldly can one communicate if the vehicle one is using is one that consists of pastiche, play, incongruity and eclecticism?

Returning to our initial point of departure: can we be so certain about the statement being made at the end of *Zabriskie Point* when the modernist house is blasted away? In the film there is a shift which can be registered between the dynamiting of the house and the ensuing images of exploding consumer items. The house itself is an example of the work of an architect such as Frank Lloyd Wright. He was hardly a purist, producing a textualized form of modernism, which made great use of building materials such as timber and stone. These blended gracefully into the natural surroundings in an eco-friendly sort of way. When the scene changes to the consumer items, the colours become artificially pastel and the music surges, underscoring the release of tension as these symbols of materialist culture are jubilantly jettisoned. Whereas the woman appeared hesitant about doing away with the villa, the other objects are relinquished without delay. Is the woman actually rejecting modernism and embracing what comes after – that is, postmodernism? She is presumably putting into practice her newly found radical politics. Can this be equated with the postmodernist theories of Jencks and Venturi who have no scores to settle with capitalism and consumer culture? Indeed, the former goes so far as to declare that today's society showers us with a superabundance of choice; according to him we are overwhelmed with an '*embarras de richesses*' and bathed in an atmosphere of 'widespread pluralism'.[34] However, Jencks then adds: 'With no recognized authority and centre of power many professional groups (and even whole countries) feel victimized by a world culture and marketplace that jumps, sporadically, in different directions.'[35]

Indeed, these 'groups' and 'even countries' who anxiously sit at the margins of an unpredictably expanding and contracting postmodern universe – suffering as they do from 'mild paranoia' – just cannot see the pleasures Jencks is trying to point out to them. They see mockery written into Ricardo Bofill's pastiche classical 'Versailles for the masses', his 'Espaces d'Abraxas' housing project at Marne la Vallée which was damningly described by Martin Filler as 'lifeless monumentality of crushing inhumanity'.[36] Equally, Venturi's assumption that

Americans especially 'feel uncomfortable sitting in a square: they should be working at the office or home with the family looking at television' could be deemed by them to be a gross generalization which leads to a regrettable neglect of public space and to a failure to foster civic identity.[37] Maybe the postmodernist architectural theorists who would have most in common with the woman's reluctant destruction of the utopian modernist project turned elitist, and her unhesitating blasting of the symbols of consumer culture, would be Jameson and Frampton. At least they are still holding on to the notion of postmodern critique which is also a postmodern counter-culture. However, to cite Jameson's concluding words, this idea might have to remain elusive. It does not give us much solid to build on:

> We have seen that there is a way in which postmodernism replicates or reproduces – reinforces – the logic of consumer capitalism; the more significant question is whether there is also a way in which it resists that logic. But that is a question we must leave open.[38]

In more recent years, debates in architecture have moved away from the issue of the modernist/postmodernist divide. Indeed, the particular 'debate' outlined above, which was such a key one for understanding the topic of postmodernism as a whole in the 1980s/1990s, is now largely only of contextual interest within a history of architectural theory. It was itself followed by a '**deconstructionist**' phase, during which architects such as Peter Eisenman interrogated the 'metaphysics of architecture', the grounding principles informing building per se, including the very concept of dwelling, and produced heavily theorized accompanying documents which drew explicitly on the work of Jacques Derrida. Such experiments were, to begin with, eagerly watched and analysed by philosophers who regarded them as possible sites of collaboration between the praxis of architecture and the often abstract world of philosophy. A later trend, which also reflects shifts in philosophical currency, is that of 'non-standard architecture': this title was adopted for the 2004 Pompidou Centre exhibition which displayed the work of architects who recurrently cite the philosophical texts of Gilles Deleuze in order to explain their exploration of 'self-organizing' topological forms, the products of sophisticated computer programs and new building materials, which are seen as transforming – rather than just deforming à la deconstructionists – structure.

However, perhaps ultimately more lasting and interesting architectural works have been produced by collaborative teams of architects and engineers which straddle the divide between 'modernism' and 'postmodernism', or rather which draw on those aspects of modernism which had been elided in the false polarity set up between modernism and the reaction against it (the 'post') that was supposed to have followed its demise. Some of the most successful recent projects – gauged in terms of their appreciation not only by the profession itself but also by the general public – such as Frank Gehry's Bilbao Guggenheim

Museum, Herzog and de Meuron's London Tate Modern, or Calatrava's Alamillo Bridge in Seville – are not to be characterized as 'anti-modernist'. Unlike postmodern architecture, they are not refusing and reacting against a homogenized concept of what modernism is, or, even worse, 'was'. Instead they draw on different strands of what is even now an eclectic and ever-changing 'tradition', or *traditions*, which continue to incorporate new building materials, such as free-form cable nets and PVC-coated Terylene, in order to develop further techniques such as tensile structures, which can themselves be dated back as far as the first Bedouin tents and the first sails used by Mediterranean mariners.

Rather than Venturi's 'postmodern' response, 'less is a bore', to Mies van der Rohe's 'less is more', maybe of more long-term interest will be Buckminster Fuller's economical – and therefore *ecological* – 'more for less'. The prolific Buckminster Fuller, whose life itself spanned the supposed divide between modernism/postmodernism, active as he was designing and writing from the 1930s to his death in 1983, continues to provide impetus not only to engineers and architects using the principle he coined, 'tensegrity', to build light-weight structures which use discontinuous compression and continuous tension to maintain themselves, but also to cultural theorists interested in synergy and intentional communities, and to biologists such as Donald Ingber researching cell structure, which uses tensegrity as its primary organizing tool – to name but a few domains which have been and continue to be influenced by Fuller's holistic vision.[39] Rather than, for instance, trying to compose architecture out of bits, compiling buildings out of an amalgam of different styles and traditions as did postmodernism, or breaking it down into its component parts as did deconstructionism, Fuller advocated a thinking of the whole – not only of a whole building, not only of a whole way of life but of Life itself – which is more than a sum of its parts. It is at this far more ambitious level, which supersedes the rather academic flavour of the 'postmodern debate' in architecture, that an engagement with globalization, both critical and affirmative, might begin.

NOTES

1 Charles Jencks, *The Language of Post-Modern Architecture*, 6th edn (London: Academy Editions, 1991), p. 12.

2 Charles, Jencks, *What is Post-Modernism?*, 3rd edn (London: Academy Editions, 1989), p. 7.

3 Ayn Rand, *The Fountainhead* [1943] (London: HarperCollins, 1994), p. 16.

4 Le Corbusier, *The Decorative Art of Today* [1925], trans. James I. Dunnett (London: Architectural Press, 1987), p. 62.

5 Le Corbusier, *Towards a New Architecture* [1923], trans. Frederick Etchells (New York: Dover, 1986), p. 138.

6 Grete Lihotzky, 'Rationalization in the Household', in Anton Kaes, Martin Jay and Edward Dimendberg, eds, *The Weimar Republic Sourcebook* (Berkeley, CA: University of California Press, 1995), pp. 462–4 (p. 463).

7 Bruno Taut, 'The New Dwelling: The Woman as Creator', *Weimar Republic Sourcebook*, pp. 461–2 (p. 461).

8 Rudolf Arnheim, 'The Bauhaus in Dessau', *Weimar Republic Sourcebook*, pp. 450–1 (p. 451).

9 Jencks, *Language of Post-Modern Architecture*, pp. 23–4.

10 Jencks, *What is Post-Modernism?*, p. 28.

11 Ibid., p. 59.

12 Kenneth Frampton, 'Towards a Critical Regionalism', in Hal Foster, ed., *Postmodern Culture* (London: Pluto, 1985), pp. 16–30 (p. 19).

13 Ibid., p. 24.

14 Jean Baudrillard, *America* [1986], trans. Chris Turner (London: Verso, 1988), p. 17.

15 Ibid., p. 125.

16 Frampton, 'Towards a Critical Regionalism', p. 28.

17 Ibid.

18 See Stelarc, 'Towards the Post-human: From Psycho-body to Cyber-system', *Architectural Design [Profile 118]*, 65:11–12 (1995), pp. 90–6.

19 See Jean-François Lyotard, *The Postmodern Condition: A Report on Knowledge* [1979], trans. Geoff Bennington and Brian Massumi (Manchester: Manchester University Press, 1984).

20 'Postmodernism and Consumer Society', in Fredric Jameson, *The Cultural Turn: Selected Writings on the Postmodern 1983–1998* (London: Verso, 1998), pp. 1–20.

21 Frampton, 'Towards a Critical Regionalism', p. 29.

22 Sigfried Giedion, *Building in France: Building in Iron, Building in Ferro-Concrete* [1928], trans. J. Duncan Berry (Santa Monica, CA: Getty Center, 1995).

23 Walter Benjamin, 'Experience and Poverty' [1933], in *Walter Benjamin: Selected Writings*, vol. 2, M. W. Jennings, ed. (Cambridge, MA: Harvard University Press, 1999), pp. 731–6.

24 Jameson, 'Postmodernism and Consumer Society', p. 15.

25 Jencks, *What is Post-modernism?*, p. 59.

26 Robert Venturi, *Complexity and Contradiction in Architecture* (New York: Museum of Modern Architecture, 1968), p. 16.

27 Ibid., p. 17.

28 Robert Venturi, Steven Izenour and Denise Scott Browne, *Learning from Las Vegas: The Forgotten Symbolism of Architectural Form*, 2nd edn (Cambridge, MA: MIT Press, 1977), p. 13.

29 Ibid.

30 Ibid., p. 7.

31 Henry-Russell Hitchcock and Philip Johnson, *The International Style*, 2nd edn (New York: W. W. Norton, 1966), p. x.

32 Venturi, *Learning from Las Vegas*, p. 7.

33 Ibid., p. 9.

34 Jencks, *What is Post-Modernism?*, p. 54.

35 Ibid.

36 Martin Filler, 'Building in the Past Tense', *The Times Literary Supplement*, 24 March 1989, pp. 295–6.

37 Venturi, *Complexity and Contradiction*, p. 131.

38 Jameson, 'Postmodernism and Consumer Society', p. 20.

39 See Richard Buckminster Fuller, 'Tensegrity', *Portfolio and Art News Annual*, 4 (1961), pp. 112–27.

12

POSTMODERNISM AND ART

COLIN TRODD

In his influential essay on Kenneth Noland, Jules Olistski and Frank Stella (*Three American Painters*, 1965), the distinguished critic Michael Fried argued that the self-critical nature of **modernist** art signalled the ethical need to embody the 'denseness, structure and complexity of moral experience'. At the same time, the 'continuous intellectual and moral alertness' of modernism must battle to avoid the fusion of art with mass culture, a place, system, and machinery denuded of all cognitive value.[1] Fried's seminal essay exemplifies a key claim of modernist criticism: digging deep into the materiality of his or her chosen medium the modernist artist produces a critique of an ideology in which things are more important than aesthetic values. By upholding a notion of order and structure Noland, Olistski and Stella are associated with the rejection of the idea that art can be assimilated into everyday life. From Fried's perspective, these defenders of modernism equate formalism with the defence of visual experience and consciousness from the seductive world of appearances and, more specifically, the ubiquitous mechanical, consumerist and media worlds of Western culture.

It is the engagement with the machinery for the construction of seeing, knowing and desiring things that marks the birth of **postmodernist** art and art criticism in the late 1960s. This fascination with the nature of sensuous life within contemporary society was coloured by the rediscovery of those modern art forms marginalized or despised by most modernist critics. Fried, developing the ideas of Roger Fry and Clement Greenberg, argued that a commitment to sensuous coherence distinguished authentic avant-garde art from the mere ad-hoc sensationalism of Dada and Surrealism. Rejecting spatial illusion in favour of flatness, which confirmed the materiality of the work as surface and picture plane, the true modernist artist equated the aesthetic process with the eviction of ordinary experience from the visual world of art. Accordingly, in denying the representational function of art, abstract forms tilted at the everyday world of visual culture, particularly advertising, television, the print media and publicity. This implies that the fact of communication in modernist art is a cultural-ethical act.

FORMATIONS OF POSTMODERN ART

The critical shift from modernism to postmodernism is seen in the work of Andy Warhol and James Rosenquist, both of whom came to prominence in the early

1960s. Their works, combining vitality and stasis, juxtapose different presenta-
tional codes in which material goods and experiences – the twin gods of advertising culture – are given equal weight and authority. The viewer stares at a
mass-media world given over to buying, spending and desiring; a world where
needs have been conflated with wants. This place of compulsion – where goods,
services and things bleed into each other – indicates that the modern world is a
paradoxical realm of spectral physicality and unrealizable desire.

Elsewhere in the late 1960s and early 1970s artists began to comment on the
regimes of perception and knowledge in **modern** life. Vision as an instrument of
power fascinated the German artist Gerhard Richter. Just as Warhol and
Rosenquist were dazzled by the world of mass consumption, so Richter was
drawn to the visual complex constituting the body or memory of the modern
state. He developed a system of painting that seemed to be more of an optical
space than a representation of a real place. Quite simply, his viewer is plunged
into a blurred and grainy world full of ghostly subjects and forms. These entities
are isolated or haunted, or washed-out by the process of being represented.
Individuation itself seems perilous, dependent on forces it cannot harness. From
'portraits', such as *Uncle Rudi* (1965), to the series of 'history paintings'
concerned with the demise of the Baader-Meinhof gang, *18 October 1977*,
Richter insists that the official language of public experience arises from a more
general condition of depersonalization. Seeing and knowing have been uncou-
pled: the impersonal world creates a plenitude of socially unknowable and
historically unanchored identities.

The idea of the transition from a world of values to a world of wants became
one way of describing the sensibility of postmodernism. Since the late 1970s,
most commentators have defined postmodernist art as a confluence of overlapping critical and artistic concerns. For many it is caught in the violated and
forlorn inscriptions of historical memory in Anselm Kiefer's paintings of
diseased myth; some point to the confusion of real and simulated mechanisms in
the dynamic surfaces of David Salle's polysemic paintings; others draw attention to the endless circuits, grids and reproductive systems of Peter Halley's
'Neo-Geo' appropriations of modernist art. To this list we can add the Walter
Benjamin-inspired photomontages of Barbara Kruger, where warring fragments of advertising and consumer culture signal that everyday experience is
subject to the language of mechanism; and the kitsch sacramentalism of Gilbert
and George, where the rhetorics of public art are grafted to the performance of
the self as manifestation of mental life.

What these practices share in common is a fascination with the multiple
conditions in which common experience enters the realm of the aesthetic to
disturb the hierarchical and classificatory procedures of modernism. By the
1990s these concerns developed into an interest with the grotesque, the detritus
of experience. For many of the Young British Artists (yBas), particularly
Damien Hirst, Jake and Dinos Chapman, Richard Patterson, Marcus Harvey,
Matt Collishaw and Tracey Emin, the materials of art are scooped and scraped

from the viscous, inchoate and disorderly material conditions of life. Here the meditativeness and detachment of high modernism is replaced by displays of unruliness – critical, formal, associative and cognitive.

Although these multiple versions of postmodernism are rooted in the exploration of the experiential apparatus of sensibility, it is unhelpful to see postmodern art in terms of a common conceptual project. Postmodernism is not a movement like Pre-Raphaelitism, Futurism or Surrealism, nor a style like Impressionism. Nonetheless, for most commentators there is a circuit between the artistic experiments of postmodernism and the activities of the postmodernist social realm. To make the same point in a different way, it is important to examine how rival and competing versions of postmodernism grapple with the social landscape of postmodernity. How do these rival visions of art comment upon the new economies of labour, leisure and consumption? Do they have anything to say about a social realm characterized in terms of the deregulation of financial markets and the consequent mobility of capital, the inexorable growth of privatization, the internationalization of the service economy, the emergence of labour flexibility, and the **globalization** of tastes, cultures and lifestyles? If we need to refer to different models of postmodernism, is it possible to say that these arise from different methods of conceptualizing social relations and social practices? In other words, to what extent does postmodernism inherit the political space left by modernism without engaging in a direct contest with its underlying concerns?

The starting point for such questions must involve an account of the legacy of modernist discourse into the 1970s and 1980s. Here the writings of Clement Greenberg were crucial. Greenberg was the great mandarin of modernism throughout the 1950s and 1960s. 'Avant-Garde and Kitsch' (1939) and 'Modernist Painting' (1961) provided the critical template for evaluating the specific critical and formal concerns of modernism.[2] In the first essay Greenberg argues that avant-garde art, the distillation of Western culture, fights to preserve its purity from the seductive but banal charms of kitsch culture and what he calls the 'Alexandrianism' (stultification) of academic culture. It does this in two ways: it operates as a process of auto-critique; and it is a model for the elimination of 'external' effects and forces. To be avant-garde is to embrace ceaseless change *and* to struggle to realize a condition of changeless aesthetic purity, which announces itself in the self-formed perfection of pristine abstraction. However, by the late 1970s and early 1980s, many artists and critics identified the social landscape of kitsch – the popular spectacles for the masses – in terms of an oceanic pleasure or plenitude, a constantly mobile realm of energies that seemed much more vivid and vital than the 'Alexandrianism' of late modernism itself. For a number of American artists, particularly Jeff Koons, Haim Steinbach and David Salle, confrontation with kitsch culture was a necessary precondition for the rearticulation of an avant-garde project where everyday experience meant more than mere visual pollution.

By questioning the Greenbergian model of modernism, postmodernist artists and critics contested the established cultural orthodoxy and developed a number of different critical strategies. Throughout the late 1970s and 1980s these 'engagements' made it possible to claim that postmodernism was iconoclastic, demotic and egalitarian. The most important of these developments included: the presentation of a variety of **text**-based processes as radical examinations of the institutional machinery of the art world; the definition of the artist with the summoning of an impure but healing creativity; and the identification of **appropriation art** as a way of trumping the idea of the unity and uniqueness of the individual cultural artefact.

What were the motivations behind these three developments? First, the site-specific and site-critical works of the Belgian Marcel Broodthaers and the German Hans Haacke were made with the intention of revealing the framing devices used by museums and art galleries. Second, the new figuration of the German painter Anselm Kiefer, in its identification of the picture-plane as a violent space where the **signs** of history are compressed and contorted, questioned modernism's residual commitment to the idea of beauty as truth. Third, in its most vivid form, that of the New York 'Neo-Geo' or **simulationist** artist Peter Halley, the appropriation of modernist masters, such as Piet Mondrian and Barnett Newman, provided a context for an examination of the relationship between modernism and the social, cultural and economic institutions of the modern capitalist state.

As these moves are interrelated – the first deals with the idea of the governmental agencies of art, the second is concerned with the communicative and expressive qualities of painting, and the third addresses the flow of power within a 'globalized' economy – the rest of this essay outlines three case studies drawn from each of these practices.

EXPERIENCING POSTMODERN ART

The first of our case studies involves a form of **installation art** based on the idea of institutional critique, a process of engagement concentrating on the material and conceptual apparatuses of the art world. This led, in the 'designs' of Broodthaers and Haacke, to questioning the belief in the purity and self-defining nature of the modernist art object. Broodthaers' work, which developed a new intensity after the *événements* of 1968, was designed to draw attention to and circumvent the intellectual division of labour that sustains and reinforces the authority of art galleries. Identifying himself with an imaginary museum – the Musée d'Art Moderne – he entangled himself in the machinery of art **discourse** by generating written accounts of his art from the position of the curatorial and cultural establishment. By conflating the realms of creativity and criticism he desired to make art 'speak' against the institutional processes in which it was framed. In this sense he wanted to focus attention on the nature of instruments of power, contract and rationality, the governmental agencies hidden from public view by official languages of curatorial display.

For Haacke, it is not only gallery-based art objects but the development, management and organization of the social networks of culture that are of importance. In his view, the contemporary artwork is a function of changes in the practices and perceptions of art. There is no formal essence to art in the way imagined by modernist communities of artists and critics. However, as power is ever present in human relations, the contemporary artist can create a counter-politics whereby the art gallery becomes a site for the evaluation of the practical and ethical contexts in which the business of culture is conducted. To this end, he produced works focusing on the relationship between art galleries and the corporations which sponsored them. Studying how business legitimizes itself through forms of cultural patronage, he set out to monitor how types of political, economic and social sovereignty are replicated or reimagined in different cultural situations. Two examples of this process are germane. In 1971 the Guggenheim Museum cancelled Haacke's planned exhibition because he declined an offer to remove a couple of controversial pieces that dealt with the practices of some of its trustees. Entitled *Real Time Social Systems*, these works comprised diagrams, maps and photographs designed to form a visual 'plan' of the interplay between economic power and cultural identity. Haacke's purpose was to reveal how the Guggenheim itself was an element of a political technology whereby slum landlords transformed themselves into respectable figures by buying into the realm of culture. These matters were revisited three years later when Haacke was invited to exhibit at the Wallraf-Richartz Museum in Cologne. Once again, in drawing attention to the management of culture within capitalist society, his work invited suppression by the cultural managers of the institution. On this occasion Haacke's installation art involved the production of a detailed history of Manet's *Bunch of Asparagus*, which the museum had recently acquired from a local industrialist. This history took the form of inverting the relationship between the object and its elucidation: the 'art' comprised a series of wall panels, all of which traced the history of the ownership of the painting. These biographical vignettes concluded with an account of Hermann J. Abs, trustee of the museum, former owner of the painting, and active supporter of the industrial and economic policies of the Third Reich.

Acting as the mediator between Haacke's interventionist form of installation art and our second case study, the so-called postmodernist '**trans-avant-garde**', we find the anarcho-spiritual performance art of Joseph Beuys. In his case, art is the medium for the enlargement of sensuous knowledge leading to the revelation of the aesthetic nature of the material world. This emphasis on the primacy of bodily experience is a noticeable feature of the work of his most celebrated student, Anselm Kiefer. Kiefer, echoing Beuys, is always in the process of declaring the redemptive quality of his art. Where Beuys' oracular rhetoric conflates a mystical version of Dada and the theatrical nature of performance art, Kiefer's art retraces some of the themes and concerns of German Romanticism, particularly its interest in tribal, folkish and national identities. Like Beuys, Kiefer equates the power of art with a condition of magical fertility and toxicity; the surfaces of his paintings are mobile forests of marks, wounds and growths. These skeins of paint – drifting, dripping and forming **nomadic** traces across the canvas – are forever entangled with new surfaces, new spaces and new morphologies. Here signs of abstraction become the means of visualizing consciousness in bodily experience. The Beuysian search for the oneness of Being becomes something much darker: painting acts a form of incantation and enchantment as precision gives way to apocalyptic expansiveness in Kiefer's boundless wilderness of vision, a vision from which the idea of belonging has been banished. This turning away from the 'universalism' of high modernism is characteristic of the other main figures associated with this mode of postmodernism. The belief that the return to painting involves a refiguring of the mythologies of national culture can be seen in the work of Kiefer's compatriots Markus Lupertz and Georg Baselitz, both of whom invoke Germanic culture in their work. Although they resist Beuys' sibylline utterances on the nature of art, they, like Kiefer, transform his 'postmodernism of immediacy' from the theatrical forms of 'body art' into a violent, dynamic expressionistic style that hovers between the mythic and the autobiographical.

The idea that painting maintains a sense of mystery in and through engagement with the magical kingdom of paint and pigment is expressed by the Italian wing of this 'trans-avant-garde', where Francesco Clemente and Sandro Chia led the return to the conventional media of oil and fresco painting. For the Italian critic Achille Bonito Oliva, the leading champion of their votive style, the neurotic lyricism of this 'nomadic' art indicates the ability of 'desire' to check the repressive forces of 'the Law'. This reintroduction of 'painting into art', a process which includes descriptive and decorative elements, allowed Oliva to claim that as Clemente and Chia simultaneously frame and fracture preceding art forms they are at once radical *and* traditional. At the same time, their work 'intentionally lacks character, does not hold heroic attitudes and does not recall exemplary situations'. As argued by Oliva, it is the unignorable virtuous humbleness of this 'weak' art, its need to distance itself from the all-seeing authority of modernism, which is the source of its restorative or 'healing' powers.[3]

These twin claims – that the artist is a spiritual healer who performs or projects those forms of sensuous experience that invoke a universal condition of expressive truth, or that art is the embodiment of the pathos of all life processes – are firmly rejected by the figures associated with appropriation art, the third of our case studies, and the one I want to examine in most detail.

Instead of relying on practices that are supposed to merge the artist with the artwork, a marked characteristic of the romanticized mythology of the trans-avant-garde, Cindy Sherman, Peter Halley, Haim Steinbach, Jeff Koons and Sherrie Levine, all of whom came to prominence in the late 1970s and early 1980s, produce work that resists the idea of unmediated individual authority and artistic creativity.

Sherman and Levine emerged in 1977 as part of a simulationist movement, a group of American artists driven by the notion that modernism had become a promotional system. Douglas Crimp, the recently appointed managing editor of *October*, the most important journal concerned with reframing art theory through the use of **poststructuralist** ideas, devised a show entitled 'Pictures', which was held at Artists' Space in Lower Manhattan, the self-styled 'alternative gallery'. In his catalogue essay, republished in expanded form in *October* in 1979, Crimp argued that the simulationists exhibited at this event subscribed to the notion that our experience of reality is organized and determined by the systems and processes in which it is reproduced, restaged and simulated. Thus, he claimed, 'to an ever greater extent our experience is governed by pictures, pictures in newspapers and magazines, on television and in the cinema. Next to these pictures, first-hand experience begins to retreat, to seem more and more trivial'.[4] For Crimp, the paradoxical power of Levine and Sherman resided in a capacity to assert that their work *lacked* all creative authority; as machines of nothingness their photographs, denuded of substantive content, demystified art by revealing the mythological nature of '**authorship**'.

Sherman's *Untitled Film Still No. 21* is a classic example of her early technique. The female figure (it is Sherman herself), photographed in black and white, appears to be involved in some form of homage to the pictorial language of depersonalization, in that Sherman's identity disappears into filmic representation of anxiety or alienation. Meaning is generic rather than specific in an image where ordinary or common experience becomes rhetorical performance rather than real action. This sense of proliferating obscurity is intensified by three factors: the framing of a figure caught from an odd, almost elliptical, angle, which suggests the operation of mechanical vision rather than human sight; the capacity of the work to stimulate and block our expectation that this inexplicable fragment of experience should be part of a repeated structure in which a story of some kind is formed, developed and rationalized; and the anonymous but symbolic naming of the work, which encourages the belief that its meaning is determined by the place it occupies in a wider structure of connected artworks.

Sherman's attitude to the issue of the referential nature of the photographic image is continued by Sherrie Levine. In her appropriation of canonical images by Edward Weston and Walker Evans, we see the conflation of the idea of simulation and gender politics. It is certainly the case that these images declare that art is forever implicated in the process of representation; that the burden of all art is its inescapable attachment to tradition and custom; and that it is somehow radical to criticize those conventions that claim to represent external reality. Here photography does not provide a window looking out into the world: it is a mirroring process involved in reflecting its own normalized codes and techniques for recording, framing and organizing the world. This interest in the 'fictive' quality of originality was continued in her 1984 show at the Nature Morte Gallery, New York, which comprised copies of drawings by Egon Schiele and Kasimir Malevich, the irreconcilable bodily and metaphysical wings of early modernism.

A similar fascination with the nature of representation is a marked feature of Peter Halley's work. Deploying cells and conduits within a grid-like geometric field, his art is informed by his reading of Michel Foucault and Jean Baudrillard. For Levine and Sherman, working through the photographic medium, representation never refers back to some pristine state of being in nature; compositions are imprisoned by those inherited codes that shape, pattern and frame them; images are entangled within visual systems from which it is impossible to escape; photographic works are copies of copies. To this interest in **representation**-as-repetition, Halley, the main painter and theorist in this group, brings his concern with the relationship between representation and power. Looking at modernism is to be confronted by models, networks, movements – the flows of matter and energy. Thus Stella's aluminium 'grid' paintings of the late 1950s, generally regarded as the zenith of late modernism, are made to reveal and express the physical and spatial logic of the massive interstate highways that traverse America.

Halley concentrates on the idea of geometry in order to ask: why does modern society associate it with freedom, light, reason and truth? In 'Notes on Painting', he identifies abstraction as a form of confinement: non-representational art, hollowed out of its utopian rhetoric, is assimilated into the visual languages of multinational corporations.[5] The modernist artefact has become part of the logic of late monopoly capitalism: in its geometrical and grid-like forms Halley discovers social, governmental and financial networks. Modernism's search for absolute visual purity is no longer 'innocent': instead of its association with idealist aesthetics, Halley connects it with the logic that 'the managerial class reserves to communicate with itself.' Accordingly, he claims that his paintings 'are a critique of idealist modernism. In the "colour field" is placed the jail. The misty space of Rothko is walled up'.[6]

Far from being a process of social enlightenment, geometry is no more than an instrument of social control. Viewed in this manner the geometric sign is an organ of the dominant form of surveillance: the grid. He writes: 'On the grid, there are no monuments. Only the grid itself is a monument to its own endless circulatory nature. ... On the grid there is only the presentness of unending movement, the abstract flow of goods, capital and information.'[7] Public space becomes less important than the virtual financial zones where life and value are measured in the selling, shuffling and reformatting of bonds, stocks and other investment instruments.

Some of these concerns with the abstraction of bodily experience from dominant definitions of the life of things and values colour *Day Glo Prison* (1982), one of his best-known paintings. Deliberately disorientating, it seems to combine elements of kitsch and abstraction, that is, junk culture and high modernism. We note both the garish, electric light colour *and* the rigour of geometric modernism. This is a weird mutation or **hybrid**: it is as if the colour scheme of a suburban home or motel has entered the 'pure' space of modern art. By appropriating the day-glo colour scheme of Stella's work from the early

1960s, he affirms that such apparently pure art is an echo of the social furniture of **post-industrial** life. By including Roll-a-tex, a mock stucco, to 'adorn' the square figure at the centre of the composition, colour becomes coloration: it is what is produced and reproduced by industrial instruments; it is that which registers the nature of its own reproduction. In other words, colour does not 'refer' to nature but to Roll-a-tex. Common experience invades the sanctified realm of abstraction to declare that it is itself a prison in which the residual forms of everyday (consumer) life are trapped or suspended.

The presentation of postmodern art as something locked into networks of leisure and consumption is continued in the work of Haim Steinbach and Jeff Koons. If Halley sees the geometric sign as the essence of modernity, both these artists are fascinated with the world of shopping. They replicate the objects of consumption as the banal and enigmatic facts of social experience. In the case of Steinbach, shopping becomes a form of urban exploration in which commodities function as souvenirs: the act of consumption is entangled in a phantastic process of nostalgia for the return of an experience that has never been known.

This simulated art takes as its reference point that most contemporary of environments: the shopping mall. A place of motion, expansion and shrinkage, the shopping mall organizes space as a system in which histories, cultures, styles, identities and experiences are knitted together in 'unique' configurations. Reproducing shopping as a leisure 'experience' through the articulation of 'themed' zones, the shopping mall blends the 'ordinary' and the 'exotic', making consumption into something 'exciting'. Here shopping becomes the dream of escape, the transformation of consumption into holiday time. Shopping, we might say, contains and re-creates the world: it is a simulation of tourism in which the shopper is an entrepreneur of (touristic) sensation.

Steinbach – who once opined 'in a sense the media have been turning us into tourists and voyeurs outside our own experience[,] ... in my case I spend a lot of time shopping' – casts the world of consumer objects as micro-environments.[8] Or, more accurately, he summons a world where the differences between perception and imagination, as well as needs and wants, are eroded. Placed on Formica shelves resembling plinths, his vacant or empty product-works suggest the 'denseness, structure and complexity' of a world in which manufacturing gives way to consumption, and industrial work is replaced by a form of capitalist pastoralism. This is another indication that this form of postmodernism is analogous to cultural anthropology in its association of the production of pleasure with particular rituals and technologies of consumption.

The product-works produced by Steinbach examine how 'empty' commodities become icons of sensibility, objects of steady-state desire. His ambition is to connect two realities: the shopping mall and the home; and to express the way in which the experience of both is built around a comforting, homely, tranquillizing banality. If objects of consumption, the commodities we buy, have become the modern equivalents of primitive totems, this may be because in our world shopping is a kind a religion: a narcotic desire for physical or social apotheosis in which the subject achieves a condition of purity to which common experience *aspires*. Steinbach displays and critiques this imaginary order of things by drawing attention to the machinery of solidity and signification. The 'substance' of his product-works is their inescapable emptiness. They form meaningless sequences of forms, which cannot be redemptive precisely because the logic of consumerism is based on the idea of the endless production-line nature of consumption.

In Britain a self-consciously whimsical or quirky attitude to appropriation is found in the work of Tony Cragg, Bill Woodrow and Edward Allington, all of whom make reference to forms of mass production, although the allusions to the world of commerce and kitsch tend to be 'poetical' rather than 'political'. Elsewhere the camp, sentimental militarism of Gilbert and George assimilates the iconic powers of medieval art and Soviet Socialist Realism, generating tableaux devoted to and obsessed by masculinity, fecundity, authority and death. In such appropriated iconography, which composes the world as a series of pictograms or isotypes, we find the pomp/banality of regimented glamour in which bodies and objects are at once physical facts and abstract ideas. Appropriation of a different kind is found in the work of Damien Hirst. From his dead cows and sheep, with their associations with Rembrandt's *The Flayed Ox*, to his 'dot' paintings, which allude to Phillip Taaffe's simulation of Op Art during the 'golden age' of New York simulationism in the 1980s, Hirst's work has acknowledged the endless entangling of 'high' and 'low' subjects in the history of post-Renaissance European art. Meanwhile, Tracey Emin fuses the alluring and the repellent, the decorative and the grotesque, in her craft-based presentations of the self as world.

POSTMODERNISM AND THE REPRODUCTION OF MODERNITY

At the beginning of this essay I asked: is there anything of value to be gained by coupling the culture of postmodernism with social postmodernity? Well, if there are no simple alignments between the processes of cultural heterogeneity and social fragmentation – alignments that enable us to distinguish between 'good' and 'bad' art – we can at least conclude our investigation by confirming that some forms of recent art establish more interesting and more critical dialogues with modernism and the social landscape of neo-liberalism and the globaliza- tion of economic life than others. Thus, in the case of the American sculptor Richard Serra we find works concerned with those public spaces that 'shopping mall' postmodernism declares to have vanished into the simulated spaces of replication and miniaturization. The sheer physicality of Serra's sculptures, which tend to inhabit the open-air urban environment, encourages spectators to reflect upon the nature of the lived experience of built space. That the nature of this art could be something other than a polite disagreement with postmodernist consumer culture can be seen in the controversy surrounding his *Tilted Arc*, which was destroyed after its removal from New York's Federal Plaza in 1989.

In its combination of brute matter and indomitable form *Tilted Arc* resisted the idea that public art should decorate, adorn or aestheticize public space. There was nothing about *Tilted Arc* to suggest it was implicated in the rhetoric of 'urban renewal'; nothing that resembled the bovine pastoralism of official public art in North America or Europe. This object was in no sense charming or convivial. Indeed, its capacity to block any real sense of spatial orientation required its audience to address its physicality or bulky ugliness. To this should be added the ghostly nature of the thing: here the matter of industrial engineering returned to a de-industrialized governmental, financial and consumer sector of the city, bringing with it the buried history of industry. This registration of the uncanny was compounded by the dimensions of a work that suggested both vertigo and claustrophobia: here was an object whose presence was both ubiquitous and elusive; at once inviting the individual to 'merge' with its form and resisting the idea of physical absorption.

More specifically, the unhomely nature of *Tilted Arc* – its ability to resist urban assimilation by registering the inescapable strangeness of urban space – brings this postmodernist work back to one of the central themes of literary and philosophical modernity: that consciousness is marked by its sense of transcendental homelessness. In the writings of Friedrich Schlegel, Charles Baudelaire, Soren Kierkegaard, Walter Benjamin, Franz Kafka, Theodor W. Adorno and Martin Heidegger we find the idea that being is a form of alienation: that life is a form of exile or the registration of an inescapable and catastrophic loss. It is, then, the simultaneous strength and weakness of art that it is generated from this experience of estrangement from the world. From this paradoxical nature, combining both utopian hope for a better world and melancholic recognition of separation from this immediate world, the most intractable or commanding works of art establish their sensuous and critical properties. In an age where museums and art galleries begin to resemble shopping malls – by processing and marketing cultural engagement as 'leisure experience', or by processing collections as '**narratives**' to be packaged, shuffled and sold as 'visitor attractions' – perhaps it is in those forms of art that reach for the utopian through the melancholic that deserve our greatest attention. Is it possible, therefore, to draw some form of **ironic** comfort from the fact that the new 'de-industrialized' postmodern classes, with their bases in the media, advertising, financial services, marketing, merchandizing, leisure and retailing, were the very groups whose campaign resulted in the destruction of *Tilted Arc*? If so, we are obliged to resist the apocalyptic or iconoclastic rhetoric of those forms of postmodernism that tell us we are condemned to be enthralled to a simulated world, and insist that the most controversial forms of contemporary art continue to engage with the most compelling themes of modernism itself.

NOTES

1 Michael Fried, *Three American Painters* (Cambridge, MA: Fogg Museum of Art, 1965), p. 7.
2 See Clement Greenberg, *Clement Greenberg; The Collected Essays and Criticism*, vols 1–4, John O'Brian, ed. (Chicago: University of Chicago Press, 1986–1993), 1, pp. 9–23; 3, pp. 98–110.
3 See Achille Bonito Oliva, 'The International Trans-Avantgarde', *Flash Art*, 104 (1982), pp. 36–43.
4 Douglas Crimp, *Pictures* (New York: Committee for the Visual Arts, 1977), p. 3.
5 Peter Halley, *Collected Essays* (Zurich and New York: Bruno Bischofberger Gallery and Sonnabend Gallery, 1988), pp. 80–91.
6 Ibid., pp. 106, 107.
7 Ibid., p. 104.
8 See 'From Criticism to Complicity', panel discussion between Haim Steinbach, Jeff Koons, Sherrie Levine, Peter Taaffe, Peter Halley and Ashley Bickerton at the Pat Hearn Gallery, New York, 2 May 1986, and published in *Flash Art*, 129 (1986), pp. 46–9.

13

POSTMODERNISM AND CINEMA

VAL HILL

Postmodern cinema has been conventionally described in terms of its bright surfaces, **intertextuality**, knowingness, referentiality, and nostalgia for past forms, genres and styles. All of this is true, and those markers have now crystal-lized into unstoppable, or rather unendable, commodities. This endless circula-tion of commodities and desire is perfectly exemplified in contemporary cinema. We see the film at the cinema, or rather the multiplex. We watch on VHS (less), on DVD (more), on our screens, digital, plasma, hung on the wall, in our 'home cinema'. The major Hollywood product, the blockbuster, is continually revised, re-edited, re-packaged. Often, within a series of films, it is not just the **narratives** that connect from film to film, but products that are outside mainstream cine-matic distribution. If you own, or are aware of, all possible objects tied to a particular title, then you will be able to make connections to or find out more about characters, flesh out obscure bits of plot, have even more 'stuff' to put on your website or say to your friends. We can watch, hire and buy prequels, sequels, soundtracks, video games, box sets, directors' cuts, producers' cuts. More recently we can buy a package which contains, as well as usual extras, versions of the film in different formats; Blu-Ray, DVD and in digital format ready to be uploaded onto our computers, or phones. We can play arcade games, buy merchandise, go to conventions, download. We, the consumers, never have the finished product; there is always another one, always another version. Finally we can watch the latest release in 3D in the cinema and at home.

Raiding the cinematic archive is yet another way in which what used to circu-late outside the **text** is raised to the level of the commodity, and becomes part of what we consume rather than part of what we produce. Quentin Tarantino is probably the most famous exponent of this tendency. His films are full of chat, anecdotes about aspects of popular culture, music, films, TV shows, actors, actresses. In *Pulp Fiction* (1994), Jules (Samuel L. Jackson) is forced to open his case by Pumpkin/Ringo (Tim Roth). The audience is never allowed to see what is inside; all we see is a golden glow reflected on the lid. The dialogue is not helpful either: 'Is that what I think it is?' 'Yes.' 'It's beautiful.' For those with sufficient cultural capital this moment, this object, invokes at least three other movies and the myth of Pandora's box: *Repo Man* (1984), *Raiders of the Lost Ark* (1981), and what has been called the last *film noir*, *Kiss Me Deadly* (1955), where the case contains the 'Big Wotsit', the Bomb (nuclear not terrorist) and the film ends with the end of the world.

Predator 2 (1990) contains a smaller but still efficient moment when the head of the Alien from the *Alien* series may be observed as one of the trophies on the wall in the Predator's spacecraft, reminding us, at the time of the film's release, of an already existing arcade game and pointing forward to a film which was about to be released, as well as constructing a galaxy that contains both species. The series of objects that form the *Matrix* (1999) commodity are worth noting. There are three films available on DVD, with extensive add-ons, commentaries and so on, especially around what became known as 'bullet time'. Indeed, *Matrix Revisited* (2001) describes itself as 'A mind-expanding look at "The Matrix" from conception to phenomenon', and promises that 'It will make you dream in bullet time'. There is also available a set of short animated films, in the style of Japanese anime. The short films tell you more about the storylines and characters in the three feature films. There is also a game called 'Enter the Matrix', where you may 'battle alongside the original motion picture cast', as well as a soundtrack CD, comics and many other bits of merchandise. What all these objects provide, apart from the obvious pleasures of consumption, is more detail about what emerges as a kind of meta-story. It is more than any or even all of the films.

There are other implications and manifestations of this postmodern know-ingness, **irony**, pastiche and blank parody, catalogued by Fredric Jameson in 'Postmodernism, or, The Cultural Logic of Late Capitalism' as filling the textual space of cinema.[1] In the first of the *Scream* (1996) series there is a sequence where the kids are sitting around drinking beer and watching *Halloween* (1978). Suddenly one of the characters pauses the movie and delivers what amounts to a lecture on the conventions of slasher films:

> That's why she [Jamie Lee Curtis] outsmarted the killer in the long chase scene at the end. Only virgins can do that. Don't you know the rules? There are certain rules that one must abide by in order to successfully survive a horror movie. For instance, number one, you can never have sex. Big no-no. Big no-no. Sex equals death. Okay, number two, you can never drink or do drugs. The sin factor. It's a sin, it's an extension of number one. And number three, never, ever, ever, under any circumstances say, 'I'll be right back', because you won't be back.

On the DVD for *Scary Movie* (2000) you can read 'The Scary Movie: Guide for the Culturally Challenged Pop Up'. This includes explanations of cultural references and insider jokes, which, as the name suggests, pop up as you are watching the film. So the commodity sucks up our chatter, our pleasures, our knowledge, and makes them part of itself. We are faced with the commodification of every-thing, from the unconscious to outer space. So what do we do, as audience, as academics? What is left for us to say if it is all on the disc or in the text?

The development of special effects, which have now almost become 'ordinary effects', is another great marker of the films of contemporary cinema; a powerful part of the marketing and the 'bonus' material on offer on DVDs. Special effects are, however, also a determinant of the content and structure of the product itself. The work of the narrative is slowed and halted by major set pieces. Indeed the narrative almost becomes a blockage to the 'true' celebration of the specificity of cinema itself. The 'cinema of attractions', the 'cinema of affect', can almost be read as the logical consequence of **globalization** and post-modernism. This has become even more marked with the advent of 3D films. The narrative of history and the specificity of social and cultural referents are lost in the shock to the senses that constitutes so much of postmodern cinema.

In the wake of these changes, postmodern film theory has celebrated the vivid intensity of the surface and the multivocal readings that postmodern cinema allows. The question needs to be asked concerning what (under)pins the text and if the position of the reader is as 'free' as has been claimed by the theorists of relativism. It is proposed that the thematic concerns produced within post-modern cinema reveal a very particular set of values. The scenarios found in many postmodern films express a number of repetitions, particularly around the issues of sexuality and ethnicity, that makes the notion of free-floating significa-tion problematic. Why, in the light of a reflexive critical sophistication towards the strictures of the text, do audience, director and critic continue to collude, most often pleasurably, in the maintenance of narrative structures which repeti-tively replay the gains and losses of '**difference**', albeit in new and mutated forms? The human body, always marked by difference, under the **sign** of post-modernism also holds the play, struggles and contradictions of difference. Under the sign of postmodernism the intensification of the signifiers of differ-ence ('more human than human') spreads itself over the majority of Hollywood productions, especially the well-funded, globally targeted blockbuster.

However, it might be useful to think of many of the Hollywood movies made between 1984 (the date of publication of the Jameson essay) and the present day as fitting into one of two categories: 'critical' and 'uncritical' postmodernism. The phrase 'critical dystopia' has been used by Constance Penley as a way of talking about films such as *Terminator* (1984), *Alien* (1979) and *Blade Runner* (1982) that use the future and the trappings of science fiction to critique the present and speculate about the impact of the present on the future.[2] By exten-sion many films of the 1980s and 1990s, and the new millennium, can be seen to use the formal and aesthetic properties of postmodernism in a way that appears to accept the analysis made by Jameson. Perversely, the same can also be said of films which might be labelled as uncritical postmodernism. The tick boxes for pastiche, blank parody, depthlessness, the decay of meaning, the end of history can all be checked in relation to films as different as *Back to the Future* (1985, 1989, 1990), *Mulholland Drive* (2001), *Kill Bill* (2003), and *Charlie's Angels Full Throttle* (2003). Many of these films work on the pleasure of recognition, and sometimes just the sheer pleasure of the experience of the cinematic; you maybe do not have to ask what it all means in the case of *Mulholland Drive*; you just let the cleverness and beauty of the surface wash over you.

The endlessly circulating commodity of postmodern cinema contains signi-fying systems that carry with them both the values of capitalism and the contradictory signs of the struggle produced within it. This means that the stories of postmodern cinema are particular stories that work through very particular themes. Now this can be said of any period of history or culture, which is precisely why it must be said about postmodern cinema. The postmodern cinematic marketplace is dominated by American products. This domination has consequences both for the form of the American film, and for other national, local and independent cinemas which tend to be absorbed, ignored or marginalized. At the same time, the American film is required to reduce its own cultural specificity in order to satisfy the demand to be 'global'. So, while the forms, codes, conventions and narrative structure possess a strong resemblance to that of the mass-produced cinema of **modernity**, the need for globalization produces both an intensification of its formal specificities and an allowed and necessary address to difference. 'Difference' is being doubly stressed here, to refer both to the organization of sexual and ethnic difference within the structure of the text and to the visibility of those representations of difference within the play of the **text**. Difference is allowed, celebrated and commodified. The cultural politics of difference becomes the cultural commodity of difference. Postmodern cinema celebrates, at surface level, its own exchange and use value. We are told how it was made, how much it cost and what it is about. This is especially true for what, in a sense, is a paradigmatic instance of postmodern cinema, the action film. In the action film the history and conventions of many Hollywood genres – the western, the thriller, the horror film, the war film, the romance and the family drama – are distilled and intensified to produce a commodity that contains all of the pleasure, all of the pain, and works in as many markets as possible – while never quite giving up on American values. I would argue that these 'intensifications' fit with the observations made by Jameson in terms of the intensity of the surface of the postmodern film. They also produce the critical emphasis on the reflexive nature of the postmodern text. The film and its audience 'know their own histories'. The pleasure of the text spills over into the audience's knowledge of other films, other performances, other musics: the referent becomes part of the treasure house of signifiers that constitute popular culture.

Some theorists, like Jean Baudrillard, originally extended this line of argument to conclude that the social world 'outside' popular culture has 'gone away'; cinema can now only refer to other signifiers of popular culture.[3] Postmodern theory speaks of the end of history, the loss of the referent, the impossibility of critical distance and the celebration of 'new-found' difference. However, if you add the first three of these to the last one, then you are forced to ask: 'What is difference?' Without history, without reference to the social, without some sense of distance (what one might call an ethics or politics) the notion of difference itself is placed under question. It is this tension between the desire to celebrate difference within the commodity form and, at the same time, the need to construct a commodity world without history or social referent or contradiction, that lets loose the kinds of difference that emerge in postmodern cinema. The weakening of the **grand narratives** releases difference from the tidy shackles of modernism – this does not, however, just mean that previously subjugated others are released into a different, more intense visibility. Indeed 'old' **binaries** themselves mutate towards a more exaggerated, almost parodic, existence or are displaced through the production of new forms of **Otherness**. Gender attributes wander across the old binary divide: Linda Hamilton in *Terminator 2* (1991) can have muscles, and we can all derive voyeuristic pleasure from Brad Pitt's butt in *Thelma and Louise* (1991). Difference itself becomes a crucial organizer and signifier within the texts of postmodern cinema.

The strong, not to say hysterical, version of masculinity, as played out by Sylvester Stallone in the action movie, embodies a desire for a fixed relation to the symbolic: the world where the law still operates, made less possible by the weakening of the grand narratives that also kept difference in place. *First Blood* (1982) could be argued to be a film in which the weight of historical trauma is borne by the body of Stallone – a new and shocking male body soon to be commodified and multiplied in the forms of Arnold Schwarzenegger, Jean-Claude Van Damme and others. The desire to win a war, in this case Vietnam, that had already been lost can itself be seen as a form of nostalgia for a present that never was. Although these bodies are on one level superhuman, too much, hysterical, they are also suffering, immolated bodies – almost to the point of death. We have become used to suffering male bodies in film genres dependent on male–male relationships, but in the post-Rambo action movies, the 'buddy' is absent, and it is not homosexuality that is defended against, but psychosis. Indeed it has been argued that if postmodernism does involve a theoretical retreat from the problem of **power** relations within capitalism, then there has to be a displacement of that antagonism onto other markers of difference, which come to bear an intolerable burden of suffering and other forms of surplus investment held in the signifiers of liberal humanism.

The contradiction within postmodern cinema's celebration of difference can be seen in the way that contradictions emerge within particular narratives. In *Predator 2* (1990) Danny Glover moves from the place of 'black sidekick who usually dies first' to that of black hero who survives. At the same time as Glover's textual liberation from stereotype, however, the Predator is con-structed as an other that carries signifiers of a more familiar representation of blackness – its 'hair' resembling dreadlocks. His figure is that of a hunter or warrior. He is seen as tribal, even within the context of high-tech space flight and weaponry. In the *Alien* 'quadrilogy' (1979, 1986, 1992, 1997) Ripley's (Sigourney Weaver) progress is significant. She moves from apparently strong single woman to good mother, to sacrificing mother carrying an alien child/queen, to child-sacrificing half-human/half-alien mother. All of the *Alien* films use the discourse of difference to carry the narrative, although the absent cause is clearly capital, present in the film in the form of the Company.

Blade Runner (1982) presents the transmutation of difference and Otherness in a more complex way, setting humans against **cyborgs**. One can read the film as if the cyborg other reproduces humanity at the point at which the human race is losing its humanity. However, the emergence of the cyborg, the unhuman, can be read differently. Cinema and other popular cultural forms of the 1980s and 1990s can contain either the fantasy of 'leaving the meat' (body) or the transformation of the body into something more, something different (*The Fly* (1986), *Nightbreed* (1990), *Lawnmower Man* (1992)). The disappearance of the human race is on the agenda in the 1990s – and maybe we should argue that this is nothing more than a coding of the imagined disappearance of white dominance. The union of Rachel and Deckard at the end of *Blade Runner* speaks of an escape from the misery of the human condition into a fantasy rural idyll (in the original released cut of the film). The twist in the tale – the possibility that they are both cyborg, and the certainty that at least one is (something not seen before as anything other than a threat) – reveals the depths of contemporary anxiety about the future of the human.

However, just as the word 'human' may be standing in for the word 'white' in relation to *Blade Runner*, so the word human, and the anxiety and pain that surrounds it, may also stand in for the masculine. The 'cost' of the gains of women in the world, or some parts of it, and the qualification of those gains, may be registered on the bodies of the female corpses that insistently haunt the screens of postmodern cinema. In the failure of the text satisfactorily to 'put things back together' in the face of the commodification of difference she/it becomes the currency through which to repay an impossible debt. In *Basic Instinct* (1992) we are 'allowed' to see a strong beautiful woman, Sharon Stone, maybe get away with murder. She is bisexual: getting both the men and women she wants. However, in order for her to achieve her ends, Michael Douglas and the ice-pick under the bed, the text produces corpses – most notably those of her girlfriend Roxy, a strongly, if conventionally, represented lipstick lesbian with a taste for voyeurism, and a female psychiatrist previously 'contaminated' by Stone's seduction. (This also shows that the free play of difference is not that free.) *Silence of the Lambs* (1991) reproduces the same pattern. The wonderful Jodie Foster, lesbian icon, wins out, but at the same time the text produces a trail of flayed female corpses. *Blue Velvet* (1986) shows us the **abjected**, less than perfect body of Isabella Rossellini; *Rising Sun* (1993) contains the digitally encoded and replayed sexual murder of an unnamed woman. A woman's corpse sutures the narrative, producing a double emptying of the female body, a double death; the weight of sexual difference is removed from the body and it becomes a thing, both a blockage and a suture – it makes sense of the narrative and compensates for a femininity 'out of place', while making no sense itself. It is as if it emerges in the real outside signification.

In the first two decades after the publication of Jameson's 1984 essay the shifts and changes in the fabric of the world have been held cinematically in two ways. There has always been a strand of critical postmodernism. Films such as *Blade Runner*, *Terminator*, *Alien* and *Brazil* (1984) and more recently *Fight Club* (1999) and *The Matrix* films (1999, 2003, 2003) show an anxiety concerning both the present and the future constructed out of the visual detritus of the past and the signifiers of historical trauma. For example, the scenes of the future catastrophe in *Terminator* could be argued to be drawing their signifiers from the Holocaust, Hiroshima or Cambodia after Pol Pot's Year Zero. Against these run uncritical postmodernism – *Star Wars* (1977), *Back to the Future* (1985), *Scream, Scary Movie,* (1996) *Down with Love* (2003), *The Fifth Element* (1997). These films conform to conventional American values, and celebrate past genres and past conventions with often crystalline perfection but with no comment. These are the blank parodies that Jameson refers to.

Reservoir Dogs (1992) is probably both one of the most extreme examples of uncritical postmodernism, and also a film in which the agenda of capital, its strains and contradictions, are worked out most tellingly in the speech and on the bodies of men. All others (almost) are held at the level of speech. The 'Dogs' worry around the signifiers of woman, black people, Jews and homosexuals. There is a resonance here between the hystericized bodies of men and the hystericized speech of men in this film and others directed by Tarantino and Scorsese. This speech is predicated on anxiety. So although we are presented with what is almost a cloning of a certain kind of white heterosexual masculinity as a defence against the postmodern condition, and given the abundant **fetishistic** pleasures of the visual and aural surfaces of the film as it attempts to defend against any suggestion of crisis, the particularities of the speech of the 'Dogs' says something else: 'What do women want?' (this was of course Freud's great question). 'Are they virgins or whores? Do they earn too much or too little? In the case of black women, are they strong or subservient to their men?' The sexuality of black men and women carries with it the intensity I have spoken of earlier; but it is actually the sexuality of black men that is the real problem for the 'Dogs', especially when combined with the 'threat' of homosexuality. The difficulty of a film full of men – a subject already well documented in modernist film theory – is displaced and projected into the **discourses** of homophobia and racism. What the narrative finally produces is their deaths; the real conditions of existence return revealing a white heterosexual masculinity in crisis.

Postmodern cinema as a useful, strong category is now shadowed by other signifiers. The words 'global' and 'imperial' might apply more usefully to the Hollywood product. Elsewhere other cinemas respond to both the invitation of the global market and the changing circumstances of world politics and history. The question of how we make films and how we understand films after 9/11, during the war against terror, is answered very differently by different nations, directors and industries. Hollywood's response is complex, and has nothing to do with temporal logic. The figures of Ripley and Clarice Starling fall and dissolve, to reveal, after the fact, the masculine figure that held the trauma, the horror – that of the serial killer. Over the time before 9/11 he had held sway over the imagination of the West in the form of Hannibal Lecter: urbane, cultured, deadly. Over time other manifestations of the serial killer have become more and more anonymous, invisible: named after any unidentified male corpse in *Seven* (1995), disappearing altogether as in *The Minus Man* (1999). In *American*

Psycho (2000) the subjectivity of the killer, the carefully constructed persona, dissolves in the gaze from the obscene objects of his own fantasy. One of the great cinematic villains of this period, Keyser Soze (*The Usual Suspects* (1995)), walks away, disappears, having constructed himself from random images, words and things that surrounded him in the police station. It is Soze who provides the link between the increasingly anonymous serial killers and Hollywood's, the West's, new villain, who, having had a past is now hesitating on the edge of **representation** (in both the film world and the 'real' world, given the elusiveness of Bin Laden and other 'usual suspects'), due to the events of 9/11 and the subsequent War against Terror: the terrorist. As Jameson says:

> 'terrorism' – the image of the 'terrorist', – is one of the privileged forms in which an ahistorical society imagines radical change; meanwhile an inspection of the content of the modern thriller or adventure story also makes it clear that the 'otherness' of so-called terrorism has begun to replace older images of criminal 'insanity' as an unexamined and seemingly 'natural' motivation in the construction of plots – yet another sign of the ideological nature of this particular pseudoconcept. Understood in this way 'terrorism' is a collective obsession, a symptomatic fantasy of the American political unconscious.[4]

This last comment is a perfect way to introduce *Fight Club* (2000). David Fincher's film starts from inside the body; it has been described as a sort of interior action movie: from the brain we travel to the bomb. We have arrived at the end, at the moment before the bang, the moment before corporate America goes up in flames in a series of images that are hard to bear after 9/11. This is maybe the same choice we confront at the end of *The Matrix* (1999), but the journey is held in a different set of signifiers. The other obvious similarity is the position of the hero, or one of them, Jack (Edward Norton). Jack works as a risk assessor: what costs less – to recall a car with a fault and thus save lives or pay the insurance? Like Neo, he works in an office, but he does not have another life as a hacker. He is Ikea Man. He is Life Style. Given that this film is another post-, post-politics, he has no union struggles. He visits support groups in an attempt to feel alive. He does have a relationship, of sorts, in that instead of looking at pornography in the toilet, he looks at the Ikea catalogue. He travels extensively, but everything is always the same. No enjoyment of the **bricolage** of postmodern life for him. The hotels are the same, the planes are the same, the food is the same – until one day he meets Tyler Durden (Brad Pitt). Durden's life is totally different: he does mundane jobs, but he subverts them. He pees in the soup, he splices pornographic stills into family films, he makes incredibly expensive soap out of liposuction detritus. He is beautiful and fearless even with a broken nose and blood streaming down his face. He lives in a derelict house on top of a toxic dump in the wonderfully named Paper Street. Durden is anti-style, anti-consumer, anti-capital: he is everything Jack is not. Together, after Tyler has blown up Jack's apartment, they form Fight Club, and then Project Mayhem –

and finally with the aid of their own warriors they blow up the skyscrapers that house everybody's credit records. The aim is to cause chaos, to go back to a financial year zero, and presumably start the revolution.

What has not been mentioned so far is the existence of Marla, who wanders between Jack and Tyler, significantly ending up with Jack after Tyler has been abolished, both watching the explosions passively, while holding hands. This film, in the spirit of Jameson's comment about the figure of the terrorist, can be seen to represent one of the many instances of post-politics. Although it is clearly critical of consumer culture, late capitalism, the film finds a way of dealing with class struggle. By holding the struggle mostly in the figures of these two men the film stays safe – except for Jack who has to expel the destructive, revolutionary figure of Tyler Durden. We are deprived of the vision of Ikea Man becoming the One. Once again the narrative produces its couple, although Tyler's existence is marked 'outside' the text in the form of interference with what appears to be the standard FBI warning, and a 'cock shot' cut in during the credits.

The place of superheroes and super villains in postmodern cinema has become increasingly problematic. It is as though they have no guaranteed status or place. There are films that seem to attempt to 'normalize' vampires and were-wolves, and these films are enormously popular (*Twilight* (2008)). Christopher Nolan's adaptation of *The Dark Knight* (2008), like *V for Vendetta* (2005), dissolves the hero, he disappears into the darkness. He has become a 'silent guardian, a watchful protector, a dark knight'. His enemy, the Joker, exempli-fies the bleak forecast of Jameson's essay. There can be no better realization of dystopic pessimism of critical postmodernism than the Joker. He reworks Nietzsche's aphorism into 'What doesn't kill you makes you ... stranger':

> [T]he Joker makes even evil seem like a puzzle too easily solved because there is nothing he can't make a joke of, and because, unlike Batman, he is not the prisoner of a traumatic past but *the inventor of one*; he can have any past he likes. ... [H]e (also) certainly terrorises people, in the movie and in the cinema. But terrorism, strictly, is a political weapon, and the Joker doesn't have any politics, any more than he has any morals. ... He is the image of everything we don't understand.[5]

So the argument has gone that not only is postmodernism no guarantee of the loosening of the reins of difference, in the end, but also that it is masculinity that is carrying the weight of the contradictions of the contemporary event. Women do not seem very visible or very important at the moment, unless it is as the ulti-mate fetish figure of Lara Croft. When we first saw the images of 9/11 many people said that it looked like a movie that we were all in some way familiar with. I would like to suggest that over time the images and sounds of 9/11 expose the specificity of cinematic construction, and even the work of sexual and ethnic difference. The films become less than those images. However, in the West, masculinity is the discourse that holds the anxiety, the trauma of the contempo-rary, unlike in the 1980s. What could be interpreted as part of an imperial or colonial fantasy in *Independence Day* (1996) or *The Siege* (1998) returns in the real – thrust there by the Twin Towers falling. What the falling of the towers seemed to deny was the possibility of representing anything, of telling any story. Retrospectively, many American movies speak to the **event**, but to speak beyond the event or even of the event is much more difficult. After the debate concerning whether or not images of the Twin Towers should be removed from existing films and TV programmes, a few directors kept them as part of the history of New York, and allowed both their absence and presence to be part of the landscape. The figuration of the contemporary crisis seems best held in the multi-Oscar-winning (including best film 2004) *The Lord of the Rings* cycle (2001, 2002, 2003). Here, the world (of the Shire) is saved, a world that is an idealized vision of rural England: saved by the sacrifices of millions and the labours of princes and hobbits. The representation of and around the War on Terror itself is surprising in that there are few spectacle-based war movies, unless they are set in the past. Even the Oscar winning *Hurt Locker* (2008) operates around small events involving the main character and his skill as a bomb disposal expert. The setting is not glamorous; it's dusty and broken. The concentration on the detail of military life of course also could be said to draw attention from a direct engagement with the political. *Saving Private Ryan* (1998) and *Atonement* (2007) both address the fragility of popular stories about war in this postmodern age. *Atonement* in particular gives the audience two versions of the ending, the happy one, and the one where the lovers never meet again. *Saving Private Ryan* is also a construction. The story of the hard work and pain of soldiering is carried by the construction of the saving of the last Ryan brother; it is a wish of the nation to ease the pain of loss. *Schindler's List* (1993) and *The Pianist* (2002) could also be seen to use devices of character and image to displace the 'real' story of the Holocaust and the Warsaw Ghetto.

The postmodern version of capitalism sets up an inclusive circuit, and maybe, in the West at least, forecloses for the moment on the idea of any kind of revolutionary or radical art. 'Everything is a copy of a copy of a copy'. Cinema doubles this capture, this inclusion, because of its temporal and spatial specificities and because of its dependence on and imbrication in language and narrative. Jameson sees postmodernity as impossible to map or represent in any way that is adequate. *Children of Men* (2006) and *V for Vendetta* are two films that fit the category of critical postmodernism. Both are set in London and show a world that, in the case of *Children of Men*, has broken down completely, and literally has no future, in that no children have been born for 18 years. *V for Vendetta*'s Britain is a fascist state. *Children of Men* may have another claim to postmodern fame in that, included in its 'extras', is a lecture by Slavoj Žižek. The lecture as video and in printed form can also be found on the official movie site. In this lecture/article Žižek talks about the way that 'history' and 'events' are the *background* in most films whereas in this film 'the background persists'. The film has:

no new gadgets, London is exactly the same as it is now, only more so[,] ... the greyness and decay of the littered suburbs, the omni-presence of video-surveillance. The film reminds us that, of all strange things that we can imagine, the weirdest is reality itself. ... *The Children of Men* is a science fiction of our present itself.

What both films also reveal is the fragile existence of the People, and the possibility of collective action, of class consciousness. Indeed in *Children of Men* the 'hero' dies, and the rescuers of the one pregnant woman in the world are anonymous. In *V for Vendetta* the ending pulls the particular action of the individual hero back on to the people – who in their action of accepting V's politics and actions, the putting on of the mask, reveal in the end, themselves, distinct, different, but part of the people.

There is now quite a body of literature denying the existence of postmodernism.[6] Or at least saying that it is over, that the trauma of the War on Terror and 9/11 has stopped it dead, helped by digitalization and globalization.[7] However I would like to suggest that James Cameron's *Avatar* (2009), the first of the new 3D movies, is maybe proof enough that postmodernism persists. Mark Fisher says, 'I would want to argue that some of the processes which Jameson described and analysed have now become so aggravated and chronic that they have gone through a change in kind'.[8] I would prefer to say that postmodernism and late capitalism have become fully developed, as Jameson claimed:

[T]his whole global, yet American, postmodern culture and superstructural expression of a whole new wave of American military and economic domination throughout the world: in this sense, as throughout class history, the underside of culture is blood, torture, death and horror.[9]

His comments prepare the ground for the complex set of reactions, from both audience and critics, to *Avatar*. Many critics and reviewers collapsed the film into a small string of other films – 'it's just like *A Man called Horse* (1970), *Dances with Wolves* (1990), *The Last Samurai* (2003)'. The film has been compared to *Heart of Darkness* and *Rambo*. There is a resemblance in that all of these films deal with a man becoming involved with an alien culture that he learns to love, generally and particularly. It is also easy to read off the colonialist ideological frame from this movie. But, there seems to be something missing from these accounts, and the weight of this omission is maybe made clear by the reaction of some audiences to it. The omission is that in the other films mentioned the indigenous culture is destroyed. *Avatar* develops a tendency visible in other postmodern films, that of the possibility of the disappearance of the human (*Blade Runner, Alien Resurrection* (1997), *I Am Legend, District 9* (2009)). In *Avatar* the humans are sent back to their dying world. The previously disabled hero, who could not afford to be healed, becomes whole as a Na'vi.

Now this has been read as the ultimate colonial fantasy, but cannot the Na'vi themselves be seen as a culture successfully embracing the first great dialectic between man and nature, and solving all of the problems that 'we' are confronted with? In a sense all of the criticisms offered can be recognized as the fact that all we have to represent our desires, our fantasies and struggles are the already available discourses of struggle. For example, Mark Fisher has suggested that:

> what we have in *Avatar* is another instance of corporate anti-capitalism[.] ... [W]hat is foreclosed in the opposition between a predatory technological capitalism and a primitive organicism, evidently is the possibility of modern, technological anti-capitalism. It is in presenting this pseudo-opposition that *Avatar* functions as an ideological symptom.[10]

What is different about *Avatar* is the utopian ending, and also the place itself, Pandora. When the film was shown in the United States it produced some extraordinary reactions. People became depressed; there are rumours of suicides. The reason given is that the world they inhabit is not Pandora. Pandora is too beautiful. The name is of course that of the first woman, an equivalent to Eve. So, not only is the planet signified as female, but the Na'vi women are strong and beautiful. The element that the Sky People (humans) were after is called Unobtanium. Some have seen this as too crude a name, but apparently it is the name given by engineers to something that it is impossible to make or obtain! The problem of perfection had previously been signalled by Smith in *The Matrix*:

> Did you know that the first matrix was designed to be a perfect human world where none suffered, where everyone would be happy, it was a disaster. No one would accept the progamme. ... But I believe that, as a species, human beings define their reality through suffering and misery. The perfect world was a dream that your primitive cerebrum kept trying to wake from.

Maybe this is what has gripped the depressed fans of *Avatar*. Žižek suggests that 'such a perfect fantasy disappoints us precisely because of its perfection. What this perfection signals is that it holds no place for us, the **subjects** who imagine it.'[11] Žižek has also suggested that if we want to change the world we should also change our fantasies. However, elsewhere, outside the West, the fantasy is good enough. Apparently Palestinians have embraced Pandora and the Na'vi, identified with them and their struggle.[12] They can be seen taking part in struggles dressed in the striking blue outfits and make-up. Their act fills the fantasy. The film ceases to be a colonial fantasy, and instead is part of a fantasy of liberation and revolution.

If postmodernism is a cultural dominant and if underneath the brilliant fragmented, parodic surface of postmodernism is blood, torture, death and horror, and if popular cinema is caught up in that; then maybe nowhere is that description more apposite than when war is a strong part of the context of cultural production.

NOTES

1 See Fredric Jameson, 'Postmodernism, or, The Cultural Logic of Late Capitalism', *New Left Review*, 146 (1984), pp. 53–92; later to become chapter 1 of *Postmodernism, or, The Cultural Logic of Late Capitalism* (London: Verso, 1991).

2 Constance Penley, 'Time Travel, Primal Scene and the Critical Dystopia', in Annette Kuhn, ed., *Alien Zone: Cultural Theory and Contemporary Science Fiction Cinema* (London: Verso, 1990), pp. 116–27 (p. 117).

3 See Jean Baudrillard, *Simulations*, trans. Paul Foss, Paul Patton and Philip Beitchman (New York: Semiotext(e), 1983).

4 Fredric Jameson, 'Periodising the 60s', in *The Ideologies of Theory: Essays 1971–1986. Vol. 2. The Syntax of History* (Minneapolis, MN: Minnesota University Press, 1988), pp. 203–4.

5 Michael Wood, 'At the Movies', *London Review of Books*, 14 August 2008, p. 32.

6 See also for doubts, critiques and elaborations: Hal Foster, *The Return of the Real: The Avant-Garde at the End of the Century* (Cambridge, MA: MIT Press, 1996); Jean-François Lyotard, *The Post Modern Condition: A Report on Knowledge* [1979], trans. Geoff Bennington and Brian Massumi (Manchester: Manchester University Press, 1984); Slavoj Žižek, 'Class Struggle or Postmodernism? Yes, Please!', in Judith Butler, Ernesto Laclau and Slavoj Žižek, eds, *Contingency, Hegemony, Universality: Contemporary Dialogues on the Left* (London: Verso, 2000), pp. 90–135.

7 Alan Kirby, *Digimodernism: How New Technologies Dismantle the Postmodern and Reconfigure our Culture* (London: Continuum, 2009); Alan Kirby, 'Successor States to an Empire in Free Fall', *Times Higher Education*, 27 May 2010, www.timeshigher education.co.uk/story.asp?storycode=411731 (accessed 8 February 2011); Karen J. Winkler, 'After Postmodernism: A Historian Reflects on Where the Field is Going', *Chronicle of Higher Education* (January 2009), http://chronicle.com/article/After-Postmodernism-A/42181 (accessed 8 February 2011).

8 Mark Fisher, *Capitalist Realism: Is there No Alternative?* (Ropley: O Books, 2009).

9 Jameson, *Postmodernism, or, The Cultural Logic*, p. 5.

10 Mark Fisher, 'They Killed their Mother: *Avatar* as Ideological Symptom', *k-punk* (6 January 2010), http://k-punk.abstractdynamics.org/archives/011437.html (accessed 8 February 2011).

11 Slavoj Žižek, 'Return of the Natives', *New Statesman*, 4 March 2010, www.news-statesman.com/film/2010/03/avatar-reality-love-couple-sex (accessed 8 February 2011).

12 Henry Jenkins, 'Avatar Activism', *Le Monde Diplomatique* (September 2009), http://mondediplo.com/2010/09/15avatar (accessed 8 February 2011).

14

POSTMODERNISM AND TELEVISION

TONY PURVIS

Postmodernity/television:
With the television image – the television being the ultimate and perfect object for this new era – our own body and the whole surrounding universe become a control screen. ... Each person sees himself at the controls of a hypothetical machine, isolated in a position of perfect and remote sovereignty, at an infinite distance from his universe of origin.

(Jean Baudrillard, 'The Ecstasy of Communication', 1985, pp. 126, 128)

Modernity/television:
Even in commercial British television there is a visual signal – the residual sign of an interval – before and after the commercial sequences, and 'programme' trailers only occur between 'programmes'. Here there was something quite different, since the transitions from film to commercial and from film A to films B and C were in effect unmarked. ... In all developed broadcasting systems the characteristic organisation, and therefore the characteristic experience, is one of sequence or flow. This phenomenon, of planned flow, is then perhaps the defining characteristic of broadcasting, simultaneously as a technology and as a cultural form.

(Raymond Williams, *Television: Technology and Cultural Form*, 1990, pp. 91–2)

(Pre)modernity/television/(post)modernity: **Simulacrum** ... has implications of a mask-like deceptiveness, of intellectual cheating, of an ideological shell-game. The word simulacrum, it seems to me, presents itself as a very suggestive one to describe an advertisement, or an over-inflated political presence, or that face on the TV screen

(Thomas Merton, *Faith and Violence*, 1968, p. 152)

TELEVISION IS (PRE)MODERN AND POSTMODERN

These three views bring together some of the contradictions which surround television and discussion of television in the context of **postmodernity**. Baudrillard sees the medium as the sign *par excellence* of a new (postmodern) era. Television makes sense of *us* by promising a sovereignty which, Baudrillard contends, is television's great deception. Williams is writing about his experience of American television in the context of his study of British culture. He sees television as a sign of **modernity**. Despite its sense of incessant flow and discontinuity, it is the medium by which we make sense of the world and, as such, it deserves to be studied methodically and critically. Finally, it is the idea of the simulacrum and the television face (the idol/image) which captivates Merton. He sees television, and again with a prescience akin to Williams, as the place of deception and falsification, a site which disseminates an unrepresentative 'ideology'. It is a medium whose very modernity resides in its (pre-modern) power to conjure images by way of illusion and defacement. The three views which preface this essay are all the more interesting because they are separated by only 15 years. In their *distinct* ways, they also share a common interest: the central place ascribed to television in modern and postmodern cultures.

They are views which, now in their ***different*** ways, hail from acclaimed critics in their respective fields: philosophy and culture; Marxist literary theory and **cultural studies**; theology and religious life. This range of comments, drawing as it does on quite disparate disciplines and languages, not only says something about the status of television in modern *and* postmodern cultures. They are scholarly disciplines, which suggests something about the study of television and media. Media and television studies are synthetic disciplines which transect the 'eras' to which Baudrillard alludes, being both modern and postmodern. Similarly, television's identity, and the genres and formats with which it works, reflect its status as a medium which is at home in modern and postmodern ways of life. Williams' experiences of television flow in Miami, Florida are in many ways prescient of the global digitalization of television in 2010. The endless flow of images, sounds, and narratives seem aptly to describe the *Freeview* (provider of free digital television in the United Kingdom) and *Sky* channels of today. Digitalization offers an agency not provided in the extra-televisual world of daily life nor even in the remote control zone of Baudrillard's (old) new era.

This collection of perspectives on television is also one which in many respects encapsulates the key tensions which continue to surround television. Baudrillard, Merton and Williams do not hold a dialogue with the other's work, yet they express a common concern about television and write about it in a lexical range which itself might be labelled postmodern. This suggests these critics have more in common with each other than their respective disciplinary boundaries might imply. But their concerns are echoed in contemporary scholarship by important critics in the field of television study itself. John Caughie, Stephen Heath, David Morley, Jane Feuer, Lynn Joyrich, and Graeme Turner and Jinna Tay, have variously taken up one or more of the preceding observations in the continuing debates surrounding the function and identity of television in postmodern conditions.[1]

TELEVISION *IS* POSTMODERN

Television is both praised and censured for being the site of fantasy, ecstasy and pleasure. Baudrillard's argument is reiterated in both postmodernist and psychoanalytic dimensions in the recent work of Slavoj Žižek, and by way of a critique of the televising of war and conflict in Paul Virilio's work on technology and knowledge.[2] Williams' contention, that television and the mass media should be studied in scholarly ways is endorsed by later theorists such as Stuart Hall[3] and echoed in the work of many scholars in today's field of media studies. At the same time, the scholarly critique of television and the media is ridiculed by both scholars and politicians,[4] something which similarly beset the academic study of English Literature at University College, London, in 1828. Finally, it is acknowledged as well as dismissed that television images hold power over audiences, so that Merton's concerns about the impact of such images and ideology continue to be discussed in contemporary media criticism.[5] These dismissals and apprehensive endorsements of television studies underline its ambiguous status in the criticism itself, but they also point to its cultural significance. Perhaps this massive variance is qualification enough that the medium be described as postmodern. Television's postmodern identity is connected precisely to its contradictoriness.

In the 'post-broadcast era',[6] however, and in the era of 'media studies 2.0' (this phrase comes from the work of Professor David Gauntlet) when self-generated user productions on sites such as *Facebook* and *YouTube* prove far more popular than television shows, and when the decoding of messages on *Twitter* and *iPhones* are far more frequent that the decoding of television ones, Baudrillard's observation might look a little dated. He writes that the television image is the perfect object of this 'new era'. Surely the new era to which he refers is the postmodern one, a one where, as Turner and Tay suggest, the 'family audience in the living room has dispersed ... into the street and onto ... mobiles'.[7] Television's identity, however, still seems tied much more to modernity, and families continue to watch it, in living rooms and at set times. It is part of the broadcast era, the period of 'media studies 1.0' when television was able to command massive audiences, and television programmes on a daily basis attracted tens of millions of viewers. Reading the observations which immediately follow his, then, Baudrillard's claims seem far more prophetic than outdated. It is in the era of postmodernity that audiences are promised new lifestyles, new choices and ecstatic futures, and it is television which has encoded this imaginary in reality programmes such as ITV's *The X-Factor* (UK, 2004–), Idol/Fox's *American Idol* (USA, 2002–; originally as *American Idol: The Search for a Superstar*), and Endemol's *Big Brother* (UK, Channel 4, 2000–10).

This 'ecstasy' of television is not Baudrillard's commendation of the medium. In that sense, he has much more in common with Merton than Williams in that Merton is the one who expressed most anxiety about television by drawing on the commanding metaphor of the face and the idol. Yet Merton is perhaps even more prescient about television and postmodernity than Baudrillard is, albeit that Merton's logic is one which perceives the postmodern as already residing in the modern, something which is taken up very significantly by Jean-François Lyotard.[8] It is Merton who draws on that most celebrated of postmodern terms, the simulacrum. Television-shopping channels today provide the illusion of ultimate control and sovereignty, but – and here Merton is surely right before Baudrillard is – always at a distance, always once-removed from the television reality which postmodern audiences are promised, and always at a cost which, using Merton's language, is not *faced*, so much as it is de-faced, in the ideology encoded in the advertisement's imagery. However (and this is where Williams' logic connects with Baudrillard's), television is a central part of media studies 1.0 (the broadcast era of media modernity) *and* media studies 2.0 (the post-broadcast era of postmodernity). How might we begin, then, to theorize and illustrate postmodern television?

TELEVISION IS OLD AND NEW: MODERN AND POSTMODERN

A constructive way to theorize television's uniqueness in the broadcast/post-broadcast era, which at the same time allows for a discussion of postmodernity, has been provided in Karen Siune and Olof Hultén's analysis of the media in general.[9] They have usefully subdivided analysis of the media into what they refer to as 'the old media' – or media more associated with modernity – and the 'new media', whose features and functions are more attuned to the more dispersed arenas of postmodernity. Here, summarized, is Siune and Hultén's structuring the relationship between old and new media:

	Old Media	New Media
Broadcasting:	Monopoly	Competition
Goals:	Democracy	Survival, success, profit
Means:	Programme production and selection of material	Selection of material and programme mix
Logic:	Responsibility	Market and economics
Selection criteria:	Political relevance	Sale
Reference group:	Citizens	Consumers
Focus:	Decisions taken/power structure and new conflict dimension	Process of policy making
Perspective:	Nation/system	Individual and global[10]

The *old* media (which remain very much in use as technologies and as media forms today) coincide with broadly Fordist-modes of production during the middle part of the twentieth century. The media are produced for mass markets. Monopolistic competition and/or state control mean that media output is less determined by audience demand and more by the collective aims of corporations or owners. Newspapers, magazines, landline telephones and AM radio (the 'wireless' of old) remain very much twentieth- and also twenty-first-century media forms. They are sometimes, however, less profitable and less popular, more costly to produce, and make sense within broadcast- or print-based paradigms. The *new* media (digital television, *iPhones*, web and **Internet**, and *Twitter*) are more focused on consumption, competition and the market, where deregulation often overlaps with periods of consumer-led demand or where production and the end product is cheaper to realize.

What is important in terms of television and postmodern culture is the medium's adaptability and versatility compared to other broadcast- or print-media forms. Television, using the above framework, is old and new, modern and postmodern. While other media forms are struggling to survive and are slowly discarded, television manages innovatively to survive. Digitization, alongside the global multiplication of Internet access, has not impaired television so much as it has enhanced and expanded its *virtual* identity. It is a medium that at any one time – and potentially without restrictions of time and space, and often without regulation or directive because of the Internet – is a home cinema, a PC, a video game, a recorder and a sound system. It is a new media form, using Siune and Hultén's template, without ceasing to be an 'old' television, an object which can be accessed for all the reasons attached to the modernity of its golden age during the 1960s to the late 1970s. Its modern identity makes television a physical technology which carries with it messages packaged into various content formats.

Its postmodern identity, however, makes it a medium of the post-broadcast era where it is accessed as a digital, multi-functional device. The social and political consensus which marked the early period of television, alongside its status as a physically static source of information and entertainment, meant television functioned mainly as a medium for families in living rooms. Phrases such as 'family-viewing', 'children's hour' and the 'watershed' make sense in relation to television in the domestic sphere.[11] The functionalities of digital television serve to extend the sphere of the living room, so that the mundane world appears extended and transformed; and its modern status also makes it a medium which, in Ernst Bloch's sense of the word, reinforces the notion of space and *heimat* ('home' and 'dwelling').[12] If representations of conflict or disaster seem to suggest such tragedy only happens to external *others*,[13] watched by audiences from a distance, popular dramas and local news continue to offer a 'modern' sense of '*at-homeness* – the taken-for-granted situation of being comfortable … with the world in which one lives … day-to-day life'. [14] How far has this sense of 'being-at-home' with television changed in the cultural arenas of postmodernity? Is television still the site through which consensus norms and values are transmitted, as they were in the period of television's modernity?

TELEVISION'S REPRESENTATIONS: MODERN AND POSTMODERN CRITICISM

Television's **representations**, whether of conflict and violence in news genres, or of home and family in popular dramas, only make sense in relation to the socio-historical spheres in which television is produced and subsequently converted into some form of meaningful **discourse**. No matter how stylistically postmodernist a televisual representation might be, or how much a programme taunts audiences' sense of historical fact or time (e.g. ITV's *The Prisoner* (UK, 1967–8); ABC's *Twin Peaks* (US, 1990–1); Twentieth Century Fox TV's *24* (US, 2001–10)), media ethnographies such as James Druckman's suggest that television audiences decode programme content with some degree of critical scepticism.[15] However, it is via television's own self-conscious and self-referential modes of representing both fact and time that critical discussion of its postmodern status has often occurred. Indeed, significant commentary on television occurs today in scholarly-critical as much fictional output (e.g. Don DeLillo's novel *White Noise* (1985); the film *The Truman Show* (1998)), intensifying, somewhat, the postmodern dimensions of television criticism. However, television criticism prior to the 1990s tends to discuss the medium in three ways. It is perceived as a producer of *texts*, a *mass medium* and a *public service* broadcaster. An outline of each approach will serve to highlight how postmodern television and criticism differ from this earlier period.

Texts: In early television criticism, programmes are analysed as discrete texts. Film and literature studies served as the structural backdrop of this criticism, as Caughie makes clear,[16] and television output tended to be dissected along lines demarcated by boundaries of genre, form and **narrative**. Television in postmodern cultures, while it continues to draw on this model, requires a supplementary critical exegesis, suggests Jeremy Butler, to understand its stylistic variation.[17] Programmes today are often marked by their blurring of generic boundaries or **hybridization**, and this is very much exemplified by reality television and docu-dramas. In addition, the seemingly playful, self-referential preoccupation with truth and fact in shows such as Chris Morris' highly controversial *The Day Today* (UK, BBC, 1994), or Sacha Baron Cohen's *Da Ali G Show* (Channel 4, UK, 2000; HBO, US, 2003–6) not only highlight some of the limitations of analysis modelled on wholly textualist approaches. Rather, these are programmes which perform a cultural-critical function, albeit controversially, by way of parody and pastiche. *The Day Today*, for instance, seriously challenges the conventions of documentary format in its treatment of sensitive moral issues in the context of the media industry's own massive investment in cultural and moral politics via the figure of the celebrity. Moreover, fictional output which has proved very popular with audiences (e.g. HBO's *The Sopranos*, US, 1999–2007; *Twin Peaks*; Twentieth Century Fox TV's *The Simpsons*, US 1989–; HBO's *The Wire*, US 2002–8) has been able to cast a critical eye on culture and tradition without an over-reliance on realist or naturalist modes of time and narrative.

Mass media: In earlier forms of criticism, television is discussed as a powerful instrument of mass technology and mass production. Serious misgivings are expressed about its ability to shape views, beliefs and opinions in the social sphere. Theories from the early to mid-twentieth century, in particular the positivistic 'effects' theory (see coverage of this in David Gauntlet; James Potter; Paul Taylor and Jan Harris),[18] as well as the critical theory of the Frankfurt School, situate television in relation to the political economy of the mass media.

These approaches have tended to imagine media in terms of *cause* (production/message) and *effect* (consumption/behaviour). Allied to the concern about effects is Theodor Adorno's important, if often misrepresented theorization of popular culture and high culture,[19] with a tendency to accord privilege to the latter's autonomy in its critique of the status quo.

In postmodern cultures, it is the axis of consumption, as suggested above, which is emphasized, though this is not something of which Frankfurt School critic Adorno was unaware. This recent emphasis, however, has prompted a range of debates, where the implicit valorization of agency and determination via consumption in some media studies, according to Marxist-feminist scholar Rosemary Hennessy, is uncritical and ill-judged.[20] This current discussion does not valorize this logic either so much as it highlights the shift to and on consumption which has occurred in late-capitalist economies. Audiences are not determined by television messages in causal ways (media messages have more than one meaning), so much as messages make sense in relation to a greater number of variables than a behavioural model takes into account. While some output impacts on a subject's sense of social relations and identity, as critics such as Morley have noted,[21] this cannot be universalized (representations are rejected or disclaimed, something which the early work of the Stuart Hall and Centre for Contemporary Cultural Studies was quick to point out).[22]

In addition, access to media has never been equal among social groups, and so any agency via new-media technologies constrains as much as it enables audience agency. Entrapment models of television, where the medium is thought to operate conspiratorially or wholly in the interests of the state or dominant group,[23] cannot always account for the media's own resistances to this group, or the media's more sympathetic reporting of counter-hegemonic movements. This was most notably observed in state television's role in Eastern Europe during the 1980s and 1990s, where stations often resisted threats and controls from specific administrations. More recently, British and American governments' foreign policies and interventions in the first decade of the twenty-first century have been called into question as much by the media as by popular anti-war movements. Governments in both countries suggested that the media, including television news, did not represent the respective government's arguments fairly and thus, by default, endorsed anti-war or anti-**globalization** lobbies. Contemporary criticism suggests there are points of inter-operation between audience and broadcast, destabilizing causal models of media-effects criticism and promoting a more liberal-**pluralist** approach to critical enquiry.[24] While media messages do impact on how audiences think and act, the evidence suggests this is far less direct than early media theory would allow.

Public Service: Finally, broadcasting is conceived in relation to television's *public service* role in the culture. The BBC in its early years was chartered to educate and inform, and to do this universally and impartially. This moral-critical dimension owes much to the founding charters of the BBC and to its founder Lord Reith, but also to the moral criticism associated with Cambridge scholar F. R. Leavis, the journal *Scrutiny* and Leavis' work on popular culture with Q. D. Leavis and Denys Thompson.[25] In addition to an approach which tended to see popular output as not worth, or worthy of, criticism, there was also a tendency to disparage popular television and the people who watched it. Postmodern cultures expose and **deconstruct** these **binaries**. Popular culture and high culture co-exist in the same social spaces *because of* television, something highlighted very strongly by Melvin Bragg, well-known UK television presenter and culture critic. In his award speech at the British Academy of Film and Television Arts (6 June 2010) he says this of television:

> [In *The South Bank Show*] I wanted to put popular arts alongside the opera and the ballet, to have pop music, and comedy, and have television drama there, and bring it all in and see what happened ... because you never know when art's going to turn up. What we decided to do was to concentrate on living artists, not the great dead – they'll basically look after themselves, and there's no risk there. But looking at living artists, people like you, people like us, people who walk the same streets, dress in the same clothes and who are part of what we are, and to bring to the screen their imagination.[26]

He talks of television as 'this most magnificent screen – this extraordinary thing – it is magnificent because it is common. It goes everywhere. Just the touch of a switch and yet look what it brings to us.'

Bragg's magazine programme *The South Bank Show*, which ran on ITV (initially London Weekend Television) from 1978 to 2009, typifies the medium's own way of trying to address the aesthetics of early-postmodern culture. The show's miscellaneous mixing of popular with high art, its eclectic approach to taste, via programmes which explored the canon of English literature as much as mass-produced paperback fiction, reflect something of the pastiche of many different elements of the culture into one programme slot. Unlike the preferred older culture of the first part of Richard Hoggart's *The Uses of Literacy*, Bragg's *The South Bank Show* looked at the contemporary cultural scene and, to use Hoggart's words, 'yield[ed] place to the new'.[27] *The South Bank Show* saw both the past and the future together, offering a postmodern slice of life to its audiences. The show represented, often in very reflexive and playful ways, the seriousness of ordinary life and popular culture. Whereas television in the past worked with fairly definite understandings of cultural and national ideals, Bragg's vision is one in which modernity and postmodernity are viewed in terms of their difference and their mutuality. In *The South Bank Show*, the boundaries between cultural forms were no longer defined simply in terms of high and low culture, or mass media and autonomous art. Nor was 'national culture' perceived as singular or monolithic. The show's representation of the new postmodern aesthetics of the 1980s and 1990s took place against the backdrop of wider concerns about values, ones which exceed those associated with the 'culture and civilization' tradition of critics such as Matthew Arnold.

Television's (un)civilized worlds

Television, as an inexpensive mass-produced consumer item, becomes the medium more than any other which brings to light the creative tensions and human conflicts which exist in 'civilized' social life. If civilization in Arnold's treatise requires a clerisy to defend its borders from the threat of anarchy,[28] television does much to deconstruct these cultural perimeters. Today, popular television output, in the form of soap operas, advertisements, popular dramas and documentaries, does not repudiate high culture or stand as its binary opposite so much as it reflects moments of borrowing, copying and continuity. Akin to postmodern fiction and art, some recent television output has challenged its audiences by way of formal innovation. Some contemporary and/or postmodern television operates by way of ridicule and satire, or by way of a nostalgic re-vision of history, as typified in history channels such as *Yesterday* (UKTV, UK, 2002–). References to the televisual and filmic past, by way of incorporation and absorption of previous forms, often characterize this output. Elements of distinct forms and genres are mixed into one form, resulting in sub- or hybrid genres such as docudramas, info-tainment and docu-soaps. Sometimes this bringing together of different elements raises obvious questions, as in the case of the BBC's *Ashes to Ashes* (UK, 2008–10) and *Life On Mars* (UK, 2006–7), where it is not clear whether or not these programmes are crime-dramas or science-fiction series.

Other output serves to distort audience perception of time, reality and fact, and invites comment and criticism by creating a sense of doubt and disbelief. In the last 15 years, 'mock-documentary' has become popular on television. This new format started its generic life as underground film but quickly became mainstream with the BBC series *The Office* (UK, 2001–3, though there are a number of exports of this show), and Comedy Central's *Reno 911* (US, 2003–9). These programmes have the feel of documentary but they are strongly inflected by reality television as well as *cinema verité*, with its familiar fly-on-the-wall filming technique. Whether 'mockumentary' acts as parody and social commentary depends on audiences' responses to the form itself. Whatever the programmes do, however, occurs on the basis of the blending a number of discrete generic elements into a new or hybrid genre whose form satirizes as much as it reports candidly, and often very credibly, on relationships at specific places of work. This blending of different elements serves to underline again the ways postmodern culture is one which, through its pastiche of multiple elements from the culture, deconstructs the binary framework which separated the popular and the mainstream from high art and Culture with a capital 'C'.

In dramas such as Paul Abbot's *Shameless* (Channel 4, UK, 2004–), HBO's *The Wire* (US, 2002–8) and AMC's *Mad Men* (US, 2007–), it makes little sense to talk about them either as popular culture or as high art if one of the aims of television studies is the analysis and greater understanding of the representation of human relation. Nor does it necessarily achieve much to treat them solely as texts to be analysed, important though such exegesis continues to be. Indeed, *Shameless* and *Mad Men* are examples of television output which confirm how both high and popular cultural forms reproduce each other far more than moral-critical or political-economy frameworks would suggest. Popular culture *is* postmodern culture to the extent that the term 'postmodernity', following Lyotard's periodization, usefully defines the current stage in late-capitalist societies. Television, as a very popular medium, is well placed to lay bare the hybrid and synthetic dimensions of the culture. Popular culture, again like postmodern culture, is additionally perceived as ironic and eclectic, at the same time as it is also anarchic, yet also accessible and mainstream. This is not to valorize popular and/or postmodern culture or one particular form over another. It is to underscore, however, the central role played by television in exposing the cultural connections and disjunctions of the period called postmodernity. These disjunctions are explored very provocatively in David Simon's *The Wire*, for example, whose postmodern cityscape stands in stark contrast to the ones constructed in day-time shows such as *Location, Location, Location* (Channel 4, UK, 2001–), or *Home and Garden Television* (HGTV, US, 1994–).

The Wire mixes very detailed depictions of city life in Baltimore, USA, with an exploration of the social and the in-depth psychological aspects of urban living surrounding daily life in the print media, the drug trade, the education sector, the port and municipal bureaucracy. The elements of crime fiction, reminiscent of the world constructed in 1930s popular American paperbacks, is placed next to images of the city which allude to Charles Dickens' dark, shaded world in *Bleak House* and *Oliver Twist*. *The Wire* is set in the present, and yet all its references to crime and detective genres are secondary, in the words of David Simon, the show's principal writer, to its concern with everyday life in the American city. Simon is interested in how people live with each other in Baltimore's contradictory postmodern terrain, one which seems uncivilized in the Arnoldian sense, but where the very paradox of culture is its seemingly *absolute* and its ominously *relative* status. *The Wire*, Simon contends, is 'about how institutions have an effect on individuals, and how whether you're a cop, a longshoreman, a drug dealer, a politician, a judge or a lawyer, you are ultimately compromised and must contend with whatever institution you've committed to'.[29]

VERY *COMMON* POSTMODERN TELEVISIONS

Dramas such as *The Wire*, *Shameless* and *Mad Men* are pieces which ponder the compromises people are forced to make. If there is sometimes a sense of anarchy depicted in the lives of dramas' fictional people, this must be placed next to the abiding presence of state apparatuses which structure the cultural backdrops of Baltimore, Manchester and New York. *Shameless* deals with poverty as experienced on a housing estate in the north of England, and greed and gender power in 1960s New York is the subject matter of *Mad Men*. Using satire and comedy in *Shameless*, Paul Abbot references high art and high culture by housing his characters on the 'Chatsworth' estate. This is in stark contrast to the English cultural heritage industry and the Derbyshire estate known as Chatsworth House. Abbot's location is a council estate, and his characters are less English and more Irish, so that the Gallagher family of the series comes to represent England's long-standing *other*. The drama's dual referencing system, which places high next to popular culture, England next to Ireland, and wealth next to poverty serves to expose the rifts which persist in all postmodern cultures. In *Shameless*, the micro-narratives and local knowledges about illegal drugs, unemployment and gritty personal relations do not undermine the macro-narratives of the national culture so much as they reveal the precise ways in which the hermeneutics of tradition is always narrativized in relation to *other* forms of knowledge.

Postmodern culture is rich simply because it is derivative, synthetic and composite. If some of the scenes are marked by bad taste, and if the northern cityscape seems uncivilized and uncouth, then Abbot has succeeded to the extent that this kind of drama exposes a postmodernity where snobbery is at work (in the construction of social difference based on class and taste) as much as mutual regard and community. It is also a drama which explores social and cultural complexity in the first decade of the UK's twenty-first century, showing how the cultural logic of late-capitalist societies is lived shamelessly on and below the surface. Similar to the postmodern culture of which *Shameless*' characters are a part, so Abbott's world is hybrid and synthetic, at once inviting (because of the characters' humour, intimacy and connectedness) and at once something audiences critique (the unemployment and poverty raise major questions about this particular representation of northern life). The drama exposes the poverty of late-capitalist economies, where some citizen-shoppers can consume on the basis of desire but where others have to seek other means by which to fulfil desire.

Drawing on the multiple traditions which comprise today's (post)modern Britain, Paul Abbott talks about how he is indebted to one tradition in particular – his family narrative. His accounts of this past not only shape how he perceives life today, but how he writes it into the drama *Shameless*.[30] He is a writer who betrays his indebtedness to a cultural terrain which is marked by the plural discourses of social class, age and gender demarcations, northern-ness and indeed Englishness. But he is also someone who, in describing Britain during a recession, trawls the micro-narratives of his own modernity (via family and region) in order to expose the synthetic dimensions of the new narratives concerned with Britain's postmodernity. Abbott's own tradition, and his own sense of modernity, is both eccentric and distinctive (in that it is uniquely his culture) and at the same time it is common and postmodern. By reflecting the postmodern cultural terrain, the drama make sense to contemporary audiences. And by being modern, this television drama is situated within a tradition which, although rooted in a past, requires regular re-vision.

NOTES

1 See John Caughie, *Television Drama: Realism, Modernism and British Culture* (Oxford: Oxford University Press, 2000); Stephen Heath, 'Representing Television', in P. Mellencamp, ed., *Logics of Television* (London: BFI, 1990), pp. 267–302; David Morley, *Television, Audiences and Cultural Studies* (London: Routledge, 1992); Jane Feuer, 'Genre Study and Television', in Robert C. Allen, ed., *Channels of Discourse, Reassembled*, 2nd edn (London: Routledge, 1992), pp. 138–60; Lynn Joyrich, *Re-Viewing Reception: Television, Gender and Postmodern Culture* (Bloomington, IN: Indiana University Press, 1996); Graeme Turner and Jinna Tay, eds, *Television Studies After TV: Understanding Television in the Post-Broadcast Era* (London: Routledge, 2009).

2 See Slavoj Žižek, *Welcome to the Desert of the Real* (London: Verso, 2002); *Violence: Six Sideways Reflections* (London: Profile, 2008); Paul Virilio, *Desert Screen: War at the Speed of Light* [1991], trans. Michael Degener (London: Continuum, 2002).

3 Stuart Hall, 'Encoding and Decoding in the Television Discourse', Occasional Paper no. 7 (Birmingham: CCCS, 1973); 'Television as a Medium and its Relation to Culture', Occasional Paper no. 34 (Birmingham: CCCS, 1975).

4 See '"Mickey Mouse" studies are no longer a laughing stock', *The Times*, 18 December 2008, www.timesonline.co.uk/tol/life_and_style/education/article5361672.ece (accessed 8 February 2011).

5 Jostein Gripsrud, *Understanding Media Culture* (London: Hodder Education, 2002); *The Dynasty Years: Hollywood Television and Critical Media Studies* (London: Routledge, 1995).

6 Turner and Tay, *Television Studies*, pp. 1–6.

7 Ibid., p. 2.

8 Jean-François Lyotard, *The Postmodern Condition: A Report on Knowledge* [1979], trans. Geoff Bennington and Brian Massumi (Manchester: Manchester University Press, 1984).

9 Karen Siune and Olof Hultén, 'Does Public Broadcasting Have a Future?', in D. McQuail and K. Siune, eds, *Media Policy: Convergence, Concentration, Commerce* (London: Sage, 1998), pp. 23–37.

10 Ibid.

11 See Dominic Strinati and Steven Wagg, *Come on Down?: Popular Media Culture in Post-War Britain* (London: Routledge, 1992) for a discussion of changes in television audience/programming.

12 Ernst Bloch, *The Spirit of Utopia* (Stanford, CA: Stanford University Press, 2000).

13 Žižek makes a very powerful intervention in this debate in *Welcome to the Desert* (pp. 5–57).

14 David Seamon, *A Geography of the Lifeworld* (New York: St. Martin's Press, 1979), p. 78.

15 See James Druckman 'The Power of Television Images: The First Kennedy–Nixon Debate Revisited', *The Journal of Politics*, 65:2 (2003), pp. 559–71.

16 Caughie, *Television Drama*.

17 See Jeremy G. Butler, *Television Style* (London: Routledge, 2009).

18 David Gauntlet, *Moving Experiences – Second Edition: Media Effects and Beyond* (London: John Libbey, 2005); James W. Potter, *On Media Violence* (Thousand Oaks,

CA: Sage, 1999); Paul Taylor and Jan Harris, *Critical Theories of Mass Media: Then and Now* (Basingstoke: Open University Press, 2008).

19 Theodor Adorno, *The Culture Industry: Selected Essays on Mass Culture*, ed. J. M. Bernstein (London: Routledge, 2001).

20 Rosemary Hennessy, *Profit and Pleasure: Sexual Identities in Late Capitalism* (London: Routledge, 2000).

21 Morley, *Television, Audiences*.

22 Stuart Hall, 'Encoding and decoding'.

23 For a discussion of this important area of media research and politics, see the work of the Glasgow Media Group (www.glasgowmediagroup.org/) (accessed 23 February 2011).

24 See the on-line scholarly journal *Participations* www.participations.org/index.htm (accessed 23 February 2011).

25 F. R. Leavis and Denys Thompson, *Culture and Environment: The Training of Critical Awareness* (London: Chatto & Windus, 1933).

26 This is the author's transcription of the speech, which can be found on YouTube, www.youtube.com/watch?v=9gWcj14YF6s (accessed 23 February 2011).

27 Richard Hoggart, *The Uses of Literacy: Aspects of Working Class Life* (London: Chatto & Windus, 1957), p. 127. Despite Hoggart's own concerns about mass culture, *The Uses of Literacy* remains massively popular and is now placed on (the free-access) 'Google' books.

28 Matthew Arnold, *Culture and Anarchy: An Essay in Political and Social Criticism* (London: Smith Elder, 1869).

29 David Simon, speaking to *Salon*, 'Everything you were afraid to ask about *The Wire*', http://dir.salon.com/ent/feature/2004/10/01/the_wire/index.html (accessed 23 February 2011).

30 'Abbott Turns his "Sub-Working Class" Life into Drama', the *Guardian*, 16 May 2003, www.guardian.co.uk/media/2003/may/16/broadcasting.channel4 (accessed 8 February 2011).

15

POSTMODERNISM AND FICTION

BARRY LEWIS

From the vantage point of the new millennium, it is clear that the dominant mode of literature in the second half of the twentieth century was **postmodernist** writing. The fiction later to be classified under this rubric emerged at around the time of the erection of the Berlin Wall in the early 1960s. By 1989, with the Wall demolished and the Cold War almost over, postmodernism had established itself as the dominant paradigm for the culture. After this point, the concept saturated the media and academia to such an extent that the term became problematic as an explanatory force due to its all-embracingness. It came to apply to virtually anything that mixed modes in a knowing manner.

It would seem, then, that the epistemic break that occurred around 1990 concerns two understandings of the concept of postmodernism in relation to literature. Before that date, it referred to an overlapping set of characteristics that applied to a particular set of novelists, bound together by their simultaneous acceptance/rejection of earlier traditions of fiction. These writers particularly contested the **representational** claims of realist writers such as Honoré de Balzac, Charles Dickens and Leo Tolstoy, whose novels were positioned as unproblematic mirrors of society. Also contested were the subjective, totalizing tendencies of the great **modernists** such as Marcel Proust, James Joyce and Virginia Woolf, and the distinctions they made between low and high culture. Inspired by the writings of Mikhail Bakhtin – particularly the concepts of dialogism, heteroglossia, polyphony, the chronotope and the carnivalesque[1] – and later theorists such as Roland Barthes and Jacques Derrida, the **texts** of the postmodernists were self-reflexive, playful and exceedingly aware of the medium of language in an attempt to revivify the novel form.

Several commentators intuited that the 'literature of exhaustion' (John Barth's phrase for the last-gasp attempt of the novel to achieve pre-eminence in the electronic global village)[2] itself became exhausted around 1990. De Villo Sloan, in his essay 'The Decline of American Postmodernism' (1987), wrote: 'Postmodernism as a literary movement … is now in its final phase of decadence.'[3] Malcolm Bradbury and Richard Ruland, in their sweeping survey *From Puritanism to Postmodernism* (1991), asserted: 'Postmodernism now looks like a stylistic phase that ran from the 1960s to the 1980s.'[4] If we take these statements seriously, it follows that the texts published between 1960 and 1990 constitute the 'first wave' of postmodernist writing and a large proportion of writing published after 1990 is part of what we might call its 'second wave'. What distinguishes the two is that postmodernism mushroomed into the widest of catch-all terms in western culture after the global shifts initiated by the collapse of Communism, the exponential spread of the media and the ubiquity of the computer. In literary terms, postmodernist fiction itself became perceptible as a kind of 'style' and its characteristic techniques and themes came to be adopted without the same sense of breaking new ground. It is as if the 'avant-garde' had become the mainstream.

Bradbury did much to chart the territory and promulgate the perception of the writing between 1960 and 1990 as a self-contained period. He admitted that the problems of mapping contemporary literature are considerable, and that its diversity presents problems for the would-be cartographer. Postmodernism was, of course, only part of the total landscape, but like a mountain range it loomed over everything else, and plodding over its peaks and valleys is no easy task. Luckily other intrepid guides have explored its contours and reliefs. The most useful textbooks are Patricia Waugh's *Metafiction*, Larry McCaffery's *Postmodern Fiction: A Bio-Bibliographical Guide*, Brian McHale's *Postmodernist Fiction*, Mark Currie's *Postmodern Narrative Theory* and Brian Nicol's *The Cambridge Introduction to Postmodernist Fiction*.[5]

Postmodernist fiction was an international phenomenon, with major representatives from all over the world: Günter Grass and Peter Handke (Germany); Georges Perec and Monique Wittig (France); Umberto Eco and Italo Calvino (Italy); Angela Carter and Salman Rushdie (Britain); Stanislaw Lem (Poland); Milan Kundera (former Czechoslovakia); Mario Vargas Llosa (Peru); Gabriel García Márquez (Colombia); J. M. Coetzee (South Africa); and Peter Carey (Australia). Yet, despite this cosmopolitanism, Malcolm Bradbury quipped that 'When something called postmodernism came along everyone thought it was American – even though its writers had names like Borges, Nabokov, Calvino and Eco'.[6] This is because the number of Stateside writers who published postmodernist fiction was large. Here are twenty names usually included in such lists: Walter Abish, Kathy Acker, Paul Auster, John Barth, Donald Barthelme, Richard Brautigan, William Burroughs, Robert Coover, Don DeLillo, E. L. Doctorow, Raymond Federman, William Gass, Steve Katz, Jerzy Kosinski, Joseph McElroy, Thomas Pynchon, Ishmael Reed, Gilbert Sorrentino, Ronald Sukenick, Kurt Vonnegut. A similar list for the post-1990 or 'second wave' of American postmodernist writers would probably include: Sherman Alexie, Mark Amerika, T. Coraghessan Boyle, Douglas Coupland, Ricardo Cortez Cruz, Mark Z. Danielewski, William Gibson, Lyn Hejinian, Harold Jaffe, Maxine Hong Kingston, Jonathan Lethem, Mark Leyner, Richard Powers, Joanna Russ, Joanna Scott, Leslie Marmon Silko, Lynne Tillman, Gerald Vizenor, William T. Vollman, David Foster Wallace. Raymond Federman states in 'Self-Reflexive Fiction' that 'it cannot be said that these [postmodernist] writers ... formed a unified movement for which a coherent theory could be formulated'.[7] It is difficult to disagree with this, as the novels and short stories of both sets of authors vary a great deal. However, the 'first wave' of postmodernist writers have more of a common end and means than the 'second wave'.

Some of the dominant features of both waves of postmodernist fiction include: temporal disorder; the erosion of the sense of time; a pervasive and pointless use of pastiche; a foregrounding of words as fragmenting material signs; the loose association of ideas; paranoia; and vicious circles, or a loss of distinction between logically separate levels of **discourse**. Traits such as these are encountered time and time again in the bare, bewildering landscapes of the original postmodernists. John W. Aldridge puts it like this:

> In the fiction of [postmodernist writers] ... virtually everything and everyone exists in such a radical state of distortion and aberration that there is no way of determining from which conditions in the real world they have been derived or from what standard of sanity they may be said to depart. The conventions of verisimilitude and sanity have been nullified. Characters inhabit a dimension of structureless being in which their behaviour becomes inexplicably arbitrary and unjudgeable because the fiction itself stands as a metaphor of a derangement that is seemingly without provocation and beyond measurement.[8]

Although Aldridge's statement could also be applied to the 'second wave' of postmodernist writers who made their impact after 1990, it should be noted that their use of these techniques is more routine than radical, as the experimentation of their predecessors became deeply absorbed into the general culture. The following brief survey will therefore concentrate mainly on the characteristic derangements of the writers who belong to the pre-1990 dispensation. It will also focus primarily on the novel. Postmodernism has, of course, infiltrated all literary forms. The paradoxes and perplexities of John Ashbery and Susan Howe, and the word games of the Language poets such as Ron Silliman and Bob Perelman, are well documented. In drama, David Mamet, Caryl Churchill, Sam Shepherd and Tony Kushner exhibit a postmodern sensibility. Yet it is within the genre of the novel that postmodernism has had the most impact. For this reason, I will focus on postmodernist fiction, although it is possible to find many of the features it discerns in other types of contemporary writing.

TEMPORAL DISORDER

Postmodernism, according to Linda Hutcheon is a 'contradictory enterprise: its art forms ... use and abuse, install and then destabilize convention ... [in] their critical or **ironic** re-reading of the art of the past'.[9] She argues further that postmodernist writing is best represented by those works of 'historiographic **metafiction**' which self-consciously distort history. This can be accomplished by several means, as Brian McHale notes in the study mentioned earlier: apocryphal history, anachronism or the blending of history and fantasy.

Apocryphal history involves bogus accounts of famous events. Thomas Pynchon's *Mason & Dixon*, for instance, implies that its two eponymous heroes were aware that their famous line, dividing Maryland from Pennsylvania, would eventually lead to civil war.[10] Anachronism disrupts temporal order by flaunting glaring inconsistencies of detail or setting. In *Flight to Canada* by Ishmael Reed, Abraham Lincoln uses a telephone, and his assassination is reported on television.[11] Tom Crick, a schoolteacher in Graham Swift's *Waterland*, blurs history and fantasy by combining his account of the French Revolution with personal reminiscences and unsubstantiated anecdotes about his own family history.[12]

Postmodernist fiction did not just disrupt the past, but corrupted the present too. It disordered the linear coherence of narrative by warping the sense of significant time, *kairos*, or the dull passing of ordinary time, *chronos*. *Kairos* is strongly associated with those modernist novels which are disposed around moments of epiphany and disclosure, such as James Joyce's *A Portrait of the Artist as a Young Man*.[13] Postmodernist novels such as *Gerald's Party* by Robert Coover chuckle at such solemnities.[14] The sheer abundance of incidents that occur over one night (several murders and beatings, the torture of Gerald's wife by the police, and the arrival of an entire theatre group) distends time beyond recognition. Realist writing specializes in *chronos*, or common-or-garden clock time, and this too is ridiculed in some postmodernist texts. Nicholson Baker's *The Mezzanine*, for instance, comprises a series of extended meditations on why the central character's shoelace snapped during one particular lunchtime.[15]

Postmodernist writing is full of these kinds of temporal disorder. Its disruptions of time anticipated a world that was soon to be 24/7. Warhol's prediction that in the future everybody would be famous for fifteen minutes was fulfilled with a vengeance by the 'reality TV shows' and blogs of the new mediasphere.

PASTICHE

The Italian word *pasticcio* means 'A medley of various ingredients: a hotchpotch, a farrago, jumble' (OED), and is the etymological root of the word 'pastiche'. Pastiching an individual writer is rather like creating an anagram, not of letters, but of the components of a style. Pastiche is therefore a kind of permutation, a shuffling of generic and grammatical tics.

The mere presence of pastiche in postmodernist writing is not in itself unique. The very infancy of the novel form was marked by a succession of parodies, from Samuel Richardson to Laurence Sterne. Yet, as John Barth points out in his essay 'The Literature of Exhaustion' (1967) and its sequel 'The Literature of Replenishment' (1968), later collected in *The Friday Book*, there is certainly something peculiar and distinctive about the mania for impersonation between 1960 and 1990.[16] However, by the year 2000 pastiche began to be almost *de rigueur* in the light of the widespread plagiarism and 'mash-up' piracy made possible by the **dot.com Internet** explosion.

Barth's earlier essay epitomizes a mood in the late 1960s, when critics such as Susan Sontag were busy greatly exaggerating rumours about the death of the novel. The traditional devices of fiction seemed clapped out, unable to capture the complexities of the electronic age. At first it was thought that Barth, by stressing the exhaustion of both realism and modernism, had not only joined the novel's funeral procession, but was volunteering to be chief pall-bearer. However, the critics overlooked his claim (reasserted in the later essay) that the corpse could be revivified by stitching together the amputated limbs and digits in new permutations: by pastiche, in other words.

Pastiche, then, arose from the frustration that everything has been done before. Contemporary artists had to face the fact that many of the stylistic possibilities had already been exhausted as permutations are finite. So postmodernist writers tended to pluck existing styles higgledy-piggledy from the reservoir of literary history, and match them with little tact.

This explains why many novels between 1960 and the turn of the millennium borrow the clothes of different forms (for example: the Western, the sci-fi yarn and the detective tale). The impulse behind this cross-dressing is more spasmodic than parodic. These genres provide ready-made forms, ideal for postmodernist miscegenation. The Western, as Philip French observes, is 'a hungry cuckoo of a genre ... ready to seize anything that's in the air from juvenile delinquency to ecology'.[17] It is already a bastardized form. Examples of the postmodern Western include *The Hawkline Monster* by Richard Brautigan, *Yellow Back Radio Broke-Down* by Ishmael Reed and *The Place of Dead Roads* by William Burroughs.[18] Science fiction was another popular source for postmodernist pastiche. Some critics claimed it to be the natural companion to postmodernist writing, because of their shared ontological occupations. (See especially *Solaris* by Stanislaw Lem, *Cosmicomics* by Italo Calvino, *Slaughterhouse-Five* by Kurt Vonnegut and the novels of the so-called '**Cyberpunk**' writers such as William Gibson and Bruce Sterling).[19] Lastly, the detective genre was another candidate for the post of true companion of postmodernism. The pursuit of clues appealed to the postmodernist writer because it so closely parallels the hunt for textual meaning by the reader. The most popular postmodernist detective fictions are *The Name of the Rose* by Umberto Eco, *The New York Trilogy* by Paul Auster and *Hawksmoor* by Peter Ackroyd.[20] Several decades on, these books have assumed the status of classics, slightly quaint in their self-conscious fusions. To the 'second wave' postmodernist writers, genre-blending is a sine qua non.

FRAGMENTATION

John Hawkes once divulged that when he began to write he assumed that 'the true enemies of the novel were plot, character, setting and theme'.[21] Certainly many authors did their best after the 1960s to sledgehammer these four literary cornerstones into oblivion. Either plot is pounded into small slabs of event and circumstance, characters disintegrate into a bundle of twitching desires, settings dwindle to little more than transitory backdrops, or themes become so attenuated that it is often comically inaccurate to say that certain novels are 'about' such-and-such.

'Too many times', as Jonathan Baumbach observes in a short story in *The Return of Service*, 'you read a story nowadays and it's not a story at all, not in the traditional sense'.[22] The postmodernist writer distrusted the wholeness and completion associated with traditional stories, and preferred to deal with other ways of structuring narrative. One alternative was the multiple ending, which resists closure by offering numerous possible outcomes for a plot. *The French Lieutenant's Woman* by John Fowles is the classic instance of this. The novel concerns the love of respectable amateur naturalist Charles Smithson (engaged to the daughter of a wealthy trader) for Sarah Woodruff, an outcast rumoured to have been scandalously involved with a French lieutenant. Although the book is set in Lyme Regis in 1867, and follows several love story conventions, it is far from being a regular historical romance.

Fowles disrupts the narrative by parading his familiarity with Marx, Darwin and others. He directly addresses the reader, and even steps into the story himself at one stage as a character. The multiple endings are a part of these guerrilla tactics. Fowles refuses to choose between two competing dénouements: one in which Charles and Sarah are reunited after a stormy affair, and the other in which they are kept irrevocably apart. He therefore introduces an uncertainty principle into the book. He even dallies with a third possibility of leaving Charles on the train, searching for Sarah in the capital: 'But the conventions of Victorian fiction allow, allowed no place for the open, the inconclusive.'[23]

Another means of allowing space for the open and inconclusive was to break up the text into short fragments or sections, separated by space, titles, numbers or symbols. The novels and short stories of Richard Brautigan, Donald Barthelme and David Markson are full of such fragments. Some authors went even further and fragmented the very fabric of the text with illustrations, typography or mixed media. As Raymond Federman puts it: 'In those spaces where there is nothing to write, the fiction writer can, at any time, introduce material (quotations, pictures, diagrams, charts, designs, pieces of other discourses, etc.) totally unrelated to the story.'[24]

Willie Masters' Lonesome Wife by William Gass does just about all these things in its sixty-odd pages, and is a postmodernist text par excellence.[25] The pages themselves come in four different colours: jotter blue, khaki green, strawberry red and glossy white. The nude woman lounging full-frontal on the title-page is Babs. She is a frustrated spouse who figuratively embodies the language/lovemaking equation examined by Gass. The layout is so eccentric it might have been designed by Marshall McLuhan. Multiple typefaces (bold, italic), fonts (Gothic, script), characters (musical symbols, accents), and miscellaneous arrangements (columns, footnotes) jostle for air alongside some visual jokes (coffee-cup stains, huge asterisk). This kind of bold collage became much easier to construct and publish post-1990, thanks to advances in word-processing software, hence the pictorial ambition of a novel such as *House of Leaves* by Mark Z. Danielewski.[26]

It is difficult not to be reminded of the famous epigraph to E. M. Forster's

Howards End which urges us to connect fragments.[27] We can counterpoint this with an utterance by a character in Barthelme's 'See the Moon?' from *Unspeakable Practices. Unnatural Acts* in which it is stated that fragments are the only trusted forms.[28] These two statements evince a crucial difference between modernism and postmodernism. The Forster phrase could almost be modernism's motto, as it points to the need to find new forms of continuity in the absence of the old linear plots. Conversely, Barthelme's gem hints at post-modernist fiction's wariness of wholeness. Yet in the age of Twitter and the instant sound bite, even fragments appear to be suspiciously holistic.

LOOSENESS OF ASSOCIATION

Another means by which many postmodernist writers disrupted the smooth production and reception of texts was by welcoming chance into the compositional process. The infamous *The Unfortunates* by B. S. Johnson, for instance, is a novel-in-a-box with instructions for the reader to riffle several loose-leaf chapters into any order.[29] Only the first and last chapter are denominated, otherwise the sections can be freely mixed. The point of this contrived format is not just to perform a cold, technical experiment. Rather, Johnson wishes to recreate the unique disposition of his thoughts on a particular Saturday afternoon, when reporting a football match in Nottingham for the *Observer*. It was the first time he had returned to the city since the death of his friend, Tony. The peculiar form of the novel mirrors his churning feelings. So, ironically, the loose leaves of *The Unfortunates* are not intended to be random at all, but strive to render the workings of the mind more naturally.

William Burroughs also forayed frequently into serendipity. The arrangement of the twenty-two individual sections of *Naked Lunch* was regulated solely by the adventitious order in which they happened to be sent to the publishers.[30] Indeed, the untidiness of the room in which the manuscript was assembled sometimes disturbed the sequence of pages. Small wonder that Burroughs confessed that *Naked Lunch* could be entered at almost any point. Burroughs wields chance less randomly in three novels from the 1960s which are often grouped together as a trilogy: *Nova Express*, *The Soft Machine* and *The Ticket That Exploded*.[31] These books make methodical use of the cut-up.

The cut-up is the brainchild of the artist Tristan Tzara, who envisaged it as a verbal equivalent to the cubist and Dadaist collages in the visual arts. Further extensions of the idea can be traced through the poetry of T. S. Eliot and Ezra Pound, and the newspaper pastiches of John Dos Passos. The cut-up involves placing excised sentences from a range of texts into a hat or other container, shaking them, then matching together the scraps of paper which are picked out at random. This rigmarole has prompted sceptical critics to make unflattering comparisons between Burroughs and monkeys with typewriters.

Another chance technique favoured by Burroughs was the fold-in, in which a page of text is folded vertically, and then aligned with another page until the two halves match. Just as the cut-up allowed writing to mimic cinematic montage, the fold-in gave Burroughs the option of repeating passages in a specifically musical way. For example, if page 1 is folded in with page 100 to form a composite page 10, phrases can flash forwards and back like the anticipation and recapitulation of motifs in a symphony.

The fold-in, like the cut-up, strained to evade the manacles of linear fiction. Burroughs' spirit of chance-taking was decidedly congenial to the postmodernist writer. In this respect he is rather like the musician John Cage, who opened up tremendous ground for exploration by later composers, although his experiments with dice and the *I-Ching* proved to be unrepeatable. Nevertheless, as Julian Cowley noted in an essay on Ronald Sukenick, in both music and writing, 'Readiness to ride with the random may be regarded as a characteristically postmodern attitude.'[32] Indeed, at the beginning of the twenty-first century, randomness is now wholly subsumed into the everyday splice-and-mix culture.

PARANOIA

Paranoia, or the threat of total engulfment by somebody else's system, is keenly felt by many of the dramatis personae of postmodernist fictions. It is tempting to speculate that this began as an indirect mimetic representation of the climate of fear and suspicion that prevailed throughout the Cold War, although following 9/11 conspiracy theory is simply a modus vivendi for the majority. The protagonists of postmodernist fiction often suffer from what Tony Tanner calls a 'dread that someone else is patterning your life, that there are all sorts of invisible plots afoot to rob you of your autonomy of thought and action, that conditioning is ubiquitous'.[33]

Postmodernist writing reflected paranoid anxieties in many ways, including: the distrust of fixity, of being circumscribed to any one particular place or identity, the conviction that society is conspiring against the individual, and the multiplication of self-made plots to counter the scheming of others. These different responses are immanent in three distinct areas of reference associated with the word 'plot'. The first meaning is that of a piece of ground of small or moderate size sequestered for some special purpose, such as a plot for growing vegetables or building a house. It is a stationary space, that is to say, and stasis is intimidating to the postmodern protagonist. Randle McMurphy in Ken Kesey's *One Flew Over the Cuckoo's Nest*, Yossarian in Joseph Heller's *Catch-22* and Billy Pilgrim in Vonnegut's *Slaughterhouse-Five* are each confined to their own 'plots' in this sense by the authorities.[34] McMurphy is committed to a mental hospital, Yossarian is conscripted to the air force, and Billy Pilgrim is interned in a German prisoner-of-war camp. A vindictive bureaucracy controls these mavericks by medication, red tape or the force of arms.

In each instance the imprisoning of the individual by outside powers propagates a panic of identity. So McMurphy's protests that he is sane prove his insanity. Pilgrim's belief that he is the subject of an experiment is belied by the offhand way his German captors treat him. To compensate for the hopelessness of their predicaments, these paranoids long for a state of complete fluidity and openness. However, their impulse towards freedom is tainted both by their terror of the actual open road and their cynicism about possible escape. McMurphy, Yossarian and Pilgrim are simultaneously safe and insecure in their 'plots' of the Oregon Asylum, the Pianosa air-force base and the Dresden slaughterhouse.

A second meaning of 'plot' is that of a secret plan or conspiracy to accomplish a criminal or illegal purpose. The protagonist of the postmodernist novel sometimes suspects that he or she is trapped at the centre of an intrigue, often with some justification. McMurphy is right to be afraid of Nurse Ratched and the Combine, who eventually force him to undergo shock treatment and an unwarranted lobotomy. Yossarian's parachute is stolen by Milo Minderbinder and replaced by a useless M & M Enterprises voucher. General Peckham sends Yossarian's squadron out on dangerous bombing missions simply to obtain decent aerial photographs for the magazines back home. Nately's whore stabs Yossarian, in the belief that he killed her lover. In *Slaughterhouse-Five*, Billy Pilgrim also correctly perceives that others wish to control his welfare. His daughter commits him to a mental institution and Paul Lazarro later kills him as a revenge for allegedly allowing Roland Weary to die.

There is but a small step from these private apprehensions to a more distressing speculation. Perhaps the whole of society is a plot against the citizen. What if all the major events of history are really side-shows orchestrated by unseen ringmasters for hidden motives? This is known as paranoid history. Thomas Pynchon is enthralled by the topic. Stencil in *V.*, Oedipa Maas in *The Crying of Lot 49*, Slothrop in *Gravity's Rainbow*, Prairie in *Vineland* and the protagonists of *Mason & Dixon*:[35] each stumble upon subterranean schemes and cabals which threaten the rights of the individual. Lawrence Norfolk presents equally entangled scenarios in *Lemprière's Dictionary* and *The Pope's Rhinoceros*.[36] The characters of Pynchon and Norfolk suspect that everything is connected. These days, thanks to the World Wide Web, everything *is* connected to everything else – at least, digitally.

The third, more mundane, meaning of plot is, of course, that of a plan of a literary work. In an interview, John Barth called this 'the incremental perturbation of an unstable homeostatic system and its catastrophic restoration to a complexified equilibrium'.[37] This humorous definition suggests that a plot has a particular shape: somebody is challenged, certain obstacles are overcome, and a new state of affairs is reached. Plot is shape, and shape is control. Postmodernist writers proliferated plot, as if to prove through zealous mastery that they were free of the straitjackets of control by outside forces. The best of these maximalist works are *Foucault's Pendulum* by Umberto Eco, *Life: A User's Manual* by Georges Perec and *Letters* by Barth himself.[38]

VICIOUS CIRCLES

Vicious circles arise in postmodernist fiction when both text and world are permeable, to the extent that we cannot separate one from the other. The literal and the metaphorical merge when the following occur: short circuits (when the author steps into the text) and double binds (when real-life historical figures appear in fictions).

The short circuits which plagued postmodernist fiction rarely occur in other forms of fiction. In realist literature, for example, there is an unbroken flow of **narrative** 'electricity' between **text** and world. The author never appears directly in his or her fictions, other than as a voice that indirectly guides the reader towards a 'correct' interpretation of the novel's themes. Conversely, much modernist fiction is motivated by the desire to expunge the author from the text altogether. Think of James Joyce's image of the artist standing behind the work, paring his fingernails. This again ensures that there is little chance of confusing the world inside the text with the world outside the text. In the postmodernist novel and short story, however, such confusion was rampant. Text and world fused when the author appeared in his or her own fiction. The best examples of this occur in Ronald Sukenick's *The Death of the Novel and Other Stories* and *Out*, and Raymond Federman's *Double or Nothing* and *Take It or Leave It*.[39]

The double bind is a concept elaborated by Gregory Bateson and others to explain an inability to distinguish between different levels of discourse. When a parent chastises a child, for instance, they may undermine the punishment by smiling as they smack. If these kinds of contradictory message are repeated obsessively, it may lead to the child experiencing increasing anxiety and possible breakdown. The boundaries separating the literal and the metaphorical will never fully form, and any moves to resolve matters result only in further ambiguity.

The equivalent of the double bind occurred in postmodernist fiction when historical characters appeared in a patent fiction. We are used to the idea of the historical novel, which shows famous people from the past acting in ways consistent with the verifiable public record. A common alternative was to sketch in the 'dark areas' of somebody's life, and again care is usually taken not to contradict substantially what we already know about them. In postmodernist writing, however, such contradictions were actively sought. So in Max Apple's *The Propheteers*, the motel mogul Howard Johnson plots against Walt Disney.[40] In Guy Davenport's 'Christ Preaching at the Henley Regatta', Bertie Wooster and Stéphane Mallarmé stand on the banks watching the boat race.[41] In E. L. Doctorow's *Ragtime*, Sigmund Freud and Carl Jung go through the Tunnel of Love together at Coney Island.[42]

To compare such distortions with the derangements of insanity, as I have done, is apt. Some major **poststructuralist** thinkers enlist ideas connected with schizophrenia in their diagnoses of postmodern society. Jean-François Lyotard, for instance, employs the metaphors of fragmentation in *The Postmodern*

Condition to convey the splintering of knowledge into a plethora of incommensurate discourses.[43] Gilles Deleuze and Félix Guattari speak of 'schizoanalysis' in *Anti-Oedipus*.[44] Lastly, Fredric Jameson's full-length study *Postmodernism, or, The Cultural Logic of Late Capitalism* employs schizophrenia as an analogy for the collapse of traditional socio-economic structures.[45] This recurrent linking of mental illness, the fractures of late capitalist society and the linguistic experiments of the postmodernists is not accidental. Temporal disorder, involuntary impersonation of other voices (or pastiche), fragmentation, looseness of association, paranoia and the creation of vicious circles are all symptoms of the language disorders of postmodernist fiction.

NOTES

1 For an overview of these Bakhtinian ideas, see Sue Vice, *Introducing Bakhtin* (Manchester: Manchester University Press, 1998).

2 John Barth, 'The Literature of Exhaustion' [1967], in Malcolm Bradbury, ed., *The Novel Today: Contemporary Writers on Modern Fiction* (Manchester: Manchester University Press, 1977).

3 De Villo Sloan, 'The Decline of American Postmodernism', *SubStance* 16:3 (1987), pp. 29–43 (p. 29).

4 Malcolm Bradbury and Richard Ruland, *From Puritanism to Postmodernism: A History of American Literature* (London: Routledge, 1991), p. 325.

5 Patricia Waugh, *Metafiction: The Theory and Practice of Self-Conscious Fiction* (London: Methuen, 1984); Larry McCaffrey, *Postmodern Fiction: A Bio-Biographical Guide* (Westport, CT: Greenwood, 1986); Brian McHale, *Postmodernist Fiction* (London: Methuen, 1987); Mark Currie, *Postmodern Narrative Theory* (London: Macmillan, 1998); Brian Nicol, *The Cambridge Introduction to Postmodernist Fiction* (Cambridge: Cambridge University Press, 2009).

6 Bradbury and Ruland, *From Puritanism*, p. 2.

7 Raymond Federman, 'Self-Reflexive Fiction', in *Columbia Literary History of the United States*, ed. Emory Elliott (New York: Columbia University Press, 1988), pp. 1142–57 (p. 1146).

8 John W. Aldridge, *The American Novel and the Way We Live Now* (New York: Oxford University Press, 1983), p. 140.

9 Linda Hutcheon, *A Poetics of Postmodernism: History, Theory, Fiction* (London: Routledge, 1988), p. 23.

10 Thomas Pynchon, *Mason & Dixon* (London: Jonathan Cape, 1997).

11 Ishmael Reed, *Flight to Canada* (New York: Random House, 1976).

12 Graham Swift, *Waterland* (London: William Heinemann, 1983).

13 James Joyce, *A Portrait of the Artist as a Young Man* [1916], ed. Chester G. Anderson (Harmondsworth: Penguin, 1977).

14 Robert Coover, *Gerald's Party* (London: Paladin, 1986).

15 Nicholson Baker, *The Mezzanine* (London: Granta, 1989).

16 John Barth, *The Friday Book* (New York: Putnam, 1984).

17 Philip French, *Westerns* (London: Secker & Warburg, 1973), p. 24.

18 Richard Brautigan, *The Hawkline Monster: A Gothic Western* (New York: Simon &

Schuster, 1974); Ishmael Reed, *Yellow Back Radio Broke-Down* (New York: Doubleday, 1969); William Burroughs, *The Place of Dead Roads* (New York: Holt, Rinehart and Winston, 1983).

19 Stanislaw Lem, *Solaris*, trans. Joanna Kilmartin and Steve Cox (London: Faber & Faber, 1961); Italo Calvino, *Cosmicomics*, trans. William Weaver (New York: Harcourt Brace Jovanovich, 1965); Kurt Vonnegut, *Slaughterhouse-Five* (New York: Dial, 1969).

20 Umberto Eco, *The Name of the Rose*, trans. William Weaver (New York: Harcourt Brace Jovanovich, 1988); Paul Auster, *The New York Trilogy* (London: Faber & Faber, 1987); Peter Ackroyd, *Hawksmoor* (London: Hamish Hamilton, 1985).

21 John Hawkes, quoted in John Enck, 'John Hawkes: An Interview', *Wisconsin Studies in Contemporary Literature*, 6 (1964), p. 149.

22 Jonathan Baumbach, 'The Traditional Story Returns', in *The Return of Service* (Urbana, IL: University of Illinois Press, 1979), p. 1.

23 John Fowles, *The French Lieutenant's Woman* (London: Jonathan Cape, 1969), p. 289.

24 Raymond Federman, 'Surfiction – Four Propositions in Form of an Introduction', in *Surfiction: Now ... and Tomorrow*, ed. Raymond Federman (Chicago: Swallow Press, 1975), p. 12.

25 William Gass, *Willie Masters' Lonesome Wife* (Evanston, IL: Northwestern University Press, 1967).

26 Mark Z. Danielewski, *House of Leaves* (New York: Pantheon, 2000).

27 E. M. Forster, *Howards End* [1910], ed. Oliver Stallybrass (Harmondsworth: Penguin, 1989).

28 Donald Barthelme, *Unspeakable Practices. Unnatural Acts* (New York: Farrar, Strauss, 1968).

29 B. S. Johnson, *The Unfortunates* (London: Panther, 1969).

30 William Burroughs, *Naked Lunch* (Paris: Olympia, 1959).

31 William Burroughs, *Nova Express* (New York: Grove, 1964), *The Soft Machine* (London: Calder and Boyars, 1968), *The Ticket That Exploded* (New York: Grove, 1967).

32 Julian Cowley, 'Ronald Sukenick's New Departures from the Terminal of Language', *Critique: Studies in Contemporary Fiction*, 28:2 (1987), pp. 87–99 (p. 93).

33 Tony Tanner, *City of Words: American Fiction 1950–70* (London: Jonathan Cape, 1971), p. 15.

34 Ken Kesey, *One Flew Over the Cuckoo's Nest* (New York: Viking, 1962); Joseph Heller, *Catch-22* (London: Jonathan Cape, 1962); Vonnegut, *Slaughterhouse-Five*.

35 Thomas Pynchon, *V.* (London: Jonathan Cape, 1963), *The Crying of Lot 49* (Philadelphia: Lippincott, 1966), *Gravity's Rainbow* (London: Jonathan Cape, 1973), *Vineland* (London: Secker & Warburg, 1990), *Mason & Dixon*.

36 Lawrence Norfolk, *Lemprière's Dictionary* (London: Sinclair-Stevenson, 1991), *The Pope's Rhinoceros* (London: Sinclair-Stevenson, 1996).

37 John Barth, *Letters* (New York: G. P. Putnam's Sons, 1979), p. 767.

38 Umberto Eco, *Foucault's Pendulum*, trans. William Weaver (New York: Harcourt Brace Jovanovich, 1988); Georges Perec, *Life: A User's Manual*, trans. David Bellos (London: Collins Harvill, 1978); Barth, *Letters*.

39 Ronald Sukenick, *The Death of the Novel and Other Stories* (New York: Dial, 1969), *Out* (Chicago: Swallow, 1973); Raymond Federman, *Double or Nothing* (Chicago: Swallow, 1971), *Take It or Leave It* (New York: Fiction Collective, 1976).

40 Max Apple, *The Propheteers* (London: Faber & Faber, 1987).

41 Guy Davenport, 'Christ Preaching at the Henley Regatta', in *Eclogues: Eight Stories by Guy Davenport* (Baltimore, MD: Johns Hopkins University Press, 1993), pp. 87–104.

42 E. L. Doctorow, *Ragtime* (London: Macmillan, 1975).

43 Jean-François Lyotard, *The Postmodern Condition: A Report on Knowledge* [1979], trans. Geoff Bennington and Brian Massumi (Manchester: Manchester University Press, 1984).

44 Gilles Deleuze and Félix Guattari, *Anti-Oedipus* [1972], trans. Robert Hurley, Mark Seem and Helen Lane (London: Athlone Press, 1984).

45 Fredric Jameson, *Postmodernism, or, The Cultural Logic of Late Capitalism* (London: Verso, 1991).

16

POSTMODERNISM AND MUSIC

DEREK B. SCOTT

Postmodernism began to have an impact upon music and musicology in the 1980s when it became evident that a **paradigmatic shift** in thought was needed in order to find answers to the theoretical impasse that had been reached in several areas.

First, the idea that a mass audience did no more than passively consume the products of a culture industry had become discredited. Yet tacit acceptance of this idea explains why, for instance, the legendary jazz saxophonist Charlie Parker did not appear in the *New Oxford History of Music* and the rock guitarist Jimi Hendrix was absent from 1980 edition of *The New Grove Dictionary of Music and Musicians.* Anyone caring to peruse the index of the *Oxford History* will indeed find Parker listed, but this is the American organist and composer Horatio Parker (1863–1919). Giving priority to the latter makes a clear state-ment of value: Horatio is of greater musical importance than Charlie. Today, it is evident that classical music is as involved in the market place as pop and jazz (conductors and singers can become superstars, and even a 'serious' composer like Henryk Górecki has appeared in record charts). Moreover, the serious *vs.* light opposition that kept mass culture theory going is also found repeated in jazz and rock – for example, 'real' jazz *vs.* commercial dance band; 'authentic' rock *vs.* superficial pop.

Second, the musical genealogical tree had needed surgery too often: lines connecting composers, charting musical developments and influences, had been redrawn too many times. One has only to consider the major reassessment of Claudio Monteverdi and Hector Berlioz in the 1960s. The linear paradigm works to include and to exclude: those who do not obviously connect are out (for example, Kurt Weill and Benjamin Britten). The related issue of the evolu-tion of musical style was now questioned: if atonality was presented as an inevi-table stylistic evolution, then clearly Duke Ellington was a musical dinosaur.

Third, the neglect of the social significance of music had become more appar-ent, especially the way cultural context often determines the legitimacy of styles of playing and singing, and changing social factors alter our response to existing works. Would we any more wish to hear John Lee Hooker attempting Giacomo Puccini's *Nessun Dorma* than Luciano Pavarotti singing Chicago bar blues?

Fourth, the impact of technology had to be considered, especially the effects that sampling and remixing had on the concept of the composer as originating mind. Furthermore, students who had grown up during the 'rock revolution' were inclined to see the **modernist** inclinations of university Departments of Music as the new orthodoxy. Perhaps more disturbing still was that it became common for a composition tutor to find students earnestly composing a type of music that they would never dream of actually going to a concert hall to hear. Other factors bearing upon the present situation were the rise of period instrument performances making old music seem new (and arguably a replacement for the new), and crossovers between 'classical' and 'popular' idioms by increasing numbers of performers and composers.

Consequently, the time was ripe for postmodernism to offer a new theoretical perspective. Its impact is discussed below under a number of headings; these are not to be taken, however, as representing a particular hierarchical order.

'ART FOR ART'S SAKE' CHALLENGED

Postmodernism ousted notions of universalism, internationalism and 'art for art's sake', and replaced them with concerns for the values of specific cultures and their **differences**. 'Art for art's sake', a nineteenth-century doctrine born of distaste for industrialization, had proved to be an insuperable obstacle to the production of music that satisfied widespread social needs. Indeed, by the time Claude Debussy was composing, the elitist attitude that 'art' is of no use to 'the masses' was common.[1] However, by the 1980s there was a growing interest in uncovering the complicity between art and entertainment rather than drawing a contrast between these two terms. Among the middle classes and the 'educated' – and among 'serious' musicians – attention drifted away from high culture to popular culture. It was no longer pressing to debate whether Pierre Boulez, John Cage or Michael Tippett represented the 'way ahead' for high culture since, to echo a well-known song, those taking the high road had been overtaken by those taking the low road. Moreover, since the 1960s there had been a remarkable similarity in marketing techniques used for the classical repertoire and for pop music.

The opposition art *vs.* entertainment is an assumption of mass culture theory and may be regarded as an ethical rather than aesthetic opposition. To choose examples from the careers of major figures in the classical canon, one can show that Wolfgang Amadeus Mozart abandoned a flute concerto in mid-composition because a commissioner failed to pay up; the same composer was persuaded by a concert promoter to change a movement of his Paris Symphony; and it was a publisher who persuaded Beethoven to replace the finale of his late String Quartet in B flat with something more conventional. More recently, Michael Nyman has not felt that associations with businesses compromise his artistic integrity: *MGV* was commissioned to mark the opening of the Paris to Lille high-speed rail link, and car manufacturer Mazda UK Ltd commissioned a concerto in 1997.

THE COLLAPSE OF HIGH AND LOW: CROSSOVERS AND NEW GENRES

The amount of 'crossover' between 'serious' and 'popular' culture has been increasing since the late 1950s. This differs from the co-opting of jazz by the French avant-garde in the 1920s and 1930s. In that case, the jazz elements were used to shock a bourgeois concert audience. The attempts of earlier avant-garde movements to place art in the service of social change had by now been abandoned. Jazz itself took over that role in 1940s Britain, when revivalist bands played at socialist rallies and accompanied the Aldermaston marches of the Campaign for Nuclear Disarmament.

The widening influence of pop music is heard in the soundtracks of films: in the 1940s Flash Gordon conquered the universe to the strains of Franz Liszt, whereas in the 1980s his crusading was accompanied by the rock band Queen. In the 1980s, performance artist Laurie Anderson had a remarkable crossover hit with 'O Superman'. In the 1990s, the violinist Nigel Kennedy tried his hand at rock, while blues guitarist Eric Clapton performed an electric guitar concerto. The Kronos String Quartet played an arrangement of Jimi Hendrix's 'Purple Haze', and opera singers of the calibre of Kiri Te Kanawa, Placido Domingo and Bryn Terfel ventured into the popular arena.

Some works now cannot easily be categorized: for example, Philip Glass's *Low* Symphony and *Heroes* Symphony (both based on albums produced in the 1970s by David Bowie and Brian Eno); *The Juliet Letters* by Elvis Costello and the Brodsky Quartet; and the peculiar mixture of medievalism and jazz in the albums *Officium* by Jan Garbarek and the Hilliard Ensemble, and *Terror and Magnificence* by John Harle. It has been claimed that shared features in the music of **minimalism** and pop are of negligible import compared to the very different ways in which minimalism is disseminated, presented and promoted, which all serve to maintain a high/low divide. Yet, there is growing evidence of omnivorous appetites on the part of listeners that clouds the issue. Taste categories in music are no longer looking as stable as they were two or three decades ago.[2] Besides, music of postmodernist character does not have to be consumed in an identical way by all.

Pop music has developed features of its own that have been greeted as postmodernist (see Chapter 18). Music videos, MTV, sampling and the phenomenon of 'world music' have received a lot of attention from postmodernist theorists. The influence of high cultural styles on popular music needs to be carefully evaluated since in some cases, such as the 'progressive' rock of the early 1970s, it may indicate modernist aspirations rather than a postmodernist play of styles.

THE END OF 'GRAND NARRATIVES'

Modernists have continually seen works as 'pointing forwards' to others, thus reinforcing a sense of self-determining progress in the arts. But can *Tristan und Isolde* really be said to point forward to the sudden and rapid developments of

1908–9, such as Richard Strauss's *Elektra* and Arnold Schoenberg's *Erwartung*? If a 50-year gap is possible, why not concede a three-hundred-year gap and allow the idea that Carlo Gesualdo pointed forward to Debussy? A major problem for 'linear modernism' is that, while Ludwig van Beethoven and Richard Wagner appear to follow an evolutionary 'progress' in their music, many otherwise impeccable modernists, like Debussy and Schoenberg, do not. What is more, modernist composers are not even reliable in their tastes: Debussy admired Charles Gounod and Richard Strauss but not Schoenberg; Igor Stravinsky admired Carl Maria von Weber and Peter Tchaikovsky but loathed Wagner.

The dominant **grand narrative** for musical modernism was that of the evolution and dissolution of tonality. Schoenberg claimed that atonal music grew out of necessity, yet this necessity was itself born of a set of particular cultural assumptions. Empirical data can be used to demonstrate that the change from extended tonality to atonality was an evolution, but it can equally well show that this was a qualitative leap. A belief in the historical necessity of atonality led to the neglect of many areas of twentieth-century music history, such as the importance of Vienna to Hollywood (Erich Korngold) or of Puccini to 'The Generation of the 1880s' in Italy. Worst of all, perhaps, was the almost complete disregard of jazz.

The BBC's thinking has for a long time been informed by modernist **metanarratives**: the corporation's admiration for 'forward-looking' composers, and of 'progressive' music is part of the left luggage from the years when Sir William Glock controlled the Third Programme's output but, all the same, dispiriting for anyone who rejects that theoretical paradigm. Nyman feels that the musical establishment has given him the cold shoulder, as evidenced by the neglect of his music by BBC Radio 3 and his lack of Proms commissions. It is erroneous to believe that an 'adventurous' style requires greater compositional skill than a 'simple and direct' style; such a position serves only to offer a facile proof, for example, that Harrison Birtwistle must be better than Arvo Pärt. As a criterion of musical value, the important thing is the relationship of style and idea.

SOCIOCULTURAL CONTEXT REPLACES AUTONOMY

The romantic and modernist interpretations of music history emphasized formal and technical values, novelty and compositional 'coups'. The stress was on the composition in itself and its place in an autonomous musical process. A well-known example of how Mozart's life and music may be interpreted through this reading of history is offered by Peter Shaffer's *Amadeus*, in which art is seen as a reflection of life (a corruption of the distinction between Romantic self-expression and the Baroque 'Doctrine of Affections'); art is perfection, the artist is a visionary (Antonio Salieri cannot understand Mozart's unique vision in the 'confutatis' of his *Requiem*), and social and political issues are cast aside (Mozart, a member, it seems, of the republican *Illuminati*, says he is 'not interested in politics', and *The Magic Flute* with its Masonic messages is described as a vaudeville). It is all too easy when constructing the history of a cultural practice to assume one is dealing with facts and not interpretation.

Raymond Williams has pointed out how lines are drawn to link together ancestors within a cultural tradition.[3] However, with the passage of time some lines become weaker, some are erased and new ones drawn in. At the beginning of the twentieth century, the reputations of Gounod, Louis Spohr and Alexander Borodin were high, but are no longer so. Since the 1960s, lines from Josquin des Pres and from Monteverdi have been strengthened, and in the 1970s eclectic modernists like Charles Ives and Edgar Varèse were brought in from the margins following the failure of attempts to establish a common practice in total serialism (an attempt to impose order on length and loudness of notes as well as their pitches).[4] This enabled the USA to take its place in the history of modernism, since a line drawn from Varèse to Henry Cowell to Cage could be used to illustrate progressively radical exploration of sound colours.

The linear paradigm works to create canonic figures and marginalize others. Canons imply an autonomous cultural development, and those who fail to participate in that particular development, or who seek alternatives, are marginalized, as were Korngold and Hans Eisler for rejecting modernism. The linear paradigm is a means of defending a single authentic culture, but that requires a common practice and modernism failed to establish one.

Aesthetics cannot always be easily divorced from social significance. Can anyone listen to those old recordings of castrati who survived into the twentieth century with an aesthetic sensibility unmoved by the knowledge that these singers were mutilated as children? Social factors affect our response to music in a variety of ways. For example, French concern at the lack of an operatic tradition, which led to the unearthing of Jean-Philippe Rameau's *Hippolyte at Aricie* early in the twentieth century, developed in the context of nationalism arising from political defeat. Changing social factors affect our response to works which may have previously provoked quite different reactions: *Così fan tutte* is not the same after the cultural impact of the Women's Movement of the 1970s, and *Peter Grimes* has become problematic due to the greater awareness of child abuse that developed in the 1980s and 1990s (we are no longer so ready to accept Grimes as a tortured idealist).

THE END OF THE 'INTERNATIONAL STYLE'

The belief in a universal aesthetics, that 'art music' transcends social and cultural context, lay behind the internationalist aspirations of modernism. Having developed his atonal style, Schoenberg gave voice to his conviction in 1910 that in ten years time every talented composer would be writing that way.[5] Modernism was never internationalist in a **pluralist** sense, but in the sense of a *single* culture with *universal* values. Composers of different nationalities and different musical traditions were shown to be moving towards the same end, usually that of embracing twelve-note music.

The ambitions of modernist music towards internationalism have been over-taken by pop, which has already become a more widely accepted international style. The social history of our times is inseparable from pop music so that, measured in terms of social significance, the twelve-bar blues may be said to have been of greater importance to twentieth-century music than the twelve-note row. Today, after all the efforts expended by ethnomusicologists, it would appear impossible to avoid the conclusion that music is no more international than other forms of cultural expression.

RELATIVISM REPLACES UNIVERSALISM

Modernism, an attempt to defend one universalist culture, was often forced to attack regionalism as parochialism, nationalism as chauvinism, and popular music as entertainment not art. The postmodern alternative is to accept that we are living in an age of **cultural relativism**. Cultural relativism, a perspective taken from anthropology, was the key to sociomusicological interpretation in the 1980s and 1990s. The argument that cultural values could be historically located was already familiar and was expanded by the recognition that significance could also be socially located. The last idea fuelled the main argument against mass culture theory: that meaning could be made in the act of consumption, rather than consumption being simply passive.

STYLES AS DISCURSIVE CODES

Contrary to Stravinsky's opinion that expressive devices are established by convention within an autonomous musical practice,[6] they are established as conventions through social practice and can be related to social changes. Musical meanings are not labels arbitrarily thrust upon abstract sounds; these sounds and their meanings originate in a social process and achieve their significance within a particular social context. Musical signifiers develop in tandem with society. The opening of Vivian Ellis's *Coronation Scot* uses no musical technique or dissonant vocabulary which would have surprised Beethoven, yet it is meaningless unless one is familiar with the sound of a steam train pulling away. The piece could not have been written before the advent of the steam locomotive. Indeed, what would boogie-woogie piano or much of the characteristic style of blues harmonica have been without trains?

Schoenberg's free atonal period can be related to the new science of psychoanalysis and Freudian investigations into the inner reaches of the human psyche. Expressionist artists envied the supposed power of music to express the composer's internal life. Just as Wassily Kandinsky spoke of 'inner necessity', Schoenberg placed his trust in 'unconscious logic'; yet, if atonality was historically inevitable, this trust was as much a corollary as a catalyst to his adopting a new musical language. Even so, it would appear odd that the development of an extreme chromatic language should coincide merely by chance with an expressionist interest in extreme emotional states.

At the same time, it is important to recognize that style codes have developed from the solidification of conventions and that these involve technical features as well as socially constituted meanings. Although style codes may be subject to further development and change, that cannot be achieved by rupturing, negating or contradicting their most important and defining attributes. The music-historical problem for jazz has been its resistance to assimilation into the Western 'art music' tradition because of fundamental aesthetic conflicts. The criteria for determining what is a beautiful or 'legitimate' style of singing and playing in jazz, for example, are frequently at odds with the criteria that prevail in 'art music'. The classical operatic voice can be related to instrumental techniques and standards of beauty of tone production within that style. Jazz has its own range of associated vocal techniques, many of which are not found in classical music – scatting, growling and smearing or bending notes – and can also be related to instrumental techniques within that style (for example, the use of a plunger mute to create a growling sound on trumpet or trombone). The existence of distinct musical style codes in the nineteenth century is made evident in the incompatibility of Beethoven's Viennese style to the Scottish airs he arranged.

An even more distinct style code, *piobaireachd* – a unique kind of bagpipe music that originated among the Gaelic communities of the Scottish Highlands and Islands – may be used to illustrate the way meaning depends on sociocultural context rather than on universally valid musical devices. The interval of the tritone (that between fah and te in tonic sol-fa) conveyed emotional anguish to seventeenth-century Venetians, as we know from their madrigals and operas; yet, it evidently did not carry this meaning to seventeenth-century Scottish Highlanders. There is an old *piobaireachd* of uncertain date bearing the title 'Praise of Marion' (*Guileagag Moraig*) which, in one variation alone, contains twenty-nine tritones within thirty-two bars.

A final example of how style codes have their own conventions and construct their own meanings is revealed by comparing Richard Strauss's 'Dance of the Seven Veils' (from his opera *Salome*) with David Rose's 'The Stripper'. In the latter, one notes the quasi-vocal slides on trombone and the wailing *tremolando* on a 'blue' seventh followed by 'jungle' drums: these were among the devices developed originally by Ellington at the Cotton Club to signify the wild and the primitive for his white patrons, and which soon became associated with wild, predatory female sexuality. The eroticism of the Strauss, on the other hand, is encoded in the sensual richness (timbral and textural) of a huge orchestra, the quasi-**Oriental** (that is, exotic) embellishment of melody, and the devices of *crescendo* and quickening pace. However, it is surely no coincidence that, despite the anachronism, the Viennese waltz with its connotations of *fin de siècle* decadence lies just below the surface of the Strauss, as the foxtrot lies below that of the Rose. There is no sense, of course, in which one of these pieces of music is really sexier than the other; each encodes eroticism in a different way and for a different function. It would be just as ludicrous to imagine Strauss's 'Dance of the Seven Veils' in a seedy strip club as to imagine Rose's 'The Stripper' incorporated into *Salome*.

MEANING AS AN EFFECT OF DISCOURSE

Seeing seven colours in a rainbow is an effect of Newtonian **discourse**, Sir Isaac Newton having added the colour indigo in his determination that a rainbow should have seven colours. Similarly, hearing an octave divided into twelve semitones is an effect of a particular Western musical discourse, that of equal temperament tuning. An empiricist would argue that a transcendental subject acquires knowledge by observing or listening, but other cultures see five or six colours in a rainbow and divide an octave into intervals that differ from the Western classical norm. If a discourse divides the spectrum into certain named coloured segments, then those are the ones that are seen. If a musical discourse – that is, a domain of musical practice or a musical style – divides an octave into quarter tones, these may be perceived in another cultural context as out-of-tune notes or 'corrected' by the ear to the nearest acceptable pitch. If a typical Western scale is conceived as seven notes, then a Chinese pentatonic melody appears to be based on a scale with two notes missing.

EMPHASIS ON RECEPTION AND SUBJECT POSITION

It has become important to ask who the implied audience might be for a piece of music. Whom do Nanci Griffith, Amy Winehouse and Angela Gheorghiu think they are singing to? The way the music sounds may indicate that it is intended, for example, for a salon, a concert hall or outdoors. If so, this may have affected the composition in terms of form and instrumentation. Beethoven's folksong arrangements for piano, violin and cello suggest he has a salon concert in mind. Certain ensembles carry greater status than others: for example, a string quartet would be regarded in some circles as more refined and 'elevated' than a saxophone quartet no matter what music was played. Some of the Edinburgh bourgeoisie may well have found Beethoven's Scottish folksong arrangements convincing, since they sought a 'refined' or 'improved' version of their musical heritage. The subject position one occupies can radically affect reception: until the 1980s, few critics in the West recognized the extent of Dmitri Shostakovitch's use of **irony** in his music.

THE DISAPPEARING 'REAL', THE SIMULACRUM AND PROBLEMS OF AUTHENTICITY

Within **poststructuralist** theory, notions of an 'inner essence' and a 'real' disappeared. In her performances, Diamanda Galás has employed a variety of extreme non-verbal vocal techniques (screaming, howling) to convey a sense of real suffering, but she has also featured in the soundtrack of a Dracula film. 'Authenticity' can be seen to be constructed as one more style: values of truth and authenticity will be set up in the dress codes and styles of singing of performers (folk singers do not wear pin-stripe suits), perhaps in the instruments they play (for example, acoustic instruments tend to signify such values better than electronic instruments). A performer who can be pinned down to a particular image, such as Bruce Springsteen, will communicate a deeper impression of authenticity than a performer who plays multiple roles, such as David Bowie. Yet, Karaoke singers can pour their hearts out in a quick succession of styles, being Sinatra for one song and Elvis for the next.

In some areas of music there are examples of Jean Baudrillard's **simulacra**, where there is not even an attempt to be real, or where reality has been appropriated by a fiction. The 'jungle music' created by Ellington's band, or Hollywood 'cowboy songs' are ready examples. A more complex matter is Orientalist music. In spite of the differences that developed over the years in Western **representations** of the East in music, the successive Orientalist styles tended to relate to previous Orientalist styles more closely than they did to Eastern ethnic practices. It is not surprising, because Orientalist music is not a poor imitation of another cultural practice: its purpose is not to imitate but to represent.[7] Representations, however, rely upon culturally learned recognition, and this may have much to do with a person's existing knowledge of Western signifiers of the East and little to do with the objective conditions of non-Western musical practices. Indeed, something new may be brought into being which displaces and stands in for the Orient. These can happen whenever music is taken from its home culture into another. Some of the Native American chants on the popular album *Sacred Spirit* of 1995 are given romantic ambient or 'chill out' arrangements, while others are 'housed up' with looped patterns and other features that lend them the character of late twentieth-century dance electronica.

The emphasis on **hybridity** in **postcolonial** studies (much indebted to the arguments of Homi K. Bhabha) demands that musical traditions be examined as mixtures and fusions of styles rather than being analysed in search of 'authentic' features, unadulterated by the impact of globalization or a former colonizing presence. Although this enables a reconsideration of, say, South African choralism or Bollywood film music, a problem remains in the term 'hybridity' since it can, itself, imply the existence of pure strains – as every gardener who has grown F1 hybrids knows.

Musicology has also had to take on board the lessons of Jacques Derrida's **deconstruction**, which is concerned with demonstrating the privileging of one term over another in metaphysical oppositions. There is no longer a case to be made for supposedly 'pure' music. Even the music of a composer like Anton Bruckner can be deconstructed to expose ideological assumptions behind what may seem to be abstract musico-logical choices. In his music, meaning is created by differing and deferring (Derrida's *différance*): minor is governed by major and therefore the minor opening of the Third Symphony is not mistaken for the dominant term; we know major will triumph. Minor is *always* the antithesis – but not a true antithesis, because Bruckner privileges major over minor.

DEATH OF THE COMPOSER AS ORIGINATING GENIUS

Music technology, especially sampling, which allows existing sounds to be recorded and re-used or manipulated at will has had a major impact on ideas of originality, creativity and ownership. So has the wide availability of pre-programmed features on sound modules, synthesizers, drum machines and keyboards. The producers and DJs in Hip-Hop, House, Techno and Underground Dance, who select parts of records, add sounds, blend features, combine tracks, restructure or remix, eat away at notions of **authorship**. Nicolas Bourriaud draws upon ideas from *Chaosmosis* by Félix Guattari to argue for the role of the artist 'as an operator of meaning, rather than a pure "creator" relying on crypto-divine inspiration'.[8] Bourriaud claims that the 'new cultural land-scape [is] marked by the twin figures of the DJ and the programmer, both of whom have the task of selecting cultural objects and inserting them into new contexts'.[9] This is the case with the 'mash-up': one of the most celebrated exam-ples (perhaps because of EMI's attempt to block its distribution) is the *Grey Album* (2004), in which Brian Burton (DJ Danger Mouse) mixed together the Beatles's *White Album* (1968) and Jay-Z's *Black Album* (2003).

We must also recognize that postmodernist theory, poststructuralism and deconstruction have strongly challenged notions of organic unity and the composer's expressive **presence** within his or her music. The use of sampling technology shifts the focus from new *creation* to new *use* of material. In her own person, Madonna has re-used existing images and taken on multiple identities in contrast to the stable identity of earlier stars (and of some of her contempo-raries, like Bruce Springsteen). Pop music revels in **intertextuality** and the circu-lation of meanings (for example, through merchandizing). Music is one among its many attributes and not always its most important one, since dance routines, fashion, image, persona creation, special effects, the performance event and its context may each take precedence at one time or another.

POSTMODERN MUSICOLOGY

The rise since the 1990s of 'feminist musicology', 'critical musicology', and 'gay and lesbian musicology' prompts the idea that, instead of there being alternative musicologies, we may be witnessing the disintegration of musicology as a disci-pline. Perhaps, the unitary concept of a discipline is part of a now discredited paradigm for musicological thought. The alternative is to view musicology no longer as an autonomous field of academic inquiry but, in the French psychoan-alyst and **semiotician** Julia Kristeva's terms, a field of transpositions of various signifying systems. Critical musicology has revealed what it means to regard musicology as an *intertextual field*, and why this, rather than the notion of a *discipline*, offers a more productive epistemological framework for research.

In the late 1980s, a New Musicology developed in the USA among concerns about the presumption in much historical and systematic musicology that music could be studied autonomously, rather than in historical and cultural context. In the United Kingdom, a Critical Musicology Group was founded (1993) to discuss the importance of critique, including the critique of musicology itself. Critical and New Musicologists wished to explore the socially constituted values of music. In doing so, a variety of methodologies and analytic tools are brought into play: these range from Marxist-influenced cultural sociology to semiotic, poststructuralist and postmodernist theories, Derrida's deconstructive manoeuvres, the discourse analysis of Michel Foucault, and the psychoanalytic insights of Sigmund Freud, Jacques Lacan and Julia Kristeva.

Postmodern musicology refuses to be restricted to analysing the formal workings of music and compiling data on the influences of one composer on another; it is keen to address questions of extrinsic meaning in music. There are those who focus on individual works, teasing out their worldly meanings, while others reject close readings, seeking, instead, a radical contextualization of musical production and a deeper understanding of how music is experienced by performers and listeners. The most recent disagreements are between those who look to the way music interacts with everyday life, and those who strive to reveal ideological meanings embedded in the music – often, the former return to empirical models of research that poststructuralism rejected (empiricism being 'the matrix of all faults menacing a discourse' for Derrida).[10]

One of the biggest problems facing current musicology is the collapse of the binary divide between pop and classical. The disintegration of high and low as aesthetic values has, of course, been felt already in other subject areas: consider how far **Cultural Studies** has encroached upon English as an academic discipline. The attention given by sociologists and musicologists to popular music in the 1990s led to several universities offering specialized degrees in this area. What musicology needs now is a new theoretical model capable of embracing all music. An outline of what this might look like is given below:

- A concern with social and cultural processes, informed by arguments that musical practices, values and meanings relate to particular historical, political and cultural contexts.
- A concern with critical theory and with developing a musical hermeneutics for the analysis of the values and meanings of musical practices and musical texts.
- A concern to avoid teleological assumptions of historical narrative (e.g. the 'inevitability' of atonality). Causal narration in musical historiography has been found problematic: genealogical lines connecting one composer (or musical style) with another are forever being redrawn or erased, and new musical styles are occasionally presented as if they sprang up fully formed (for example, New Orleans jazz).
- A readiness to engage with, rather than marginalize, issues of class, generation, gender, sexuality and ethnicity in music, and to address matters such as production, reception and subject position, while questioning notions of genius, canons, universality, aesthetic autonomy and **textual** immanence.
- A readiness to contest the binary divide between 'classical' and 'popular', since both may be perceived as intimately related to the same social formation.

- A readiness to study different cultures with regard to their own specific cultural values, so that a cultural arbitrary is not misrecognized as an objective truth, but also to recognize the necessity of extending the terms of such study beyond explicit cultural self-evaluation.
- A readiness to consider that meanings are intertextual, and that it may be necessary to examine a broad range of discourses in order to explain music, its contexts and the way it functions within them. For example, questions of music and sexuality cannot be considered in isolation from political, biological, psychological, psychoanalytical and aesthetic discourses. There may be no intention, however, to document each area comprehensively.
- A readiness to respond to the multiplicity of music's contemporary functions and meanings (for example, the fusions of practices variously described as 'time-based arts' and 'multimedia arts'). This may be achieved by adopting the epistemological position and methodology outlined above (one requiring intertextual study and the blurring of discipline boundaries); it contrasts with a narrow discipline-based study of music as performance art or as composition (typically represented by the printed score).

NOTES

1 Claude Debussy, 'Monsieur Croche the Dilettante Hater', in Claude Debussy, Ferruccio Busoni and Charles Ives, *Three Classics in the Aesthetics of Music* (New York: Dover, 1962).

2 Richard A. Peterson, 'The Rise and Fall of Highbrow Snobbery as a Status Marker', *Poetics*, 25 (1997), pp. 75–92.

3 Raymond Williams, *The Long Revolution* (Harmondsworth: Penguin, 1961), p. 69.

4 Robert P. Morgan, 'Rewriting Music History – Second Thoughts on Ives and Varèse', *Musical Newsletter*, 111:1 (January, 1973), pp. 3–12.

5 Arnold Schoenberg, *Letters*, trans. Ethne Wilkins and Ernst Kaiser, ed. Edwin Stein (London: Faber & Faber, 1964), p. 28.

6 Igor Stravinsky, *Poetics of Music* [1942] (Cambridge, MA: Harvard University Press, 1974).

7 Derek B. Scott, *From the Erotic to the Demonic: On Critical Musicology* (New York: Oxford University Press, 2003), p. 174.

8 Nicolas Bourriaud, *Relational Aesthetics* [1998], trans. Simon Pleasance and Fronza Woods (Dijon: Les presses du réel, 2002), p. 93; Félix Guattari, *Chaosmosis: An Ethicoaesthetic Paradigm*, trans. Paul Bains and Julian Pefanis (Bloomington, IN: Indiana University Press, 1995).

9 Nicolas Bourriaud, *Postproduction: Culture as Screenplay*, trans. Jeanine Hernan (New York: Lukas & Sternberg, 2002), p. 13.

10 Jacques Derrida, *Writing and Difference* [1967], trans. Alan Bass (Chicago: University of Chicago Press, 1978), p. 364.

17

POSTMODERNISM AND PERFORMANCE

SUSAN MELROSE

> Stelarc is not a conceptual artist. He is not interested in communicating ideas
> *about* the body. What he is interested in is experiencing the body as concept. ...
> The ideas he takes as his medium ... do not pre-exist their physical expression.
> ... It was only after the manifestation of the ideas began in the body that they
> were able to be disengaged enough from it to enter speech and writing.
>
> (Brian Massumi, *Parables for the Virtual*, 2002, p. 89)

Why start with so many negatives, above, in an attempt to account for **postmodern** performance? Jean-François Lyotard: 'I have favored a certain pro-
cedure [in *The Postmodern Condition*]: emphasizing facts of language and in
particular their pragmatic aspect.'[1] What's in a name – Stelarc, Massumi,
Lyotard? And what is the effect of a suffix – as in postmodern-*ism* – when our
concern here, it appears, is with performing the postmodern/postmodern performances? What do we *do with* names, if and when we pronounce or write (that is,
perform) them, and what, once again, is *performed* if we add the suffix '-ism' to
the noun 'the postmodern', or '-ist' to the qualifier 'postmodern'? Naming itself
is a word game, rather than a straightforward reference to *the way things are*.
Nominalization, some have argued, has an 'ontologising' force[2] – as though
through the event of naming itself, a speaker or writer can summon or conjure
what is named into being, almost as though it is already 'in being', already exists,
and can simply be called forth, once again. This essay suggests that while its
name is widely spoken and written, 'postmodern-*ism*' has not yet been
performed, in the times and spaces of performance itself – which does not mean,
however, that postmodern performances have not taken place, nor that the
postmodern has not been performed: they have been, and I would argue that
they continue to be, although these may no longer be postmodern in the sense of
the term specific to its earlier emergence and reception by spectators. Plainly,
this essay is discipline-specific, to the extent that 'performance' names a complex
set of practices, relational and internally differentiated, each of which, nonetheless, conforms to a certain plane of consistency, on which basis we tend to
cluster them together, in certain registers of writing.

As far as academic writing is concerned, you might have noted, I have chosen
above to emphasize not only 'facts of language and in particular their pragmatic
aspect', but also the problematic relationship between that 'pragmatic aspect'
of language and performances, to which Massumi, translator with Geoff

Bennington of Lyotard's *The Postmodern Condition*, draws our attention. Massumi's concern in his book *Parables of the Virtual* is with knowledge itself – recalling, in this, Lyotard's late 1970s 'report on knowledge'– and with certain erasures, practised in theoretical writing over preceding decades, to the end of a major debunking of conservative institutions. In Massumi's terms, then, much of the critical-theoretical writing in 'academic' registers of the later twentieth century, is one word game among others, albeit one that tends to assert its authority over others; its relationship to that other complex game that is post-modern performance remains in question, as Massumi argues above, in the case of Stelarc's performance.

Massumi, one might argue, summons 'Stelarc' into being, above, by performing the name of the artist, in order to attempt to achieve certain ends: to bring about a change in the established 'academic' orders of being, according to which 'ideas' are better articulated in speech and writing – in, for example, that writing gathered under the name of 'Performance Studies' – rather than in performances themselves; better articulated by performance theorists, for example, than by those practitioners upon whose work the theoretical writer also depends. Massumi's project, in the early twenty-first century, in its stated concern with movement, affect and sensation, has been of keen interest to ways of seeing, doing and understanding in the arts in general, but I would argue that it is of keen interest to performance in particular. It was identified and posi-tioned, in 2001, in the following terms: 'to explore the implications for cultural theory of this simple conceptual displacement: body(movement/sensation)-change', in the face of 'postmodern celebrations of **aporia**'.[3] In that focus on movement, affect, sensation, and in his brief allusion to 'postmodern aporia', one might argue, the writer provides us with a notion of the postmodern and of a twenty-first century *post*-**postmodern** that challenges certain excesses of the discourses of 'Performance Studies' of the later decades of the twentieth century – typified, perhaps, by the notion of a postmodern *performance without repre-sentations*, which found its *raison d'être* in Gilles Deleuze's 1968 text **Difference and Repetition**. Recalling the *idea* of theatrical performance in traditions of phil-osophical writing, Deleuze called for acts that might:

> put metaphysics in motion[,] ... make it act, and make it carry out immediate acts ... of producing within the work a movement capable of affecting the mind outside of all representation[,] ... vibrations, rotations, whirling, gravitations, dances or leaps which directly touch the mind.[4]

In terms of Lyotard's 'facts of language and in particular their pragmatic aspect', what we might note of the lines quoted above is that they are action-heavy, but curiously and pointedly, as far as material performances are concerned, they lack an active subject – for example, the (grammatical) agency of an artist – a performer, a choreographer, a director. They take as their target 'the mind', rather than the live spectator, willingly positioned in a performance space and time, of which they are in part constitutive. In terms of performance action, and of that constitutive relationality (performer-spectator), Deleuze's explicit *philosophical* orientation, in the late 1960s, was to a 'pure staging without author, without actors and without subjects', or, at least, with actors and subjects who are 'larvae, since they alone are capable of sustaining the lines, the slippages and the rotations' that 'directly touch the mind'.[5]

I cite this tradition of academic writing that is in name at least apparently 'about theatre/performance' here, not because, to my mind, it conjures up realities of (postmodern) performances – which I am likely, instead, to experience/ have experienced in the theatre work of the UK companies, 'Forced Entertainment' and 'Blast Theory', the American and Canadian artists and companies, Robert Wilson, Robert Lepage and Goat Island and in the performance work of Stelarc and the recent Abramovic. Instead, I am concerned in this chapter to sketch out a still striking curiosity of the performance disciplines – especially in the case of what Jon McKenzie has called 'aesthetic performance'[6] – which is its simultaneous recourse to the human expertise of a performer, and to a live spectator, on the one hand, and, on the other, a distaste, in many later twentieth-century performance-theoretical writers, for precisely that human **presence** and expertise, active in performance-designated times and spaces. Theatre institutions, Jill Dolan once asserted, male, middle-aged, white and conservative, were performed, in precisely those terms, in such a way that it seemed that the institution itself needed to be challenged, accused, interrogated, exploded, side-stepped, ignored.[7] Yet experimental counter-performances in 'non-designated' spaces and times, auto-reflexive and playful, liminal and subversive as they strove to be, as long as they retained that constitutive performance relationality identified above, were hard-pressed to escape what was then entailed in the humanist tradition, without simultaneously losing their audience.

We return below to the issue of the historical placing of the early postmodern, to its relationship to an apparently invasive technological change in the early decades after the Second World War, to early notions of loss and nostalgia for that loss, and to more recent post-postmodern performance. This latter has taken rapid technological change as a widely marketed given,[8] normalized and naturalized, rather than 'new', and has returned, after the fall of the Berlin Wall and the illegal invasion of Iraq, to an explicit relationship with 'history' – without, however, a simultaneous return to subservience to the authoritative explanatory discourses, the practices, the aspiration and the belief in scientific progress identified in the earlier twentieth century with the modern. On a similar basis, it will be difficult in terms of the historical to avoid the double question of the incomplete project of **modernity** (Jürgen Habermas)[9] and its implications for arts-practitioners and spectators. Nor, if we are concerned with historical circumstance and the emergence of postmodern practices, can we overlook the role of performance in the *événements* of May 1968, which provided not just a socio-political context to the collaboration of Deleuze and Guattari but a backdrop to Lyotard's report published some ten years later.[10]

I would argue, to return to my opening question, that whenever the qualifier 'postmodern-*ist*' is used in connection with performance, that use tends to be critical and **writerly**, positioned in the zone of spectating and often after its event, rather than in those of performance-making and its times and processes; that its use is borderline-pejorative, with regard to whatever is being qualified by the performance-maker's **other**. Yet a number of writers on the postmodern seem almost carelessly to use these suffixes – as though the postmodern and postmodernism, the modern, modernity and **modernism** were interchangeable. They are not. To begin this essay with naming *as a mode of performance* ('how to do things [and how to cause things to happen] with words')[11] within what might now be called a 'post-postmodern scene', might seem to be a strange way to enter into an account of historically specific changes in performance-making and spectating, yet as we have already seen, naming itself, an everyday and banal activity as well as one of interest to philosophers, *performs* something. Use of the term 'the postmodern' in the final decades of the twentieth century actually *performed* a shift in established relationships with knowledge, whereas I am arguing that use of the term 'postmodernism' did and does not. The notion of such a shift in relationships with knowledge in the second half of the twentieth century and thereafter engages us, in the university at least, with that 'report' on knowledge initially proposed by Lyotard.

Plainly Lyotard's written 'report' on knowledge, however ingenious the noetic leap it also performed, was already reflective: it *re*-flected his and others' perceptions of 'tendencies' in the arts and in cultural practices more generally in relationship to changing technologies, and the 're-' of 'reflect' demonstrates an orientation to the past in the present. It was 'already historical', in that it looked back at the recent past, even as it outlined its own present circumstance, as well as prescient. How the terms and issues outlined in his report (or reports of his report), came to the attention of performance-makers, or crystallized 'something' of which performance-makers were already aware, remains a question of some keen interest to those of us who are concerned with art-making and makers, as well as with, or as distinct from, spectating. This reference to moments of historical emergence (post-Second World War) and to the recent past needs to be qualified by an equally important point, which is that qualities identifiable in terms of the performance postmodern can be traced to earlier incidents of twentieth-century experimentation in the arts, and to different cultural contexts. Expert invention in creative practice tends to pre-date written reflection upon it – whence the qualifier 'experimental'. Yet many artist-performance-makers whose work has been identified in terms of the early postmodern, have seemed to share, with Lyotard's 'report on knowledge', the philosopher's concern with some of the implications of the (mis-)use of technological and scientific 'advancement', typified in the Second World War by the Holocaust (where the identification of indices of racial and religious identity led to extermination of the Jewish people) and the nuclear bombing by Allied forces of Hiroshima.

In Johannes Birringer's *Theater, Theory, Postmodernism*, indicatively, the writer recounted his experience in 1969 in Frankfurt of Joseph Beuys's action event *Iphigenia/Titus*, in which Beuys 'sat inside an enclosure with a white horse that quietly ate hay and gazed at us', vital but indifferent to the onlookers; and of Beuys's 'shift toward a pedagogical action or sculpting process' in his *Show us your Wound* (1979), which, according to Birringer at least, 'clearly referred to the destructiveness of the concentration camps and the Holocaust'.[12] In this case, for Birringer as spectator-writer, at least, performance, in Beuys's case, marking a shift in the use of the personal self in performance – the self performed by the artist becomes a vehicle for a knowledge practice – was at the same time irretrievably positioned, historically and politically. That performance and its use of self, for Birringer, was bound irresistibly back to moments of a historical as well as a personal trauma; it was bound-in, by the same token, to an eternal return to the ways those traumatic circumstances impact upon the artist and spectator implicated. Yet Joseph Beuys's pedagogic 'post'-performances and his 'sculpting', identified by Gregory Ulmer as shamanistic:

> turns out to be descriptive of a major trend in modern art, beginning with the 'primitivism' of the early modernists [sic] (Gauguin, Picasso) and extending through to contemporary 'abreaction' and 'ritual' modes of performance and body art (Vito Acconci, Dennis Oppenheim) equally find its place and time within a twentieth century avant-garde.[13]

The 'post-' of performance, in other words, tends to be unable to avoid continuity with its own disciplinary past, to the extent, in part, that a relationally constitutive spectator participates in its event, recuperating discontinuities – often enough in order to 'make [a] sense of them'. In terms of naming, with which this essay began, 'post'-performance retains the latter term as disciplinary identifier, despite the later twentieth-century concern, not least among Performance Studies theorists, with the (anonymous and banal) performances of everyday life.[14] Some writers make a distinction between performances qualified as 'aesthetic' and those identified as 'cultural',[15] without effectively identifying the markers of the one and the other, and without letting go of the notion of performance as actional, taking its (relational) place in time, thereby making itself available to the actions of spectating of an **other**. Performance, 'post-' and 'post-post-', continues to take its place and time as complex action, bound-in to and orientated to spectating, regardless of that widely cited and heady Deleuzian anticipation in *Difference and Repetition*, cited above, according to which a newly *theatricalized* philosophy (or a philosophical theatricality?) would entail that pure staging without author, actors and subjects.

Post-postmodern performances continue to employ (in all senses of the term) *performers*, whatever the nature of the latter; and whereas the 'body-ness' of the avatar might seem to provide a perfected example of the Deleuzian '**body without organs**', I would argue that it remains the case that a spectatorial

semiotic engagement will tend to be organized in part, however discontinuous her or his attempt, to attribute a role and often a responsibility in its making to a creative human **subject** or subjects, in whose name/s, thereafter, judgements of taste and value continue to be made. Efficacity in performance continues to be required to the extent that performances require of spectators an investment of and in time.

A spectatorial drive to identify and/or constitute indices of the human self remains, whether or not as spectators one attributes that selfhood to performer or directorial figure or function, regardless of the accusation that such a quest binds the quester unwittingly in, to a tradition of self-referentiality. Hence the performance project of 'body artist' Stelarc, as Massumi pointed out above, would be a double bind: a 'body artist', working within performance, who 'is not a conceptual artist' concerned with ideas '*about* the body', but is instead 'interested in ... experiencing the body *as* concept'. Before I continue here I need to intervene in terms that might recall my opening query: when we are concerned with performance-making by expert artist-practitioners, among whom Stelarc is included, it is worth observing that Stelarc's concern, as Massumi puts it, can only lie with 'the body' to the extent that – not entirely unlike Beuys, above – he engages his own body, and all that goes with (and within) it – including the self-referentiality hard to separate from much artistic action – in this enquiry. The point is vital: although the visual arts more generally have taken 'the body' as a privileged site of enquiry, the performing arts are particular in the sense that the starting-point as far as 'the performer' is concerned is 'whole human' and active or action-focused, in the performance-relational framework, orientated, in the majority of circumstances, to equally present spectatorly bodies. It is only on the basis of this relational circumstance that we can grapple with the performance problematic of the postmodern: the body present/presented – performer and spectator – brings with it, and engages actively, whatever one may know of, experience, and take to be the parameters of the self.

> PROJECT: 'extend intelligence beyond the earth';
> MEDIUM: the body.
> *Correction*: the body is obsolete.[16]

The assertedly obsolete body of a performer, referenced by Deleuze, above, yet performed for its other – not *wholly* unlike the widely distributed self in multi-authored electronic arts where that distributed self is a vehicle for a differently modulated knowledge practice – does nothing, *in the event* (taken literally) to erase the drive, in a spectator-other, to identify and to recuperate self from that dispersion and from that performed obsolescence. Indeed, the relational unit – self and other – that is constitutive to performance, modern or 'post-', would seem to guarantee to performance a particular and a continuous identity across history/histories. To the extent that performance decision-making is constitu-tively relational and calculated in terms of an other – whether or not the artist/s acknowledge/s that constitutive relational specificity – 'the body' of 'the spec-tator' explicit or implicit in the act, refutes obsolescence in its performer-other. To the extent that I, as spectator, intuit the role of a mind implicit in both the body of my spectating and in the activity of my performer-other, then perfor-mance itself simultaneously allows and confounds some of the excesses of the artist.

One answer to my initial question above, then, might well be that to add the suffix '-ism', to the 'postmodern' – or to the 'modern', for that matter – is itself a modern*ist* strategy, whose implications lean toward the pejorative. I would argue that its easy use *converts* (it is, in Austinian speech act terms, felicitously *performative*) what is named into a fixed, generalized and uniform category of knowledge, viewed historically, by which I mean that its naming and classifica-tion tends to occur after the moment of the emergence of the practice/s thereby categorized. Use of the suffix itself, in other words, is almost effortlessly objecti-fying and historicizing. Its addition in naming tends to fix dynamic and often barely wordable, borderline or challenging practices into a manageable knowl-edge category, and it tends to convert those practices and the 'objects' (or 'knowledge objects') concerned into stereotypical examples of the same cate-gory. In Derridean terms, its uses practice closure upon the dynamic, the chal-lenging and the deferred. I would go so far as to intimate that the addition of the suffix, and the conversion that it performs, is almost effortlessly abusive of what it seems/seeks merely to name. Used by the critic-spectator, it classifies, objecti-fies and – effectively – it *others* the work of the artist. Despite this, the suffix is widely used, apparently innocently of these sorts of implications. In Birringer's *Theater, Theory, Postmodernism*, once again, the comma used in place of the simple conjunction ('*and* Postmodernism) mimics a postmodern principle of composition, whereas the suffix apparently irresistibly renders the final term categorical, classificatory. (Writing has its own traps, when it comes to post-modern practices: the use of the clause and the sentence are obedient to the rules (hence to the authority) of grammar as master code.)

While the 'report on knowledge' that Lyotard published in 1979 is, unavoid-ably, historically specific – it concerns 'a transition' that Lyotard identified, in the late 1970s, as having 'been underway since at least the end of the 1950s' – the 'Postmodern Perspective' he identified depended then and still depends today on the impact of technological change on ways of seeing, doing and knowing more generally:

> These technological transformations can be expected to have a considerable impact on knowledge. Its two principal functions – research and the transmission of acquired learning – are already feeling the effect, or will in the future ... [G]enetics provides an example that is accessible to the layman: it owes its theoretical para-digm to cybernetics. ... [It] is common knowledge that the miniaturisation and commercialisation of machines is already changing the way in which learning is acquired, classified, made available, and exploited.[17]

Yet Lyotard's use of tense here – 'can be expected to have' – articulated the technological specificity of the time of writing, and cannot readily be transferred to this twenty-first-century context of reading and writing: it is tied to its own present moment, and is now history. Nonetheless, his identification of a 'condition' was at the time a masterly turn, itself rich in postmodern implications, in the sense that it is almost impossible to boundary-mark, classify or catalogue everything that constitutes a condition. His *Report on Knowledge* was neither a manifesto, nor did he identify it as a treatise. After all, its writer might well have wanted – and needed – to avoid some of the trappings of authority in writing, which authority he had nonetheless mastered. My *sense* – and I use the term deliberately – is that what use of the noun 'condition' *performs* was quite deliberately targeted: a 'condition' (most are familiar with the hackneyed 'human condition') can range – almost viral in its progression – across not only all sorts of aspects of contemporary life, but has no clear beginning, middle or end; in addition, it is not necessarily terminal. Moreover, one 'condition' can conceal and indeed co-exist with another: its identification does not exhaust the ways contemporary culture can be understood, by which I mean that a postmodern condition can co-exist with and has co-existed with Habermas's identification, in the 1980s, of the incomplete project of modernity.

In spite of the gloom, warnings and nostalgia of those in the early post-Second World War decades who anticipated the inroads of rapid technological change on the self as it was experienced and understood, more recent writing suggests that the techno-future foreseen by Lyotard in the late 1970s, in which the 'thorough exteriorisation of knowledge with respect to the "knower"' would give rise to a level of participation in, access to, transfer and sharing of knowledge in all of its registers including the personal and intimate', is already here[18] – *and is performed*, in performance registers that retain their engagement with that plane of consistency through which performances are identified and named as such. If it is 'posthuman', in the terms N. Katharine Hayles set out,[19] it is no less concerned – arguably it is more concerned – with the human and the humanist. Its operations on and the widespread understanding of the processes, mechanism and apparatuses of the digital, its revealing of the meta-plane in the organization and operations of knowledge, have allowed the similarly widespread recognition of networks and systems, options and modes of engagement as such. Nancy Baym's *Personal Connections in the Digital Age* suggests that ICT may well not have brought about the sorts of transformational effects that writers in the 1970s and later decades predicted, in terms of self, professional self and relational other.[20] In arguing, in what might be described as post-Kantian mode, that *life gets in the way*, Baym identifies a resistant humanism that stands up to techno-determinism; which means that while we may use ICT in all sorts of ways, the self, continuous with twentieth-century senses of that late modern self, remains more or less intact and active. Contextualization, in personal and societal terms, is vital to our demonstrating that in spite of greater **complexity**, changes are less radical than 1970s writers might have supposed. The predictions for knowledge, in Lyotard's terms, have not been realized wholesale.

In the title itself of his *Postdramatic Theatre*, Hans-Thies Lehmann (and/or his English translator) adroitly combine/s the name of a discipline ('Theatre'), with a qualifier that includes the 'post'-mark widely associated with the challenge to or interrogation of another disciplinary category ('drama', 'dramatic', 'postdrama').[21] Certainly by his decision to foreground the discipline of theatre – and of dramatic theatre, at that (the 'post'-mark always also references the tradition) – Lehmann simultaneously locates his enquiry in a quite precisely delineated area of performance and/or performance theory: this is not, that is to say, a book 'about performance', and nor does it seem to be 'about' postmodern performance or performances. After all, if, in the Goffman tradition 'everything (every action) is performance', or performed, only a few of these performances might be described as dramatic-theatrical.[22] The whole world is not, in other words, a stage, or at any rate not a theatre stage, regardless of postmodern interdisciplinary slipperiness.

I raise these issues of naming, discipline and the 'post'-(mark), once again, in part because Lehmann does so too, in a work already described, at the moment of its first publication in English (1999), as a European classic; in part because I am interested in what might be called the 'performance of the performance-theoretical' in writing, and in the question of whether a 'performance-post-*theoretical*' might be better performed theatrically. That is, the performance-post-theoretical might be better performed in a divided space in which skills other than those peculiar to academic published *writing/writers* engage with their audiences. One thing we can't say of Lehmann's text is that it is 'postbook', 'postgrammatical' or 'postacademic', because it *works* (its *work* is) entirely conventional in grammatical, academic and publishing terms. Nor is it 'post-theoretical', since the writer's mode of engagement remains 'theoretical': he is an expert spectator, not a creative practitioner. What this series of 'non-post' marks means – to me at least – is that whereas a supremely professional, expert-theoretical writer like Lehmann can write persuasively and in an illuminating manner 'about' the postdramatic theatrical, for an academic audience, he cannot be said to perform it, and nor, by the same token, do his readers experience it.

NOTES

1 Jean-François Lyotard, *The Postmodern Condition: A Report on Knowledge* [1979], trans. Geoff Bennington and Brian Massumi (Manchester: Manchester University Press, 1984), p. 9.
2 See, for example, Peter Osborne, *Philosophy in Cultural Theory* (London: Routledge, 2000), p. 18.
3 Brian Massumi, *Parables for the Virtual: Movement, Affect, Sensation* (Durham, NC: Duke University Press, 2002), pp. 1, 69.
4 Gilles Deleuze, *Difference and Repetition* [1968], trans. Paul Patton (London: Athlone Press, 1994), p. 8.

5 Ibid.

6 Jon MacKenzie, *Perform or Else: From Discipline to Performance* (London: Routledge, 2001), p. 9.

7 Jill Dolan, 'Geographies of Learning: Theatre Studies, Performance and the Performative', *Theatre Journal*, 45:4 (1993), pp. 417–41.

8 Widely marketed, but not universally available, which tends to mean that 'we' are not yet, as Hayles has claimed, 'posthuman' (see N. Katharine Hayles, *How We Became Posthuman: Virtual Bodies in Cybernetics, Literature, and Informatics* (Chicago: University of Chicago Press, 1999)).

9 Jürgen Habermas, 'Modernity – An Incomplete Project', in Hal Foster, ed., *Postmodern Culture* (London: Pluto, 1985), pp. 3–15.

10 See, for example, Gilles Deleuze and Félix Guattari, *A Thousand Plateaus: Capitalism and Schizophrenia* [1980], trans. Brian Massumi (London: Athlone Press, 1988).

11 J. L. Austin, *How To Do Things With Words* (Oxford: Clarendon, 1962): along with the work of Erving Goffman (for example, *The Presentation of Self in Everyday Life* [1959] (Harmondsworth: Penguin, 1990)) on the performance of self and more recent writing on performativity, this post-Second World War text in linguistics and philosophy identified language use as having performative potential and force, felicitous or infelicitous.

12 Johannes Birringer, *Theater, Theory, Postmodernism* (Bloomington, IN: Indiana University Press, 1993), p. 13.

13 Gregory Ulmer, *Applied Grammatology: Post(e)-Pedagogy from Jacques Derrida to Joseph Beuys* (Baltimore, MD: Johns Hopkins University Press, 1985), p. 30.

14 This trend was crystallized in the work of Richard Schechner, in his *Performance Theory* (New York: Taylor & Francis, 1988).

15 See, for example, McKenzie, *Perform or Else*, p. 9.

16 Massumi, *Parables*, p. 89.

17 Lyotard, *Postmodern Condition*, p. 4.

18 Ibid.

19 See Hayles, *How We Became Posthuman*.

20 Nancy K. Baym, *Personal Connections in the Digital Age* (Cambridge: Polity Press, 2010).

21 Hans-Thies Lehmann, *Postdramatic Theatre* [1999], trans. Karen Jürs-Munby (London: Routledge, 2006).

22 See Goffman, *The Presentation of Self*.

18

POSTMODERNISM AND POPULAR CULTURE

JOHN STOREY

Most contributions to the debate on **postmodernism** agree that whatever else it is or might be, postmodernism has something to do with the development of popular culture in the late twentieth century in the advanced capitalist democracies of the West. That is, whether postmodernism is seen as a new historical moment, a new sensibility or a new cultural style, popular culture is cited as a terrain on which these changes can be most readily found.

It is in the late 1950s and early 1960s that we see the beginnings of what is now understood as postmodernism. In the work of the American cultural critic, Susan Sontag, we encounter the celebration of what she calls a 'new sensibility'. As she explains: 'One important consequence of the new sensibility [is] that the distinction between "high" and "low" culture seems less and less meaningful.'[1]

The postmodern 'new sensibility' rejected the cultural elitism of **modernism**. Although it often 'quoted' popular culture, modernism was marked by a deep suspicion of all things popular. Its entry into the museum and the academy as official culture was undoubtedly made easier (despite its declared antagonism to 'bourgeois philistinism') by its appeal to, and homologous relationship with, the elitism of class society. The response of the postmodern 'new sensibility' to modernism's canonization was a re-evaluation of popular culture. The postmodernism of the late 1950s and early 1960s was therefore in part a populist attack on the elitism of modernism. It signalled a refusal of what Andreas Huyssen calls 'the great divide ... [a] **discourse** which insists on the categorical distinction between high art and mass culture'.[2] Moreover, according to Huyssen: 'To a large extent, it is by the distance we have travelled from this "great divide" between mass culture and modernism that we can measure our own cultural **postmodernity**.'[3]

The American and British pop art movement of the 1950s and the 1960s, with its rejection of the distinction between popular and high culture, is postmodernism's first cultural flowering. As pop art's first theorist Lawrence Alloway explains:

> The area of contact was mass produced urban culture: movies, advertising, science fiction, pop music. We felt none of the dislike of commercial culture standard among most intellectuals, but accepted it as a fact, discussed it in detail, and consumed it enthusiastically. One result of our discussions was to take pop culture out of the realm of 'escapism', 'sheer entertainment', 'relaxation', and to treat it with the seriousness of art.[4]

Seen from this perspective, postmodernism first emerges out of a generational refusal of the categorical certainties of high modernism. The insistence on an absolute distinction between high and popular culture came to be regarded as the 'unhip' assumption of an older generation. One sign of this collapse can be seen in the merging of art and pop music. For example, Peter Blake designed the cover of the Beatles' 'Sergeant Pepper's Lonely Hearts Club Band'; Richard Hamilton designed the cover of their 'white album'; Andy Warhol designed the cover of the Rolling Stones' album 'Sticky Fingers'. We can also see this in the way the 'pop' of Bob Dylan and the Beatles was taken seriously as a new art form.

By the mid-1980s, the postmodern 'new sensibility' had become a condition and for many a reason to despair. According to Jean-François Lyotard the post-modern condition is marked by a crisis in the status of knowledge in Western societies. This is expressed as 'incredulity toward **metanarratives**', such as God, Marxism, scientific progress.[5] Steven Connor suggests that Lyotard's analysis may be read 'as a disguised allegory of the condition of academic knowledge and institutions in the contemporary world'. Lyotard's 'diagnosis of the postmodern condition is, in one sense, the diagnosis of the final futility of the intellectual'. Lyotard is himself aware of what he calls the contemporary intellectual's 'nega-tive heroism'. Intellectuals have, he argues, been losing their authority since 'the violence and critique mounted against the academy during the sixties'.[6] Iain Chambers makes much the same point but from a different perspective. He argues that the debate over postmodernism can in part be understood as:

> the symptom of the disruptive ingression of popular culture, its aesthetics and inti-mate possibilities, into a previously privileged domain. Theory and academic discourses are confronted by the wider, unsystemized, popular networks of cultural production and knowledge. The intellectual's privilege to explain and distribute knowledge is threatened.[7]

Like Chambers, Angela McRobbie welcomes postmodernism, seeing it as 'the coming into being of those whose voices were historically drowned out by the (modernist) metanarratives of mastery, which were in turn both patriarchal and imperialist'. Postmodernism, she argues, has enfranchised a new body of intel-lectuals: voices from the margins speaking from positions of **difference** – ethnic, gender, class, sexual preference; those whom she refers to as 'the new generation of intellectuals (often black, female, or working class)'.[8] Kobena Mercer makes a similar point, seeing postmodernism as in part an unacknowledged response to 'the emerging voices, practices and identities of dispersed African, Caribbean and Asian peoples [who have] crept in from the margins of post-imperial Britain to dislocate commonplace certainties and consensual "truths" and thus open up new ways of seeing, and understanding'.[9]

For Jean Baudrillard, **hyperrealism** is the characteristic mode of postmoder-nity. In the realm of the 'hyperreal', the 'real' and the imaginary continually implode into each other.[10] The result is that reality and what Baudrillard calls '**simulations**' are experienced as without difference – operating along a roller-coaster continuum. Simulations can often be experienced as more real than the real itself – 'even better than the real thing', in the words of the U2 song. The evidence for hyperrealism is said to be everywhere. For example, we in the West live in a world in which people write letters addressed to characters in soap operas, making them offers of marriage, sympathizing with their current difficulties, offering them new accommodation, or just writing to ask how they are coping with life. Television villains are regularly confronted in the street and warned about the possible future consequences of not altering their behaviour. Television doctors, television lawyers and television detectives regularly receive requests for advice and help. Baudrillard calls this 'the dissolution of TV into life, the dissolution of life into TV'.[11] This happens every time we take a tour of a place based on the fact that the place has featured in a media **representation**. For example, the *Sex and the City Tour* of New York, invites us to experience a real place through the frame of a fiction. This is now a fairly common aspect of organized tourism.

John Fiske claims in *Media Matters* that postmodern media no longer provide 'secondary representations of reality; they affect and produce the reality that they mediate'. Moreover, in our postmodern world, all **events** that 'matter' are media events. He cites the example of the arrest of O. J. Simpson:

> Local people watching the chase on TV went to O. J.'s house to be there at the showdown, but took their portable TVs with them in the knowledge that the live event was not a substitute for the mediated one but a complement to it. On seeing themselves on their own TVs, they waved to themselves, for postmodern people have no problem in being simultaneously and indistinguishably livepeople and mediapeople.[12]

These people knew implicitly that the media do not simply report or circulate the news, they produce it. Therefore, in order to be part of the news of O. J. Simpson's arrest, it was not enough to be there, one had to be there on television. In the hyperreal world of the postmodern, there is no longer a clear distinction between a 'real' event and its media representation. In the same way, O. J. Simpson's trial cannot be neatly separated into a 'real' event that television then represented as a media event. Anyone who watched the proceedings unfold on TV knows that the trial was conducted at least as much for the television audience as it was for those present in the court. Without the presence of the cameras this would have been a very different event indeed.

Fredric Jameson is an American Marxist cultural critic who has written a number of very influential essays on postmodernism. According to his account postmodernism is a culture of pastiche, disfigured by the 'complacent play of historical allusion'.[13] Postmodern culture is 'a world in which stylistic innovation is no longer possible, all that is left is to imitate dead styles, to speak through the masks and with the voices of the styles in the imaginary museum'.[14] Rather than a culture of pristine creativity, postmodern culture is a culture of quotations. Instead of 'original' cultural production, we have cultural production born out of other cultural production. It is a culture 'of flatness or depthlessness, a new kind of superficiality in the most literal sense'.[15] A culture of images and surfaces, without 'latent' possibilities, it derives its hermeneutic force from other images, other surfaces. Jameson acknowledges that modernism itself often 'quoted' from other cultures and other historical moments, but he insists that there is a fundamental difference – postmodern cultural texts do not just quote other cultures, other historical moments, they randomly cannibalize them to the point where any sense of critical or historical distance ceases to exist – there is only pastiche.

Perhaps Jameson's best-known example of the postmodern culture of pastiche is what he calls the 'nostalgia film'. The category could include a number of films from the 1980s and 1990s: *Back to the Future I* and *II* (1985, 1989), *Peggy Sue Got Married* (1986), *Rumble Fish* (1983), *Angel Heart* (1987), *Blue Velvet* (1986). He argues that the nostalgia film sets out to recapture the atmosphere and stylistic peculiarities of America in the 1950s. But the nostalgia film is not just another name for the historical film. This is clearly demonstrated by the fact that Jameson's own list includes the *Star Wars* films (1977, 1980, 1983, 1999, 2002, 2005). Now it might seem strange to suggest that films about the future can be nostalgic for the past, but as Jameson explains in 'Postmodernism and Consumer Society', *Star Wars* 'does not reinvent a picture of the past in its lived totality; rather, [it reinvents] the feel and shape of characteristic art objects of an older period'.[16]

Films such as *Raiders of the Lost Ark* (1981), *Independence Day* (1996), *Robin Hood, Prince of Thieves* (1991), *Lord of the Rings* (2001, 2002, 2003), *Pirates of the Caribbean* (2003) and *The Mummy* (1999), operate in a similar way to evoke a sense of the **narrative** certainties of the past. In this way, according to Jameson, the nostalgia film either recaptures and represents the atmosphere and stylistic features of the past and/or recaptures and represents certain styles of viewing of the past. What is of absolute significance for Jameson is that such films do not attempt to recapture or represent the 'real' past, but always make do with certain cultural myths and stereotypes about the past. They offer what he calls 'false realism': films about other films, representations of other representations (what Baudrillard calls simulations). In this way, history is effaced by 'historicism ... the random cannibalization of all the styles of the past, the play of random stylistic allusion'.[17]

Austin Powers: The Spy Who Shagged Me (1999) could be cited as an example of the random cannibalization of the past. As Mike Myers (the film's writer, producer and principal star) himself explains, 'I'm a police composite of every comedian I've ever liked, Peter Sellers, Alec Guinness, Dan Aykroyd, John Belushi, Woody Allen, *Monty Python*, *The Goodies*, the British TV show *Some Mothers Do 'Ave 'Em*, *On the Buses*, the *Carry On* films'. Moreover, Myers' account of the origins of *Austin Powers* could also be cited as evidence of Jameson's argument about the random cannibalization of the past:

> I just love the conventions of James Bond and sixties movies. *Wayne's World* [1992] is everything I was, growing up in the suburbs of Toronto in the mid-seventies, *Austin Powers* is everything I watched [on TV in the late sixties]. My parents were from Liverpool, and there's no one more English than an Englishman who no longer lives there. Every molecule of British culture that came across the Atlantic was tasted and worshipped. Around 1994, I was driving and listening to Burt Bacharach's 'The Look of Love', which is so sixties. And it made me think of all those cult TV shows. I went back home and I wrote the original *Austin Powers* script in just three weeks. ... I mean, this stuff is coming direct from my child-hood.[18]

Similarly, Quentin Tarantino describes *Kill Bill* (2003, 2004) as a combination of kung fu movies, Japanese pop samurai cinema, Chinese wuxia films, spaghetti westerns, female blaxploitation flicks, along with revenge movies in general.

Popular culture (television, pop music, cinema, fashion, etc.) has always recycled its own history (remakes, revivals, cover versions, comebacks, etc.). Rapid advances in technology (for example, the technologies of 'sampling', the introduction of cable, satellite and digital television, the film-on-video/DVD market) have in recent years rapidly expanded and accelerated this process. But are the textual results best understood using the term pastiche? 'Sampling' is a favourite example of what Jameson (and those who share his perspective) understand as postmodern pastiche. But, as Andrew Goodwin points out, with particular reference to pop music, what is often missed in such claims is the way in which sampling is used:

> [T]hese critical strategies miss both the historicizing function of sampling technologies in contemporary pop and the ways in which textual incorporation cannot be adequately understood as 'blank parody'. We need categories to add to pastiche, which demonstrate how contemporary pop opposes, celebrates and promotes the texts it steals from.

Goodwin insists that sampling is often 'used to invoke history and authenticity' and that 'it has often been overlooked that the "quoting" of sounds and styles acts to historicize contemporary culture'.[19] In the main, pop music still tends to operate with an aesthetic that drifts between Romanticism's tortured genius and modernism's avant-garde artist. Because of this, sampling is rarely, if ever, done as a form of pastiche (or even parody); samples are incorporated into the 'organic whole' in much the same way as occurs in T. S. Eliot's classic monument to modernist poetic practice *The Waste Land*.[20]

There is a sense in which what is being claimed as postmodern about popular culture is really only an acceleration and intensification of what has been happening in the traditions of popular entertainment since at least the nineteenth century. In other words, what Jameson (and others like him) identify as postmodern culture has always been a feature of modern popular culture. As David Chaney observes:

> the privileged qualities of postmodernism – parody/pastiche, depthlessness, allegory, spectacular show, and an **ironic** celebration of artifice – have all been central to the submerged traditions of popular culture. One has only to think of the traditions of music and vaudeville, the fair-ground, the circus and pantomime, the melodramatic theatre and the literatures of crime and romance to find all these qualities clearly displayed.[21]

Elizabeth Wilson makes a similar point with regard to fashion: 'some of the themes and hallmarks of what is today termed postmodernism have been around for a long, long time'. She maintains that 'Fashion [which she describes 'as the most popular aesthetic practice of all'] ... has relied on pastiche and the recycling of styles throughout the industrial period'. More generally, she contends:

> This evidence [especially Hollywood film from the 1920s onwards] from the past that pastiche and nostalgia have been pervasive in popular culture throughout the twentieth century and indeed earlier appears to contradict Jameson's belief that 'nostalgia mode' is peculiarly a feature of his postmodern era.[22]

The play of, and playing with, **intertextuality**, a feature shared by both the **texts** of the postmodern and the traditions of popular entertainment, is not, therefore, something which can be understood using only the concepts of pastiche or nostalgic recycling. As Chaney observes:

> Popular entertainment may be structured by the reiteration of certain formulas and genres which provide staple narrative forms, and there may be endless nostalgic regression in re-cycling previous eras and styles, but even so there will be an overwhelming need for novelty in performance, styles and manners. The history of popular music since the development of cheap recordings as a medium of mass entertainment specifically targeted at youth audiences has shown this clearly.[23]

The intertextual understood as a form of borrowing from what already exists is always also (at least potentially) a making new from combinations of what is old. In this way, popular culture is, and has always been, about more than a pastiche or a nostalgic recycling of what has been before. I quoted earlier, in a discussion of Jameson's notion of pastiche, Mike Myers' account of the origins of *Austin Powers*. Other things he has to say about how he came to write the two films point to something more complex than pastiche – a certain kind of parody, not of the sixties but of a particular way of understanding the sixties. As Myers explains:

The movie isn't about the 60s. If anything it's about straight culture's view of the 60s. It's like Matt Helm [secret agent played by Dean Martin in *The Silencers* (1965), *Murderer's Row* (1966), *The Ambushers* (1967) and *The Wrecking Crew* (1969)]. Dean Martin was a man of the 40s and 50s thrust into the context of the 60s and having to deal with all these liberated young people. That was his response to it, it wasn't pot it was booze. It's something I noticed with my dad. He had mutton chops and dyed hair and he put in a bar downstairs at our house. He was like, 'Hey, I'm still a swinger.' It's the whole world of straight culture going, 'I'm with it. Like the kids, you know?' That's what the whole *Austin Powers* thing is about ... *Austin Powers* is like a huge in-joke that I never thought anyone else would get.[24]

There may, therefore, be a certain (postmodern) irony in Jameson's complaint about nostalgia effacing history, given that his own critique is structured by a profound nostalgia for modernist 'certainty', promoted, as it is, at the expense of detailed historical understanding of the traditions of popular entertainment.

According to Jim Collins, part of what is postmodern about Western societies is the fact that the old is not simply replaced by the new, but is recycled for circulation together with the new. As he explains, 'The ever-expanding number of texts and technologies is both a reflection of and a significant contribution to the "array" – the perpetual circulation and recirculation of **signs** that forms the fabric of postmodern cultural life.' He argues that 'This foregrounded, hyper-conscious intertextuality reflects changes in terms of audience competence and narrative technique, as well as a fundamental shift in what constitutes both entertainment and cultural literacy in [postmodern culture].' As a consequence of this, 'Narrative action now operates at two levels simultaneously – in reference to character adventure and in reference to a text's adventures in the array of contemporary cultural production.'[25]

Collins argues that the appeal of films that self-consciously make reference to and borrow from different genres of film is that they appeal to (and help constitute) an audience of knowing bricoleurs, who take pleasure from this and other forms of **bricolage**. Similarly, Brooker and Brooker, following Collins, see the development of 'a new historical sense[,] ... the shared pleasure of intertextual recognition, the critical effect of play with narrative conventions, character and cultural stereotypes, and the **power** rather than passivity of nostalgia'.[26]

Peter and Will Brooker argue that Quentin Tarantino's films, for example, can be seen as reactivating jaded conventions and audience alike, enabling a more active nostalgia and intertextual exploration than a term such as 'pastiche', which has nowhere to go but deeper into the recycling factory, implies. Instead of 'pastiche', we might think of 're-writing' or 're-viewing' and, in terms of the spectator's experience, of the 're-activation' and 're-configuration' of a given generational 'structure of feeling' within a more dynamic and varied set of histories. They point to the ways in which Tarantino's work presents an 'aesthetic of recycling ... an affirmative "bringing back to life", a "making new"'.[27]

The widespread eclecticism of postmodern culture is encouraging and helping to produce what Collins calls the 'sophisticated bricoleur' of post-modern culture. For example, a television series like *Twin Peaks*, both consti-tutes an audience as bricoleurs and in turn is watched by an audience who celebrate its bricolage:

> Postmodernist eclecticism might only occasionally be a preconceived design choice in individual programs, but it is built into the technologies of media-sophisticated societies. Thus television, like the postmodern **subject**, must be conceived as a *site* – an intersection of multiple, conflicting cultural messages. Only by recognizing this interdependency of bricolage and eclecticism can we come to appreciate the profound changes in the relationship of reception and production in postmodern cultures. Not only has reception become another form of meaning production, but production has increasingly become a form of reception as it rearticulates ante-cedent and competing forms of representation.[28]

In a similar way, Umberto Eco, drawing on Charles Jencks' notion of **double-coding**, identifies a postmodern sensibility exhibited in an awareness of what he calls the 'already said'. He gives the example of a man who cannot tell his lover 'I love you madly', out of fear that it might produce only ridicule, and so says instead: 'As Barbara Cartland would put it, "I love you madly"'.[29] Given that we now live in an increasingly media-saturated world, the 'already said' is, as Collins observes, 'still being said'; for example, in the way television (in a effort to fill the space opened up by the growth in satellite and cable channels) recycles its own accumulated past, and that of cinema, and broadcasts these alongside what is new in both media. But how the past is articulated in the present is always as much to do with the present as the past. Collins provides this example of different strategies of articulation:

> The Christian Broadcasting Network and Nickelodeon both broadcast series from the late fifties and early sixties, but whereas the former presents these series as a model for family entertainment the way it used to be, the latter offers them as fun for the contemporary family, 'camped up' with parodic voice-overs, super-graphics, re-editing designed to deride their quaint vision of American family life, which we all know never really existed even 'back then'.[30]

There can be little doubt that similar things are happening in, for example, music, television, advertising, fashion and in the different lived cultures of everyday life. It is not a sign that there has been a general collapse of the distinc-tions people make between, say, high culture/low culture, past/present, history/ nostalgia, fiction/reality; but it is a sign that such distinctions (first noticed in the late 1950s and early 1960s, and gradually more so ever since) are becoming increasingly less important, less obvious, less taken for granted. But this does not of course mean that such distinctions cannot be, and are not being, articulated and mobilized for particular strategies of social distinction. The presence of the past in the present is the result of many different articulations, and we should not take any of these at face value; we must always be alert to the what, why and for whom something is being articulated, and how it can always be articulated differently, in other contexts.

Postmodernism has disturbed many of the old certainties surrounding questions of cultural value. It has become somewhat of a commonplace to demonstrate how canons of value form and re-form in response to the social and political concerns of those with cultural power. To the less watchful eye, the changes often seem insignificant – changes at the perimeters, relative stability at the core – but even when the canonical texts remain the same, how and why they are valued certainly changes. So much so that they are hardly the same texts from one historical moment to the next. As the Four Tops put it, in a slightly different context: 'It's the same old song/But with a different meaning since you've been gone.' Or to put it in a less danceable discourse, the cultural text under the sign of the postmodern is not the source of value, but a site where the construction of value – variable values – can take place.

Perhaps the most significant thing about postmodernism for the student of popular culture is the recognition that there is no absolute categorical difference between high and popular culture. This is not to say that one text or practice might not be 'better' (for what/for whom, etc., must always be decided and made clear) than another text or practice. But it is to say that there are no longer any easy reference points that will automatically preselect for us the good from the bad. Some might regard such a situation (or even the description of such a situation) with horror – the end of standards. On the contrary, without easy recourse to fixed categories of value, it calls for rigorous, if always contingent, standards, if our task is to separate the good from the bad, the usable from the obsolete, the progressive from the reactionary. As John Fekete points out in *Life after Postmodernism*:

> The prospect of learning to be at ease with limited warranties, and with the responsibility for issuing them, without the false security of inherited guarantees, is promising for a livelier, more colourful, more alert, and, one hopes, more tolerant culture that draws enjoyment from the dappled relations between meaning and value.[31]

Fekete's point is not significantly different from the argument made by Susan Sontag in *Against Interpretation* at the birth of the postmodern 'new sensibility'. As she explains:

> From the vantage point of this new sensibility, the beauty of a machine or of the solution to a mathematical problem, of a painting by Jasper Johns, of a film by Jean-Luc Godard, and of the personalities and music of the Beatles is equally accessible.[32]

Postmodernism has certainly changed the theoretical and the cultural basis on which to think about popular culture. In fact, the collapse of the distinction (if this is the case) between high and popular culture may signify that at last it may be possible to use the term popular culture and mean nothing more than culture liked by many people.

NOTES

1 Susan Sontag, *Against Interpretation, and Other Essays* (New York: Dell, 1966), p. 302.
2 Andreas Huyssen, *After the Great Divide: Modernism, Mass Culture, Postmodernism* (Bloomington, IN: Indiana University Press, 1986), p. viii.
3 Ibid., p. 57.
4 Lawrence Alloway, quoted in John Storey, *Cultural Theory and Popular Culture: A Reader*, 5th edn (London: Pearson, 2009), p. 183.
5 Jean-François Lyotard, *The Postmodern Condition: A Report on Knowledge* [1979], trans. Geoff Bennington and Brian Massumi (Manchester: Manchester University Press, 1984), p. xxiv.
6 Steven Connor, *Postmodernist Culture: An Introduction to Theories of the Contemporary* (Oxford: Blackwell, 1989), p. 41.
7 Iain Chambers, *Popular Culture: The Metropolitan Experience* (London: Methuen, 1988), p. 216.
8 Angela McRobbie, *Postmodernism and Popular Culture* (London: Routledge, 1994), p. 15.
9 Kobena Mercer, *Welcome to the Jungle* (London: Routledge, 1994), p. 2.
10 Jean Baudrillard, *Simulations*, trans. Paul Foss, Paul Patton and Philip Beitchman (New York: Semiotext(e), 1983), p. 3.
11 Ibid., p. 55.
12 John Fiske, *Media Matters* (Minneapolis, MN: University of Minnesota Press, 1994), p. xxii.
13 Fredric Jameson, *The Ideologies of Theory: Essays 1971–1986. Vol. 2. The Syntax of History* (Minneapolis, MN: University of Minnesota Press, 1988), p. 105.
14 Fredric Jameson, 'Postmodernism and Consumer Society', in Hal Foster, ed., *Postmodern Culture* (London: Pluto, 1985), pp. 111–25 (p. 115).
15 Fredric Jameson, 'Postmodernism, or, The Cultural Logic of Late Capitalism', *New Left Review*, 146 (1984), pp. 53–92 (p. 60).
16 Jameson, 'Postmodernism and Consumer Society', p. 116.
17 Jameson, 'Postmodernism, or, The Cultural Logic', pp. 65–6.
18 Mike Myers, quoted in John Storey, *Culture and Power in Cultural Studies: The Politics of Signification* (Edinburgh: Edinburgh University Press, 2010), p. 60.
19 Andrew Goodwin, 'Popular Music and Postmodern Theory', *Cultural Studies*, 5:2 (1991), pp. 174–90 (p. 175).
20 T. S. Eliot, *The Waste Land* [1922], in *The Complete Poems and Plays of T. S. Eliot* (London: Faber & Faber, 1969).
21 David Chaney, *The Cultural Turn: Scene-Setting Essays on Contemporary Cultural Theory* (London: Routledge, 1994), p. 204.

22 Elizabeth Wilson, 'Fashion and Postmodernism', in John Storey, ed., *Cultural Theory*, pp. 444–53 (p. 445).

23 Chaney, *Cultural Turn*, p. 210.

24 Mike Myers, quoted in Storey, *Culture and Power in Cultural Studies*, p. 66.

25 Jim Collins, 'Genericity in the Nineties', in Storey, ed., *Cultural Theory*, pp. 454–71 (p. 459).

26 Peter Brooker and Will Brooker, eds, *Postmodern After-Images: A Reader in Film, Television, and Video* (London: Edward Arnold, 1997), p. 7.

27 Ibid., p. 56.

28 Jim Collins, 'Postmodernism and Television', in Robert C. Allen, ed., *Channels of Discourse, Reassembled: Television and Contemporary Criticism*, 2nd edn (London: Routledge, 1992), pp. 327–53 (p. 338).

29 Umberto Eco; quoted in Collins, 'Postmodernism and Television', p. 333.

30 Ibid., p. 334.

31 John Fekete, *Life After Postmodernism: Essays on Value and Culture* (London: Macmillan, 1987), p. 17.

32 Sontag, *Against Interpretation*, p. 304.

19

POSTMODERNISM, MODERNITY AND THE TRADITION OF DISSENT

LLOYD SPENCER

It is perhaps characteristic of our age – the age of designer labels, when almost every aspect of culture and identity seems amenable to 'packaging' – that there should still be a fuss over the label '**postmodern**'. As the novelist and critic, Gilbert Adair notes, few 'isms' have provoked as much perplexity and suspicion as postmodernism.[1]

The very term 'postmodern' is a paradox and a provocation. **Modernity**, in the sense of the 'now' which surrounds us, is not something we can be 'post'. But the modernity referred to is not the 'now' of the thoroughly modern. Modernity is more usefully thought of as a long epoch of historical change, fuelled by scientific and technological development and dominated by the spread – *extensively* across the world and *intensively* into every nook and cranny of the soul – of the capitalist market economy. Throughout the modern era, cultural, philosophical and political debates have marked out an intellectual space between the declining authority of the church on the one hand and, on the other, the economic and technical imperatives forcing the pace of change.

Modernity, even in this sense of a centuries-old tradition of change and debate about change, can hardly be said to have come to an end. In the industrial West the declining role of religion and the pace of economic and technological change are factors which will shape the future as decisively as they have shaped our past. But something has changed in the very nature of tradition and in the way that we relate to the past. Every aspect of the past is made accessible, available. But it is *made* available, mediated, packaged, presented and re-presented. Postmodernism could be described as that variant of **modernism** which has given up hope of freeing itself from the ravages of modernity or of mastering the forces unleashed by modernity.

Modernity – however it is conceived – had a history several centuries old before it came to be formulated under the label of 'modernity'. Modernism in art was echoed in the debates that arose in philosophy and social theory. But it should not be forgotten that there were reactionary modernisms as well as progressive, and that most forms of modernism were a compound of quite disparate, ill-assorted, even contradictory, ideas. If modernism implies enthusiasm about some aspects of modernity, it was usually accomplished – in the same writers, in the same works – by despair at other aspects of modernity. Modernism is as much an antidote to modernity as it is its party programme.

If we choose to call these times we live in 'postmodern' then we have to recognize as 'postmodern' intellectuals of an equally wide variety of cultural and political orientations. That at least should be clear from the variety of positions and postures, beliefs and commitments evidenced in this volume. If 'postmodernity' is a way of describing the times in which we live, then we may justly characterize as 'postmodernism' a diverse range of responses to those times. We use labels such as 'modernity' and 'modernism' to refer to historical epochs and trends which we feel constrained to grasp *in their complexity*. The 'postmodernity' of our own time demands similarly to be viewed in its complexity.

Our own postmodern age is extraordinarily self-conscious. It subjects itself to the most glaring scrutiny and to endless commentary. Writers, theologians and artists have their part in this process, as do academics and other intellectuals. So far the cast-list of these scrutinizers and commentators is a familiar one. What has changed is the role of these agents in the age of the mass media. The postmodern era is one in which cultural activity is dominated by media industries capable of appealing directly to a public (itself the beneficiary of 'mass education') over the heads of any cultural elite.

Mass media and the culture industries, informatics and cybernetics, **virtual reality** and an obsession with 'image' – the changes in the increasingly synthetic fabric of social life are mapped by postmodernists and their detractors in remarkably similar ways. Postmodernists present postmodernism as the set of critical tools needed to grasp and criticize new and changing circumstances. For critics of postmodernism the very 'appropriateness' of postmodernist ideas is the ground for suspicion. Some postmodernists (Jean Baudrillard is the obvious example) write in a style that is ostentatiously 'postmodern' when they write about postmodernism. The close fit between the tools of criticism and the circumstances criticized opens postmodernists to the accusation – which has been often repeated – that their thinking is itself symptomatic of the ills which need to be diagnosed.

Postmodernism, like modernism before it, has produced a profusion of definitions and redefinitions. Readers who come to this volume in search of clear and stable definitions may begin to feel a sense of vertigo as they explore the entries. Not only does what counts as 'postmodern' change from writer to writer, but what is 'meant' by most other terms depends on who is doing the 'meaning', and what they mean by 'meaning'.

One of the symptoms of the 'postmodern condition' is a hypersensitivity to the ways in which words are strategically defined and polemically deployed. In the early years of the twentieth century, the poets of high modernism seemed each to produce their own virtual thesaurus of the language. Now, towards the end of the century, sociologists and other theorists have been made aware of the constraints imposed by language and engage in related processes of linguistic gymnastics (or linguistic mud-wrestling).

Not only are 'postmodernism', 'postmodernity' and 'the postmodern' difficult to define, but like their ('modern') counterparts, they refer to processes of definition and redefinition. At the heart of debates concerning modernism/post-modernism lies the question of 'meaning' itself (or of *The Meaning of 'Meaning'*) and a host of heated arguments over the meanings of particular key terms (including the various cognates of 'the modern' and 'the postmodern'). The result is that in many contemporary debates these labels, and their cognates, obscure more than they clarify. Inherently vague, ambiguous and slippery, these terms are continually used in conflicting and even contradictory ways. Even when this confusion is acknowledged, there seems to be no simple way out of the maze – and no route back to a simpler clear view of the intellectual landscape.

Dissenting from postmodernity is difficult for at least three, interrelated reasons. First, postmodernity is still so amorphous. Although it is all but ubiquitous it remains ill-defined. Second, the 'postmodern' emerges into fierce debates about the role of language and almost all commentators self-consciously deploy their terms and definitions with strategic, often combative intention. On all sides, agreeing the terms of the debate is less important than acting politically on and in the domain of language itself. The result is a multiplicity of competing definitions of postmodernity. Third, dissent from postmodernism is especially difficult because postmodernism – the awkward label announces this at very least – is itself so thoroughly imbued with the spirit of dissent. By constantly striking an attitude of dissent, postmodernism both declares its **difference** from a previous tradition of dissent – modernism – and at the same time accentuates the attitude which it shares with its predecessor. Postmodernism is always having it both ways: it is both the definitive end and overcoming of modernism and, at the same time, modernism under new management.

Although it has become established in cultural and intellectual discussion over recent decades, the term 'postmodernity' has never gained any precise or clear definition; it has gained currency instead as a vague and all-embracing notion referring to a wide variety of ways in which we have succeeded to the ambiguous legacy of modernity and of its late apologists, the modernists. Postmodernism is much less a programme or intellectual framework than it is a mood or *Stimmung* – the Zeitgeist, a 'feeling in the air'.

If postmodernism can be most accurately described as a certain mood or *Stimmung*, then it is one characterized by ambivalence and uncertainty, or what Jean-François Lyotard calls a 'slackening'.[2] Postmodernism did not announce itself bravely and proudly but seems to have slunk onto the horizon, and it has been characterized by dissent and disillusionment in equal measure. Although some of the products or manifestations which are grouped under the heading of postmodernism are playful or joyous, 'postmodernism' always seems to revert to an attitude more often associated with that of an awkward and petulant teen-ager, continually wavering between anger and revolt on the one hand and sullen reproach and refusal on the other. Postmodernism presents itself as a 'historical complex' – complete with its neuroses and obsessions. And legions of therapists and counsellors are constantly at work on the personality disorders of the Zeitgeist.

Throughout its long history 'modernity', in all its guises, has been characterized by the tension between impulses which were critical or sceptical – destructive or negative – and other impulses which were more positive and affirmative – of hope and longing. The dynamic of modernity stems from the intertwining of these constructive and **deconstructive** tendencies.

Postmodernism can be seen as an extension of the critical, sceptical, dissenting – even nihilistic – impulse of modernity. It is treated in this way by many of its critics. And for many critics of postmodernity this is exactly the problem. Under the 'postmodern condition' dissent becomes generalized: it can seem to involve 'dissent in principle' or even 'dissent from everything possible'.

At the same time, postmodernism is sometimes claimed to be a new form of realism. Postmodernism also includes the call for a return to common sense, for pragmatism in the face of the wilder utopian visions indulged in by modernism. As such it is reproached by its critics, especially Marxist ones, as leading to easy assimilation or accommodation with the status quo. Listen to this attack on Baudrillard by Douglas Kellner:

> Baudrillard is still read and received as a political radical, and those who are becoming increasingly attracted to his thought generally perceive themselves as 'radicals' of some sort. ... Baudrillard is the latest example of critical criticism which criticizes everything, but rarely affirms anything of much danger to the status quo. ... A court jester of the society he mocks, he safely simulates criticism, advertises his wares and proceeds to enjoy the follies of the consumer and media society.[3]

Postmodernity = 'dissent' minus 'danger'?

It is a recurrent gesture of the 'postmodern' moment to be 'critical' – of Western rationality, **logocentricism**, humanism, the legacy of the **Enlightenment**, the centred **subject** and so on. The most frequent refrain among dissenters from postmodernism is 'critique in the name of what?' Richard J. Bernstein offers one of the most eloquent explorations of this quandary: '[T]he very "grammar" of critique requires some standard, some measure, some basis for critique. Otherwise there is – as Habermas claims – the danger of the critical impulse consuming itself'.[4] And he goes on to cite Jacques Derrida, so often claimed by friends and foes as a prototypical postmodernist: 'I cannot conceive of a radical critique which would not be ultimately motivated by some sort of affirmation, acknowledged or not.'[5]

Nihilistic, subjectivist, amoral, fragmentary, arbitrary, defeatist, wilful: the terms sound familiar. They constitute some of the core vocabulary used in the criticism of postmodernism. It is worth pausing to reflect that these terms are not only in wide circulation today – they have much justification – but that they have a surprisingly long and respectable pedigree.

In the first half of this century disapproving critics, such as Georg Lukács, deplored the tendencies (nihilism, **irony**, fragmentation) of *modernist* literature (Fyodor Dostoevsky, Franz Kafka, Robert Musil) in just these terms. In doing so they – intentionally – echoed the warnings issued a hundred years earlier by G. W. F. Hegel against the subjectivism of his Romantic contemporaries (Novalis, the brothers Karl and August Schlegel, Friedrich Schleiermacher and Jakob Fries).

The fact that postmodernism – or at least the nihilistic tendency it contains – has such a long tradition is fully recognized by leading postmodernists. In diagnosing what he called the 'Postmodern Condition', Lyotard presented it as one that occurs again and again throughout history:

> What, then is the postmodern? ... It is undoubtedly a part of the modern. ... A work can become modern only if it is first postmodern. Postmodernism thus understood is not modernism at its end but in the nascent state, and this state is constant.[6]

Lyotard has unearthed many worthy precursors of the postmodern. In considering the criticisms levelled at postmodernism it might be worthwhile to follow his example and to examine an important precedent.

Denis Diderot (1713–84) gave 20 years of his life to editing the great French *Encyclopédie*, and was at the centre of French Enlightenment circles. In *Rameau's Nephew* Diderot drew a portrait of the new man.[7] Rameau's nephew is a *philosophe* like himself and like his former friend, Jean-Jacques Rousseau. He is an assertive, self-conscious and self-ironizing citizen of the republic of letters. Rameau's nephew has absorbed all of the (**'anti-foundational'**) arguments against traditional forms of moral authority: the church, the state. The result is that Rameau's nephew declares himself to be utterly amoral, absolutely self-seeking and nihilistic.

Rameau's nephew is the classical prototype of the nihilist tendencies which have drawn fire from the critics of postmodernism. But Diderot's tale gives the devil the best tunes and offers no effective antidote to the dangerous amoralism and subjectivism so successfully evoked. So the tale itself could be claimed for the very postmodernism it attacks.

Diderot himself felt the tale so dangerous that he left it unpublished. His most personal reflections show how very much he wanted to be a good man, a moral person. But they show, too, hiss awareness that if moral codes were not handed down from above then moral awareness will inevitably involve uncertainty, ambiguity and doubt.

That a moral impulse can and must survive in the postmodernist landscape is a message repeated in book after book by Zygmunt Bauman. Bauman's postmodern ethics – which include the notion that we must not attempt to eradicate ambiguity but instead must learn to face it and to live with it – would be well understood by his Enlightenment precursor, Diderot.

When postmodernism is advanced in a thoughtful, non-polemical form – such as in the writings of Bauman[8] – it demands a new asceticism and modesty. It demands that we be scrupulously responsible not only about our actions but even about our hopes and dreams. To dissent from the prevailing postmodern disenchantment with all previous theoretical frameworks, programmes and social movements appears to make one guilty of wanting to resuscitate worn-out illusions, to re-enchant one's world, or at least one's outlook on it.

One way of drawing the line between postmodernism and its critics is to focus on postmodernism's refusal of the utopian, dream-like elements which have accompanied the constant change of modernity. Modernisms, including Marxism, dreamt of a better world. Legislating for this world on the basis of this dream of a better one is seen as the cardinal sin of that modernism which post-modernism seeks to go beyond.

The antagonism between many postmodernists and many neo-Marxists revolves around this fraught issue. Postmodernists treat the authoritarianism of communist regimes as being a result of having tried to realize an unrealizable dream, or having tried to lay hands on utopia and to engineer it in actually existing societies.

Karl Marx himself criticized what he ridiculed as the 'utopian' socialists, always respecting the Jewish prohibition on investigating the future. But, for Marx, his refusal to speculate on a future communist society was an aspect of the 'scientific' nature of his socialist social science.

It could not be clearer that, for Marx, capitalism – the unique object of his historical materialism – is a *moral* issue. Throughout his life, Marx's thinking expressed his fierce political commitment. And the question of the relation of theory to practice has always been a crucial one within the Marxist tradition. For 70 years after Lenin's victory in Russia this question increasingly became an entangled and intransigent one for Western Marxist intellectuals. Although many Western Communist Parties and trade unions developed authoritarian forms of organization, the totalitarian form of communism established in Soviet Russia attracted relatively few supporters among leading Western Marxist intellectuals. On the other hand, Chinese communism, and especially the 'Cultural Revolution' initiated by Mao, was viewed with some enthusiasm by many during the student protests of the late 1960s.

Many of the leading figures associated with French postmodernism, including Lyotard and Baudrillard, emerged from Marxist and **'post-Marxist'** groupings. Reaction against totalitarianism within the Soviet Union had its parallels in reaction against the closed minds and authoritarian practices within the French left. By the late twentieth century both Marxism and modernism had become easy targets for the dissenting impulse within postmodernism. Both had been institutionalized and associated with an 'establishment' – even where this was the 'establishment' of oppositional groups, trade unions, party organizations and academic faculties.

Today the very notion of Marxist political practice has a paradoxical ring to it. On the other hand, Marx's theoretical insights and achievements are now so widely accepted that they have long since ceased to be the property of any particular political orientation or grouping. Whoever seeks to understand society today in sociological and historical terms will find themselves borrowing, correcting and extending Marx's ideas.

Not surprisingly much of the fiercest criticism of postmodernist trends has come from writers who feel that they continue to work within the Marxist tradition in one way or another: Alex Callinicos, for example, is a Marxist who stresses that the nature of exploitation remains fundamentally unchanged.[9] In order to understand the changes taking place in society it is essential to begin by analysing the mechanisms whereby surplus-value is extracted. Fredric Jameson has developed a Lukácsian or Hegelian-Marxist perspective on historical development and treats postmodernism as expressing the 'logic of late capitalism'.[10] In other words, postmodernism is treated as symptomatic of the capitalist system at a particular phase in its development. In order to develop a critical perspective appropriate to our consumerist cyber-society Douglas Kellner has argued that the critical theory tradition of the Frankfurt School has more to offer than currently fashionable French theory:

> I am not sure that we have now transcended and left behind modernity, class politics, labor and production, imperialism, fascism and the phenomena described by classical and neo-Marxism, as well as by other political and social theories which Baudrillard rejects out of hand.[11]

Kellner, like Jameson, has conducted a very serious engagement with postmodern thought and shows in his own analyses of contemporary society that he has drawn a great deal from the postmodernists. Nevertheless, he insists, French postmodernists have been over-hasty in their dismissal of the neo-Marxist tradition of cultural analysis:

> New French Theorists like Baudrillard, Lyotard and Foucault have made a serious theoretical and political mistake in severing their work from the Marxian critique of capitalism precisely at a point when the logic of capital has been playing an increasingly important role in structuring the new stage of society which I conceptualize as a new stage of capitalism – capitalism as techno-capital.[12]

For the postmodernists, Lyotard represents the view that in all the advanced societies '[socialist] struggles and their instruments have been transformed into regulators of the system'.[13] Against the postmodernists, neo-Marxist critics allege that postmodernist criticism is always already complicit in the system which it criticizes.

Postmodernism is a label one can attach to cultural manifestations across the entire globe. Postmodernism in philosophy and cultural theory, however, has had a distinct French accent. Leading cultural theorists such as Baudrillard and Lyotard developed away from variants of Marxism with which they were familiar in Paris. Unfortunately there has been no sustained attempt on the part of French intellectuals to engage seriously with the way in which the Marxian tradition was developed in the German-speaking realm. It has largely been left to English-speaking writers such as Jameson, Kellner and Bernstein to bring the two traditions into critical engagement with one another.

The one notable exception to this generalization would seem to be the way in which Lyotard's French theory has defined itself in opposition to the thinking of the German social theorist, Jürgen Habermas. In *The Postmodern Condition*, Lyotard developed his most often quoted definitions of postmodernism (as a suspicion of **metanarratives**) as an explicit critique of Habermas's ambitious intellectual project. Habermas was singled out for this unique distinction because his aims remain unashamedly synthetic and constructive (rather than analytical and de-constructive). Habermas acknowledges ideals (albeit highly abstract ones) which he claims as universal, and his social theory is continually related to accounts of human evolution (including the phases of history). Particular difficulty has surrounded Habermas's notion of an 'interest in consensus', which occupies a crucial role at the heart of his extensive theorization of communication and **discourse**. Habermas, for whom the concept of modernity is central, is frequently taken to be the boldest defender of the unfinished project of modernity, a forceful champion of the Enlightenment legacy.

Habermas presented an early response to postmodernism in social theory in an essay entitled 'Modernity versus Postmodernity' in which he drew comparisons between postmodern theory and neoconservatism.[14] A more sustained and substantial treatment of what Habermas sees as the flaws and dangers of postmodernism was presented in his twelve lectures on *The Philosophical Discourse of Modernity*.[15] But here, too, the engagement is anything but direct. Habermas speaks of Michel Foucault and Derrida as well as the antecedents of postmodern thinking in Friedrich Nietzsche, Martin Heidegger and the surrealist Georges Bataille. But he is more concerned to trace what he sees as a more promising basis for understanding modernity (and postmodernity) through the insights of Hegel and the theorization of late capitalism (and late modernism) by Max Horkheimer and Theodor W. Adorno. Richard Rorty gives a succinct summary of the way in which Habermas and Lyotard talk past one another:

> Anything that Habermas will count as retaining a 'theoretical approach' will be counted by an incredulous Lyotard as a 'meta-narrative'. Anything that abandons such an approach will be counted by Habermas as 'neoconservative', because it drops the notions which have been used to justify the various reforms which have marked the history of the Western democracies since the Enlightenment, and which are still being used to criticize the socio-economic institutions of both the Free and the Communist worlds. Abandoning a standpoint which is, if not transcendental, at least 'universalistic', seems to Habermas to betray the social hopes

which have been central to liberal politics. So we find French critics of Habermas ready to abandon liberal politics in order to avoid universalistic philosophy, and Habermas trying to hang on to universalistic philosophy, with all its problems in order to support liberal politics.[16]

As Bernstein has reminded us in *The New Constellation*, the 'most fundamental, powerful – and perhaps seductive – theme in Hegel's philosophy is the promise and fulfillment of reconciliation (*Versöhnung*)'.[17] Habermas's treatment of communication and discourse partakes of this spirit and on this basis seeks to transcend 'systematically distorted communication': 'The "postmodern" celebration of contingency, fragmentation, fissures, singularity, plurality, and ruptures (that defy reconciliation) are profoundly anti-Hegelian gestures.'[18] From Hegel to Habermas (and beyond in many other traditions still active) there persists the hope of reconciliation not only among the living but also with the dead. The postmodernist attitude of citing, parodying, pastiching, using and reusing the past is surely a significant symptom of our times. The postmodernist intellectual metropolis is one without a cemetery – there is no 'dead centre' to its town.

At the start of the eighteenth century a great debate raged between the 'ancients' and the 'moderns'. The 'ancients' held that the classical civilizations of Greece and Rome were the source of all standards and all literary ideals. The 'moderns' contended that new times required new standards and new forms of expression. What we should remember in this context is that this was a debate between men raised on Greek and Latin. Even those who belonged to the 'modern' camp, from whom emerged the leading figures of the Enlightenment, were steeped in the classics. All the participants to the debate were on familiar terms with Aristotle and Aristophanes, with Tacitus and Cicero.

Our 'modern' sense of feeling superior to, and hence cut off from, all of our ancestors is an extraordinarily disorientating and alienating experience. We have always felt the need to acknowledge the authority of at least some of the ancients. Throughout modernity the canon of 'classics' has been continually recreated. But, until fairly recently, the search always led back to the huge variety of prototypes and precedents played out in the ancient world. From this stems both the universalism and the elitism which characterizes various forms of modernism, from the reforming zeal of the Enlightenment *philosophes* to the aesthetic experiments of the twentieth-century avant-garde.

The evolution of mass education is one of the key factors in shaping the social history of the twentieth and twenty-first centuries. Education is the one 'great hope' which we have not entirely given up. One precondition (and effect) of universal education was a dramatically reduced role for Latin, Greek and 'classics'. For the first half of the twentieth century, modernism operated in an intellectual landscape in which the 'classics' still represented an active, if ambivalent, legacy. 'Classics' came more and more to be the cornerstone of a privileged education, allowing access to the heritage of the past. At the same time among disaffected, yet almost always 'well-educated', intellectuals, the perennial sub-versiveness of classical authors and classical themes (myths and mythemes) fuelled the radical universalism of modernism.

Meanwhile the demands of the market turn yesterday's fashions into something already ancient, utterly out-of-date – into something ripe for revival as 'classic'. The cycles of history are driven by the mandarins of a commercial culture, in order that they, and others, might turn a profit. Among all of the culture industries, it is the heritage industry which experiences the most sustained boom.

The radical avant-garde wish was to overcome the gulf between art and society or between art and everyday life. The aestheticized world prophesied by a modernist avant-garde in the earlier half of the twentieth century has, in our own time, become all too real: it has become the *hyperreal*. And this state of hyperreality has been achieved not by the artistic avant-garde but by commodities and the countless creative workers who sustain our consumer culture. No new aesthetic movements of collective importance, operative across more than one art form, emerged either, after surrealism. As Kellner has pointed out, post-modernism is continually parodying the revolutionary gestures of the avant-garde earlier in the twentieth century. This is true at least of one brand of postmodernism which, when it came on the market, announced itself with shrill insistence as something utterly new:

> [A]lmost every discussion of Baudrillard in English seems to presuppose that he is right, that we are in something like a postmodern condition, that we have left modernity behind and are in a qualitatively new society where the old categories and old distinctions no longer hold. Such a vision rests, I believe, partly on wishful thinking.[19]

We have lately learnt to be more modest in our modernity, more cautious in our hopes, more sceptical of the promise of the future (the credit crunch has concentrated minds in this respect). We cannot any longer take the project of modernity simply on trust. Even this postmodern tentativeness is no longer new. Postmodernity is ready to enter dictionaries and encyclopaedias as it has already entered into countless textbooks. Debates over the traditions of modernity, late modernity, postmodernity will continue, and will continue to generate sober reflection on where we have come from and where we are going.

NOTES

1 See Gilbert Adair, *The Postmodernist Always Rings Twice: Reflections on Culture in the 90s* (London: Fourth Estate, 1992).
2 Jean-François Lyotard, *The Postmodern Condition: A Report on Knowledge* [1979], trans. Geoff Bennington and Brian Massumi (Manchester: Manchester University Press, 1984), p. 71.

3 Douglas Kellner, *Jean Baudrillard: From Marxism to Postmodernism and Beyond* (Cambridge: Polity Press, 1989), p. 216.

4 Richard J. Bernstein, *The New Constellation: The Ethical-Political Horizons of Modernity/Postmodernity* (Cambridge, MA: MIT Press, 1990), pp. 6–7.

5 Ibid., p. 7.

6 Lyotard, *Postmodern Condition*, p. 79.

7 Denis Diderot, *Rameau's Nephew* [1761], trans. Leonard Tancock (Harmondsworth: Penguin, 1976).

8 See, for example, Zygmunt Bauman, *Intimations of Postmodernity* (London: Routledge, 1992).

9 See for example, Alex Callinicos, *Against Postmodernism: A Marxist Perspective* (Cambridge and Oxford: Polity Press and Blackwell, 1990).

10 See Fredric Jameson, *Postmodernism, or, The Cultural Logic of Late Capitalism* (London: Verso, 1991).

11 Kellner, *Jean Baudrillard*, p. 217.

12 Douglas Kellner, 'Boundaries and Borderlines: Reflections on Jean Baudrillard and Critical Theory', *Illuminations: The Critical Theory Web Site*, www.uta.edu/huma/ illuminations/kell2.htm (accessed 8 February 2011).

13 Lyotard, *Postmodern Condition*, p. 13.

14 Jürgen Habermas, 'Modernity versus Postmodernity', *New German Critique*, 22 (1981), pp. 3–14.

15 Jürgen Habermas, *The Philosophical Discourse of Modernity* [1985], trans. Frederick Lawrence (Cambridge: Polity Press, 1987).

16 Richard Rorty, 'Habermas and Lyotard on Postmodernity', in Richard J. Bernstein, ed., *Habermas and Modernity* (Cambridge: Polity Press, 1985), pp. 161–75 (p. 162).

17 Bernstein, *New Constellation*, p. 293.

18 Ibid., p. 307.

19 Kellner, 'Boundaries and Borderlines'.

Part II
CRITICAL TERMS

A

ABJECTION A term coined by the French psychoanalytical theorist and **semiotician** Julia Kristeva. In 1982 she published *Powers of Horror: An Essay on Abjection*, in which she argued that the 'abject' constitutes anything that is excluded from the symbolic order, the site of the social and unambiguous subjectivity. In order to take up a position within such an order, the **subject** must repress that which reminds it of its own material nature by categorizing it as unclean or disgusting. This attempt at exclusion can only ever be partially successful, and thus the abject preserves an ability to render the subject's inclusion in the symbolic order problematic. At moments when the subject is forced to recognize this, the resultant reaction is one of extreme repulsion – what Kristeva terms an 'act of abjection'. [SG]

ALTERITY 'Alterity' is often used interchangeably in **poststructuralist discourse** with '**Other**'. The 'Other' in the work of Michel Foucault, for instance, consists of those who are excluded from positions of **power**, and are often victimized within a predominantly liberal humanist view of the **subject**. Much of Foucault's work is therefore dedicated to retrieving for history and philosophy those who have been excluded from intellectual consideration, and have consequently had their political rights either ignored or erased. The 'Other' in this context are homosexuals, women, the clinically insane, non-whites and prisoners. These figures, collectively and individually, are seen by poststructural and **postmodern** thinkers to exist on the margins of Western society, and are often the negative opposition in **deconstructive** discourse. [DW]

ALTERMODERN A term coined by the French art theorist Nicolas Bourriaud to describe art that is attempting to transcend the **binary opposition** of **modernism** and **postmodernism**. In Bourriaud's view, much contemporary art practice no longer conforms to the postmodern aesthetic, with its liking for pastiche and **double-coding**, and is in many ways closer to modernism in spirit. Bourriaud approves of the adventurous, subversive side of modernism, but does not advocate a return to it as it was. Instead, he envisages a synthesis being constructed between modernism and **postcolonialism** that would enable artists to break free of the constraints that past theories had tended to impose on them. He suggests that artists should think of themselves as **nomadic** rather than as being in the service of any particular 'ism'. His views were put into practice in the exhibition entitled 'Altermodern' that he curated at the Tate Gallery in London ('Tate Triennial', 2009), where his catalogue introduction spoke of the need to go 'beyond the postmodern' to discover new ways of capturing the changes occurring in contemporary culture. [SS]

ANTI-CAPITALISM A highly vocal anti-capitalist movement has developed in recent years to protest against the unfairness of **globalization** as a system for international trade. Nations in the developing world, for example, can find themselves in a neo-colonial relationship with the West, their resources and labour forces being ruthlessly exploited in order to produce cheap goods for the Western market. Campaigners such as Naomi Klein, in her best-selling book *No Logo* (2001), have been particularly critical of the multinationals' role in creating this state of affairs, charging them with unethical behaviour.

Anti-capitalists have targeted high-profile international bodies such as the World Trade Organization (WTO), turning several of their meetings into open conflict between protestors and police. The movement could be seen as an example of Jean-François Lyotard's **little narrative** notion, being very much a grassroots phenomenon, the aim of which is to challenge political power structures rather than become a political party in its own right. In that sense anti-capitalism could be claimed as **postmodern**, since it is not in the service of any **grand narrative**. It could also be said, however, that it demonstrates the problematical side of postmodernism as a political position in that it is easier to say what it is against than what it would put in its place. [SS]

ANTI-ESSENTIALISM Postmodernist thinkers invariably describe themselves as anti-essentialist, meaning that they reject the notion of there being any essence to phenomena such as truth, meaning, self or identity. Traditional philosophy is taken to be essentialist in believing that there is such a thing as absolute truth underpinned by logical formulae such as the law of identity ($A = A$, or a thing equals itself). This law has been challenged by postmodernists, who claim that it does not always hold (a thing might not equal itself in all senses if it is in a continuous process of change over time, for example). Traditional philosophy also tends to posit an essential self (as in the case of René Descartes, where the mind is the essence of selfhood: 'I think therefore I am'), which postmodernism has similarly called into question. Self is in fact seen to be a very fluid entity in postmodernist thought, particularly in feminist circles, where the notion of an essentialist self is regarded as part of the system of patriarchal oppression. [SS]

ANTI-FOUNDATIONALISM To challenge the grounds of someone's system of belief, or thought, is to be anti-foundationalist. **Poststructuralist** and **postmodernist** thinkers tend to be self-consciously anti-foundational in outlook. Jacques Derrida, as a case in point, has challenged the validity of the law of identity (that a thing equals itself, $A = A$), arguably *the* foundation to thought and argument in the West. The basic problem is that any system of thought, indeed any system aspiring to make value judgements of any kind (true or false, good or evil, etc.), requires a starting point, or initial assumption (say, that $A = A$) that is self-evidently true and beyond all possible doubt. Anti-foundationalists point out that the starting point itself requires a prior assumption. Poststructuralism and postmodernism are merely more extreme versions of positions that have been outlined earlier in the history of Western philosophy. Sceptics in general, such as the eighteenth-century philosopher David Hume, are anti-foundationally inclined in that they are less concerned with what their opponents say than their ground of authority for making any kind of value judgement at all. Anti-foundationalism in recent times has argued that foundationalism is authoritarian in intent, and it has become a rallying cry for an attack on the status quo and the establishment. [SS]

APORIA From the Greek, meaning, literally, 'the absence of a passage', and hence a perplexing difficulty or state of being at a loss, aporia denotes in rhetoric a figure in which the speaker or writer expresses doubt about how or where to begin a **discourse**, or how to overcome a particular problem or obstacle. For **deconstructive** criticism, it is precisely around such moments of doubt or apparently unresolvable problems that reading orientates itself. For Jacques Derrida, as for the criticism of Paul de Man, it is these **textual** gaps or stumbling-blocks to which we must pay attention.

The term is also an apt one to describe the kind of 'impossibility' of judgement which Jean-François Lyotard identifies in the aesthetics of the **sublime** and the avant-garde, with which he identifies the **postmodern**. For Lyotard, the moment at which political judgement takes place is an aporetic one, analogous with the disjunction between the faculties of reason and imagination in the sublime, and with the avant-garde injunction to create, but in the absence of any rules for the production of art. [BD]

APPROPRIATION In art, appropriation involves the inclusion of real objects or existent art into works which are then claimed as new on the grounds of recontextualization. There is a definite strand of this in the **modernist** movement, as in cubist collages and Marcel Duchamp's readymades. Andy Warhol's assemblages of Campbell soup cans suggest a similar motivation. **Appropriation art** became a critical term in the 1980s to mark out the work of artists such as Sherrie Levine, who appropriated paintings by Claude Monet among others.

Appropriation can be found across the arts, with popular music a good example through its use of techniques such as sampling, where previously recorded material is openly assimilated into new recordings by other artists (a standard device in rap and hip-hop). Sampling exemplifies the **postmodern** aesthetic of pastiche, which actively encourages creative artists to raid the past in order to set up a sense of dialogue between it and the present. Postmodern architecture incorporates older building styles and features to the same end. The postmodern suspicion of **originality** also helps to promote such practice, although critics would see the resulting creations as raising some tricky questions about authenticity – not to mention copyright in many cases. [SS]

APPROPRIATION ART A term used to describe works by Sherrie Levine, Barbara Kruger, Cindy Sherman, Richard Prince and those artists for whom the real was coterminous with the image world of contemporary social life. Levine, Sherman and Prince were represented at the seminal *Pictures* exhibition, held at the Artists' Space gallery in Lower Manhattan in 1977. The influential art critic Douglas Crimp, writing in the catalogue, waxed lyrical about artists for whom 'skill' meant **simulation** rather than emulation, repetition rather than **originality**, and confiscation rather than creation. [CT]

ARCHAEOLOGY Archaeology, the scientific study of the remains of the past, is a potent metaphor for excavations of a more subjective nature. Sigmund Freud famously used the image of a city to picture the relation between the conscious and the unconscious. Like the city of Rome, the thinking **subject** is composed of many different layers of awareness and susceptibility. Destructive drives and desires may emanate from buried parts of the self, and the analyst must help the analysand to dig deep and expose repressed memories and fears to the light of waking day. Michel Foucault uses a similar concept to describe the investigation into the unconscious of the **episteme**, which is shorthand for the 'epistemological field' of assumptions, expectations, values and beliefs of a society at a particular historical moment. His *The*

Order of Things: An Archaeology of the Human Sciences (1966), for example, seeks to uncover the formational rules and systematic shaping factors which are common to scientific **representations** of the classical period. The **text** is an 'open site', another archaeological metaphor which refers to the necessary incompleteness of the project. So Foucault's speculations should not be read as if they were by a historian of science, but with a **postmodern** provisionality. [BL]

ARTIFICIAL INTELLIGENCE On the one hand, artificial intelligence (AI) forms a powerfully attractive motor for the artificial evolution of human reality into science fiction; on the other, it is a research programme attracting funds from military and corporate sponsors that seeks, for the first time, to place a new created or manufactured species of intelligent life on the Earth. If this still sounds somewhat intoxicated, we need only remember AI guru Marvin Minsky discussing the possibility of real artificial intelligences: 'Of course they're possible; that's not the problem. The real problem is that the first hundred or so are going to be clinically insane.' As contemporary phenomena such as **cyberpunk** demonstrate, AI, along with **artificial life**, forms a haunting cultural threshold beyond which Frankenstein's monster already has us in his virtual grasp.

As Minsky does, however, it is necessary to insist that these virtual monsters are also real. In AI research proper, then, there are two basic models: the first, top-down, approach seeks to develop software that can capture the core cognitive functions that define human intelligence, and thereafter to upload them into a single central processor that stands in for the human brain. Broadly speaking, this is the model pursued in the production of 'expert systems' and the chess computers against which so many humans have pitted their

wits and failed. The other, bottom-up, approach seeks to create machines that learn. Variously called 'parallel distributed processing', 'neural nets', or 'connectionism', this model allows many processors to interact in order to develop a collective response to random phenomena. Over time, such parallel machines establish pathways and **fuzzy** rules for connections in exactly the same way, it is argued, as organic, human brains do: rather than being given a set of rules and parameters as a program that an expert system then applies, neural nets select the best from many options, so that the rules the system learns 'emerge' from its functioning.

While the top-down approach is by now all but redundant, the success enjoyed by neural nets has generated new approaches to the philosophy of mind, generally called 'connectionist' theories. Like the model of the neural net, connectivity and interaction become more important tools for the development of human intelligence than the centralized idea of the mind-brain as a whole. Perhaps, if this trend continues, the question as to which intelligence is derived from the other will be harder to pose than it currently seems, in a world that, temporarily at least, is devoid of artificial intelligences. [IHG]

ARTIFICIAL LIFE Along with **artificial intelligence**, one of the two contemporary sciences of the artificial, artificial life (AL), is a truly bizarre confluence of technology, science and **simulacra**. Generating 'organisms' from algorithms, AL researchers seek not so much to model 'real-life' evolutionary processes, as to extend them into the artificial environment of computer memory. Thomas S. Ray, at the Fourth International Conference on Artificial Life in 1994, suggested that his Tierra, a program that, like a digital simulation of our own primal soup, 'evolves' independent life-forms in a computer, be released onto the **Internet** to 'breed' new species all over the (virtual) world. While Tierra is an example of AL software, AL researchers also investigate hardware – the construction of artificial life-forms such as robots, aiming eventually at the ideal of realizing the self-replicating but abstract 'von Neumann machine' in material form – and wetware – the attempt to create artificial life in a test tube. AL software involves writing programs that perpetually feed back the information they produce into the production of further information, creating an informational complexity from which, it is hoped, artificial life-forms will emerge. Key to the process, therefore, is its 'bottom-up' strategy rather than the 'top-down' approach initially adopted by artificial intelligence research, meaning that more emerges from AL's new, silicon-based evolutionary ecosystems than was programmed in at the start. [IHG]

AURA A term associated with the German cultural critic Walter Benjamin. In an important essay entitled 'The Work of Art in the Age of Mechanical Reproduction' (1936), Benjamin argues that, prior to mechanization, art had a non-reproductive quality which conferred upon it a unique status, or 'aura'. This aura, which signified the artwork's autonomy, had been destroyed in modern times by soulless automation. For Benjamin, the mysticism that he associates with the unique work of art has been 'withered' as a result of the machine age, and art and its artefacts have become divorced from tradition, leading to a 'liquidization of the cultural heritage'. [DW]

AUTHOR From **structuralism** through to **postmodernism**, there has been a downgrading of the author's reputation in **continental philosophical** thought, particularly in France. Roland Barthes' 'death of the author' notion announced the end of the author as an authority figure responsible for the meaning of his or her work, shifting the balance of **power** towards the reader instead. Authority figures are generally frowned upon in postmodernism, and the notion of the author as cultural icon has accordingly been challenged. There is little support among postmodernist theorists for the idea that any one individual should (or in any practical way can) exert control over what a **text** means; hence it is held to be pointless to seek out an author's 'intentions' (see also **death of the author**). [SS]

B

BIG BANG COSMOLOGY The 'big bang' model is the current mainstream cosmological description of the origin and evolution of our universe, based on work in the early twentieth century by Albert Einstein (general **relativity**), Aleksandr A. Friedmann and Georges Lemaître (expanding universe), Edwin Hubble (red shift expansion observations), and others. It asserts that around twelve to fourteen billion years ago the area of the universe we can see today was only a few millimetres across and that it expanded extremely rapidly from its initial incredibly hot dense state into the much cooler and very much larger expanse we currently inhabit. There wasn't an explosion in the conventional sense, but rather space-time itself underwent a rapid expansion, forming only the very light atomic elements hydrogen, helium and lithium in the process, with all the heavier elements produced in the stars subsequently. Observations such as the isotropic distribution of cosmic microwave background radiation (CMB) left over from the initial very hot phase lend strong credibility to the underlying assumption that matter is distributed uniformly and homogeneously throughout the universe (the cosmological principle).

The standard big bang theory cannot explain the birth and existence of stars and galaxies. However, a recent modification to the model incorporates the concept of an initial rapid inflationary phase in which exponential expansion allowed **quantum** fluctuations to grow and become small variations in the distribution of matter, leading eventually to stars and galaxies. Inflation also helps to account for measured fluctuations in CMB and the low proportion of ordinary detectable matter (see **dark matter**). Recent measurements indicate that expansion of the universe is not constant but appears to be speeding up, suggesting the need for a cosmological constant in the form of **dark energy,** which would also stretch current estimates of the age of the universe. This is fortunate since at present some of our older stars appear to be older than the current predicted age of the cosmos.

A combination of improved measurement resolution, wider theoretical developments and perhaps the effects of **postmodernism** loosening the certainties of **modernist** science has recently fuelled interest in different cosmological models (multiverse, super-inflation, wave function, evolutionary, quantum bounce, etc). Cosmology will always be of central interest to any philosophy, especially one such as postmodernism, concerned as it is with investigating foundational aspects, since boundary conditions and initial assumptions inevitably form a critical component of any theoretical cosmological framework. [BW]

BINARY OPPOSITIONS The use of binary oppositions in analysing phenomena is highly characteristic of **structuralism**, and one of the aspects of its methodology that is most vigorously attacked by **poststructuralist** critics. Thus, in Claude Lévi-Strauss, 'nature' and 'culture' are set in opposition to each other as mutually exclusive categories, such that given examples of human behaviour must belong to one or other category – but not both. Lévi-Strauss proceeds to run into problems with the incest taboo, which he is forced to concede *does* seem to belong to both categories. For Jacques Derrida, this is an admission that calls into question the whole structuralist project, the methodology of which is seen to be faulty. Poststructuralists like Derrida also consider that the principle of binary opposition (*either* one thing *or* its opposite number) depends on a notion of fixed identity that is no longer tenable; as far as they are concerned, identity is a much more fluid phenomenon than structuralists would like to believe. [SS]

BIOPOLITICS A concept devised by Michel Foucault to describe how modern governments (roughly from the **Enlightenment** period onwards) have put the processes of human life at the centre of politics, using this as a way of regulating the behaviour of the population so that they can exercise control over it – or 'biopower'. As Foucault conceived it: '**modern** man is an animal whose politics places his existence as a living being in question'. It is effectively the development of biopower that Foucault is dealing with in works like *Madness and Civilization* (1964) and *Discipline and Punish* (1975), where he explores the rationale behind the foundation of asylums and the modern prison system respectively.

A central concern of Foucault's oeuvre is the issue of **power** and how it can be resisted, and biopower might seem to set special problems in this regard. Yet despite its success it nevertheless offers up the possibility of resistance, since biopolitics gives us a greater awareness of our potential as individuals and our ability to construct new forms of relationship that could subvert the biopolitical machine. Jean-François Lyotard's notion of the **little narrative** is very similar, with its insistence that

grand narratives can always be challenged, no matter how all-powerful they might consider themselves to be. [SS]

BLACK CRITICISM With its emphasis on tradition, and on experience, often authenticated through the autobiographical voice, black writing seems inimical to a good deal of **postmodern** theory with its talk of the **death of the author**, the fluidity of **subjectivity** and of the end of history. Yet some of the most familiar critical concepts in the postmodern lexicon – marginality, **difference**, **otherness** – have given a powerful impetus to the exploration of black **texts**, though not without controversy among black scholars themselves. Black American writing is a good example of the tensions between the demands of political and aesthetic expression. Black criticism sees race as a fundamental category of cultural analysis. The publication of self-authored narratives by ex-slaves in the antebellum period was a profoundly political as well as aesthetic act. While many displayed an exuberant 'literariness', they were written as part of the propaganda war against slavery since, as a number of critics have pointed out, literacy was the principal sign of reason, a faculty that white supremacists denied black people possessed. Art would be put in the service of politics from the Harlem renaissance of the 1920s, when critics called for a literature that would show the black race at its best, in the 1940s and 1950s by communist fellow travellers arguing for reform and integration, and in the 1960s by black nationalists in such books as Addison Gayle's *The Black Aesthetic* (1972), which called for revolution and a cross-class alliance of black Americans. In the 1970s Gayle's essentialism and chauvinism were challenged by growing numbers of black feminist critics and by the emergence of **poststructuralist** analysis. In the postmodern world, critics still value concepts of blackness and tradition, though they are no longer identified by authorial skin colour, but through the very language of the texts themselves. [PD]

BLACK HOLES Despite their being entirely hypothetical or theoretical entities, black holes remain powerfully attractive to cosmologists and astrophysicists such as Stephen Hawking and Roger Penrose. For all astrophysics based (as in fact it all is) on general **relativity**, light is the limit velocity of the universe; nothing, in other words, travels faster than light. The first theoretical account of black holes stems from J. R. Oppenheimer and H. Snyder's application in 1939 of the principles of general relativity to the life cycles of stars. A black hole is a collapsing star of such mass that the velocity required to escape its gravitational field exceeds the velocity of light – which, by the principles of general relativity, is impossible. A black hole is therefore black because it emits no light, and a hole because within it all matter, and even space-time, is destroyed. Black holes are 'expected' to arise when the mass of a neutron star (not all stars will attain the violent end of the neutron star; our Sun, for example, will not) reaches a density so high as to create a gravitational field so strong that even the matter-energy of which the star consists will collapse under its own gravity. Many properties stem from this. One is the notion of the 'event horizon' of a black hole: the limit point of the black hole's gravitational field. As this event horizon is approached, since light is unable to escape it, time slows until within it nothing happens: neither matter nor even space-time survives the event horizon of a black hole.

Some cosmologists have hypothesized that the isolated space-time of black holes turns them, to all intents and purposes, into separate universes, each competing with others, through intense gravitation, for resources in order to realize the 'best of all possible worlds' on the evolutionary basis suggested by the fact that stars have life cycles. It is both tempting and appropriate to suggest that the theoretical physics of black holes, a multiverse composed of timeless and spaceless dematerialized yet physical absences, separated by unbridgeable event horizons the one from the other, provides a genuinely physical instantiation of the **postmodern** condition. [IHG]

BODY WITHOUT ORGANS A term used by Gilles Deleuze and Félix Guattari to describe all those forces that hinder the free expression of desire and **libidinal** energy. For the authors, the body without organs – which they also refer to as 'the body without an image' – is sterile and unproductive, and they identify it with the forces of repression in society. Capital, for example, is to be regarded as the body without organs of the capitalist, which appropriates the production of individual **desiring-machines** (in this case wage labourers) for its own ends. Production (a term encompassing the expression of desire and libidinal energy) is a positive force for Deleuze and Guattari, and bodies without organs are to be resisted because they restrict its range while channelling what is left into their own projects (the creation of profits for themselves, for example). [SS]

BRICOLAGE In *The Savage Mind* (1966) Claude Lévi-Strauss differentiated between primitive and advanced thought, by describing the former as less structured and theoretically sophisticated than the latter. Just as a *bricoleur* (handyman) might improvise with whatever materials were available to him if mending a broken object or appliance, so the world-view of primitive tribes was constructed out of recycled ideas and beliefs rearranged as needed. The scientist or technologist, on the other hand, approached problems in a highly theoretical manner, and if necessary could invent new tools or methods in search of solutions. Bricolage thus stands in opposition to **modern** thought patterns, being ad hoc in character instead of rigorously systematic.

The sense of improvisation that bricolage carries appeals to the **postmodern** theorist, since it suggests an arbitrary, undetermined quality to creative activity in which the end is not specified in advance. Where a modern thinker might see lack of order or method, his or her postmodern counterpart would see a welcome exercise of spontaneity. The postmodern enthusiasm for pastiche, whereby creative artists ransack the past for inspiration, underlines this commitment to bricolage as an aesthetic ideal. Most postmodern theorists would also want to argue that there is far more bricolage going on in scientific thought than is generally acknowledged. [SS]

C

CATASTROPHE THEORY Apocalyptic similarities with **chaos theory** notwithstanding, catastrophe theory shares little with the latter beyond both implying, through their names, that mathematics by our day has become a technical code devoted to the analysis of some glamorously crash-and-burn apocalypse. Invented by mathematical 'sorcerer' René Thom in *Structural Stability and Morphogenesis* (1972) there is in fact little catastrophic about the theory. Instead, the overt strategy of catastrophe theory is to demonstrate a formal, mathematizable continuity between states in a dynamical system despite gross apparent discontinuities between those states. An ice age, for example, does not appear to be part of the mesh of interconnected systems of life on a temperate Earth, but rather its end. Catastrophe theory seeks to demonstrate that what appear to be catastrophes that change everything are, at the level of mathematical form – *morphogenetically* – profoundly continuous. A catastrophe is not the end of a system, but an inherent, predictable and mathematizable component of it.

So stated, emphasizing continuity over discontinuity, catastrophe theory seems anything but **postmodern**; it is paradoxical, then, that Jean-François Lyotard derives some of the more celebrated theses of *The Postmodern Condition* (1979) from this body of theory. Just as, for example, Lyotard famously insists that '**postmodernity** is incredulity towards **metanarratives**', so Thom declares that 'the era of grand cosmic synthesis is at an end' and that science can no longer be characterized as the investigation of the ultimate nature of reality. Accordingly, catastrophe theory recognizes the impossibility of the quantitative global model aspired to by Euclidean geometry, and frames its analyses within the local parameters of the dynamical system under study. Catastrophe theory's emphasis on formal continuity is therefore both local and abstract, the sequence of models amounting to nothing more than 'the play of pure forms' – morphogenesis. Following this abstract line, catastrophe theory thus broaches territories long since barred to mathematics, including sociology, linguistics and **semiotics**, so that it feeds directly into the arenas where postmodernism is currently contested. [IHG]

CHAOS THEORY A chaotic system is one that shows a sensitive dependence on initial conditions. If chaos theory can be said to have a beginning, it was the discovery by Edward Lorenz in 1960 that tiny errors in equations he was using to model weather systems resulted in enormous and apparently unpredictable variations in the outcome of the equations. The consequences of this seemed fatal to any attempt to make long-term weather forecasts – minute differences in the initial conditions could mean the **difference** between flood and drought. This has become known as the butterfly effect – the flapping of a butterfly's wings in China could create a causal chain, the final outcome of which is a hurricane in Indonesia.

Postmodernists have embraced chaos as a counter to the expansive truth-claims of science. Chaos seems, superficially, to throw an element of uncertainty into the activity of the material world: it has been argued that it would require a computer bigger than the universe itself to predict the behaviour of all the chaotic systems it contains.

This is, however, to ignore the constructive side of chaos theory. When data from chaotic systems are plotted, complex but recognizable patterns emerge – the consequence of what are known as strange attractors. These patterns in chaotic behaviour make it possible to make short-term predictions and to predict general trends. The quest to find order in chaos has led to the creation of another new field – the science of **complexity**.

Chaos theory has been used to help explain the baffling orbits of certain satellites, to understand fluctuations in animal populations, to track the movement of the market and to model the beating of the human heart. There are, however, those who claim that there has been precious little real achievement to justify the hype. [AM]

CHORA In Plato's *Timaeus*, chora is the unnameable, unstable receptacle existing prior to the nameable form of the One. Generally, in **postmodern** usage, chora designates a site of undifferentiated being, connoting the experience of continuity with the maternal body as an infinite space. Specifically in Julia Kristeva's work, chora specifies the presignifying traces which underlie and at times break through the order of signification. Hence the shared bodily space of mother and child resists **representation**, yet is experienced as desire, the uncanny or the mystical. The chora as maternal desire threatens to destabilize the finite unity and autonomous identity of the **modern** 'man'. [PSA]

COMPLEXITY THEORY The world is full of complex systems, from the internal structure of single-celled organisms to the

working of the stock exchange. Complexity theory has attempted to define these 'self-organizing' systems, and then to find the general principles that underlie them, with the goal of producing a unified law of complexity. Although the search for a unified law betrays a deep-seated reductionist bias, there is also a counterbalancing holism in that the behaviour of complex systems cannot be simply deduced from their constituent parts. Complexity therefore calls for new principles, new modes of analysis.

Although there is no consensus among researchers, the nearest thing to a common definition of complexity involves the '**edge of chaos**' hypothesis. The distinguishing feature of complexity, in this view, is high informational content, and informational content is maximized in systems that exist at the border between highly stable states (crystalline structures, regular planetary orbits) and chaos.

Complexity theorists typically spend their time producing computer models of natural behaviours. Shapes squirm and wriggle across computer screens in **simulations** of bacteria or antelope, struggling for survival, competing for resources in harsh environments, evolving, dying. This '**artificial life**' research attempts to find the simple laws that generate both the complexity and the emergent order. Researchers argue that if you can create complex behaviour in a computer from a small number of simple rules, the corresponding behaviours in the 'real' world must equally be the product of a small number of simple rules. If it is countered that there is a fundamental **difference** between real-world organisms and the blips on a computer screen, complexity theorists tend to suggest that the parallels are so close that the 'virtual' organisms should be granted the same status as their flesh and blood cousins. This blurring of real and virtual worlds is, of course, very **postmodern**. [AM]

CONTINENTAL PHILOSOPHY Philosophy in Europe (particularly in France and Germany) has been felt by many to have developed in a radically different way in **modern** times from that in the English-speaking world, and the term 'continental philosophy' has increasingly come to be applied as a way of differentiating it from what is taken to be the philosophical mainstream. Many would date continental philosophy back to Immanuel Kant (in particular to his *Critique of Judgment* (1790) and its theory of the **sublime**), but in a more recent sense it refers to movements such as phenomenology, existentialism, **structuralism**, **poststructuralism**, **postmodernism** and **difference feminism**. Edmund Husserl and Martin Heidegger's phenomenology is one of the critical influences on later twentieth-century continental philosophy (nearly every major poststructuralist and postmodernist thinker acknowledges their influence), which has also drawn freely on such intellectual traditions as Marxism and Freudianism, and such maverick philosophical figures as Friedrich Nietzsche.

The English philosopher David Cooper has usefully defined continental philosophy as having the following major concerns: (1) cultural critique; (2) concern with the background conditions of enquiry; (3) 'the fall of the self' (that is, a loss of belief in the notion of a unified personal identity or **subject**). Although such concerns can also be found in the work of English-speaking philosophers, they hardly ever dominate debate in the way they do on the continent, where they recur obsessively in the work of such recent figures as Michel Foucault, Jacques Derrida, Gilles Deleuze and Jean-François Lyotard.

Although it is identified with French and German thought, it is nevertheless possible to be defined as a continental philosopher outside those traditions – the American philosopher Richard Rorty being one such

example. Continental philosophy is to be regarded as a particular 'style' or 'mood' of philosophical **discourse** rather than a specific cultural or national tradition as such. [SS]

CREDIT CRUNCH Modernity as a socio-political phenomenon has been heavily committed to the notion of progress, particularly economic progress that visibly demonstrates improvement in the general standard of living. **Postmodernism** notwithstanding, our economic life has still been dominated by this idea, and the assumption has been that such progress can continue almost indefinitely. But the credit crunch that broke in 2007 has raised severe doubts about the ideology behind this, since it has revealed some serious structural contradictions in our socio-economic system, which has been achieving its spectacular results of the last couple of decades largely on the basis of the creation of a vast debt mountain that eventually proved to be unsustainable. This could be said to provide ammunition for postmodern theorists in their critique of modernity since the **market fundamentalist** ethos that drives our economic life could certainly be classified as a **grand narrative**. It would have to be admitted, however, that specific recommendations as to how to reorder our economic life are rather thin on the ground in postmodern thought. [SS]

CULTURAL MATERIALISM Cultural materialism is the term used by critics Jonathan Dollimore and Alan Sinfield to describe their work (and that of like-minded critics). They argue that culture is inseparable from its conditions of production and reception in history. The term was originally coined by Raymond Williams in the early 1980s to describe 'the analysis of all forms of signification ... within the actual means and conditions of their production'. Cultural materialism's 'key axiom', as

Sinfield calls it, is 'culture is political'. For Dollimore 'there is no cultural practice without political significance'. Their method of analysis takes the form of politically engaged and theoretically informed close readings of, for example, Shakespeare's plays, which would take issue with more conservative readings that make the dramas vessels of universal, timeless values. In this respect cultural materialism is akin to American **new historicism**, though this is a more pessimistic method of analysis that looks to Michel Foucault rather than to Karl Marx, and suggests, as many postmodern critics do, that 'subversion' in Renaissance drama is finally contained and may have been a ruse of **power** to consolidate itself all along. Dollimore finds this work 'salutary', but argues that to contain a threat by rehearsing it at least gives it a voice. [PD]

CULTURAL RELATIVISM Perhaps the first explicit statement of the concept of cultural relativism occurs in Book III of *The Histories* when Herodotus observes that we all follow the customs of the society into which we are born, and that, as a consequence, all such customs should be respected. The following two thousand years saw that principle sadly neglected. While it might be acknowledged that other cultures operated with different value systems, it remained the orthodox view in Western culture from late antiquity to the nineteenth century that alien cultures (African, Oriental, Native American) could be judged from the vantage point of Western 'rationality'.

A fully developed theory of cultural relativism had to wait until the rise of **modern** anthropology in the early twentieth century. A number of American anthropologists began to attempt to understand non-Western cultures 'from the inside'. The proper investigation of other cultures came to involve a complete immersion in the values, traditions and beliefs of those cultures. Other societies came to be seen as self-contained, self-validating 'organic' forms. The corollary of this was a thoroughgoing moral relativism: what is right or wrong is defined within each culture, and there is no objective position from which two different cultural/moral systems might be assessed. [AM]

CULTURAL STUDIES Cultural studies works with an inclusive definition of culture. That is, it is a 'democratic' project in the sense that rather than study only what Matthew Arnold called 'the best which has been thought and said' (*Culture and Anarchy*), cultural studies is committed to examining *all* that has been thought or said. To put it simply, culture is how we live nature (including our own biology): it is the shared meanings we make and encounter in our everyday lives. Culture is not something essential, embodied in particular '**texts**' (that is, any commodity, object or event that can be made to signify), it is the practices and processes of making meanings with and from the 'texts' we encounter in our everyday lives. In this way, then, cultures are made from the production, circulation and consumption of meanings. To share a culture, therefore, is to interpret the world – make it meaningful – in recognizably similar ways.

To see culture as the practices and processes of making shared meanings does not mean that cultural studies believes that cultures are harmonious, organic wholes. On the contrary, cultural studies maintains that the world and all the things in it can be made to have meaning in many different ways. Given this, conflict over making the world mean – insisting on the 'right' meaning(s) – is almost inevitable. It is this conflict – the relations between culture and **power** – which is the core interest of cultural studies.

If meaning is not something fixed and

guaranteed in nature, but is the result of particular ways of expressing nature in culture, then the meaning of something can never be fixed, final or true; its meaning will only ever be contextual and contingent and, moreover, always open to the changing relations of power. This is not to deny that the world exists in all its materiality but to insist that it is only made meaningful in culture. Moreover, dominant ways of knowing the world – making it meaningful – produced by those with the power to make their ways of knowing circulate **discursively** in the world, generate ways of seeing, thinking and acting, which may come to assume authority over the ways in which we see, think and act; that is, provide us with 'scripts' from which meanings can be made and actions carried out. This makes practices and processes of signification a key concern in cultural studies' focus on the relations between culture and power. [JS]

CYBERPUNK Cyberpunk is a term loosely applied to a variety of recent science fiction. It was first used by critics to describe William Gibson's influential science-fiction novel *Neuromancer* (1984) and then such writers as Bruce Sterling, John Shirley, Pat Cadogan and Elizabeth Vonarburg, who present a grimly commodified dystopian future. Stylistically, cyberpunk is an eclectic collage of influences, among them the film *Blade Runner* (1982), William Burroughs, Thomas Pynchon, Raymond Chandler, *film noir* and the 'psychological' science fiction of late 1960s counterculture: J. G. Ballard, Philip K. Dick and Samuel Delany. 'Cyber' comes from control and communications systems and 'punk' from the relative youth of the writers and their indebtedness to popular music and TV.

Cyberpunk is interested primarily in the interface (a favourite word) between humans and new technologies such as 'virtual reality' and cloning, and in the psychological and philosophical consequences of the blurring of such distinctions as human/machine and illusion/reality. Seen as quintessentially **postmodern** by many critics, the world of cyberpunk is a bleak Baudrillardian one of **simulation**, where image and reality have imploded. However, many women writers have been drawn to the genre to explore, through the virtual disembodiment of **cyberspace**, different constructions of gender and gender relations. [PD]

CYBERSPACE Take the mouse on your computer. Remove a document from a file and throw it away. Once upon a time you would have typed DOS (disk operating system) instructions to do this. The graphic user interface (GUI) which spatializes the process is a version of cyberspace, a virtual space that exists nowhere and is made of millions of pieces of information. It is where your money is. What if you could put on a certain kind of headset and dissolve the distinction between you and your computer, entering the information site through your mind? And what if more than one of you could enter the (non-) space and could interact? This is the premise of *Neuromancer* (1984), William Gibson's hugely influential **cyberpunk** novel. Gibson invented the term 'cyberspace' in the novel and describes it as 'a consensual hallucination experienced daily by billions of legitimate operators in every nation. A graphic representation of data extracted from the banks of every computer in the human system. Unthinkable complexity.' Cyberspace is a non-space that is everywhere and yet nowhere. This space exists: it is called the **Internet**, the decentralized and global network of networks. We do have interaction: it is called a multi-user domain (MUD). We can make porous the human/machine interface: it is called **virtual reality**. All that makes Gibson's book science fiction is the nature of the interface, which is of an interactive complexity we have not yet achieved. Cyberspace is a world of **postmodern simulation**, where image and reality, human and machine implode, become porous.

While for some, cyberspace throws up profound epistemological and ontological problems, for many the democracy of the Internet is a potential liberation, not least from the sexual, racial and bodily identities they live with in the corporeal world. [PD]

CYBORG The term cyborg was coined in 1960 by Manfred Clynes, a research space scientist. A combination of 'cybernetic' and 'organism', it is used to describe a hybrid being who is half human, half machine. Cyborgs have been a staple motif in science fiction since the 1920s. However, they have gained a new position in the popular imagination since the success of such cult films as *Terminator* (1984). Beneath its playing out of familiar macho fantasies, *Terminator* also communicates the anxiety inherent in the concept of the cyborg, whose technological modifications, combined with the emotionlessness of a machine, make him an invincible instrument of destruction. In its iconic role, therefore, the cyborg acts as a symbol of the fear that humanity itself is in danger of becoming absorbed into a wholly technological future within which the machine becomes the paradigm by which the organic itself functions.

On a more mundane plane, however, cyborgs already exist, for mechanical body parts are now routinely used as a replacement for human organs, joints and limbs. For **postmodernist** techno-theorists such as Donna Haraway, it is these less dramatic manifestations of the cyborg that demonstrate that a future in which the boundaries between the organic and the technological are being transgressed every day is one we already, inescapably, inhabit. [SG]

D

DARK MATTER AND DARK ENERGY Neither dark matter nor dark energy has yet been observed. Indeed, they may not even exist, but simply be an unanticipated consequence of our present incomplete and possibly erroneous theoretical cosmological model. Even so, most present estimates put the composition of the universe at around 22 per cent dark matter, 74 per cent dark energy and only 4–5 per cent conventional atomic matter. Hence the urgency with which cosmologists are computing and searching.

Since the mid-1930s repeated astronomical and cosmological measurements of increasing resolution on spiral galaxies and clusters of galaxies, alongside gravitational lensing effects, have all suggested strongly that there is some force in addition to the normal visible matter that we can see that is influencing our observations. Equations of motion derived from our understanding of Einstein's general **relativity** suggest that the missing matter must be around five times greater than the ordinary every-day atomic matter with which we are familiar. The term 'dark matter' was coined since the missing material appears totally transparent and does not interact with normal atomic (baryonic) matter or electromagnetic radiation in any way, shape or form. However, as for much else on the boundaries of our understanding, dark matter may have a real, but as yet undiscovered, physical existence, or else it may simply be a ghostly presence thrown up by our provisional understanding of the physics involved that would evaporate under a different theoretical framework.

In general the difficulty is one of trying to understand physical behaviour at extremely large astronomical and small atomic scales simultaneously, requiring recourse to both relativity and **quantum mechanics** through what has come to be known as quantum gravity. All previous attempts to come up with a theory of quantum gravity have thrown up unexpected twists, suggesting that the conceptual models employed were incompatible at a fundamental level. Most recently **M-theory** (successor to **string theory**) has looked to the use of additional hidden dimensions to couple effects at the quantum level and 'borrow' matter into our own dimensions, thus removing the need for dark matter. Quantum loop gravity, on the other hand, posits that even empty space is made up of a kind of linked and looped energy that is in effect crumpled up to form matter in which the effects are distributed wider than the specific location.

Dark energy is a more challenging problem still. Observations indicate that the expansion of the universe has started to speed up in the last few billion years. To explain this, physicists have invoked the inherent energy of the vacuum of space-time – otherwise known as dark energy, or the energy of nothingness. However, all our current theories of **particle physics** predict the strength of this dark energy to be about 120 orders of magnitude larger than actually observed, and general relativity cannot explain the discrepancy. This is an area of cosmology in which apparently small changes to the structure of present equations can have widely divergent consequences. The area would seem ripe therefore for a fundamental reappraisal.

Both dark matter and dark energy are of interest to **postmodernists** in that such huge variations in predictions, their consequences and general perceptions of the world can arise from subtly differing fundamental structures. In particular, postmodernists' attraction to the **sublime**, the unknowable or always incompletely knowable is aroused by physicists' and cosmologists' struggle at the interface between perception and prediction; understanding as an elusive chimera always just around the next theoretical corner. As with so much in the history of science it isn't what is directly revealed that seems to endure, but the nature of the new questions we learn to ask in the process. [BW]

DEATH OF THE AUTHOR Roland Barthes' notion of the death of the author is one of the rallying cries for **poststructuralism** in its insistence that the author is not to be regarded as the final arbiter of a **text**'s meaning. In Barthes' view, **authors** had come to be considered as authority figures, thus placing the reader in an inferior position. He called for the death of the author (more precisely, the death of a certain conception of the author, the author as authority figure) in order to free the reader to be creative. Reading was no longer to be considered a passive process, but instead an active one in which the reader was fully engaged in the production of textual meaning. The birth of the reader, as Barthes put it, was to be achieved at the expense of the author.

The major thrust of Barthes' attack is against the **modern** tendency to treat authors as cultural icons (the Author rather than the author, with the capital 'A' signalling the importance accorded this figure), rather than authorship as such, and the death of the author is an implicitly anti-traditional notion much in keeping

with the liberationist tenor of the 1960s when it was devised. [SS]

DEATH OF MAN (DEATH OF THE SUBJECT) Michel Foucault is somewhat notorious for proclaiming the death of man (for which we are to read the death of a particular conception of man), and this politically charged idea is certainly prevalent in **poststructuralist** and **postmodernist** thought. (Another way of putting this is to speak of the death of the '**subject**'.) In Foucault's view, man is a recent, and not particularly noteworthy, invention that will be erased by the passage of time. His target is the humanist conception of man (the dominant one in the West for the last few centuries), where the individual is regarded as the focal point of the cultural process.

Earlier versions of the notion can be found in **structuralist** thought, with Claude Lévi-Strauss providing one of the best-known examples: for Lévi-Strauss it is the system, not the individual, that is of importance. Structural Marxism too, with its emphasis on the critical role played by institutional structures in determining the ideology of Western society, assumes the death of man as a starting point for its cultural analyses, which it openly declares to be anti-humanist. Critics of this movement have spoken of it as giving us 'history without a subject'. [SS]

DECONSTRUCTION Deconstruction is a term coined by the French philosopher Jacques Derrida in the late 1960s to offer a mode of reading which is attentive to a **text**'s multiple meanings. Rather than attempting to find a true meaning, a consistent point of view or unified message in a given work, a deconstructive reading *carefully teases out*, to use Barbara Johnson's words, 'the warring forces of signification' at play and waiting to be read in what might be called the textual unconscious. As a mode of reading, then, which exposes a text's internal differences and attends to its repressed contradictions or inherent vulnerabilities, its strategy is also interventionist, and as such, despite many a claim to the contrary, deconstruction is political. This is not only because of the ways in which a deconstructive reading can turn a text's logic against itself by showing how the logic of its language can differ from and play against the logic of its **author**'s stated claims, but also because deconstructors tend to seize on the inconsistencies, inequalities or hierarchies which are expounded or glossed over either by a text, by a whole **discourse**, or even by an entire system of beliefs. For instance, the structure of hierarchy which Derrida sees as implicit in the kinds of '**binary oppositions**' which have traditionally informed, organized and ranked Western thinking, and have therefore led us to value a concept such as 'order' more highly than its opposite, '**chaos**', makes it imperative for Derrida to re-examine other such binary couplets. What the privileging of one term over and above the other (such as good over evil, light over dark, reason over emotion, male over female, master over slave, model over copy, original over reproduction, literature over criticism, high culture over popular culture, etc.) reveals is that the preference for one term always works at the expense or exclusion of the other, subordinated, term. **Difference feminists** have drawn on this kind of analysis to question not only the position of women vis-à-vis men, or the **subaltern** vis-à-vis the Westerner, but moreover to deconstruct the very system of conceptual opposition which has enabled, and still perpetuates, such metaphysical and ideological values in Western society.

Deconstruction then is the very means, Derrida suggests, by which to expose, reverse and dismantle binary oppositions with their hierarchies of value; that is, to render untenable the logic which, while pitching one term against the other, fails to recognize that each term both *differs* from and *defers* to the other term (Derrida's '**différance**' captures both senses of this movement simultaneously), and thus also fails to acknowledge that even though 'good', for example, is distinct from 'evil', as the privileged term 'good' also depends for its meaning on its association with its subordinate opposite, 'evil'. This suggests not only a degree of contamination between opposite terms, each a kind of **trace** of the other, but concomitantly also indicates the impossibility of ever maintaining a clear-cut division in the form of an opposition, hence pointing up once more the unstable nature of meaning. [KL]

DESIRING-MACHINE Individuals constitute desiring-machines in Gilles Deleuze and Félix Guattari's terminology. In *Anti-Oedipus* (1972) they argue that we have transcended such traditional categories as man and nature, and are now in a society that consists of various kinds of 'machine' – for example, desiring-machines, producing-machines and schizophrenic-machines. It is the point of **modern** psychoanalysis (summed up under the blanket heading of **Oedipus**) to repress desiring-machines and, indeed, the expression of desire in general. The desiring-machine is driven by **libidinal** energy rather than reason, and lacks the unity normally associated with individual identity in Western culture. It is therefore seen by the ruling authorities as a threat to social order. [SS]

DETERRITORIALIZATION Gilles Deleuze and Félix Guattari's book *A Thousand Plateaus* (1980) argues the case for **nomadism** as a way of overcoming the oppressiveness of **modern** culture. From this perspective post-**Enlightenment** society has an obsessive concern with territorial boundaries (**territoriality**), enclosing a national domain where the writ of the ruling class applies and the populace is kept in a state of subjection, its behaviour strictly monitored and controlled. Nomadism is designed to subvert this system by achieving a condition of deterritorialization, where there is no settled place of existence and thus no need for a centralized authority which will invariably become a power base for vested interests. To be deterritorialized (as much an intellectual as a physical state for these thinkers), is to create space for the expression of individual desire, and effectively to opt out of modernity as we have known it. [SS]

DIFFÉRANCE Différance, a term coined by Jacques Derrida, both signals how language works and is also another term for the manoeuvres and movements of **deconstruction**. As a descriptive term, Derrida uses it to illustrate, following the Swiss linguist Ferdinand de Saussure, how any word always depends for its meaning not on its natural bond with the real, as if it were its stand-in, but on its association with other words along a whole chain of significations, to which it refers but also from which it is different, thus indicating perpetual movements as well as potential slippages of meaning in language. As a neologism, created from the French verb *différer* which means both 'to differ' and 'to defer', différance, referring to both senses simultaneously and therefore deliberately ambiguous, demonstrates that language is always indeterminate, and that meaning is always undecidable and thus endlessly deferred. As such, différance not only describes linguistic functions, it also performs them. As an interchangeable term for deconstruction it also, however, fulfils another function. While undermining any sense of unity, it can never simply be conceived as its opposite; for, to conceive of différance in op*position* to another

term, such as unity, would be to fix it in a certain *position* and thus curtail what characterizes it: suspension, movement, deferral. Thus, as its very operations illustrate, it is an alternative term for both unity *and* difference. [KL]

DIFFERENCE Difference, as a term in **deconstruction** and **poststructuralism**, signals that a **text** is not an ideal unity, but always subject to indeterminacies inherent in language, which resist interpretive closure of meaning, thus illustrating that although there is a difference between texts, there is also difference within 'one' text. While **postmodernism** tends to celebrate difference, schools of thought following G. W. F. Hegel seek to overcome it. Thus for Hegel difference is something to be mediated, which results in the dialectical synthesis between two terms in an opposition, to produce an altogether new and different third term. For Jacques Derrida, on the other hand, to overcome difference is to subsume two opposing terms in one fusion and reduce them from two into one, without preserving their radical **alterity** from, or difference from, each other, and without respecting each 'one' in its 'many-ness'. For this reason, Derrida suggests, as a third term, the notion of **différance**, which as an alternative to both unity and difference is always marked by an excess, resisting the pull to be unified, to be assimilated into one. Derrida's suspicions in *Altérités* (1986) of the Hegelian tendency to gather and fuse that which is dispersed is a reaction to, as he sees it, the dangerous willingness of thinkers such as Jürgen Habermas either to find or to impose unity or consensus, respectively. In common with Jean-François Lyotard, Derrida believes that to force agreement where there is disagreement, to will consensus where there is dissent, is also to level difference, to efface **otherness** and to eliminate multiplicity. [KL]

DIFFERENCE FEMINISM A highly contentious concern with **difference** is one of the contemporary characteristics of **postmodern** thought. A similar concern also emerged in the 1970s from the practical domain of an emergent feminist politics. Within the second wave of feminism, difference came to signify all the theoretical complexities arising from the sociological observation that women do not possess a uniform social identity. Postmodern thought and difference feminism come together in a fragile alliance: both recognize the practical and epistemological significance of women being variously situated, like men, in a network of many dimensions of identity and **power**.

However, in the context of feminist psychoanalytic theory, 'difference' is used in a narrower sense: it signifies specifically male–female sexual difference. Unlike a feminist psychoanalytic ethics of sexual difference, difference feminism represents a decisive split within feminism itself over the exclusionary dominance of a white, middle-class perspective. Yet this split raises the hope that a new sort of feminist politics will strive for solidarity without doing violence to the intricacies of social identity, the goal being a transformation of the politics of gender in becoming aware of various relations of oppression.

Difference here is not a description of the attributes of a group, but a function of the relations between groups, intending emancipation rather than exclusion. A positive sense of group difference is emancipatory insofar as it is a creation, and not an assertion, of a singular identity given with certainty by experience. The group 'women' has overlapping experiences with such group differences as race, class, religion and ethnicity. To preserve difference without creating new entrenched forms of identity, difference feminists articulate a politics in which the meaning of difference itself becomes a terrain of political struggle. [PSA]

DIFFEREND To Jean-François Lyotard, a differend is a dispute that arises when each party is employing a form of language (or **discourse**) **incommensurable** with the other. Thus an employee being exploited by an unscrupulous employer cannot find redress from that employer in a court set up according to the laws of a society which specifically sanctions economic exploitation of employees by employers. The dispute is irresolvable, except in the sense that one party can use its greater **power** to enforce its will on the other (as happens, for example, in colonial situations). Differends are, therefore, normally suppressed by means of brute power, but Lyotard wants them to be acknowledged, and not taken advantage of by the stronger party. It is the duty of philosophers to help the weaker parties to disputes to find the language (or 'phrase-regimen', as Lyotard refers to it) in which their grievance can be framed.

In a geopolitical sense, recognizing the differend would mean acknowledging the rights of exploited peoples and minority groups to be heard (acknowledging the claims to landownership of the native peoples in North America or Australia, for example), and in general backing away from 'solutions' to political problems based on the mere exercise of power. [SS]

DISCOURSE In Michel Foucault's writings, discourse refers to self-contained systems of thought, belief, or social or political practices, governed by internally accepted regulations and procedures. Foucault pointed out how medicine, for example, became a discourse in **modern** times, but we can also speak of politics or art – or even sexuality – as discourses, with particular concerns and conventions in given periods. From that point of view Marxism is a discourse, as is **modernism** in the arts (and then various sub-branches within modernism itself, such as cubism). The sum of all the discourses in a historical period, say the

Enlightenment, constitutes what Foucault calls an **episteme**.

It is a critical point about discourses that they can come and go; they contain no universal truths that hold over time. They are based on **power** relations, and these can alter. Thus, for Foucault, humanism is merely another discourse, which will one day pass away, 'like a face drawn in sand at the edge of the sea', as he put it at the close of *The Order of Things* (1966). In Foucault's scheme, most discourses are repressive and deserve to be challenged, as he himself challenged the discourse of compulsory heterosexuality in Western culture in his monumental trilogy *The History of Sexuality* (1976–84). [SS]

DISSEMINATION As outlined in the book of the same name by Jacques Derrida (1972), dissemination is a method of reading involving the **deconstruction** of certain highly influential **texts** in the Western philosophical tradition – such as Plato's *Phaedrus.* The concern, as so often in Derrida's work, is with challenging the view that speech is privileged over writing, the latter being a standard assumption of **discourse** in the West. The *Phaedrus* takes the customary Platonic form of a dialogue, in which Socrates listens to a speech written by Lysias which is in the possession of Phaedrus. In his response to Phaedrus, Socrates relates the story of Theuth, the inventor of writing. Much of Derrida's discussion turns on the term 'pharmakon', which Plato uses to refer to writing, and which has been variously translated as both poison and remedy. Derrida points to the deeply ambivalent nature of the term, and from this demonstrates that in his condemnation of writing Socrates borrows from the very tools he disparages, thus undermining his arguments. [DW]

DOT.COMS Dot.coms refers to **Internet**-based companies, taking advantage of the new technology to create a new type of company trading exclusively over the Internet, with largely service-based rather than product-based businesses. The move from production to service – post-Fordism as it is called – is characteristically **post-modernist** in ethos. Although many dot.coms have been and continue to be successful, they have not in general lived up to the expectations they aroused in investment circles in the 1990s. Then, a dot.com bubble occurred, with many companies drawing in massive investment through the stock market way in excess of their actual value. This was thought to be the future for business, with investors seemingly unperturbed by the initial losses of most dot.coms, treating them as worthwhile longer-term bets that would overtake conventional business structures. Many dot.coms soon crashed, however, carrying a huge amount of investment capital with them. Others, such as the online bookseller Amazon, managed to survive, but few have delivered the profit margins that investors were hoping for. [SS]

DOUBLE-CODING Double-coding, according to Charles Jencks, describes a defining characteristic of **postmodern** architecture. In *The Language of Post-Modern Architecture* (1977) he refers to double-coding as 'the combination of **modern** techniques with something else (usually traditional building)'. Among the many examples Jencks uses is British architect James Stirling's addition to the Staatsgalerie in Stuttgart. While obviously a contemporary building, it echoes and plays with past art and architecture, including classical and pop art. Jencks sees this kind of postmodernist building as a way of opening up the minimalist language of modernism to history, context and **difference**.

During the 1980s, Jencks expanded his theory of double-coding into other areas of culture. In art, Jencks sees the return of

representational painting, self-conscious allegory, eclecticism and **hybridity** as signs of ubiquitous postmodern double-coding. In fiction, Jencks admires writers who neither repudiate nor slavishly imitate the experimental modernist writers of the early years of the century, but who, like John Barth and Umberto Eco for instance, give us the traditional pleasures of plot and work on a number of other levels too. Theories of postmodern fiction such as Linda Hutcheon's 'historiographical **metafiction**' have put Jencks' concept to interesting use. [PD]

E

EDGE OF CHAOS **Chaos theory** posits a world in which randomness and determinism can co-exist within the same system. The tension between the two phenomena is most keenly felt at what has been dubbed the edge of chaos: the state in which the system is only just preventing itself from lapsing into chaos. For many commentators, this is the optimum condition for systems to be in, since it encourages innovation and ingenuity to keep chaos at bay. Without that tension, systems (such as species or societies) stagnate, and eventually die out. [SS]

ENDISM Endism refers to the various theories circulating in the last few decades proclaiming the end of phenomena such as history. Francis Fukuyama is notorious for arguing that the collapse of communism signals the end of history in the sense that liberal democratic capitalism has now won the global political struggle, and that henceforth it is the only viable political system. Daniel Bell had earlier proclaimed that we had moved beyond industrialization to what he called a '**post-industrial**' culture, an idea that influenced thinkers like Fukuyama. Jean Baudrillard fits into this developing tradition of endist thought, being happy to abolish history, because, as one of his typically provocative arguments puts it, if we are only alienated in history, then the end *of* history must constitute the end of our alienation.

Postmodernism in general is somewhat ambivalent about endism. On the one hand, postmodernist thinkers are fond of claiming that we have passed over a watershed to a new kind of cultural formation; on the other, postmodernism is often a self-conscious dialogue with the past, in the sense of a recovery of older artistic forms (novelistic realism, figurative painting, pre-**modernist** architecture, etc.) or ideas (the '**sublime**', for example). [SS]

ENLIGHTENMENT PROJECT Historians use the term 'the Enlightenment' to refer to the 'long' eighteenth century which stretches from England's 'Glorious Revolution' (1688) to the outbreak of the French Revolution (1789). But the Enlightenment was not only a historical period; it was also an intellectual project brought into focus by the group of French intellectuals – the *philosophes* – involved in the publication of the *Encyclopédie*, edited by Denis Diderot over a period of 20 years from 1751. The ideals of this group were increasingly shared by educated men and women across the globe.

To understand the relevance of what is repeatedly referred to in **postmodernism** as the 'Enlightenment project', it is vital to distinguish between a critical, often polemical, element and its more progressive, constructive and sometimes prescriptive developments.

Enlightenment was defined as the project of dispelling darkness, fear and superstition; of removing all the shackles from free enquiry and debate. It opposed the traditional powers and beliefs of the church (branded as 'superstition') and raised questions of political **legitimacy**. All received or traditional notions, and social relations, were to be made subject to the scrutiny of the public, and therefore, collective – or intersubjective – use of 'reason'. The comparatively liberal social arrangements which characterized politics and commerce in eighteenth-century England were one important model or inspiration for Enlightenment thinkers. The other was the fantastic achievements of science and technology, in the wake of Sir Isaac Newton's scientific revolution. This was the epoch which first came to terms with extensive and tangible improvements in many areas of life affected by the application of science, giving rise to the dream of a world radically improved, ordered, engineered, mastered. The idea of the improvement of the human race, and of 'moral progress', was born. The desire to master nature developed into the dream of mastering society and history. The dark, nightmarish side of this dream was analysed by Theodor W. Adorno and Max Horkheimer in *Dialectic of Enlightenment* (1947), whose opening reads: '[T]he Enlightenment has always aimed at liberating men from fear and establishing their sovereignty. Yet the fully enlightened earth radiates disaster triumphant.'

One shorthand way to define postmodernism is as the end of the Enlightenment dream of mastery and a definitive improvement to human society through knowledge and technology. In recent years the eighteenth century has become the focus of intensive historical research. The results, recorded in fascinating biographies and penetrating monographs, could go a long way to correcting the caricature of the Enlightenment which the 'postmodernism' debates have tended to circulate. The eighteenth century saw traditional certainties dissolve. Even the most optimistic thinkers were plagued by doubt and even despair. It was a time of constant experimentation, not of complacent self-confidence. [LS]

EPISTEME For Michel Foucault, episteme stands for a historical period and all the cultural beliefs and practices it contains.

Those beliefs and practices are expressed within various **discourses** (the law, politics, the arts, for example), and the sum total of all those historically bound discourses constitutes an episteme. All those discourses stand in relation to the dominant ideology of the time, which has the **power** to decide what will count as knowledge, or acceptable practice, within the culture in question. For the **postmodern** historian or cultural critic, it is the power relations within an episteme that are of overriding interest; any analysis of a given period will home in on these, as Foucault himself did in works such as *The Birth of the Clinic* (1963) and *Madness and Civilization* (1964). [SS]

ERASURE Erasure is a **deconstructionist** technique whereby a word or term is used, but what it commits one to (its meaning, as well as the theory of meaning lying behind it) is denied, or, as Jacques Derrida puts it, placed 'under erasure' (*sous rature*). This enables Derrida to claim that he can use the language of Western philosophy without that use committing him to a belief in its concepts or any of its principles. The practice is derived from Martin Heidegger, who in *Zur Seinsfrage* used the word 'being' with a line drawn through it, in order to signal that he did not want to be drawn into debates about the concept, since that would imply his acceptance of Western philosophy's metaphysical assumptions about being. Erasure is one of the ways Derrida attempts to answer what has become a standard criticism of his work: that he relies on language to put his arguments across, while simultaneously claiming that language is unstable and meaning indeterminate. Critics have pointed out that Derrida's critique of language could not be understood unless language and meaning were at least relatively stable. Seen from that latter perspective, the technique of erasure is something of a confidence trick. [SS]

ÉVÉNEMENTS In May 1968, the *événements* (the '**events**') shattered the banal peace of urban Paris. While they may not have achieved the overthrow of Charles de Gaulle's government – although, but for the intervention of the unions, they might well have done so – they *practised* the revolution of everyday life according to the theoretical forecasts and personal dreams of many unorthodox Communist Party members and Marxist theoreticians. Following the arrest of the activist leaders of the National Committee for Vietnam, students at the University of Paris formed the 22nd March Movement and, under the emerging leadership of Daniel Cohn-Bendit, occupied its Nanterre campus and vociferously condemned the education regime as a factory for turning out the bureaucrats of everyday life. Similar occupations and demonstrations followed all over France. Meanwhile, union unrest was also growing, with the major unions rejecting government pay policy and sparking protest marches and strikes throughout the country. The unions themselves, however, began to condemn the activist tendencies of both the workers and the students, opening up the rift between the protesters and their union representatives that would eventually see these populist movements caught in a government-union axis. The spark came when, on 3 May 1968, the Paris riot police, the CRS, surrounded and sealed Nanterre before bombarding the campus with tear gas and invading it. The French Communist Party (PCF), meanwhile, condemned the student occupations, prompting a final break between the students and the left-wing political parties. This break is decisive for the widespread sense of the failure of the Marxist project, since its PCF vanguard effectively colluded with the government and the unions to bring an end to the *événements*, rather than supporting their revolutionary aims. For the first time, decisively for the politics of **postmodernism** in France, Marxism was revealed as a bureaucratic machine for the suppression rather than the advancement of revolution.

Following a massively successful general strike, the workers, students and the angry and the dissident intellectuals of the **Situationist** International took over the streets of Paris. After a month of barricades and immediate revolution, the government forces eventually put down the insurgents while the trade unions swiftly negotiated a return to work. The *événements* nevertheless mark the closest a modern first world state has come to complete dissolution at the hands of popular revolution. [IHG]

EVENT Jean-François Lyotard refers to an 'event' as the change in perspective that takes place after a particularly significant cultural occurrence. The most frequently cited example of this in Lyotard is Auschwitz, which he argues irrevocably altered our perception of human nature and the world in which we live (Theodor W. Adorno had also spoken of the difficulty of writing poetry after the facts of Auschwitz had become known). The 1968 *événements* in Paris are another example of an event which irrevocably altered the world-view of a specific social group, in this case a whole generation of French intellectuals. What was shattered was that generation's belief in the moral supremacy of Marxism, as enshrined in the French Communist Party (PCF). The collusion of the latter with the forces of the state in bringing down the alliance of workers and students that had briefly challenged the state's authority was felt by many French left-wing intellectuals, including Lyotard, to have compromised Marxism to the point where it had lost all credibility. Lyotard speaks of the need to be 'open' to the event, meaning to be able to approach new experiences without bringing with us the prejudices of outmoded theories such as Marxism. [SS]

F

FETISH An object believed to contain magical powers. In **discourse**, it has at least two slightly different implications. In Marxist usage ('commodity fetishism') it suggests a magical **aura** that disguises from those who use it or value it the true nature of an object and the social relations that bring it into being. Thus the material object of a banknote is believed by its fetishistic users to contain value whereas it is in fact a token whose true nature subsists in a complicated system of social relationships. By contrast, in Lacanian usage a fetish provides for the **subject** a substitute for something that is missing (strictly speaking something that fills out the void of the missing maternal phallus). Slavoj Žižek explains this in terms of the pet of a deceased lover that acts as a fetish by subliminally allowing the bereaved partner to act on the basis of a partially repressed belief that the loved one is not dead. Politically, Žižek argues that fetishes can be objects that allow subjects to operate in a supposedly cynical-realist capitalist social order, and that enable them to (pretend to) accept reality 'the way it is'. An example of this might be the phenomenon in UK politics of the State Opening of Parliament in which politicians in suits surround themselves with people in quasi-medieval costume and the trappings of feudalism, thus allowing the participants and spectators to believe that they are part of a stable and unchanging political and economic order validated by antiquity. [PG]

FRACTALS Fractal geometry, a field invented by Benoit Mandelbrot, builds on work begun but discontinued at the turn of last century by the French mathematicians Henri Poincaré, Pierre Fatou and Gaston Julia. Both Mandelbrot and Julia have fractal sets named after them: sets that have served as a cultural icon of **chaos**. There are three basic types of fractal: linear self-similar (or 'self-repeating'), random self-similar, and fractal or 'chaotic' attractors. The first is best illustrated by a phenomenon known as a 'Sierpinski gasket': take a triangle and subdivide its area into smaller triangles. Following this first subdivision, repeat or 'reiterate' the operation on these smaller triangles, and so on ad infinitum. Such a figure is linearly self-similar because each part of the object is exactly like the whole from which it is derived.

Random fractals are found in natural phenomena such as coastlines, mountains and clouds. One of Mandelbrot's earliest explorations of what he then called 'fractional dimension' was entitled 'How Long is the Coastline of Britain?' (1967). His paradoxical thesis in that paper is that since a coastline is not a pure curve but a random series of indents and excrescences, the coastline does not have a line that can be measured, but an infinite series of fractional dimensions that cannot be finally measured. If we regard a coastline from the air, it appears jagged and random. From ground level, a different dimension of randomness is revealed. Microscopically, the randomness is different again, and so on. Hence the various dimensions of randomness revealed by studying coastlines, clouds and mountains are randomly self-similar, since each dimension repeats randomness, but repeats it differently.

Third, chaotic fractals, such as the Mandelbrot set itself, model the behaviour of complex systems. Such systems are really chaotic rather than self-similar since each iteration reacts upon the previous one to produce endless bifurcations. The figure produced by the Mandelbrot set, the most familiar image of chaos, consists of a series of 'blobs' each of which repeats the core blob from which the set starts. With each fractal iteration of the blob, however, a new fractal dimension is produced that does not resemble the whole. This system is therefore complex, both linearly self-similar and random, depending upon which fractal dimension of this nonlinear, dynamical system is studied. [IHG]

FUNDAMENTALISM **Postmodernist** philosophers may argue that **grand narratives** are in decline, but the popularity of religious fundamentalism around the world suggests this may be an over-optimistic assessment. Most of the major world religions have fundamentalist movements: Christianity and Islam are the most prominent, but Hinduism and Judaism have their committed activists as well. Fundamentalism was coined as a term to describe radical Protestant evangelism in early twentieth-century America. Christianity was reduced to a set of fundamental beliefs (such as the virgin birth of Christ) that could not be questioned by adherents. Central to this outlook was the Bible, which in the more militant forms of fundamentalist thought is taken to be literally true. There are similar attitudes in Islam with regard to the Q'ran.

Fundamentalism is to some extent a reaction to postmodern scepticism towards authority, and has been described as an 'authority-minded' movement. Whatever the complexities of the relationship between these two cultural movements, it is clear there is a larger market for traditional systems of belief, and the security they can provide for individual believers, than postmodernist theorists have been claiming. [SS]

FUZZY LOGICS Otherwise known as 'vague' or 'multivalent' (many-valued), fuzzy logics have been developed since the 1920s, when Jan Lukasiewicz, a Polish logician, formalized a continuum of possible states. Lukasiewicz's impetus came from Werner Heisenberg's uncertainty principle, which postulated that no observer can measure both the position and the velocity of a given electron. In other words, the more precisely the electron's velocity is delineated, the more vague its position becomes. **Quantum mechanics** therefore demanded a more flexible mathematical model, not in order to resolve the uncertainty, but, on the contrary, to account for it.

More recently, fuzzy logics have found a niche in **artificial intelligence** research, where neural nets 'grow' fuzzy rules from fuzzy data, rather than computers getting it wrong with unerring precision. Fuzzy logics allow computers to learn rather than simply to act upon pre-programmed instruction, exactly in the way that humans learn within a context of real-world fuzziness: humans do not act in accordance with formal rules so much as by approximation and adjustment. Thus Bart Kosko's *Fuzzy Thinking* (1993) contrasts the fuzziness of everyday life with the artificial, black-and-white, 1 or 0, binary world long championed by science and philosophy, and even goes so far as to suggest that fuzziness has a history repressed by the avatars of precision that, since Aristotle, have acquired an unshakeable prestige under Western science. The logical basis of such models of scientific certainty ('true or false', but not both) was formulated by Aristotle in the fourth century BC as the law of the excluded middle, which states that a thing cannot be both x and not-x at the same time. In reality, of course, things are frequently x and not-x. At what precise point, for example, does a half-eaten apple cease to be an apple; at what point does the apple cease to be red and become not-red? Fuzzy logics therefore replace the two-value abstractions (black or white, x or not-x) of the law of the excluded middle with a multivalent, 'fuzzy' principle of '*both* x and not-x'. What this means in practice is that precise, quantitative points are replaced by qualitative shifts, a phenomenon that, according to many mathematicians, aligns fuzziness with, for example, the new mathematics of **fractal** objects. [IHG]

G

GENEALOGY Genealogy denotes the tracings of the origin of a phenomenon, and is associated principally with Friedrich Nietzsche. Whereas Immanuel Kant had looked for the conditions of knowledge, and asked 'how is x possible?', Nietzsche wished to add a second question to this, namely, 'why is x necessary?' Genealogy is therefore an investigation into the combined possibilities and necessities of a form of life. Nietzsche's most sustained exploration into origins is *Toward a Genealogy of Morals* (1887). Here he tracks the formation of notions of 'good' and 'bad', and 'good' and 'evil', and the corresponding states of responsibility, guilt and bad conscience which usually accompany those terms. Nietzsche's project is not primarily etymological. Rather, he is careful to stress that the evolution of a thing is not directed towards a single purpose, but is subject to changing pressures and circumstances.

More recently, Michel Foucault has engaged extensively with the work of genealogy. In *Discipline and Punish* (1975), he presents a history of how Western society has dealt with crime. He illustrates a shift from practices involving bodily mutilation and public humiliation, common at the time of Shakespeare, to punishments since the eighteenth century involving incarceration or financial reparation. Again it is the non-continuities and complex transactions between institutions and their **discursive power** that are highlighted. [BL]

GENERATION X Asked by a publisher to write a guide to the twenty-something generation, Douglas Coupland turned in a novel, the phenomenally successful *Generation X* (1991), noted for capturing the mindset and language of privileged young 1990s Californians. A good deal of the novel's energy comes from the marginalia – a whole series of Zeitgeist-defining neologisms, asides and summaries which generalize the main characters' experience. Generation X-ers are young, well-educated, under-employed post-babyboomers who despise the corporate ideology of the 1980s, but have little to put in its place. In this vacuum, they affect a **postmodern** superficiality, an all-pervasive 'knee-jerk **irony**', spending their time practising an ironic form of cultural snobbery by one-upping each other with knowledge of TV trivia ('obscurism') when not doing low-paid, low-esteem, no-future, service-sector work ('McJobs'). They get by through personally tailored but wildly uninformed philosophico-religious beliefs ('Me-ism') and settle for 'lessness' – reconciling themselves to diminishing expectations. If, for some, these modes of living disguise a romantic longing for a form of authentic experience often associated in classic American literature with nature, then other X-ers might say (if they would admit to reading him): 'Nature? How *Ralph Waldo Emerson*.' [PD]

GLOBAL WARMING There is a clear consensus within the scientific community that the Earth's average temperature is rising as a consequence of massively increased carbon emissions (in the main from fossil fuels) being pumped into the atmosphere in recent years and that some fairly drastic, as well as urgent, action is required to counter this. The argument is that the progressively higher levels of carbon dioxide are creating a 'greenhouse effect' that will soon project us past a series of critical environmental 'tipping points'. Some dire warnings have been issued about what this could mean for humankind's future, such as dramatic rises in sea levels (with figures as high as seventy-five metres being postulated) that would lead to the loss of the world's coastal cities and a likely breakdown in the global political system.

The warnings are based on computer predictions, and there is still controversy as to how accurate these can be considered. A vocal anti-global warming lobby has grown up (particularly in the business world, which has a vested commercial interest in the continued consumption of carbon-emitting products) that is highly sceptical about the predictions, claiming that global warming is a natural phenomenon, caused by solar cycles rather than human activity, and that its likely effects are being wildly exaggerated. Since all the proposed solutions to date (a wholesale switch-over to green energy, various highly speculative and untested geo-engineering schemes, etc.) look prohibitively expensive to put into practice, such arguments tend to carry a lot of weight in political circles, and as yet almost nothing substantial has been done to address the issue.

If the predictions prove to be correct, however, then the environmental effects will have to be seen as a direct consequence of **modernity** and the cult of material and technological progress it promotes. The **grand narrative** of modernity will stand revealed as unsustainable in the longer term. This is an argument that the **Green movement** has been putting forward for some time now, and it has a definite resonance for the general critique being conducted of modernity by **postmodernists**. [SS]

GLOBALIZATION Globalization strives to create a worldwide economic market in which the nation state has an increasingly peripheral role. It is possible to see globalization either as an aspect of, or a threat to, **postmodern** ideals. The **power** of the nation state has certainly been weakened by the ability of multinationals to outsource their production to the lowest bidder: few of the products consumed in the West are actually manufactured there any more. Reducing the power of the nation state is a long-running objective of libertarians, who feel this will increase individual freedom. But if power passes to the multinationals instead, the individual is in many cases left worse off – multinationals, after all, do not have to answer to the voters in elections. The **anti-capitalist** movement has bitterly opposed this shift in power, arguing that it simply reduces the living standards of workers worldwide, even in the developing world, where most of the production is transferred. Globalization tends to favour **market fundamentalism** (unregulated capitalism) as its method of operation, which many see as a threat to the ideals of postmodernism. [SS]

GRAMMATOLOGY The term 'grammatology' first came to prominence with the publication of Jacques Derrida's *Of Grammatology* in 1967, and describes a science of writing that puts into question the inherent value of the linguistic **sign**. Derrida's use of the term is part of a critique of Western philosophy for giving precedence to speech over writing. Western philosophical **discourse** is held to be committed to phonetic writing: the kind of writing that attempts fully to represent speech. Grammatology as a science of writing is part of a general tendency in Derrida's work to redress this balance. Central to this process is the refutation of the **structuralist** notion that signifier and signified form an organic unity. Speech is regarded as an original **presence** in structuralist linguistics and writing an invasion of purity. **Logocentric** writing (the reproduction of the phoneme or the voice), is distinguished by the grammatologist from écriture, or grammatological writing, which is concerned with characterizing those actions that create language. Following Derrida, the grammatologist argues that 'there is nothing outside the **text**', and that language is open to myriad interpretations that continually defer meaning. This involves a rejection of the possibility of an absolute truth fixed by a transcendental signifier. Such a position has affinities with the **postmodern** dismissal of **grand narratives**. [DW]

GRAND NARRATIVE Jean-François Lyotard described as grand narratives theories which claim to provide universal explanations and trade on the authority this gives them. A prime example would be Marxism, which processes all human history and social behaviour through its theory of dialectical materialism. According to dialectical materialism all human history has been the history of class struggle, and it denies the validity of all other explanations, laying sole claim to the truth. The ultimate goal of human history is the 'dictatorship of the proletariat', where class struggle has been eliminated for the common good and individuals are no longer exploited. Most religions offer a similarly all-embracing explanation of human history to fit their particular schemes. Lyotard's contention is that such schemes are implicitly authoritarian, and that by the late twentieth century they had lost all claim to authority over individual behaviour. It is part of living in a **postmodern** world that we can

no longer rely on such grand narratives (or '**metanarratives**'), but must construct more tactically orientated '**little narratives**' instead if we wish to stand up against authoritarianism. In Lyotard's view, we have now seen through grand narratives and realized that their claims to authority are false and unsustainable. [SS]

GREENS (GREEN MOVEMENT) The increasing threat to the environment posed by **modern** industrial and technological processes (resulting in, for example, the phenomenon of **global warming**) has led to the formation of pressure groups to resist, and, if possible, arrest this cultural trend. Collectively, such groups have been dubbed the 'Greens', and have had a significant impact on Western culture. It is not just the processes that the Greens have called into question, however, but also the socio-economic and political systems they derive from, with their seemingly insatiable demand for technological progress and ever higher levels of consumption.

Although they have enjoyed a certain amount of success in local and national elections across Western Europe, the Greens function most effectively as a pressure group. In this latter guise they have managed to make most of the continent's major political parties and public institutions pay at least lip-service to Green principles, such as the need to protect the environment by restricting car usage and controlling the disposal of industrial waste. The Green movement can be regarded as **postmodern** in its generally sceptical attitude towards progress, as well as in the way that it cuts across existing political party lines to challenge the prevailing **power** structures in Western society. [SS]

H

HEGEMONY The concept of hegemony was most notably used by the Italian Marxist theorist Antonio Gramsci as a way of explaining how the ruling class in a capitalist society managed to impose its ideology on the mass of the population – most of the time without recourse to force. Thus the belief system of bourgeois capitalism could be communicated through the arts and the media, which could present the principles of that ideology as ideals to be aspired to by the general population – or, more simply, as the 'natural' order of things (it is 'natural' for human beings to compete, etc.).

The **structural** Marxist theorist Louis Althusser later built on Gramsci's ideas to suggest that Western societies consisted of various 'Ideological State Apparatuses' (ISAs), and a 'Repressive State Apparatus' (RSA). It was the role of the ISAs (the educational system, the arts and the media, for example) to disseminate the ideological principles of the ruling class, such that they became part of everyday life for the bulk of the population to the point where the population no longer even recognized that it was being indoctrinated. The RSA (the government, police and army) was there to impose order by violent means if the ISAs failed in their objective.

In **postmodernist** thought, the concept of hegemony has been revised by Ernesto Laclau and Chantal Mouffe, who in *Hegemony and Socialist Strategy* (1985) emphasized its *contingent* nature, pointing out that it had been devised to explain away (in somewhat ad hoc fashion) some apparent failings of Marxist theory. Historical necessity, one of the cornerstones of classical Marxist thought, dictated that the working class eventually *ought* to have risen up against its exploiters; hegemony explained why it generally did not, but in so doing cast doubt on the validity of the classical Marxist conception of historical necessity itself. Neither did Laclau and Mouffe believe in the working class as a homogeneous 'totality' in the manner of classical Marxism, but instead as liable to fragmentation. They concluded that what hegemony demonstrated was the need to develop a **pluralist** Marxism, which would involve the many new social movements that had arisen in the later twentieth century (the **Greens**, for example, as well as various ethnic and sexual minorities). [SS]

HIGH ENERGY PARTICLE PHYSICS Early concepts of particle physics can be traced back to the sixth-century BC Greek 'atomist' philosophers Leucippus and Democritus, re-emerging again with European **Enlightenment** physicists such as Robert Boyle and Sir Isaac Newton and maturing with John Dalton in the nineteenth century. The **modern** atomic era post-World War II has seen the growth of particle accelerators capable of colliding streams of atoms together at extremely high speeds – and hence energies – to break them down into smaller components to investigate the structure of sub-atomic particles. Some of the resulting sub-atomic entities, such as the more familiar electrons, protons and neutrons, are stable constituent components of atoms, whereas others are very unstable and short lived, decaying or interacting extremely rapidly back to more stable forms.

After decades of practical and theoretical research elementary particles have been categorized into families such as Quarks, Leptons and Bosons with a range of family properties termed variously as spin, strangeness, charm, colour and so on. The term 'particle' is actually misapplied in many respects because the dynamics of particle physics are governed by **quantum mechanics** which also implies distributed wave-like properties, often loosely described as 'wave-particle duality'. Physicists have erected a 'standard model' to explain the various experimental results, properties and inter-relationships in a structured way. At the moment discovery of the predicted Higgs Boson is eagerly awaited from experiments at the Large Hadron Collider (LHC) at CERN in Geneva and Fermilab's Tevatron in Batavia (USA). The Higgs Boson is a vital – but as yet undetected – component of the standard model responsible for particles having intrinsic mass and so is central to its validation. A number of theoreticians unhappy with various aspects of the standard model are exploring other approaches, such as **M-theory** (successor to **string theory**) aimed at a 'grand unified theory', often popularly termed a 'theory of everything'.

Particle physics is of necessity a foundational activity of modern science and therefore naturally attracts the attention of **postmodernists**, especially because of its strong reductionist approach. Theory formation is at the centre of all philosophical constructs, and particle physics provides a fertile arena in which science and philosophy are naturally forced into intimate contact. [BW]

HOMOSOCIALITY Although it is by no means a particularly **postmodern** phenomenon, homosociality does have implications for how we perceive and construct gender relations now. The term refers to single-sex relationships that do not necessarily include the element of sexual relations, as occurs in the activities of both male bonding and female bonding. Clearly, bonding of this nature has gone on throughout history, and indeed feminists argue that male homosociality is still a major barrier to the achievement of gender equality. Most workplaces and institutions are controlled by men, and there is a decidedly masculinist culture operating overall in the worlds of business and politics. In this regard male homosociality often functions much like a **grand narrative**.

It is the relationship between male homosociality and **power** that needs to be addressed, therefore, rather than the condition itself, which in most other respects could be considered relatively benign. It is only when homosociality discriminates against **difference** and diversity that significant socio-political problems arise. [SS]

HYBRIDITY The concept of hybridity is central to the **discourses** of **postcolonial** theory and **cultural studies**. Hybridity refers to the ambivalent conceptual 'space' between adversarial, polarized perspectives and/or ideologies. Challenging the notion that any political ideology can claim transcendent or metaphysical authority for itself, the discourse of hybridity counters notions of the **metaphysics of presence**, and facile **binary oppositions**, by foregrounding the interstices or fault lines where identities are performed and contested.

Theorists such as Homi K. Bhabha, Paul Gilroy, Stuart Hall and Gayatri Chakravorty Spivak have written on the concept. Bhabha in particular has developed the idea in relation to the identity of the colonised **Other**. In *Signs Taken for Wonders* (1985) he argues that: 'The display of hybridity – its peculiar "replication" – terrorizes authority with the ruse of recognition, its mimicry, its mockery'. He locates the 'hybrid moment' in the interstitial 'third space' wherein meaning is always in between, in process, contestatory and resistant to closure. Critical of essentialist notions of identity with their connotations of fixity and repression, hybridity, for Bhabha, captures the liberatory potential of resistant cultures, by subverting dualistic categories and initiating 'mutual and mutable' identity formations 'in between' the static binarisms of colonizer and colonized. [AY]

HYPERMEDIA is the name given to an interactive network of media with hyperlinks provided for ready access online. **Text**, graphics, audio and video can be connected in this manner, giving the user a wide range of related material and modes of presenting it. It represents a development of the idea of **hypertext**, which allowed the user to move out of the main text being read online in order to gain more information on specific details of that text by means of hyperlinks; other related texts could be accessed, for example, or images that were mentioned in the original text but not reproduced there. Once the process is underway the chain of hyperlinks could go on almost indefinitely.

The concept of hypermedia, with its non-linear form of operation, is quintessentially **postmodern**. There is no overall plan as to how to proceed, no specific route mapped out. Instead, the links can be deployed in any order the user wants, in an associative fashion, often taking her far away from her starting point. From a postmodern perspective there is no **grand narrative** dictating what should be done, and the concept of **authorship** is problematized, since the shape of the **narrative** created in each case depends on the associations made by the individual user, who thereby controls the direction of its flow. [SS]

HYPERREALITY The term hyperreality is used by Jean Baudrillard to indicate the 'loss of the real', where distinctions between surface and depth, the real and the imaginary no longer exist. The world of the hyperreal is where image and reality implode. Baudrillard suggests that we no longer need models of analysis such as Marxism with its language of surface and depth, for there are no depths. Marxism, which sees the market *behind* everything, must give way to the idea that the market is *in* everything but *behind* nothing. In a famous example, Baudrillard chooses Disneyland as an illustration of a third-order image, a magical space which masks the absence of the real. He argues that, just as prisons exist to mask the fact that society *itself is* one, 'Disneyland is presented as imaginary in order to make us believe that the rest is real, when in fact all of Los Angeles and the America surrounding it are no longer real, but of the order of the hyperreal'.

While Baudrillard's concept may be criticized in any number of ways, it seems to capture something of the flavour of the commodified and mediated nature of contemporary life. [PD]

HYPERTEXT Hypertext is electronic text that provides links between key elements, allowing the reader to move through information non-sequentially. Now the key technology of the worldwide web, the idea of hypertext can be traced back to an article published in 1945 by Franklin D. Roosevelt's wartime science adviser, Vannevar Bush. Bush envisaged mechanically linked machines for the storage and retrieval of information, allowing scholars, researchers and others access to large amounts of information without having to deal with the cumbersome storage and classification methods of traditional archives and libraries. Bush proposed a device called the Memex, with translucent screens, levers and motors, which would allow the user to annotate and link information on microfilm.

The term itself was coined by Theodore H. Nelson in 1965: 'By "hypertext", I mean non-sequential writing – **text** that branches out and allows choices to the reader, best read at an interactive screen.' Nelson envisaged hypertext in utopian fashion as an encyclopaedic gathering together of all printed texts in a global hypertext publishing system called 'Xanadu'.

For some critics and theorists, the non-linearity, linkage and decentredness of hypertext appear to demonstrate empirically the insights regarding reading and textuality advanced by such thinkers as Jacques Derrida, Roland Barthes and Michel Foucault. George P. Landow in his book *Hypertext: The Convergence of Contemporary Critical Theory and Technology* (1992), claims that 'critical theory promises to theorize hypertext and hypertext promises to embody and thereby test aspects of theory, particularly those concerning textuality, **narrative** and the roles or functions of reader and writer'. At the same time, critics like Landow and J. David Bolter claim that hypertext encourages a more 'natural' and associative way of reading. The inherent utopianism of much hypertext theory has recently come under attack: while the *analogies* between hypertext and the works of Derrida, for example, are clear, it is unclear what the 'realization' or 'fulfilment' of a philosophy like **deconstruction** (not a *project* in any traditional sense) could mean. [BD]

INCOMMENSURABILITY Many **postmodernists** hold to a version of the 'Sapir-Whorf hypothesis'. In its strongest form it is the claim that linguistic structures condition thought patterns and *determine* our perception of the world. This could be taken to mean that speakers of different languages in a sense inhabit different worlds. Incommensurability is a term taken from mathematical theory where it refers to two qualities or magnitudes which have no common measure. The notion has been loosely transferred to debates about the role of language. Two languages are incommensurable if their structures make exact translation between them difficult or impossible. The term 'incommensurability' has gained currency together with a view (or speculative hypothesis) that all languages are incommensurable one with another.

The most precise formulation of this view is presented by the philosopher Willard van Orman Quine as part of a more general scepticism about the very idea of meaning. Quine dramatized what he termed 'the indeterminacy of translation'. This is not the same as the platitude that there are shades of meaning which might be lost in the process of translation; instead, it implies that the very notion of shades of meaning which are uncaptured is pointless. Each language posits a different set of objects, and maps the world in a different way. Thomas Kuhn's work deals with scientific paradigms. At its most basic, a paradigm is simply an exemplary model. But in the context of scientific theories it is also taken to refer to the interrelationships between a whole system of concepts. There are many postmodern writers on the philosophy of science who suggest that competing scientific paradigms are in principle incommensurable.

The notion of incommensurability reappears in Jean-François Lyotard's concept of the '**differend**'. The differend is incommensurability politicized. Each party inhabits not simply their own language, and thus their own world; they inhabit a 'phrase regimen', embodying interests and objectives. One phrase regimen exerts dominance over another. Incommensurability captured the idea of opacity between languages. The differend suggests an opacity, and a deformation, created by the action of one language – or phrase regimen – on another. [LS]

INSTALLATION ART came into vogue during the late 1960s and 1970s to describe works by Marcel Broodthaers, Hans Haacke, Daniel Buren and Michael Asher that drew attention to or challenged the cultural, institutional, political dimensions of the art gallery. These matters were dealt with in a number of ways, but Haacke's exploration of the politics of communication via the incorporation of corporate logos and advertising copy into the artwork coloured subsequent works by a wide range of artists including Terry Atkinson, Peter Kennard, Susan Hiller and some of the 'Young British Artists' (yBas). [CT]

INTERNET An electronic space that **cyberpunk** author William Gibson has called a 'consensual hallucination', in many ways the Internet, combining a technological reality with immense politically hallucinatory potential, is *the* exemplary **postmodern** object, and arguably even the architecture of postmodern culture. Its technological roots lie in a system developed by the American Advanced Research Projects Agency to link their computers into a network, forming ARPAnet, which went online towards the end of 1969. Since then it has grown geometrically, and has been championed as the source and – although geography is a problem in **cyberspace** – the site of a new, utopian political order, marking the rise of what Howard Rheingold has famously called 'virtual communities' where information flows without property relations and where anyone can have access to anyone else.

In consequence many of the political conflicts associated with postmodernism, and even the posts one ought to inhabit within postmodern and **post-industrial** societies, are now being contested on the Net. For example, Jean-François Lyotard's call, as *The Postmodern Condition* (1979) draws to an end, for the public to be given access to all databases stems from his thesis that, in a computerized society, information is **power**. Lyotard's pronouncement echoes the Internet ideologues' credo 'information wants to be free'; meanwhile, however, corporate concerns have set about the commercialization of the Internet, ensuring that the days of democratized information flow are running out.

This is not, however, a change of direction following the origins of the Internet; rather, the whole purpose of the ARPAnet was to find a means whereby, in the event of a nuclear strike, no single node or post in the network would be responsible for the continuing functioning of the entire net. In other words, the absence of central control on the Net, championed as its chief political virtue by Internet activists, derives from the military necessity that the defence grid remain functional even if some of the nodes in the Net are taken out. To this extent, the democratic impetus of Lyotard's proposals, the anarcho-syndicalism of virtual communities and the ideological sloganizing of the informational libertarians seem, in the long run, doomed to lose their political naivety. The Internet is not beyond war and capital; rather, their territories and markets have been uploaded into cyberspace. [IHG]

INTERTEXTUALITY Many classic literary texts, from François Rabelais' *Gargantua and Pantagruel*, through Robert Burton's *Anatomy of Melancholy* and on to Laurence Sterne's *Tristram Shandy*, are woven from other texts: references, citations and quotations tumbling together in disorientating superabundance. However it was only with Julia Kristeva's *Semiotike* (1969) that it was claimed that *'every'* text takes shape as a mosaic of citations, every text is the absorption and transformation of other texts'.

The concept of intertextuality derived from the **poststructuralist** claim that signifiers refer always and only to other signifiers: that language can be transformed, translated, transferred, but never transcended. Words gain their meaning not by referring to some object present to the mind of the language user but from the never-ending play of signification. To use the word 'love' is not to refer to some extra-linguistic biological or psychological object but, consciously or unconsciously, to join in a conversation that takes in the lays of the troubadours, Shakespearean tragedy, romantic lyrics and the songs of the Beatles.

Postmodernism embraces an extreme notion of intertextuality, in which the play of meaning is infinite, in which anything goes. The limits of interpretation are set only by the boundaries of the imagination. [AM]

IRONY We are all familiar with irony as a figure of speech in which the intended meaning is the opposite of that expressed by the words used. In the form of sarcasm or ridicule, irony can express a degree of hostility. It is common in jokes which sometimes separate 'insiders' (who share the joke) from those being laughed at (who do not 'get it' – that is, do not see the irony). Irony is always connected with a requirement not to take things (including ourselves) too seriously, or at least not to take things at face value. Nothing is so characteristic of the current **postmodern** 'mood' as its ironic, detached self-consciousness. Umberto Eco has characterized postmodernism as an attitude in which we cannot give up our cherished hopes and beliefs, but at the same time can no longer embrace them with unqualified or wholehearted adherence. In *Contingency, Irony, and Solidarity* (1989) Richard Rorty sketches and recommends the figure of the 'liberal ironist'. 'Ironists' face up to the contingency of their beliefs; 'liberal ironists' are aware that among these lie such things as 'their own hope that suffering will be diminished'. [LS]

J

JOUISSANCE No adequate translation exists for the French term *jouissance*. *Jouir de* implies the ability to profit from pleasure; *jouissance* connotes the bliss of sexual orgasm. In **postmodern discourse** this psychoanalytic term gains significance from its opposite, the lack accompanying desire. Julia Kristeva suggests the existence of a feminine *jouissance* that exceeds the bounds of patriarchal language, remaining within woman's vision but beyond articulation; this pleasurable experience is associated with the child's joyful continuity with the maternal. Luce Irigaray defines a 'hysterical' *jouissance* that would not be 'paternal', but would be unrepresentable – remaining forever a lack within patriarchy. [PSA]

L

LANGUAGE GAMES In *Philosophical Investigations* (1953) Ludwig Wittgenstein treated language as a series of games, each having its own internal conventions that we learn to deploy. The key aspect to pay attention to was how words were used rather than their meaning, and usage could change, as the rules of any game could. The implication of this was not lost on the **poststructuralist/postmodernist** community, for whom it provided reinforcement of their view that meaning was not fixed and stable but rather indeterminate. That community pushed the notion further than Wittgenstein, with meaning becoming the most transitory of phenomena for such as Jacques Derrida, whose claim was that words always contained **traces** of other words that varied from individual to individual and from each instance of usage to the next.

Jean-François Lyotard drew heavily on Wittgenstein in *The Postmodern Condition* (1979), arguing that although there had to be rules in any particular game, these were to be considered contractual only and carried no authority in themselves. In *The Differend* (1983) he developed this line to conceive of language as a series of 'phrase regimens', where each phrase that is made constitutes a link to some previous phrase, inviting further links in its turn. The critical point, however, is that those links only work within their own regimen and cannot be transferred into another. Whatever meaning is ascribed to the links ceases to apply when we move outside their home regimen. [SS]

LEGITIMATION To speak of the legitimation of a theory or political system is to speak of what gives it authority. Thus Marxism regards itself as based on scientific principles, as opposed to mere ideologies which set out to excuse the domination of one part of society by another: what legitimates Marxism is its status as a 'science of society', rigorous in execution and free of sectional interest. Similarly, Western liberal democracy takes its authority from a particular conception of the individual human being as the possessor of certain inalienable rights (right to equality before the law, to own property, to sell one's labour on the open market, etc.); the political system of Western societies is legitimated by its protection of those rights.

Thinkers like Jean-François Lyotard consider that there is a crisis of legitimation in the **postmodern** world, in that theories such as Marxism (**grand narratives** or **metanarratives** in Lyotard's terminology) have had their authority called into question to the point where there is open incredulity towards them. We can no longer rely on grand narratives to solve all our sociopolitical problems; rather, we have to realize that they are the *source* of most of these problems, by arousing hopes that they cannot fulfil. Marxism also demands uncritical acceptance of certain key principles (the desirability of the dictatorship of the proletariat, etc.), and for Lyotard this is authoritarian and a suppression of individual creativity. Generally speaking, postmodernist thinkers are suspicious of most means of legitimation in the twentieth century, tending to find authoritarianism lurking behind the scenes in some guise or another. [SS]

'THE LETTER ALWAYS ARRIVES AT ITS DESTINATION' A concept from Jacques Lacan used by Slavoj Žižek to explain the process whereby the **subject** recognizes/ misrecognizes herself as the object of ideological interpellation. This can be manifested in the form of an unrecognized piece of circular reasoning such as the concept of predestination ('my present situation has been designated for me by history: it is the only possible outcome of an incalculable and inevitable series of causes which define who I am and what I must do'). Žižek illustrates this by reference to a story in the Arabian Nights in which the hero, lost in the desert, stumbles into a cave where he finds three old wise men who are woken by his entry and greet him by saying, 'At last! You have arrived! We have been awaiting your arrival for three hundred years!'. These words appear to be addressed personally to the hero but could, of course, be addressed to anybody who had stumbled into the cave. The roots of the concept are in Lacan's 'Seminar on "The Purloined Letter"' and are wedded to the psychoanalytic idea that nothing a patient/analysand says on the couch is irrelevant. To suggest, as Jacques Derrida did, that it might be possible for a letter to fail to arrive is to misunderstand the concept: as Žižek develops it, the concept is used to explain the way in which messages generated by the symbolic order (and which necessarily have no specific addressee) are interpreted by the subject through a process in which she subconsciously writes her own name on what is otherwise a blank envelope. [PG]

LIBIDINAL ECONOMY Libidinal economy is Jean-François Lyotard's term for the various drives within human beings that resist the workings of logic and reason. These are

to be seen as analogous to the subconscious drives identified by psychoanalytical theorists such as Sigmund Freud, although Lyotard is perhaps more openly in favour of their free expression than most psychoanalytical theorists, and more prone to celebrate their anarchic, socially disordering effect. One of Lyotard's major objections to Marxism is that it fails to allow any place for these drives within its theories, seeing them as irrational and unpredictable, and therefore to be resisted. For Lyotard, however, the denial of libidinal drives in this way is an authoritarian act, and one that ultimately can only be unsuccessful: the drives will always find some means of expression and cannot be suppressed indefinitely. He goes so far as to suggest that the working class in the nineteenth century identified with industrialization as a massive outburst of libidinal energy, and that where Marxists saw simply exploitation the workers instead saw excitement, variety and change.

Libidinal economy is therefore to be regarded as a direct attack on Marxism as both a philosophy and a cultural project. In a more general sense it also constitutes a rejection of philosophy's rationalist heritage, to the extent that it has been dubbed a **post-philosophical** and even antiphilosophical notion. The context of the theory is important to note: Lyotard's book *Libidinal Economy* was published in 1974; that is, in the aftermath of the 1968 *événements* when many French left-wing intellectuals had become severely disenchanted by Marxism, largely as a result of the failure of the French Communist Party to support the anti-state cause. *Libidinal Economy* represents one of the most vicious attacks on Marxist thought of the period, and charts a sea change in Lyotard's own career. [SS]

LITTLE NARRATIVE In the **grand narratives** of Jean-François Lyotard (all-embracing explanatory theories such as Marxism or Hegelian dialectics) individuals are oppressed and find themselves being sacrificed to the objectives of those controlling the grand narrative. Thus Marxism in its Soviet model demanded that all individuals follow the Communist Party line since the Party was assumed to be the repository of all truth. Lyotard points out how this destroys individual initiative, leading to a totalitarian society where dissent is ruthlessly repressed and creativity stifled. The failings of grand narratives had, however, been well recognized by the late twentieth century (thus the collapse of the Soviet Union and its client states), and what we should now be supporting is little narratives. These are tactical groupings (or coalitions of interest) which seek to oppose specific social ills. Little narratives, of which the worker–student collaboration in the 1968 *événements* in Paris remains an outstanding example for Lyotard, are not designed to last, but merely to achieve limited, short-term objectives. One might regard the individual as the ultimate little narrative seeking to resist the **power** of authoritarian grand narratives, such as the state or multinational corporations. [SS]

LOGOCENTRICITY Logocentricity is the assumption that words can unproblematically communicate meanings present in individuals' minds such that the listener, or reader, receives them in the same way as the speaker/**author** intended. Words and meanings are therefore considered to have an internal stability. This is a standard assumption of **discourse** in Western culture, but one that has come under attack from the **deconstructionist** movement. Jacques Derrida in particular regards this as an unsustainable position to adopt, on the basis that words always carry **traces** of previous meanings, as well as suggesting other words which sound similar to the one being used. [SS]

M-THEORY Continuing the twentieth-century journey down through the sub-atomic world, physicists faced difficulties developing a **quantum** theory of gravity to integrate with a quantum field approach to electromagnetism and both the strong and weak nuclear forces to achieve a 'grand unified theory'. Many theoretical paths were plagued with problems as energy summation over all possibilities created troublesome infinities that couldn't be mathematically renormalized as before, resulting eventually in a 'standard model' that satisfied almost no-one and worried everyone. Exploring a super-symmetry theory of quantum gravity – very similar to the earlier '**string theory**' – in which particles are not viewed as points, but patterns of vibrations on very small one-dimensional strings embedded within ten dimensions, managed to avoid most of the renormalization problems.

Eventually it was realized that the five different competing versions of super-string theory and super-gravity were all related, each version valid in different circumstances. The proposed underlying theory is termed M-theory, where M is often taken to refer to 'membrane'. M-theory requires eleven dimensions (seven more than the commonly recognized four) and the way in which these extra dimensions are curled at the quantum levels of internal space give rise to different apparent laws of nature – about 10,500 possibilities in all. However, only in a very few cases would carbon-based life-forms as we know them be able to exist.

M-theory is not a single theory but rather a group of theories, each one of which is good at describing **events** within a certain range. No single theory within the group is able to describe every aspect of the universe, but where these ranges overlap the various theories agree. While this situation cannot satisfy the **modernists**' traditional quest for a single unified theory, it is considered acceptable within a framework based around 'model-dependent realism' according to Stephen Hawking.

M-theory is attractive to physicists despite the fact that it has so far failed Karl Popper's requirement of being able to make testable predictions. If modernism's long-held focus on 'testability and prediction' has to give way at this level of generality to a more **pluralistic** approach in which physicists' expectation of a single unified theory of everything becomes unworkable at the quantum level, then it will have strong implications for **postmodernism**. Having to abandon the notion of a single unique set of physical laws governing the behaviour of our universe would signal an end to the **Enlightenment** model of Newton and around 300 years of scientific modernism. [BW]

MAGIC REALISM As the term itself suggests, magic realism is a form founded on the juxtaposition of two modes of **representation** which normally exist in opposition: realism and the fantastic. Although the term is now almost exclusively associated with literature, it was originally coined by Franz Roh in 1925 to describe a form of art that portrayed scenes of fantasy and imagination through the use of clear-cut, 'documentary' painting techniques. It is, however, primarily identified with the writing of Latin America, where authors such as Gabriel Garcia Márquez, Carlos Fuentes and Octavio Paz create **narratives** in which the realistic elements of the **text** are continually being undercut by the intrusion of impossible or inexplicable **events**. In this context, magic realism is also a politicized term, since it charts the contradictory responses of a **postcolonial** culture that is engaged in the process of recovering a lost past, while remaining unable completely to escape the lingering influence of its more recent colonial history.

Since the 1970s, however, magic realism has become a fashionable label for any writing that subverts realistic expectations, and has been particularly associated with the work of writers such as Salman Rushdie, Angela Carter and Jeanette Winterson, all of whom exploit the disruptive potential of fantasy in order to pose a challenge to cultural perceptions of 'normality'. [SG]

MARKET FUNDAMENTALISM The term coined by the financier George Soros to describe the unregulated capitalism favoured by institutions such as the World Bank and the International Monetary Fund (IMF). As several commentators have pointed out, market fundamentalism involves the same kind of closed mind and unquestioning commitment to basic principles that are to be found in religious **fundamentalism**. For market fundamentalists, the market has an almost divine status: its will is law and it must be left to its own devices, with the so-called 'invisible hand' providing a self-correcting mechanism. Government intervention is strongly resisted, and national economies are expected to find their own level in competition with all others. Market fundamentalism wants to reduce the public sector to a bare minimum, and feels that the private sector is not just more efficient but morally superior.

The application of such principles in debtor countries, as a price for receipt of IMF and World Bank aid, has often had disastrous consequences, as witness the plight of Argentina in the late 1990s, when the currency and banking system collapsed, plunging the nation into political anarchy. In its belief in the authority of the market, market fundamentalism runs counter to the **postmodern** scepticism towards authority, although some postmodernist thinkers would see the market as a way of undermining traditional social and political values. [SS]

METAFICTION Postmodern literature is often described as metafictional, meaning that it has a self-conscious, self-referential quality that blurs – or at the very least explores – the distinction between the fictional world and reality. The **author** may choose to disrupt the **narrative** in a variety of ways to draw attention to its fictive status, self-consciously playing games with the reader in the process. The act of writing itself is foregrounded, with the author insisting that we recognize the artifice involved in constructing a narrative.

Although used widely of postmodernist fiction (as in the case of novelists such as John Barth, Donald Barthelme, Thomas Pynchon and Kurt Vonnegut) the term can also be read back into literary history, with Laurence Sterne's *Tristram Shandy* (published 1759–67), for example, often being cited by critics as a metafictional **text**. [SS]

METANARRATIVE Jean-François Lyotard's term (used interchangeably with **grand narrative**) for any theory claiming to provide universal explanations and to be universally valid. Marxism is probably the outstanding example of the phenomenon.

Lyotard is resolutely opposed to metanarrative, considering it to be authoritarian and restrictive to individual creativity. [SS]

METAPHYSICS OF PRESENCE The **deconstructionist** Jacques Derrida considers that the history of Western philosophy, and by implication the history of all **discourse** in the West, is marked by a commitment to what he calls '**presence**'. This is the assumption we make that we can grasp meaning in its entirety, and that when we hear a word or phrase it is totally 'present' to us in our minds. Presence is therefore an unacknowledged metaphysical assumption that we make when we engage in communication with others. Behind the metaphysics of presence lies a belief in the inherent stability of words and meanings, which, to a **poststructuralist** thinker like Derrida, invites attack. Derrida's point is that language is much more slippery than believers in presence care to admit, and that, in effect, any given word has a cluster of associations around it that undermine its supposed purity. What language features, to Derrida, is instability and indeterminacy of meaning: never any moment of full presence. Part of the reason for this inability of words to achieve full presence can be found in the nature of time. Derrida makes great play of the fact that time rolls remorselessly on, and that words are constantly being exposed to new states of affairs. There can never be any moment at which full presence, or for that matter full identity, is possible.

Full presence and full identity are two of the main assumptions on which discourse in the West is based, and by his critique of the metaphysics of presence Derrida is calling into question an entire intellectual tradition, which in his opinion is built on an illusion. In the absence of the metaphysics of presence communication appears a much more erratic and anarchic activity than we are normally led to believe, although for the deconstructionist it is also a more creative affair. [SS]

MINIMALIST MUSIC The movement towards minimalism in music began in the early 1960s in America. This movement, which was pioneered by Terry Riley, Steve Reich and Philip Glass, soon spread to Europe where it was further developed by composers such as Michael Nyman.

Minimalism can be seen as a reaction against the **modernist** aesthetics of the post-war avant-garde which came to be the norm within 'serious' concert music of the 1960s and 1970s. The minimalists rejected modernist music on the following grounds: (a) it was often complex for the sake of complexity and lacked an accessible surface level (thus modernist composers, in alienating their audiences, often harboured elitist attitudes, showing nothing but contempt for the average listener); (b) it maintained the division between 'high' and 'low' art and relegated the role of popular, jazz or folk musics to that of mindless entertainment; (c) the emphasis on dissonance, atonality and loss of regular pulse contradicted the fundamental axioms of music and, again, alienated audiences.

Minimalist music was, for the most part, ignored or vilified by the 'classical' music establishment who often labelled it 'banal', 'retrogressive' or 'not worthy of serious consideration'. Even today, a significant number of European university music departments do not include it in their undergraduate modules, regarding minimalist music as unworthy of serious academic study.

The genre has been diversifying and developing over the past few decades (the term post-minimalism often being employed to describe more recent works), but the original features of the music were: *repetition* (often, small musical fragments, maybe only one or two bars long, would be repeated (and developed) over long periods of time); *static harmony* (a sense of stasis was achieved by remaining not just within one key or mode but often on one chord for long periods of time); *rhythmic complexity* (the simplicity of the harmony was often contrasted with complex poly-rhythmic and polymetric structures); *process and impersonality* (the composers deliberately avoided self-expression and emotionalism, and maintained a detachment from the music by setting up processes which then generated the flow and structure of the music – this is most evident in the 1960s music of Steve Reich); and *cultural eclecticism* (the composers, not content to draw solely on the art tradition, often made studies of jazz, rock and non-Western musics which then informed their own work). [AB]

MISE-EN-ABYME Originally a heraldic term denoting an escutcheon bearing in its centre a miniature replica of itself, *mise-en-abyme* was used by André Gide to describe the same technique in literary **narratives**. In contemporary criticism, it has been used since the 1950s in a more general sense to describe self-reflexivity or self-consciousness in fiction. The term first gained currency in descriptions of the *nouveau roman*, particularly in the criticism of Lucian Dallenbach and Jean Ricardou.

A good example of the technique is provided by John Barth's collection *Lost in the Funhouse* (1968), in the title story of which the narrator, Ambrose, describes the difficulty of writing a story called 'Lost in the Funhouse', about a character called Ambrose who is lost in the funhouse. Other examples are the novels described in Vladimir Nabokov's *The Real Life of Sebastian Knight* (1941), the novels-within-novels of Flann O'Brien's *At Swim-Two-Birds* (1939) and Italo Calvino's *If on a Winter's Night a Traveller* (1979). The technique is not only to be found in twentieth-century fiction: Miguel de Cervantes and

Laurence Sterne contain early novelistic uses of the *mise-en-abyme*. It has become important for **postmodernism** as a way of denoting the self-reflexive nature of **representation** in general, as this is taken – accurately or otherwise – to be a central tenet of **deconstruction** and postmodern philosophy. [BD]

MODERNISM Modernism usually refers to a constellation of intellectual and, especially, artistic movements which emerged around the middle of the nineteenth century. Charles Baudelaire provided early but clear and far-reaching formulations of the doctrines of modernism. Karl Marx's dream of the global abolition of capitalism by means of a proletarian revolution is, in a sense, a modernist vision. Modernist movements included impressionism, symbolism, cubism, futurism, art nouveau, imagism and so on. By the beginning of the twentieth century, modernist doctrines came to dominate and define the whole of the literary and artistic landscape.

More specifically – if more intangibly – modernism refers to an impulse within artistic and literary circles. For modernism, one's response to the challenge of the 'modern' has become a fundamental issue. Confusions in our terminology result from the fact that modernism is a relatively late development in the history of **modernity**. By the middle of the nineteenth century, modernity had so thoroughly established itself that the sense of scandal and challenge which it once suggested has to some extent been displaced by a belief in progress and evolution. Modernism is a response to these developments which keeps alive an awareness of the conflict, upheaval and even destruction involved in modernity and modernization. With the emergence of modernism, modernity entered a new, conflict-ridden and self-conscious phase. Modernism and **postmodernism** are intimately interrelated responses to the crises of modernity. In most of its forms, modernism has been characterized by the (often desperate) hope of solving the problems of modernity, by a heightened, more radical (more absolute, more utopian) form of the 'modern'. All too often modernism has been seduced by the vision of a 'final solution' to the problems of history, and of modernity. Postmodernism's even more final solution is to give up the hope of finality. It is thus both a strict and logical continuation of modernist thought and its thoroughgoing revision or reversal. [LS]

MODERNITY **Postmodernism** is inevitably confused in its definition by being counterpoised to a whole series of impulses and ambitions which have emerged during the last, say, 500 years. Postmodernism, **postmodernity**, the postmodern: these are often treated as synonymous. Their 'modern' counterparts cannot be. Historians commonly refer to the 'early modern' as that broad period in history which encompasses the rise of capitalism, science and technology. Each new expression of these forces represented a challenge to traditional and relatively settled ways of life. In addition they brought with them challenges to the traditional authority of the Christian church and to the **legitimacy** of political power. Modernity in this sense is the precondition of the emergence of comparatively liberal regimes as well as of political theories of liberalism.

Equally characteristic of modernity, however, is the emergence of the modern state, and with it the more efficient, and sometimes more ruthless, exercise of political power. During the seventeenth century, Protestant countries, such as England and The Netherlands, suffered political upheavals and religious wars, but also succeeded in capitalist and imperial expansion

and put themselves in the vanguard of modernity. During the **Enlightenment**, modernity became an explicit and central theme of almost all significant thinkers. Modernity, in other words, came to consciousness of itself. It should be remembered that the Enlightenment, the great cultural project of the eighteenth century, was constantly defined in opposition to the continuities of traditional ways of life. It set itself against the arbitrary personal authority of political rulers and the church's dogmatic (and sometimes violent) defence of superstitious and mysterious rituals. A vision opened up of nature and eventually society (and history) being brought under human control. The Enlightenment proposed one – secular and liberal – route to modernization. Another form of modernization was represented by the absolutism of the French kings, Louis XIV, XV and XVI.

By the nineteenth century, change, transformation and periodic upheaval were increasingly seen as the norm. Doctrines of progress and evolution were and are confronted by revolutionary visionaries and the theorists of crisis and convulsion. Industrial capitalism, and subsequently (and in total opposition) communism, can both be seen to represent the historical movement of modernity. Even until very recently the 'modern' (in the form of new technology, new scientific discoveries, new patterns of behaviour) has generally been the source of enormously inflated hopes. In recent years – at least from the 1974 oil crisis – we have become much more aware of the costs and the burdens associated with modernity. Postmodernity in this sense could be characterized as the growing awareness that the 'modern' is something to which we are condemned. [LS]

N

NANOTECHNOLOGY Nanotechnology is the generic term for technology down at the nano scale of 10^{-9} metre (or one millionth of a millimetre), often involving direct manipulation and control of individual atoms and molecules to create materials with novel properties. Working at the nano scale of 1–100nm can bring you into contact with life's building blocks themselves, as a double helix of DNA has a diameter of typically 2nm. The birth of nanoscience is usually taken as the 1980s with the discovery of fullerenes and carbon nanotubes, although a possible route for working at the nanoscale had been described over 20 years earlier by the physicist Richard Feynman.

Preparation of nanomaterials proceeds in two contrasting ways: building them upwards from molecular components, often through chemical properties of 'self-assembly', or attempts to create super-miniaturized copies of machines and devices from the larger microscopic scale, as with nanoelectromechanical systems, nanoelectronics and nanorobots. Materials at the nanoscale often display significant changes from their bulk properties, so, for example, copper becomes transparent and normally inert materials such as gold can become reactive. Novel nanomaterials can be used for bulk applications and it is in this area that medical and pharmaceutical companies are interested, as with the use of titanium dioxide in suncreams and cosmetics, silver in disinfectants, clothing and food packaging for example. One of the present concerns is over environmental consequences such as downstream contamination from bulk nano-preparations, as many of them can be absorbed through the skin relatively easily with potentially worrying, but as yet largely unknown, consequences.

Nanotechnology attracts the interest of **postmodernists** as it can readily be viewed as the apogee of **modernism**'s attempts to command, control and manipulate nature down to its most fundamental level; even as a further step along the path of merging humans and technology in a vision of the modernist cybernetic organism (**cyborg**). [BW]

NARRATIVE Roland Barthes was one of the first to recognize just how narrative-based our culture had become, remarking in his essay 'Introduction to the Structural Analysis of Narratives' (1966) that 'the narratives of the world are numberless' (the list could even include stained-glass windows for Barthes). It was through narrative that we made sense of our world. Jean-François Lyotard has also made a strong case for the central cultural role of narrative, arguing in *The Postmodern Condition* (1979) that it enables traditional societies to evolve methods of value judgement without having to resort to any overarching **grand narrative** as a method of validation. Lyotard distinguishes between **little narratives** and grand ones, recommending that our culture should be based on the former rather than the latter, since, unlike grand narratives, they do not attempt to exert control over others.

The Postmodern Condition claims that grand narratives are in decline, but the dramatic growth of religious **fundamentalism** around the globe, especially since

Lyotard made his pronouncement in the late 1970s (not to mention **market fundamentalism**), casts more than a little doubt on this assessment. Preventing narratives from being turned into grand narrative remains, however, one of the major tasks of **postmodern** philosophy and cultural critique. [SS]

NEGATIVE DIALECTICS *Negative Dialectics* (1966) was the title given by Theodor W. Adorno to his philosophical magnum opus. The huge ambitions of the work include both a summation and a **deconstruction** of the legacy of what Adorno regards as the tradition of Western philosophy – stretching from classical Greece up to G. W. F. Hegel and Karl Marx. In particular, negative dialectics presupposes and incorporates the achievements of Hegel's dialectical philosophy. At the same time, Adorno seeks to hold Hegel's thought at a distance, and indeed to subject it to a painstaking deconstruction. Hegel's philosophy is historical through and through. It constitutes itself through a historical recapitulation of the ideas and principles which have constituted the whole history of the world as reflected by philosophy. Hegel's thought is dialectical in that it effects a 'reconciliation' of the whole and the part, of unity and **difference**, of individual and society, of particularity and totality. Adorno affirms the need to think in these Hegelian terms because, under late capitalism, the world tends to take on the characteristics of an integrated totality. On the other hand, Adorno asserts the need for dialectics to be thoroughly 'negative' in the sense that it should be alive to the extent of (social) oppression and (individual) repression in the integration of the 'administered world'.

Negative dialectics are needed to allow thought to think the relationships which make up the totality without itself succumbing to the totalitarian tendencies within thought itself. Adorno reverses many of Hegel's dictums. Where Hegel believed only the whole to be true, Adorno (basing himself on the state of the world as he saw it) declared, 'The whole is untrue.' In restoring the critical tension to Hegelian thinking, Adorno believed he was able to represent the perspective of suffering.

Hegel's philosophy depends on a logic which proposes 'the identity of identity and non-identity'. Negative dialectics seeks to remain true to the 'non-identical', or to that which is subjugated by thought. [LS]

NEO-MODERNISM Jürgen Habermas has argued that **modernity** is an 'unfinished' project, and there are many thinkers and artists who would agree with this claim and consider themselves as carrying forward that project's ideals. Any attempt to do so, however, has to contend with the challenge of **postmodernism**, which calls into question the ideals of modernity and **modernism** – ideals such as cultural progress and the cult of **originality** and formal experimentation in the arts. The term 'neo-modernism' has been applied to this trend, which tends to be deeply suspicious of the postmodern ethos, regarding it as lazy and lacking in creative inspiration. For Habermas, this is enough to dismiss postmodernism as neo-conservative. [SS]

NEW HISTORICISM The new historicism that emerged during the 1980s insists upon the necessity of studying literature within its historical and social contexts. Centring around the figure of Stephen Greenblatt and his journal *Representations*, new historicism's critical heartland is early **modern** culture. Prominent in new-historicist accounts of Renaissance literature are Greenblatt himself, Jonathan Goldberg and Louis Montrose. New-historicist strands are also to be found in Romantic studies (notably in the work of J. J. McGann, Marjorie Levinson and Alan Liu) and criticism of American literature (most notably

Walter Benn Michaels). A transatlantic cousin of American new historicism is the '**cultural materialism**' of British critics Jonathan Dollimore and Alan Sinfield.

New historicism repudiates new criticism's formalist tendency to address a work of art as a self-sufficient object divorced from its cultural setting. Simultaneously, new historicists argue that the American theoretical orthodoxies of the 1970s, notably **poststructuralism** and **deconstruction**, were as ahistorical in their methodologies as the critical schools – new criticism and myth criticism – which they challenged and replaced. What distinguishes the new historicism from more traditional historical criticism is its problematizing of the division between literary foreground and political background. Following Michel Foucault, it foregrounds the concept that 'history' is itself textually mediated, and problematizes the mimetic model of previous historicist criticism which viewed a **text** as simply reflecting the history around (and thus still outside) it. To use Montrose's phrase, new historicism insists upon the 'the historicity of texts and the textuality of history'.

For Greenblatt, literary works are not 'a stable set of reflections of the historical facts that lie beyond them'; they are 'places of dissension'. From this premise is developed a number of readings of Renaissance literature, many of which address issues of **power**. For some, such writings offer a subversive riposte to the dominant structures of authority, while for others their dissident potential is contained by the power of the state. Renaissance new historicism, though it quarrels with the ahistorical aspects of **postmodernist** theory, borrows heavily from some of its techniques. Greenblatt's founding document, *Renaissance Self-Fashioning* (1980) is heavily dependent upon deconstructionist terminology ('origins', 'rupture', 'inscription', etc.). The new historicism is an attempt to fuse the supposedly dissonant tendencies of post-modern thought with literary historical enquiry. Equally important is the adaptation of critical sources hitherto neglected in historicist writing, notably the work of Foucault, Lacanian neo-Freudianism and the anthropological theory of Clifford Geertz. For new historicism of the Romantic period, the French structural Marxism of Louis Althusser and Pierre Macherey is also an important influence. However, there is no systematic theoretical methodology evident in new-historicist writing: Greenblatt has argued, against two of the major figures in postmodern thought, that the 'historical relation between art and society … does not lend itself to a single, theoretically satisfactory answer of the kind that Fredric Jameson and Jean-François Lyotard are trying to provide'. Nonetheless, one can discern certain key preoccupations within this body of writing: structures of authority, the subversion/containment debate, the tendency to use anecdotes to initiate a wider cultural **narrative**, the inscription of the body within **discourse** and the social construction of identity; and, throughout all, the devotion to Jameson's injunction: 'Always historicize!'. [JStr]

NOMADISM In *Anti-Oedipus* (1972) and *A Thousand Plateaus* (1980) Gilles Deleuze and Félix Guattari put forward nomadic existence as a socio-political ideal. Nomads inhabit no fixed territory (they are '**deterritorialized**'), thus lack all the social and political structures that traditionally go along with the nation state: structures that Deleuze and Guattari consider to be repressive. Nomadism is as much an intellectual as a physical condition for these authors, representing a refusal to commit oneself to an authoritarian system of belief. It can thus be considered something of a **postmodern** ideal, and has functioned that way for many other thinkers, such as the feminist theorist Rosi Braidotti. [SS]

OEDIPUS Gilles Deleuze and Félix Guattari's term for the body of theories, processes and institutional structures by which modern psychoanalysis sets about repressing desire (or **desiring-machines**, as they refer to individual human beings). The Oedipus complex itself (with its source in classical myth) is only one aspect of this repressive mechanism, which attempts to force individuals into socially conformist behaviour such that they are more easily controlled by the political authorities. Psychoanalysis in this reading is an ideologically motivated activity, and Oedipus becomes symbolic of the authoritarianism (and even fascism) felt by the authors to be endemic to **modern** social existence. [SS]

ORIENTALISM Edward Said's pathbreaking work, *Orientalism* (1978), leans on Michel Foucault's discussion of knowledge/**power** as well as Jacques Derrida's insistence that we should '**deconstruct**' certain privileged **binary oppositions**. The words for 'Orient' and 'Occident' derive simply from Latin words for sun rising (*oriens*) and sun setting (*occidens*). Orient and occident are thus by nature entirely relative to the positioning of the observer (for inhabitants of Tokyo the sun rises in the east over Hawaii). However, as Said explains, a huge and ancient historical regime has taken this necessarily mobile and relational positioning and reduced it to a fixity, specifying, for example, the 'Near', 'Middle' and 'Far East' posed in opposition to a supposedly originary point in Europe.

Placed at this imaginary centre, Europe claims to be a **subject** able to know the 'Orient', the entire non-Western world, as an object, so exercising power over it (in his epigraph to the book, Said cites Karl Marx: 'They cannot represent themselves; they must be represented'). By bracketing the question of what may or may not be true about 'the Orient', Said opens for interrogation an extraordinary range of writing – 'not only scholarly works but also works of literature, political tracts, journalistic **texts**, travel books, religious and philological studies'.

This manoeuvre for categorizing and denigrating the Orient secures a particular notion of identity for the West: 'European culture gained in strength and identity by setting itself off against the Orient as a sort of surrogate and even underground self.' If Westerners are, as Said says, 'rational, peaceful, liberal, logical, capable of holding real values, without natural suspicion', then what he terms 'Arab-Orientals' are 'none of these things'; and of course if the Oriental is classified as none of these things this ensures that the Western subject is 'rational, peaceful, liberal' and so on.

Thus the West established a good image for itself by disavowing irrational feelings which are then projected on to an Oriental **Other**. But the repressed returns: for the West the Orient becomes the place of the unconscious itself – it must, as Said points out, open on to 'terrors, pleasures, desires', an Other which is both seductive and terrible.

Said must risk the accusation of functionalism, for in his account orientalism works only too well, perfectly hailing subjects into fixed positions (as Western or Eastern) which they are forced to take up.

Homi K. Bhabha asserts that 'there is always, in Said, the suggestion that colonial power and **discourse** is possessed entirely by the coloniser' and in response he looks for resistance to the power of orientalism. Bhabha draws on psychoanalysis to propose that orientalizing is a struggle always liable to fail since the colonial subject is constructed in 'a repertoire of conflictual positions'; these render him or her 'the site of both fixity and fantasy' in a process which cannot but be uneven, divided, incomplete (Bhabha details mechanisms through which orientalism always threatens to undo itself).

Said's analysis has been extended as a way to understand how any cultural, ethical or racial group may be 'known' and so dominated by a more powerful bloc. For example, his argument that no generalization (about 'races, types, colours, mentalities') remains a neutral description because it always makes an 'an evaluative interpretation' has been foundational for multiculturalism in the United States. [AE]

ORIGINALITY Modernist aesthetics actively encouraged originality, regarding it as one of the main criteria for assessing aesthetic value: Ezra Pound's exhortation to 'make it new' resounded throughout the movement in this respect. **Postmodernist** aesthetics, on the other hand, has tended to play this factor down, making the case instead for pastiche and **double-coding**, whereby a dialogue is opened up with the past and older artistic forms are revived. The cult of originality in modernism had not always gone down well with the general public, who could find it very alienating, especially given the lengths that modern creative artists were driven to in order to keep finding something new to say (abstract art, twelve-tone music, etc.). Postmodernism suggested that this rift could be overcome by using materials that the general public were familiar with, thus making it possible to connect with a wider audience – a practice which has enjoyed considerable success. There has been the beginnings of late, however, of a reaction against what might now be seen as the cult of pastiche by such as the **altermodern** movement, which has sought to recapture at least some of the spirit of modernism in its practice. [SS]

OTHER Postmodernists are firmly committed to defending otherness and **difference**, which they consider to be under permanent threat from the dominant ideology in our culture. Multiculturalism notwithstanding, there is still a noticeable tendency towards cultural standardization in Western societies, meaning that certain groups and belief systems can find themselves being excluded from the mainstream on a fairly regular basis. Jean-François Lyotard was very much exercised by this problem, which he treated at length in *Heidegger and 'the jews'*. The Jewish race becomes symbolic to him of the homogenizing tendency in Western culture, and of its ingrained distrust of otherness and difference, which at its worst expresses itself, as in Nazi Germany, in a defence of racial purity and then the attempt to eradicate all trace of those that are 'Other' from the historical record.

That the Other is a politically loaded concept in postmodern thought also comes through strongly in the work of Michel Foucault, whose historical investigations ('**archaeologies**' as he calls them) home in on periods when otherness is being suppressed by those in positions of **power**. Foucault proceeds to outline, for example, how the mentally unstable were locked up in asylums from the seventeenth century onwards, and how the prison system was developed to deal with criminal activity. His overall claim is that policing of social behaviour becomes institutionalized in the **modern** state, to the explicit benefit of the ruling class. To impose order in this fashion is to marginalize the Other to the point where they are rendered all but invisible within everyday life and **discourse**. [SS]

P

PAGANISM Jean-François Lyotard uses this term for the state where we make judgements without criteria. In effect, this describes the **postmodern** condition, since in that condition we no longer have any universal theories to fall back on in order to validate our criteria. Without such universal theories (whether they be theories of truth or politics) we are reduced to making judgements on a case-by-case basis, which for Lyotard is the only honest way to proceed. Lyotard finds a precedent for this method of making judgements in the work of Aristotle, whom he considers to be a particularly pragmatic thinker. Lyotard wishes to introduce this kind of pragmatism into our public life in a more general way, since it moves us away from an uncritical and slavish reliance on universal theories (**grand narratives**). In his reading of recent history, it has been this uncritical reliance which has been the source of most of our socio-political problems, in that it has sanctioned such horrors as Auschwitz and the many inhuman things done in the name of theories such as Marxism, communism and socialism. A 'pagan' society would reject such authorities and examine each demand for political action on its own merits, the assumption being that this would result in a more just society than one based on rigid rules and regulations. Judgement without preconceived criteria thus becomes one of the defining characteristics of a postmodern society. [SS]

PARADIGM SHIFT In the work of Thomas Kuhn, a paradigm is a framework of thought within which scientific enquiry takes place in any given era. Thus scientists are constrained by institutional and peer pressure to conduct enquiry within the guidelines laid down by currently accepted theories and their prescribed models of practice. This is what Kuhn refers to as 'normal science'. It is in the nature of scientific experiment, however, to generate anomalies that cannot always be explained away by current theories, and when such instances become frequent enough, science finds itself in a state of crisis that can only be resolved by the creation of a new paradigm. The new paradigm is usually **incommensurable** with the old and we then speak of a paradigm shift, or radical change in perspective. The shift from Ptolemaic to Copernican astronomy – from the Earth as the centre of the universe to the Sun as the centre – is presented by Kuhn as a classic instance of paradigm shift, where one can believe in one theory or the other, but not both.

Kuhn's theory can be applied outside the sciences, and the notion of cultural paradigm shifts is now widely accepted. One such shift might be from **modernity** to **postmodernity**, although it is also part of the postmodern outlook constantly to challenge the authoritarianism felt to be encoded within almost *any* paradigm. Postmodern thinkers are, as a rule, more concerned with contesting the validity of frameworks of thought in general than upholding their authority. [SS]

PLURALISM It has become all but an article of faith in **postmodernism** to argue against absolute notions of truth or authority, and to encourage plural interpretations of **texts** and situations instead. Thus for

Jean-François Lyotard there is no overriding **grand narrative** (or universal explanatory theory) in the political domain any more, but rather a plurality of **little narratives** seeking to achieve limited objectives. Roland Barthes argues in *S/Z* (1970) that texts are no longer to be seen as having central meanings that critics should be striving to reveal, but instead as sources of plural interpretations. **Poststructuralism** in general has encouraged that view. The idea that there can be any unquestionable central authority (whether in the political or intellectual domain) has been vigorously resisted by poststructuralists and postmodernists alike. Even truth is seen as plural: that is, not reducible to one central meaning that excludes all others, but as relative to the interpreter and situation at hand. Friedrich Nietzsche provides much of the inspiration for this view in his insistence that truth is simply an army of metaphors, available to be wielded on behalf of a specific cause. For poststructuralists and postmodernists there is no one privileged interpretation of any situation, but rather a plurality of possible interpretations. [SS]

POLYSEMY Polysemy initially referred to a single word with two or more meanings, for example 'pen' which, according to context, can mean either 'a writing instrument' or 'a small enclosure for domestic animals'. More recently, literary theorists have extended the term to include larger units of sense, such as an entire fictional work. The classic demonstration of this is *S/Z* (1970) by Roland Barthes. In this study, Barthes dissects the text of Honoré de Balzac's short story 'Sarrasine' into 512 fragments, or lexias. He then shows how five arbitrary codes (hermeneutic, proairetic, semic, cultural and symbolic) multiply meaning in each fragment. [BL]

POSTCOLONIALISM 'Colonialism' is the conquest and direct control of another people's land, a phase in the history of imperialism, which in turn is the **globalization** of the capitalist mode of production from the sixteenth century onwards. In the context of cultural production, 'postcolonialism' is 'writing after empire': the analysis of both colonial **discourse** and the writings of the ex-colonized. In relation to British imperialism, this work would have once been called 'Commonwealth literature', but the field has been transformed by the use of a variety of **postmodern** theories concerning language, gender, **subjectivity** and race. The proliferation of full-length studies, readers and conferences on the subject testifies to its importance over a range of **cultural studies**.

The two most important dates in postcolonial studies are 1947, which marks the beginning of a massive decolonization of the British Empire, and 1978, when the founding **text** of postcolonial studies was published: Edward Said's ***Orientalism***. Drawing upon the work of Michel Foucault and others, Said examines the **representation** of the Orient in Western discourse and finds there 'Europe's deepest and most recurring image of the **Other** ... a Western style for dominating, restructuring and having authority over the Orient'. Though much criticized, this book gave an impetus to the study of the culture of post-independent states, from Africa and the Caribbean to South and South-East Asia. It ushered in a period in which the literature of colonial struggle and nationalism, most importantly the writings of Frantz Fanon, was reread from various postmodernist perspectives.

More recently, 'postcolonial' has come to mean something other than 'post-independent', and includes writing that resists colonialism in all its forms. This allows postcolonial critics to examine the work of influential anti-colonialists such as Fanon and the huge body of culture affected by the imperial process from the moment of colonization to the present day. [PD]

POST-FEMINISM Post-feminism has appeared as a result of contemporary manoeuvres to discredit feminism as passé and bad. The post-feminist contention is that the dangers and damage of feminism 'prove' women are wrong to seek equality with men in a man's world. In particular, the mass media both pronounce the official equality of women and catalogue the ills that this equality brings. Post-feminist doctrine in the media encourages women to blame feminism for their exhaustion and disillusionment with equality. For instance, women's magazines make post-feminist assertions such as the following: feminism spoiled women's right to be sexually attractive, to flirt, to enjoy domestic bliss; it damaged the family, leaving young children to grow up without correct moral standards; it resulted in violence against women and by women. However, acceptance of such messages reveals the public's failure to recognize a political structure that profits, literally, from the inequalities it promotes.

Post-feminism may claim to promote 'the new', for example the new femininity or the new monogamy. But the reality is the opposite. It claims that feminism's anti-family stance has destroyed what most people see as the essential foundation of a healthy and just society, while supporting a return to traditional values. Portraying feminism as the disease of 'the terminally single woman', and women's liberation as the source of an endless catalogue of contemporary personal, social and economic evils, post-feminism creates a backlash. It defends men against blame for the oppression of women, and so produces reversals of freedom and justice: the movement for women's liberation is made to appear tyrannical and unrepresentative of the demands of women. If there is any lesson to be learned from post-feminism, it is that the openness and celebration of **postmodern** relativism can be co-opted into its opposite: an uncritical and absolutist stance. [PSA]

POSTHUMANISM One of the implications of **postmodern** thought is that we are now deemed to live in a posthumanist age as well. Humanism is identified with the discredited **Enlightenment project**, and in particular with its concentration on the cultural importance of the individual. The individual **subject** was held to be a being with a unique essence, whose goal was self-realization. It was regarded as one of the primary objectives of culture to provide the basis for such self-realization, by guaranteeing the freedom of the individual through the establishment of appropriate institutional structures (governmental, legal, educational, etc.). Various French theorists such as Claude Lévi-Strauss, Roland Barthes and Michel Foucault have argued against this conception of the subject, and can be seen to contribute in their own particular way to the dismantling of the humanist ideal. The **structuralist** Marxist philosopher Louis Althusser gave a particular boost to the development of a posthumanist consciousness by openly declaring himself to be an anti-humanist – that is, to be in opposition to the Enlightenment vision of mankind as the centre of the universe.

More recent **poststructuralist** and postmodernist thinkers such as Jean-François Lyotard, Gilles Deleuze and Félix Guattari have also consciously distanced themselves from the humanist tradition of thought, which they see as an integral component of **modernity**; as do **difference feminists**, for whom humanism is part of the patriarchal ideology they are actively seeking to shake off. [SS]

POST-INDUSTRIALISM A post-industrial society relies on service industries, knowledge production and information technology to create wealth, rather than, as in most Western societies from the time of the Industrial Revolution onwards, heavy industrial manufacture. Post-industrialism can be identified with the **postmodern,** in much the same way that industrialism, with its commitment to exploitation of the environment in the name of social progress, can with **modernism.** A concern with knowledge production is in fact now seen as one of the hallmarks of a postmodern society.

One of the great proponents of the notion of post-industrialism is the American sociologist Daniel Bell, whose highly influential study *The Coming of Post-Industrial Society* (1973) outlined the likely characteristics involved. Bell envisaged a society where there was a dramatic shift away from manufacturing to services; science-based industries took on a central role; and new elites based on services and science-based industries arose, thus altering the balance of power in that society. Most of the advanced economies in the West can now be described as post-industrial in some sense, in that they have moved significantly towards a position where services, knowledge and information have become the most valuable commodities for trading purposes. [SS]

POST-MARXISM The term 'post-Marxist' can be applied in two specific ways: to those who have rejected Marxist beliefs, and to those who have attempted to open up Marxism to more recent theoretical developments such as **poststructuralism, postmodernism,** feminism and the various new social protest movements (such as the **Greens**) that rose to prominence in the later decades of the twentieth century. In the terminology of Ernesto Laclau and Chantal Mouffe, arguably the leading theorists of post-Marxism, this would equate to being either *post*-Marxist or post-*Marxist*.

In both its main senses, post-Marxism

has become an increasingly important theoretical position from the later twentieth century onwards, with such key events as the 1968 *événements* and the collapse of the Soviet bloc in the 1980s serving as catalysts for its development. A whole generation of French intellectuals, including such high-profile figures as Jean-François Lyotard, Gilles Deleuze and Michel Foucault, took a post-Marxist turn in the aftermath of the former event, and proceeded to argue vigorously against what had hitherto been one of the major paradigms of post-war French thought. Lyotard, in *Libidinal Economy* (1974) unleashed a vicious attack on Marxist doctrine, which in many ways sounded the death-knell of the theory as a major factor in French intellectual life.

Deleuze and Guattari's *Anti-Oedipus* (1972) also represented a highly symbolic move away from uncritical acceptance of Marxist doctrine in the period. Laclau and Mouffe's *Hegemony and Socialist Strategy* (1985), with its call for a new kind of politics structured around the objectives of the new movements, as well as rejection of many key Marxist principles as outmoded, created considerable controversy in Marxist circles when it was published. The Marxist establishment has tended to argue that to incorporate ideas from other sources is to compromise the integrity and authority of Marxism itself. [SS]

POSTMODERN SCIENCE In Jean-François Lyotard's terms of reference, **postmodern** science is that form of science which seeks to discover the unknown rather the known, and is less interested in solving problems than revealing uncharted territories. Prime examples of this kind of scientific practice would be **catastrophe theory** (which Lyotard relies on heavily in his most famous work *The Postmodern Condition* (1979)), **chaos theory** and **complexity theory**. Such theories feature a host of mysterious entities (strange attractors, **dark matter**, **black holes**, etc.) that seem to defy any possibility of rational explanation, although of course we cannot prove that they will always do so. [SS]

POSTMODERNISM Postmodernism is a wide-ranging cultural movement which adopts a sceptical attitude to many of the principles and assumptions that have underpinned Western thought and social life for the last few centuries. These assumptions, which constitute the core of what we call **modernism**, include a belief in the inevitability of progress in all areas of human endeavour, and in the power of reason, as well as a commitment to **originality** in both thought and artistic expression.

As a cultural ethos, modernism is uncompromisingly forward-looking and, at least implicitly, makes the assumption that present civilization is to be considered superior to that of the past in the extent of its knowledge and the sophistication of its techniques. As an aesthetic, modernism promotes the view that originality is the highest state of artistic endeavour, and that this can best be achieved by experimentation with form. Postmodernism has turned such ideas on their head, by calling into question modernism's commitment to progress, as well as the ideology underpinning it, and encouraging a dialogue between past and present in thought and the arts. Postmodernism has therefore involved a rejection of the modernist commitment to experiment and originality, and a return to the use of older styles and artistic methods – even if this is done in an **ironic** manner. The characteristic postmodernist style is pastiche, with **authors** returning to a realist style of novel-writing, artists moving away from abstraction and back to figurative painting, and architects freely mixing old and new styles in building. Charles Jencks has spoken of the latter practice as '**double-coding**', and regards it as a way of overcoming the alienating effect of much modern architecture, which was geared towards professional practitioners rather than the public. Jean-François Lyotard has encouraged us to see postmodernism as a rejection of all-encompassing cultural theories (such as Marxism), and has argued for a much more pragmatic attitude to political life and artistic expression that simply ignores the oppressive rules laid down by **grand narrative**. Postmodernism is therefore as much an attitude of mind as a specific theoretical position in its own right.

In general, postmodernism can be regarded as part of a longer-running philosophical tradition of scepticism, which is intrinsically anti-authoritarian in outlook and negative in tone: more concerned with undermining the pretensions of other theories than putting anything positive in their place. Lyotard himself sees postmodernism and modernism as cyclical movements which alternate throughout the course of history. [SS]

POSTMODERNITY Postmodernity describes the cultural situation we are now assumed to inhabit, in the wake of **modernity**'s collapse as a cultural ethos. Modernity represented a culmination of several trends in Western culture, including the belief in economic and social improvement and, in a general sense, the inevitability of progress in human affairs (each generation having greater knowledge and technological sophistication than its predecessor). A commitment to progress was built into the politics of modernity, whether this took a capitalist or socialist form, the assumption being that the quality of life could indefinitely be improved, and that science and technology could be utilized to guarantee this. There was in effect an ideology (or **grand narrative**) of progress accepted by most nations, including those in the impoverished third world.

Postmodernity, on the other hand, is the state where scepticism is expressed about notions like the inevitable march of progress, or the necessity to continue exploiting the environment around us irrespective of the long-term effect (from that point of view the **Green Movement** can be seen as a postmodernist phenomenon). It is one of the characteristics of postmodernity that there is a decline in belief in universal theories, and a greater commitment to pragmatism in political affairs. This is accompanied by a generalized suspicion of authority and its grand narratives, and a concern to encourage diversity and cultural **difference**. Against that, it could be argued that grand narratives are still very much with us in the postmodern world in the form of religious **fundamentalism**.

How long postmodernity will last is an open question: as far as theorists like Jean-François Lyotard are concerned, the modern and the postmodern alternate over time, in which case our current phase of postmodernity may be no more than a temporary respite before another outbreak of modernity. [SS]

POST-PHILOSOPHY Reflection upon the future direction of philosophy has been a fundamental of philosophical **discourse** since the time of Socrates. But an unusually menacing aura accompanied the repeated announcements of the end of philosophy from Friedrich Nietzsche to Martin Heidegger and Jean-François Lyotard, ultimately rendering problematic the very possibility of **postmodern** philosophical discourse. At the least, post-philosophy means after philosophy conceived according to the ideals of autonomous rationality, historical progress and metaphysical truth. Post-philosophy designates the postmodern situation in which these **Enlightenment** ideals have come under criticism. But different responses can be given to this situation. The

post-philosopher queries: has philosophy come to an end or a transformation? The alternative answers offer both strong and weak versions of what comes after philosophy.

Those who seek to transform philosophy admit that an autonomous, fully transparent **subject** of rationality is no longer beyond critique, that the hoped-for progress of history under the guidance of Enlightenment philosophy has resulted in its own failure, and that a grand truth as the outcome of metaphysical reflection is wisely replaced with the 'local' character of truth. Yet these same metaphysical ideals were already being questioned by Enlightenment philosophers such as Immanuel Kant. For this reason, Kant's critiques offer a useful framework for many in the post-philosophy debates.

Those who make the stronger claim to a decisive end of philosophy find support in a radical critique of the necessity that characterizes Kantian reason. These post-philosophers insist upon the contingency of the rules, criteria and results of what counts as rational thought and action at any given time and place. They give priority to the empirical and fallible over the a priori and certain, to heterogeneity over unity, to the fragmentary over the total and to the irreducible **plurality** of **incommensurable** language games over the universality of philosophical discourse. [PSA]

POST-POSTMODERNISM Whether such an entity as post-postmodernism actually exists is open to debate, but some cultural theorists have taken to using the term to argue that we have passed beyond **postmodernism**, which in this reading becomes an essentially late twentieth-century phenomenon that has run its course. Jean-François Lyotard saw **modernism** and postmodernism as much more general terms, describing cultural movements which continually replaced each other over time in serial fashion. From that perspective post-postmodernism might be simply modernism in a new guise. More worryingly, however, given the rise of religious **fundamentalism**, post-postmodernism might instead be a regression to a much more dogmatic society of the type that modernity replaced. [SS]

POSTSTRUCTURALISM Poststructuralism is a generic term used to refer to all those theories that came to reject the principles of **structuralism**, which, from the 1950s through to the 1970s, constituted one of the most powerful movements of French intellectual enquiry. Among the theories that came to challenge the stranglehold of the structuralist paradigm were **deconstruction**, feminism and **postmodernism**, all of which can be considered as poststructuralist in that they challenged the assumptions on which structuralism was based. Structuralists had held that underlying all phenomena were deep structures that dictated how those phenomena developed (we might think of deep structure as being something in the nature of a genetic programme), and that the world was organized into a series of interlocking systems, each with its own 'grammar' of operation. All systems were amenable to structuralist analysis, given that their grammars were seen to operate in similar ways, and structuralism became an exercise in classification whose goal was the comprehensive mapping of all systems. In principle, at least, the world was completely knowable through the analysis of its systems and their grammars.

For poststructuralists this was at once too neat and also oppressive, since it seemed to allow little room for either human agency – individuals being assumed to be mere channels through which deep structure operated – or the workings of chance (an increasingly important factor in scientific enquiry in the later twentieth century). Against this essentially orderly picture of the world, deconstructionists offered a far more anarchic alternative, where **difference** rather than similarity was the defining characteristic, and where there were assumed to be many gaps and paradoxes in the workings of systems, which were not as predictable as structuralists would have had us believe. Jacques Derrida spoke of the 'innocence of becoming' rather than the predetermined working out of deep structural patterns, meaning that the future was always to be considered open and unknown. From a deconstructionist perspective structuralism was to be considered authoritarian, since the theory prescribed exactly how systems had to operate. Postmodernists, too, have reacted against the rigidity and apparent authoritarianism of the structuralist model, and have expressed similar sentiments to the deconstructionists – that is, a commitment to the open-endedness of cultural processes, and to the notion of the 'innocence of becoming'. Once again the thrust of the argument is against theories that claim to offer universal explanations of phenomena, and this dislike of totalizing theory has been a constant feature of the poststructuralist outlook. [SS]

POWER For most **postmodernist** theorists, politics is a question of power rather than morality, and their cultural analyses are often geared to revealing how the former tries to masquerade as the latter in order to present a more acceptable face to the general public. Michel Foucault's work is centrally concerned with this issue, and how the dominant group in **modern** societies has created a series of institutions – asylums, hospitals, the prison service, for example – to maintain its control over the mass of the populace. The **discourses** that resulted were based on power relations rather than any moral considerations. Political **grand narratives** (liberal democracy, Marxism, etc.)

may present themselves as a set of ideals that we all share, but in reality they are a means of keeping certain groups in power. Postmodern politics is dedicated to disrupting the power relations that had become entrenched within modernity as a cultural movement. [SS]

PRESENCE Jacques Derrida argues that Western thought in general is based on the notion of presence: that is, that the full meaning of words (or concepts) is 'present' to us in our minds when we think them, and that there is no 'slippage' between word and meaning. For Derrida, this is a metaphysical assumption that we are unjustified in making (see also **metaphysics of presence**). [SS]

Q

QUANTUM MECHANICS/PHYSICS Below the atomic level physics becomes very strange and counter-intuitive, at least when measured against everyday experience in our macro-world. In the realm of **particle physics** energy levels are not continuous, but become quantized into discrete levels – hence the term quantum mechanics. This new quantum view of the sub-atomic world came of age at the 5th Solvay conference in 1927 where topics such as the line spectra, quantized electron orbitals, double-slit interference, wave functions and electron exclusion were heatedly discussed, evolving into what is usually termed the 'Copenhagen Interpretation' of quantum mechanics; a position Albert Einstein never seemed fully to accept.

In the quantum world particles can display wave-like properties and waves display particle-like properties, as in the double slit experiment in which a beam of sub-atomic particles is fired at a pair of narrow slits beyond which there is a detection screen. The resulting interference pattern detected on the screen is highly suggestive of wave-like behaviour – like ripples passing through a grating – rather than the behaviour of particles, leading to the notion of wave-particle duality. According to Erwin Schrödinger, quantum events only exist as wave functions until we force them into behaving one way or the other by the nature of our experiment. Werner Heisenberg's uncertainty principle also places a fundamental limit on the precision with which we may simultaneously measure the position and speed of quantum particles such as electrons.

Quantum physics recognizes that to make an observation on a system you must interact with it – perhaps using a beam of light – and this stream of photons could considerably alter the behaviour of quantum particles under observation. In a Newtonian universe the past exists as a definite series of events, whereas in a quantum universe no matter how detailed our observations in the present, the unobserved past, like the future, is indefinite and exists only as unactualized possibilities. At the quantum level there is therefore no single past or history. For 'post-decision' experimental interventions action in the present has influenced an event in the past, raising interesting questions about our notions of causality.

Quantum physics offers plentiful scope for **postmodern** enquiry, especially as it stands in regard to classical physics as postmodernism does to **modernism**, and important questions relating to the nature of epistemology are raised at every turn. However it must be remembered that quantum effects take place primarily at the sub-atomic level – not in our macro-world. [BW]

QUEER THEORY In the early 1990s, there were a number of articles, conferences and special issues of journals that dealt with lesbian and gay culture by embracing the stigmatized term 'queer'. This was both to remind the reader of homophobic prejudice and to suggest a form of criticism that uses a pejorative signifier of transgressive desire and sexual instability as a metaphor to describe a category that goes beyond categories. Heavily marked by **deconstruction**, queer readings use a variety of **postmodern** theories 'to destabilize the entire system of sex regulation, that undoes **binary oppositions** such as gay/straight', as Judith Butler has argued. Identity, rather than being the essence of our being, is a '**simulation**', a contingent, provisional performance.

Queer theory produces a disturbing, profoundly philosophical kind of criticism that argues not for alternative forms of identity, but for identity's confounding. For Butler and other influential theorists of queer reading such as Eve Kosofsky Sedgwick and D. A. Miller, identity, and in particular sexual identity, is non-essentialist and formed in a material reality that is mediated through **discourse**. Some critics have argued that this formidable body of criticism plays down sexual **difference** and that its sceptical stance forbids it producing any useful or emancipatory knowledge. [PD]

R

RADICAL DEMOCRACY Ernesto Laclau and Chantal Mouffe, arguably the major theorists of **post-Marxism**, put forward the notion of radical democracy in their controversial book *Hegemony and Socialist Strategy* (1985). Their critique of Marxism argued that it was failing to cater for the many new protest movements springing up around the globe in the later twentieth century (representing ethnic and sexual minorities, for example, as well as various ecological initiatives). Marxism was held to have become a very inflexible theory incapable of adapting to changing cultural circumstances. Laclau and Mouffe wanted to maintain the spirit of Marxism in its concern to overcome social injustice, but to lose its doctrinaire quality – and radical democracy was the outcome.

Radical democracy was to involve dialogue and joint action between socialism in the broader sense and those emerging protest groups, in order to campaign for a more **pluralist** form of politics than was to be found under either communism or liberal democracy. The goal was to ensure there was a forum for minority views to be heard, instead of being marginalized by the mass political parties and the system they had built up to protect their own interests. Even commentators sympathetic towards the theory have had to concede, however, that it is rather thin on how to engineer a shift to radical democracy in the face of the opposition to be expected from entrenched political powers. [SS]

READERLY TEXTS Roland Barthes in his later, **poststructuralist**, phase (roughly from the publication of *S/Z* in 1970 onwards) distinguished between readerly and **writerly texts**. The former were taken to impose a meaning on the reader, whereas the latter invited the reader to engage in the production of textual meaning. Barthes argued in *S/Z* that readerly texts encouraged passive consumption, being designed to constrain the exercise of the reader's imagination. In such cases the **author** was exerting **power** over the reader, and readerly texts therefore played a part in maintaining the cultural status quo. It is difficult to be precise as to what constitutes a readerly text, but nineteenth-century realist novels, with their carefully worked-out plots, omniscient narrators and overt moral purpose, are probably good candidates. In these cases, as Barthes sees it, the reader is forced to respond in a predetermined way and to accept the author's world-view as expressed through the **narrative**. Reading becomes passive consumption, but passive consumption in the service of a particular socio-political structure. To argue in favour of writerly texts (where the reader is assumed to be actively involved in the production of textual meaning) is therefore to take a stance against the prevailing political and intellectual order. [SS]

RELATIVITY The underlying principle of Albert Einstein's special theory of relativity is that the laws of physics (including the speed of light *in vacuo*) must appear identical to all observers in uniform motion with respect to one another. His 1905 publication was based on the earlier failure of the

Michelson-Morley experiment to detect any difference in the speed of light arriving at earth along orthogonal paths, ruling out the possibility of a preferred frame of reference that was at rest with the previously proposed 'luminiferous ether'. From this Einstein concluded that the measurement of time intervals depends on the observer undertaking the experiment. Special relativity predicts that a clock runs faster according to an observer at rest with respect to the clock than for an observer in motion with respect to that particular clock. In effect Einstein showed that time cannot be absolute, as Newton thought, but that time and space are intimately linked together as 'space-time' and that matter and information cannot travel faster than the speed of light. Einstein's famous equation $E = mc^2$, showing the relationship between mass and energy, was also one of the conclusions of special relativity.

It took Einstein a further 11 years to incorporate the effects of observers in accelerated motion under the influence of gravity into his general theory of relativity by proposing that mass and energy distort space-time by curving it. Among the predictions of special relativity are that: clocks run slower in regions of lower gravitational potential; light bends in the presence of a gravitational field; and planetary orbits behave in a way unexpected by Newtonian gravity. These predictions have been tested extensively and found to be as accurate as the measurements themselves. On a contemporary note, errors in GPS navigation systems would make them of little use without relativistic corrections.

Einstein's theories pose tantalizing questions for **postmodernist** commentators by their foundational attack on preferred frames of reference and **discourse** on relativity. It is often overlooked that Einstein's theories are essentially a piece of classical physics *par excellence*, perhaps

the apotheosis of **modernist** philosophy expressed through science. By 1927 **quantum mechanics** was becoming well established, and this generally offers fertile ground for informed postmodernist enquiry. Einstein disliked certain probabilistic aspects of quantum mechanics, but of course it was his own work that had in effect opened the door to it. [BW]

REPRESENTATION Postmodern theories of representation take many forms. In painting, for instance, the 1970s and 1980s are said to have witnessed the reintroduction of representation accompanied by **irony**, illusion and disbelief, where content rather than form was deemed to be of central importance. These are ideas primarily associated with American theorists of painting, such as Donald Kuspit and Lawrence Alloway. In continental Europe, however, representation is figured in very different terms by philosophers of the **post-structuralist** school, with Jean-François Lyotard and Jacques Derrida, for example, pointing to the impossibility of representing reality. In their denial of 'reality' as such, works such as Lyotard's *The Postmodern Condition* (1979) and *The Differend* (1983) emphasize that the 'unpresentable' (or the **sublime**) exists. Attempts to represent the unpresentable are considered to be the defining characteristic of the avant-garde artist.

Following Derrida, **deconstructionists** concentrate on the slippery and ambivalent nature of language, and are similarly negative about the possibility of representing reality. Deconstructionist analyses of representation are **anti-foundationalist** in intent, and attack the idea that the Western philosophical tradition provides a transcendental set of beliefs which are 'truthful'. Michel Foucault, on the other hand, draws attention to the pervasiveness of **power** inside representation, particularly as it relates to institutions, and the manner in which certain representations of power are favoured at the expense of others. Consequently, a Foucauldian analysis of representation engages in a more direct fashion with questions of gender, race and class. Postmodern theorists on the left – Jean Baudrillard and Fredric Jameson, for example – argue that representation in the arts has been made impossible by the cultural **hegemony** of capitalism. [AE]

RETRO As part of its campaign against **modernism** and **modernity**, and their cult of the new and **original**, **postmodernism** has encouraged dialogue with the past. Perhaps most famously, this change of attitude towards the past can be found in Charles Jencks' notion of **double-coding**, where a deliberate attempt is made to appeal to both specialists and the general public by mixing together old and new architectural styles in one building. Such reappropriation and recontextualization of older forms and styles, often referred to as retro, has become a hallmark of the postmodern aesthetic and features prominently in areas such as art, music and fashion. In keeping with the postmodern ethos, retro often involves an **ironic** attitude towards the earlier style, and is not a simple act of homage or mere imitation – more a case of a critical comment on the cult of originality for originality's sake. [SS]

RHIZOME In *A Thousand Plateaus* (1980), Gilles Deleuze and Félix Guattari put forward the notion of the rhizome as a model for how systems should work in a **postmodern** world. Prime examples of rhizomes in the natural world would be tubers or mosses, and it is characteristic of a rhizomatic system that, as Deleuze and Guattari put it, any point on it can be connected up to any other (as in the intertwining of mosses). Rhizomes are contrasted to trees and roots, which, in Deleuze and Guattari's opinion, 'fix an order', and are thus implicitly restrictive and authoritarian. The implication is that since rhizomes do not feature the linear development pattern of trees and roots, they are more democratic and creative, thus forming a better basis for systems in a postmodern world than the tree-like hierarchies most Western societies tend to favour.

In common with their **poststructuralist** and postmodernist peers, Deleuze and Guattari are firmly opposed to hierarchy and authority, and concerned to find alternative methods of constructing networks. Something like the rhizome idea can be found in the **Internet**, which similarly allows for connections to be established between any two points of the system, as well as having no clearly identifiable 'centre', or central authority. **Hypertext** and **hypermedia** work in the same fashion. [SS]

S

SCHIZOANALYSIS A form of anti-psycho-analysis devised by Gilles Deleuze and Félix Guattari in their controversial study *Anti-Oedipus* (1972), based on the experience of the schizophrenic. The theory is that the schizophrenic provides a better model for resisting authority (as embedded in the procedures of psychoanalysis, for example), than such types as the neurotic – and resisting authority is all but an article of faith for **postmodernists** such as Deleuze and Guattari. Schizophrenics, with their multiple identities, are seen to defeat the efforts of the psychoanalyst to make them conform (that being the point of psycho-analysis, as far as Deleuze and Guattari are concerned), whereas neurotics are more likely to be induced to co-operate, thus helping to perpetuate an authoritarian system.

Psychoanalysis is regarded by the authors as a form of politically inspired social control, and the ability of schizophrenics to frustrate the process turns them into postmodernist role models. Loss of ego amounts to a politically subversive act in this respect. (See also **Oedipus**.) [SS]

SEMANALYSIS A synthesis of **semiotics**, Marxism, and Freudianism put together by Julia Kristeva in her first major work of theory, *Semiotike: Recherches pour une semanalyse* (1968). Kristeva's contention was that **semiotics** was both a critical science in its own right and a critique of science itself. She coined the term semanalysis to describe semiotics in this new critical-political role that she had designed for it, and saw her project as being very close in spirit to the structural Marxism of Louis Althusser and his disciples, with its concern to turn Marxism into a hard-edged 'science of society'. The inspiration behind the development of semanalysis, designed to provide a scientific basis for the study of all **sign** systems, came from such formal sciences as mathematics and logic. [SS]

SEMIOTICS Semiotics (or semiology) is for a **structuralist** the science of **signs**, but for a **postmodernist** merely the study of them. Ferdinand de Saussure first broke from the study of language through its history (philology) to investigate language as a structure (linguistics). For Saussure, and all subsequent semioticians, a word is made up of a material component, such as a sound, or a mark on a page, which he terms the *signifier*, and a mental component, the concept or idea represented by the signifier: the *signified*. The signifier and the signified together form a *sign*. Saussurean linguistics became the model for the investigation of all patterned human communication. If a semiotician gives her boyfriend a bunch of roses she knows that it is a sign that can be broken down into the matter of the roses, their petals and leaves – the signifier – and the message they convey: 'I love you' – the signified.

After Saussure, semiologists have concentrated on showing the influence of signs, their **power** and ubiquity. One classic illustration of the semiotic method is Roland Barthes' *Mythologies* (1957). Barthes takes various aspects of French popular culture – car adverts, wrestling, soap-powders – and analyses them to reveal the subtle meanings they convey – often sinister, conservative and repressive.

The emergence of **poststructuralism** towards the end of the 1960s meant a shift in emphasis from the signified to the signifier. In the work of Jacques Derrida and Julia Kristeva, the links between signifier and signified are broken, replaced by the **intertextual** free interplay of signifiers. Structuralists had sought to find *the* meaning of **texts**; poststructuralists revel in multiple meanings, none of which can be allowed priority.

Postmodernism takes this process one stage further. For Jean Baudrillard, present-day society is so saturated with signs pumped out by the media that it is no longer possible to distinguish between signs and reality. [AM]

SIGN In Saussurean linguistics, the sign is constituted by the union between a signifier (word) and signified (concept). This union takes place in the individual's mind, and its end product is a recognition of the meaning of the word in question. This meaning is held to be a more or less stable entity, which does not change arbitrarily or at any given individual's whim. It is shared, therefore, by all the members of a given linguistic community at a particular historical moment, although it can change over time. Saussure regarded language as a sign system, which elicited common responses from individuals, and his linguistic theories went on to form the basis for **structuralism**. Structuralist theorists took Saussurean linguistics as the model for the study of all other sign systems, demonstrating how, for example, literary genres were made up of signs (or **narrative** conventions) that signalled to readers to respond in a particular manner.

Poststructuralist theorists such as Jacques Derrida have taken a very different view of the sign, regarding it as a fractured entity which can never capture the 'full' meaning of words. One commentator on Derrida, Gayatri Chakravorty Spivak, has spoken of the sign as being 'half not there, and half not that', and as such being open to a wide range of interpretations by individuals. The sign is therefore an *unstable* entity in poststructuralist thought, and meaning shot through with ambiguity. [SS]

SIMULACRA, SIMULATION Jean Baudrillard's theories relating to simulation stem from his early work on **sign** systems in the 1970s, where he argued that commodity and sign had combined in order to form a self-referential loop within a closed 'object system'. While the collective imagination may be deceived into thinking that such signs refer to something real and solid outside the system, this is an illusion. What is being generated is a 'simulacrum', which, although the product of the system, also acts as the external referent by which it justifies its function.

In *Symbolic Exchange and Death* (1976), Baudrillard organized the history of the production of simulacra into three parts. In the 'classical' era (from the Renaissance to the Industrial Revolution), simulation takes the form of counterfeiting. This is followed by the 'industrial' era, in which techniques of mass production allow an order of infinitely reproducible objects. Finally, in our contemporary **postmodern** order, new cybernetics and communications technologies have absorbed human **subjectivity** itself into a network of busily self-replicating digital systems.

In *Simulations* (1983), Baudrillard sums up the status of the 'real' in the postmodern world. Transformed into the '**hyperreal**', which bears no relation to any reality whatsoever, it has disappeared entirely into the process of simulation, and become 'its own pure simulacrum'. [SG]

SIMULATIONISM A term used to describe a type of post-Warholian American art of the late 1970s and 1980s that explores how the mass media makes experience 'real' or' truthful'. Peter Halley, Sherrie Levine, Phillip Taaffe, Ross Bleckner, Jeff Koons and Ashley Bickerton, most of whom were influenced by the writings of Michel Foucault, Jean Baudrillard and Guy Debord, were interested in displaying a world where production meant the production of images and appetites rather than things. Two assumptions colour many of the works by these artists. First, the idea that the contemporary social order is structured by the **representations**, **signs** and values embedded in the processes of consumption. Second, the belief that the most appropriate setting for contemporary art entails engaging with or unmasking how pleasure or knowledge is transmitted in visual form.

Just as Halley, Bleckner, Taaffe and Levine replicated the styles of Barnett Newman, Frank Stella, Robert Ryman, Piet Mondrian and Kasimir Malevich, so their acts of mimicry were designed to rebut the prevailing theory that art generates its own formal purity. This enabled them to argue against the view that **modernism** was the opposite of capitalism. In abstract art, concerned as it is with fundamental orders and optical regimes, they saw the technocratic geometries of circuits, networks and other signs of the material logic of the social order. From these conceptual foundations two forms of practice were developed. On the one hand, Bickerton's self-styled 'defiant complicity' – where the cybernetic **hybridity** of the object as total platform attempts to assimilate all aspects of the infrastructural world of art. (Bickerton wanted his object to invoke 'every station of its operational life, i.e. storage, shipping, gallery access, rack reproduction'.) On the other hand, Halley's simulated **sublime**, where the painting, composed of grids, nodes, conduits and cells, confirms the priority of abstract codes and languages within a **post-industrial** social system where reality has become co-extensive to the duplication of signs within the simulated spaces of computer circuitry. [CT]

SINGULARITY In physics, a singularity is a point (described as being of infinite density) from which a series of effects unfold, but which is not itself 'caused' by anything else. The '**big bang**' theory of the universe presupposes one such singularity, claiming that it is pointless to ask what caused the big bang, or existed before it, since the big bang *itself* was the beginning of space and time – and thus of causal sequences. Some theorists have speculated that the universe might ultimately collapse back into a singularity again. There are also held to be singularities at the centre of **black holes**.

Singularities have something like the properties traditionally attributed to divinity in that they transcend physical explanations, such as those of cause and effect (the Christian God similarly creates a universe where there was not one before). The notion of singularity, with its insistence that there are limits to explanation (rather as there are with the **sublime**), appeals to the **postmodern** mind in that it provides one solution to the problem of foundations – although, philosophically speaking, it could be said to constitute rather too neat a solution to that problem. [SS]

SINTHOME Jacques Lacan's term for an irreducible quantum of enjoyment essential to the **subject**'s ability to sustain some kind of consistency, without which a patient/analysand would collapse psychologically. In French, the term constitutes an elaborate play on words which is not only a pun on 'symptom' itself but can also indicate 'Saint Tom' (i.e. Saint Thomas Aquinas), 'synthetic human' and 'healthy tone'. Lacan developed the concept to explain those symptoms which could not be dispelled by even the most thorough analysis. Sinthomes, unlike symptoms, are not coded messages from the unconscious, but packages of enjoyment which, as Slavoj Žižek puts it, are 'like a tic we compulsively repeat'. Lacan's main illustration of a sinthome is in his characterization of the manner in which James Joyce pursued his literary art (particularly the 'epiphanies') which Lacan explained as a solution to the problem of the radical absence in Joyce's early childhood of the Name-of-the-Father. For Lacan, the whole purpose of the psychoanalytic process is for the patient/analysand to achieve an identification with the symptom because the alternative would be a collapse into autism. [PG]

SITUATIONISM Formed in Italy in 1957, the Situationists were a loose grouping of disputatious political activists, writers and artists who played a significant role in the Paris uprisings of May 1968. The most prominent members of the group were Guy Debord, political theorist and author of *The Society of the Spectacle* (1967), and the artist Asger Jorn. Debord edited the group's journal, which carried articles on Vietnam, urban geography, and cultural and political issues and was full of examples of the Situationists' distinctive and influential approach to graphic design, using political slogans and doctored images from the popular press and advertising. Debord's Marxist-influenced *The Society of the Spectacle* suggests that social relations themselves are mediated through images and that we have become spectators in our own lives, while Jorn's technique of *détournement* ('over-painting' found images with political messages) was used extensively by the late 1960s underground press and by punk bands and fanzines in the 1970s. Situationism both prefigures and inaugurates important elements of **postmodern** thinking; Jean Baudrillard's **'hyperreality'** has similarities

to Debord's spectacle, while the Situationists' concept of the *dérive*, a psychogeographical 'drift' through an urban landscape, becomes the philosophical 'drifting thought' of Jean-François Lyotard. [PD]

STRING THEORY Haunted by the incompatibility of general **relativity** and **quantum mechanics**, twentieth-century physics' most recent 'theory of everything' is string theory. To combine these theories, superstring theorists explain, we need to explore the sub-atomic world at a much smaller scale, one-thousandth of one-billionth the size of a nucleus. As we descend the scale of sub-atomic particles, the theory goes, we find that the smallest – quarks – are composed of oscillating strings. Each string vibrates at a particular frequency and assumes a particular tension, like a violin string, producing quarks that will form neutrons, protons, electrons and so on, depending on the string's particular frequency. As we ascend the scale, everything dances to 'the music of the strings'. Apart from its successes in explaining '**high-energy' particle physics**, advocates of string theory hold that its mathematics also make sense of the 'low-energy' planetary gravity to which Einsteinian relativity applies.

However, in order to explain sub-atomic particles in terms that make equal sense of cosmic gravity, string theory suggests that at sub-quark scales strings 'unfold' into at least six extra dimensions. Since the energies required to observe real strings in the four dimensions we inhabit would be at least ten million billion times as high as current particle accelerators are capable of, strings remain elegant mathematical fictions that must yet explain how ten 'stringy' dimensions fold up into our apparently four-dimensional world. [IHG]

STRUCTURALISM When, in the early years of the twentieth century, Ferdinand de

Saussure began to study language as a system of interlinked units, each of which had a meaning only in relation to the system as a whole, he inaugurated one of the great movements in Western intellectual history. Saussure sought the underlying rules of language, the deep structures that must exist if language is to perform its function. These deep structures are independent of the human agents who use language, and this displacement of the human **subject** from the focus of interest is one of the characteristics of structuralism.

For Saussure, language was a system of **signs**. A sign was made up of a 'signified' – a mental component (a concept) – and the 'signifier' – a physical component (for example a sound, or a mark on paper). Each took its place in a rigid and relatively stable system of **differences**. The sound 'dog' is only capable of carrying a meaning because it is different from the sound 'dig'. Convention then ties the sound 'dog' to the image of man's best friend.

Structural linguistics became a model for researchers in the humanities who were attempting to make sense of the complex products of human cultures. The anthropologist Claude Lévi-Strauss was among the first to realize the potential of the structuralist approach. He analysed the intricate rules determining kinship relationships and, later, the myths of 'primitive' peoples in terms of simple **binary oppositions**. In both cases the linguistic/cultural structures produced by these binary oppositions are a reflection of mental structures: the shape of the social world is determined by the structure of the human mind.

After Lévi-Strauss, Roland Barthes, Michel Foucault and Jacques Lacan applied structuralist modes of analysis to, respectively, literary studies, cultural history and psychoanalysis. In each case, the aim was to find the underlying system of relationships, the structure, within which

any individual **event** could come to have a meaning.

By the late 1960s, however, a radical reaction to structuralism's ambitious claims to have explained the world had set in. Jacques Derrida and other **poststructuralists** launched a series of devastating critiques of structuralist poetics, anthropology and historiography, focusing on the inability of structuralists to understand the radicalism inherent in their own view of language. Derrida emphasized the fragility of the conventional link between signifier and signified, thus rendering 'meaning' a more elusive and slippery beast than the structuralists had supposed. [AM]

SUBALTERN THEORY *Webster's Dictionary* defines subaltern thus: 'A commissioned officer below the rank of captain/a person holding a subordinate position/particularly with reference to a related universal.' This links subalternity with the notions of *marginality* and Jacques Derrida's notion of *presence* as the subaltern **subject** is, owing to either race, class or gender, marginalized and placed in a subordinate position in relation to the determining authority of 'the centre'. In other words, the centre is designated an invariable 'presence'; it is a point of reference or authority from which norms are established. That which is outside the centre or in the margins is designated '**Other**'.

Postcolonial theorists such as Gayatri Chakravorty Spivak and the Subaltern Studies Group led by Ranajit Guha examine this process of 'Othering' by examining the way in which the signifying system of the centre, that is, colonialist discourse, renders the experience of the subaltern, or colonial subject, as irrelevant as it is outside the system of normality and convention. Thus the colonial subject is 'muted' owing to its being constructed within a disabling master **discourse**. The alternative to this silencing is espoused by Homi K.

Bhabha in his notions of 'mimicry' and 'parody' in which the subaltern's voice is characterized by inappropriate imitations of the master discourse of the centre.

Subaltern studies can be viewed as a form of postcolonial historiography which interrogates the centre from the margin using **deconstructive** and **poststructuralist** practices. It focuses attention on the function of the centre as a site of the operation of **power** and thus confers insight on the marginalized or subaltern by exposing the oppressive nature of this discourse. [AY]

SUBJECT **Postmodernism** has rejected the concept of the individual, or 'subject', that has prevailed in Western thought for the last few centuries. For that latter tradition, the subject has been a privileged being right at the very heart of cultural process. Humanism has taught us to regard the individual subject as a unified self, with a central 'core' of identity unique to each individual, motivated primarily by the **power** of reason. **Modernity** encouraged the notion of the entrepreneurial subject exploiting the world of nature and bringing it under his (the pronoun being appropriate in this case, given the patriarchal bias of modernity as a cultural movement) domination. Rights and privileges could be ascribed to that subject, whose development and self-realization came to be regarded as a central objective (if not *the* central objective) of Western culture.

This model of the subject as a rational, unified, powerful and controlling being has come under increasing attack from the days of **structuralism** onwards and, particularly in France, there has been a concerted move on the part of theorists to destabilize this model. Claude Lévi-Strauss spoke of the **death of man**, arguing that deep structures worked *through* mankind, using it as a channel; Roland Barthes spoke of the **death of the author** as a controller of **textual** meaning (the reader becoming the key element instead); Michel Foucault spoke of the modern conception of the subject as something that could be erased quite easily, rather as marks made in the sand could be. For **poststructuralists** and postmodernists, the subject is a fragmented being that has no essential core of identity, and is to be regarded as a process in a continual state of dissolution rather than a fixed identity or self that endures unchanged over time. The old model of the subject is held by such thinkers to inhibit creativity and cultural change; as Gilles Deleuze and Félix Guattari put it, 'there is no fixed subject unless there is repression'. [SS]

SUBLIME As an aesthetic concept the sublime can be traced back to classical times and the work of Longinus, but in its modern manifestation it dates from the eighteenth century and the work of Edmund Burke and Immanuel Kant. It has since come into prominence again in **postmodern** theory, particularly in the work of Jean-François Lyotard, for whom it has become an increasingly important concept in his later philosophy (much of which is a conscious dialogue with Kant).

In Burke and Kant the sublime represents a force larger than the human, which holds human beings in a state of awe. Essentially, the sublime cannot be comprehended by individuals, who can at best come to recognize the incomprehensibility of its magnitude and **power** (as in the case of the power of nature), and their inferiority before it. For Lyotard the sublime is the 'unpresentable', the element which always militates against the possibility of any complete understanding of the world. **Grand narratives** (or universal theories) always try, ultimately unsuccessfully, to deny the existence of the sublime. Great art, on the other hand, makes us aware of the unpresentable, and Lyotard proceeds to judge works of art in terms of their attitude to the unpresentable. [SS]

SUPPLEMENT In its **poststructuralist** sense, the term originates from Jacques Derrida's *Of Grammatology* (1967) and his reading of Jean-Jacques Rousseau, who is accused of devaluing writing in favour of speech. Rousseau's contention is that writing is a supplement to speech, is inessential and therefore inferior. By this reckoning, writing adds nothing affirmative to speech and is in itself unnatural, creating, according to Rousseau, a distance between those in communication, and distorting intention and meaning. Rousseau's **logocentrist** discourse is then **deconstructed** by Derrida, for whom speech and writing exist as **binary oppositions** in a 'violent' hierarchy, in which positive value is always accorded to the first term.

The French verb *suppléer* (root of *supplément*) has two meanings: in the first instance it means 'to make up' (as in adding to); it can also mean 'to take the place of' or 'to substitute'. The distinction in what seem to be oppositions is, however, difficult to maintain upon close analysis. The supplement appears as a replacement and/or addition for the terms that the deconstructionist herself has 'violently' reversed. In the endless process of deconstructive reading, the instability of the **sign** ensures that as the newly inverted hierarchy begins to take shape it too is subverted by the supplement. Other examples include active/passive and good/evil; the first term is deemed 'natural', but is subverted by the second, which is in turn supplemented by another. [DW]

T

TERRITORIALITY In Gilles Deleuze and Félix Guattari's *A Thousand Plateaus* (1980), a territoriality is any entity or institution that restricts the free flow of individual desire. The family and the state count as prime examples of territorialities, and they conspire to produce the modern **subject** – the controlled and, as Deleuze and Guattari see it, inhibited subject of liberal humanism and the **Enlightenment project**; 'there is no fixed subject unless there is repression', they insist. They argue that desire needs to be '**deterritorialized**', and they treat **nomadic** existence as some kind of ideal of deterritorialization. [SS]

TEXT In **postmodern** thought, 'text' refers not only to written materials but also to painting, architecture, information systems and to all attempts at **representation**, whatever form this may take. Jacques Derrida's famous dictum that 'there is nothing outside the text', for instance, has been badly misrepresented as a call for a kind of super-formalism. This reading of Derrida's key works has been advanced by members of the so-called Yale School, such as Geoffrey Hartman, whose work on the use of the pun in literature has been highly influential in the American academy. There is, however, more to postmodern usage of the word 'text' than an endless game of word-play. For postmodernists, it would be more accurate to state that the world is constituted by text. [DW]

TRACE As a translation of the French for a track or footprint, 'trace' indicates something that is no longer present, yet has left its mark. Understood as a structure of **difference**, trace marks a relation to what is not present. Following Emmanuel Levinas and Jacques Derrida, the structure of every linguistic sign is determined by the trace of that **other** which is forever absent. Breaking with the classical sense of an empirical mark standing for an original non-trace, its origin is equally a trace. A lack of nostalgia for what has been lost gives the term its **postmodern** distinctiveness: its differential relation to a non-origin. [PSA]

TRANS-AVANT-GARDE The term trans-avant-garde was invented by the Italian critic Achille Bonito Oliva to distinguish the works of Anselm Kiefer, Francesco Clemente, Sandro Chia, Georg Baselitz and Markus Lupertz from their **modernist** predecessors. According to Oliva, who became an important cultural commentator in the 1980s, this group of European painters, eschewing the utopian rhetoric of modernism, had escaped the burden of art history by using it as a critical platform for their elaborations of myth, will and self-expression. In place of the universalism of modernism, the trans-avant-garde would reveal the magical roots of art in the conflation of ego and symbol, thus producing a new generation of shamanic-bohemian and culturally '**nomadic**' artists. [CT]

VIRTUAL REALITY The oxymoron 'virtual reality' was coined by Jaron Lanier in 1986 to describe technology that attempts to create computer-generated interactive environments, in which users can immerse themselves by means of 3D goggles and gloves which act as computer-input devices. Initially developed in the late 1960s, virtual reality is now an increasingly common phenomenon in the world of entertainment, art, and scientific and medical research. However, in the popular imagination it still has more than a hint of the science-fictional about it, and it is therefore not surprising that the concept is capable of arousing feverish speculation and paranoia far beyond what its current capabilities would allow.

Virtual reality is certainly a common theme in contemporary science fiction, where it becomes the focus of both horror and celebration. David Cronenberg's film *Videodrome* (1982), for example, led the way in portraying it as an invasive technology which hijacks the human brain, making it incapable of distinguishing between the virtual and the real. *Videodrome* anticipates by two years what is probably the most famous fictional evocation of virtual reality: William Gibson's *Neuromancer*

(1984). Gibson's vision of the world within the computer is more equivocal than Cronenberg's, however, for he invests the concept of computer-generated worlds with a sense of vertiginous freedom, in which, free of the body's 'meat', the disembodied mind can traverse the limitless realm of **cyberspace**.

The concept of virtual reality, therefore, is inherently double-edged, offering us a window into a world of imagination and exciting possibility, while also threatening us with its implicit challenge to our assumptions concerning 'authentic' reality. With good enough technology, perhaps no one will be able to tell where the computer **simulation** ends and reality begins. Indeed, who would want to accept the limitations of the 'real', anyway, when one can be and do anything one wants in the world behind the screen – even if it means sacrificing a society of human interaction? It is such speculations that continue to energize the work of science-fiction writers and film makers, and make virtual reality a potent motif through which the increasingly tenuous status of reality within **postmodern** culture can be foregrounded and problematized. [SG]

WRITERLY TEXTS Roland Barthes divides **narrative** fiction into two main types in his **poststructuralist** study *S/Z* (1970): writerly and **readerly**. The latter comprises narratives that promote passive consumption on the part of the reader, whereas the former invites the reader to participate in the production of **textual** meaning. **Modernist** texts are good examples of the writerly category, in that the reader frequently has to fill in gaps in the narrative, thus, in Barthes' terms of reference, becoming part of the production of textual meaning. Such texts are to be regarded as 'open' to the exercise of the reader's invention and imagination. Readerly texts, on the other hand, are designed to prevent such invention and imaginative play. A candidate for this category would be the nineteenth-century realist novel, which, with its meticulously structured plot, omniscient narrator and overt moral agenda, severely constrained the nature of the reader's response.

Readerly texts are therefore in the service of the cultural status quo, whereas writerly ones help to undermine it by calling into question the extent of the **author**'s control over interpretation. Many critics have taken the line, however, that writerly texts are just as manipulative in their way as the readerly texts that Barthes accuses of being ideologically suspect. [SS]

Z

ZAPPING The technique of rapidly cutting between television channels using a remote control device, or 'zapping' as it is colloquially known, can lay claim to being one of the most characteristically **postmodern** acts. The channels themselves are treated like some kind of continuous **narrative** which can be connected together in any order at all, according to the whims of the individual viewer. There are clear similarities in this respect with the way that hypertext or the **Internet** work. The effect of zapping is to break up the flow of linear narrative and, arguably, to empower the viewer to a certain extent by giving her control over the sequencing, if not the content, of her viewing. If nothing else, the **grand narratives** of the programme makers, which demand passive viewers who consume what is given to them in a relatively uncritical manner, is challenged by the process of zapping. [SS]

BIBLIOGRAPHY

The following is a bibliography of all the texts referred to in the Preface and Part I. The original date of publication is given in square brackets after the title where appropriate.

'Abbott Turns his "Sub-Working Class Life" into Drama', *The Guardian*, 16 May 2003, www.guardian.co.uk/media/2003/may/16/broadcasting.channel4 (accessed 8 February 2011).

Abelove, Henry, 'Some Speculations on the History of "Sexual Intercourse" During the "Long Eighteenth Century" in England', in A. Parker, M. Russo, D. Sommer and P. Yeager, eds, *Nationalism & Sexualities* (London: Routledge, 1992), pp. 335–42.

Ackroyd, Peter, *Hawksmoor* (London: Hamish Hamilton, 1985).

Adair, Gilbert, *The Postmodernist Always Rings Twice: Reflections on Culture in the 90s* (London: Fourth Estate, 1992).

Adam, Ian and Tiffin, Helen, *Past the Last Post: Theorizing Post-Colonialism and Post-Modernism* (Hemel Hempstead: Harvester Wheatsheaf, 1991).

Adorno, Theodor W., *The Culture Industry: Selected Essays on Mass Culture*, ed. J. M. Bernstein (London: Routledge, 2001).

Ahmad, Aijaz, *In Theory* (London: Verso, 1992).

Aldridge, John W., *The American Novel and the Way We Live Now* (New York: Oxford University Press, 1983).

Allen, Robert C., ed., *Channels of Discourse, Reassembled: Television and Contemporary Criticism*, 2nd edn (London: Routledge, 1992).

Anderson, Pamela Sue, *A Feminist Philosophy of Religion: The Rationality and Myths of Religious Belief* (Oxford: Blackwell, 1998).

Anderson, Pamela Sue, ed., *New Topics in Feminist Philosophy of Religion: Contestations and Transcendence Incarnate* (London: Springer, 2010).

Anderson, Pamela Sue and Clack, Beverley, eds, *Feminist Philosophy of Religion: Critical Readings* (London: Routledge, 2004).

Apple, Max, *The Propheteers* (London: Faber & Faber, 1987).

Armour, Ellen, 'Beyond Belief: Sexual Difference and Religion after Ontotheology', in John Caputo, ed., *The Religious* (Oxford: Blackwell, 2001), pp. 212–16.

Arnheim, Rudolf, 'The Bauhaus in Dessau', in Anton Kaes, Martin Jay and Edward Dimendberg, eds, *The Weimar Republic Sourcebook* (Berkeley, CA: University of California Press, 1995), pp. 450–1.

Arnold, Matthew, *Culture and Anarchy: An Essay in Political and Social Criticism* (London: Smith Elder, 1869).

Asad, Talal, *Genealogies of Religion: Discipline and Reasons of Power in Christianity and Islam* (Baltimore, MD: Johns Hopkins University Press, 1993).

Auster, Paul, *The New York Trilogy* (London: Faber & Faber, 1987).

Austin, J. L., *How to Do Things with Words* (Oxford: Clarendon, 1962).

Badiou, Alain, *Saint Paul: The Foundation of Universalism*, trans. Ray Brassier (Stanford, CT: Stanford University Press, 2003).

Baker, Nicholson, *The Mezzanine* (London: Granta, 1989).

Bakhtin, Mikhail, *Rabelais and his World* [1965], trans. Helen Iswolsky (Bloomington, IN: Indiana University Press, 1984).

Barth, John, 'The Literature of Exhaustion' [1967], in Malcolm Bradbury, ed., *The Novel Today: Contemporary Writers on Modern Fiction* (Manchester: Manchester University Press, 1977).

Barth, John, *Letters: A Novel* (New York: Putnam, 1979).

Barth, John, *The Friday Book* (New York: Putnam, 1984).

Barthelme, Donald, *Unspeakable Practices. Unnatural Acts* (New York: Farrar, Strauss, 1968).

Barthes, Roland, *Image-Music-Text*, trans. and ed. Stephen Heath (London: Fontana, 1977).

Baudrillard, Jean, *The Mirror of Production* [1973], trans. Mark Poster (St Louis, MO: Telos Press, 1975).

Baudrillard, Jean, *Simulations*, trans. Paul Foss, Paul Patton and Philip Beitchman (New York: Semiotext(e), 1983).

Baudrillard, Jean, 'The Ecstasy of Communication', in Hal Foster, ed., *Postmodern Culture* (London: Pluto Press, 1985), pp. 126–34.

Baudrillard, Jean, *America* [1986], trans. Chris Turner (London: Verso, 1988).

Baudrillard, Jean, *Cool Memories* [1987], trans. Chris Turner (London: Verso, 1990).

Baudrillard, Jean, *Seduction* [1979], trans. Brian Singer (Basingstoke: Macmillan, 1990).

Baudrillard, Jean, *Baudrillard Live: Selected Interviews*, ed. Mike Gane (London: Routledge, 1993).

Baudrillard, Jean, *Symbolic Exchange and Death* [1976], trans. Iain Hamilton Grant (London: Sage, 1993).

Baudrillard, Jean, *The Transparency of Evil: Essays on Extreme Phenomena* [1990], trans. J. Benedict (London: Verso, 1993).

Baudrillard, Jean, *The Perfect Crime*, trans. Chris Turner (London: Verso, 1996).

Baudrillard, Jean, *Fatal Strategies* [1983], trans. Philip Bietchman and W. G. Niesluchowski (London: Pluto Press, 2008).

Bauman, Zygmunt, *Freedom* (Milton Keynes: Open University Press, 1988).

Bauman, Zygmunt, *Intimations of Postmodernity* (London: Routledge, 1992).

Baumbach, Joseph, *The Return of Service* (Urbana, IL: University of Illinois Press, 1979).

Baym, Nancy K., *Personal Connections in the Digital Age* (Cambridge: Polity Press, 2010).

Beauvoir, Simone de, *The Second Sex* [1949], trans. H. M. Pashley (Harmondsworth: Penguin, 1972).

Beck, Ulrich, *Risk Society: Towards a New Modernity* (London: Sage, 1992).

Bell, Bernard Iddings, *Postmodernism and Other Essays* (Milwaukee, WI: Morehouse, 1926).

Bell, Daniel, *The End of Ideology* (Cambridge, MA: Harvard University Press, 1960).

Bell, Daniel, *The Coming of Post-Industrial Society: A Venture in Social Forecasting* (London: Heinemann, 1974).

Benjamin, Walter, *Walter Benjamin: Selected Writings*, vol. 2, M. W. Jennings, ed. (Cambridge, MA: Harvard University Press, 1999).

Berger, Roger, 'Review of *Past the Last Post*', *Postmodern Culture*, 2:2 (1992).

Bernstein, Richard J., ed., *Habermas and Modernity* (Cambridge: Polity Press, 1985).

Bernstein, Richard J., *The New Constellation: The Ethical-Political Horizons of Modernity/Postmodernity* (Cambridge, MA: MIT Press, 1990).

Berry, Philippa, and Wernick, Andrew, eds, *Shadow of Spirit: Postmodernism and Religion* (London: Routledge, 1992).

Best, Steven, and Kellner, Douglas, *Postmodern Theory: Critical Interrogations* (New York: Guilford Press, 1991).

Best, Steven, and Kellner, Douglas, *The Postmodern Turn* (New York: Guilford Press, 1997).

Bhabha, Homi K., *The Location of Culture* (London: Routledge, 1994).

Bilimoria, Purushottama and Irvine, Andrew B., eds, *Postcolonial Philosophy of Religion* (Dordrecht: Springer, 2009).

Birringer, Johannes, *Theater, Theory, Postmodernism* (Bloomington, IN: Indiana University Press, 1993).

Bloch, Ernst, *The Spirit of Utopia* (Stanford, CA: Stanford University Press, 2000).

Boje, David M., *Storytelling Organizations* (London: Sage, 2008).

Boje, David M., Gephart Jr, Robert P. and Thtachenkery, Tojo J., eds, *Postmodern Management and Organization Theory* (London: Sage, 1996).

Bordo, Susan, 'Feminism, Postmodernism, and Gender-Scepticism', in L. J. Nicholson, ed., *Feminism/Postmodernism* (London: Routledge, 1990), pp. 133–56.

Bornstein, Kate, *Gender Outlaw: On Men, Women, and the Rest of Us* (New York: Vintage, 1995).

Bourdieu, Pierre, *Outline of a Theory of Practice* [1972], trans. Richard Nice (Cambridge: Cambridge University Press, 1977).

Bourriaud, Nicolas, *Postproduction: Culture as Screenplay*, trans. Jeanine Herman (New York: Lukas & Sternberg, 2002).

Bourriaud, Nicolas, *Relational Aesthetics* [1998], trans. Simon Pleasance and Fronza Woods (Dijon: Les presses du réel, 2002).

Bourriaud, Nicolas, 'Altermodern', in Nicolas Bouriaud, ed., *Altermodern: Tate Triennial* (London: Tate Publishing, 2009), pp. 11–24.

Boyne, R. and Rattansi, A., eds, *Postmodernism and Society* (London: Macmillan, 1990).

Bradbury, Malcolm, ed., *The Novel Today: Contemporary Writers on Modern Fiction* (Manchester: Manchester University Press, 1977).

Bradbury, Malcolm and Ruland, Richard, *From Puritanism to Postmodernism: A History of American Literature* (London: Routledge, 1991).

Bragg, Melvin, speech at British Academy for Film and Television Awards, 6 June 2010, www.youtube.com/watch?v=9gWcj14YF6s (accessed 23 February 2011).

Braidotti, Rosi, *Nomadic Subjects: Embodiment and Sexual Difference in Contemporary Feminist Theory* (New York: Columbia University Press, 1994).

Braidotti, Rosi, *Metamorphoses: Towards a Materialist Theory of Becoming* (Cambridge: Polity Press, 2002).

Brautigan, Richard, *The Hawkline Monster: A Gothic Western* (New York: Simon & Schuster, 1974).

Bray, Alan, *Homosexuality in Renaissance England* (London: GMP, 1982).

Bristow, Joseph, and Wilson, Angie, eds, *Activating Theory: Lesbian, Gay, Bisexual Politics* (London: Lawrence & Wishart, 1993).

Brooker, Peter and Brooker, Will, eds, *Postmodern After-Images: A Reader in Film, Television, and Video* (London: Edward Arnold, 1997).

Brooks, Ann, *Post-Feminisms: Feminism, Cultural Theory and Cultural Forms* (London: Routledge, 1997).

Brown, David, *Tradition and Imagination: Revelation and Change* (Oxford: Oxford University Press, 1999).

Burrell, Gibson, and Morgan, Gareth, *Sociological Paradigms and Organisational Analysis* (London: Heinemann, 1979).

Burroughs, William, *Naked Lunch* (Paris: Olympia, 1959).

Burroughs, William, *Nova Express* (New York: Grove, 1964).

Burroughs, William, *The Ticket That Exploded* (New York: Grove, 1967).

Burroughs, William, *The Soft Machine* (London: Calder and Boyars, 1968).

Burroughs, William, *The Place of Dead Roads* (New York: Holt, Rinehart and Winston, 1983).

Butler, Judith, *Gender Trouble: Feminism and the Subversion of Identity* (London: Routledge, 1990).

Butler, Judith, 'Gender Trouble, Feminist Theory, and Psychoanalytic Discourse', in L. J. Nicholson, ed., *Feminism/Postmodernism* (London: Routledge, 1990), pp. 324–40.

Butler, Judith, 'Imitation and Gender Insubordination', in D. Fuss, ed., *Inside/Out: Lesbian Theories, Gay Theories* (London: Routledge, 1991), pp. 13–31.

Butler, Judith, 'Revisiting Bodies and Pleasures', *Theory, Culture & Society*, 16:2 (1999), pp. 11–20.

Butler, Judith, 'Is Kinship Always Already Heterosexual?', *Differences: A Journal of Feminist Cultural Studies*, 13:1 (2002), pp. 14–44.

Butler, Judith, *Undoing Gender* (London: Routledge, 2004).

Butler, Judith, Laclau, Ernesto, and Žižek, Slavoj, eds, *Contingency, Hegemony, Universality: Contemporary Dialogues on the Left* (London: Verso, 2000).

Callinicos, Alex, *Against Postmodernism: A Marxist Perspective* (Cambridge and Oxford: Polity Press and Blackwell, 1990).

Calvino, Italo, *Cosmicomics*, trans. William Weaver (New York: Harcourt Brace Jovanovich, 1965).

Caputo, John D., ed., *The Religious* (Oxford: Blackwell, 2001).

Caputo, John D. and Scanlon, Michael J., eds, *God, The Gift, and Postmodernism* (Bloomington, IN: Indiana University Press, 1999).

Caughie, John, *Television Drama: Realism, Modernism and British Culture* (Oxford: Oxford University Press, 2000).

Chambers, Iain, *Popular Culture: The Metropolitan Experience* (London: Methuen, 1986).

Chaney, David, *The Cultural Turn: Scene-Setting Essays on Contemporary Cultural Theory* (London: Routledge, 1994).

Chodorow, Nancy, *The Reproduction of Mothering: Psychoanalysis and the Sociology of Gender* (Berkeley, CA: University of California Press, 1978).

Clough, Patricia Ticineto, *Feminist Thought: Desire, Power and Academic Discourse* (Oxford: Blackwell, 1994).

Collins, Jim, 'Postmodernism and Television', in Robert C. Allen, ed., *Channels of Discourse, Reassembled* (London: Routledge, 1992), pp. 327–53.

Collins, Jim, 'Genericity in the Nineties', in John Storey, ed., *Cultural Theory and Popular Culture: A Reader* (London: Pearson, 2009), pp. 454–71.

Collins, Patricia Hill, 'The Social Construction of Black Feminist Thought' [1989], in B. Guy-Sheftall, ed., *Words of Fire: An Anthology of African-American Thought* (New York: New Press, 1995), pp. 338–57.

Comte, Auguste, *A General View of Positivism* [1848], trans. J. H. Bridges (London: George Routledge, 1908).

Connor, Steven, *Postmodernist Culture: An Introduction to Theories of the Contemporary* (Oxford: Blackwell, 1989).

Cooper, Robert and Burrell, Gibson, 'Modernism, Postmodernism and Organizational Analysis: An Introduction', *Organization Studies*, 9:1 (1988), pp. 91–112.

Coover, Robert, *Gerald's Party* (London: Paladin, 1986).

Cowburn, Malcolm and Dominelli, Lena, 'Masking Hegemonic Masculinity: Reconstructing the Paedophile as the Dangerous Stranger', *British Journal of Social Work*, 31:3 (2001), pp. 339–415.

Cowley, Julian, 'Ronald Sukenick's New Departures from the Terminal of Language', *Critique: Studies in Contemporary Fiction*, 28:2 (1987), pp. 87–99.

Crimp, Douglas, *Pictures* (New York: Committee for the Visual Arts, 1977).

Crockett, Clayton, *A Theology of the Sublime* (London: Routledge, 2001).

Crockett, Clayton, 'Gilles Deleuze and the Sublime Fold of Religion', in Philip Goodchild, ed., *Rethinking Philosophy of Religion: Approaches from Continental Philosophy* (New York: Fordham University Press, 2002), pp. 267–80.

Crockett, Clayton, 'The Plasticity of Continental Philosophy of Religion', in Anthony Paul Smith and Daniel Whistler, eds, *After the Postsecular and the Postmodern: New Essays in Continental Philosophy of Religion* (Newcastle upon Tyne: Cambridge Scholars Publishing, 2010), pp. 299–315.

Crowley, H. and Himmelweit, S., eds, *Knowing Women: Feminism and Knowledge* (Cambridge: Polity Press, 1992).

Currie, Mark, *Postmodern Narrative Theory* (London: Macmillan, 1998).

Danielewski, Mark Z., *House of Leaves* (New York: Pantheon, 2000).

Davenport, Guy, *Eclogues: Eight Stories by Guy Davenport* (Baltimore, MD: Johns Hopkins University Press, 1993).

Debord, Guy, *The Society of the Spectacle* [1967], trans. Donald Nicholson-Smith (New York: Zone Books, 1994).

Debussy, Claude, Busoni, Ferruccio and Ives, Charles, *Three Classics in the Aesthetics of Music* (New York: Dover, 1962).

Deleuze, Gilles, *Difference and Repetition* [1968], trans. Paul Patton (London: Athlone Press, 1994).

Deleuze, Gilles, 'Seminar on Spinoza/Cours Vincennes 25/11/1980', www.webdeleuze. com/php/texte.php?cle=17&groupe=Spinoza&langue=2 (accessed 8 February 2011).

Deleuze, Gilles and Guattari, Félix, *Anti-Oedipus* [1972], trans. Robert Hurley, Mark Seem and Helen Lane (London: Athlone Press, 1984).

Deleuze, Gilles and Guattari, Félix, *A Thousand Plateaus: Capitalism and Schizophrenia* [1980], trans. Brian Massumi (London: Athlone Press, 1988).

DeLillo, Don, *White Noise* (London: Picador, 1986).

Delmar, Rosalind, 'What is Feminism?', in J. Mitchell and A. Oakley, eds, *What is Feminism?* (Oxford: Blackwell, 1986), pp. 8–33.

Derrida, Jacques, *Of Grammatology* [1967], trans. Gayatri Chakravorty Spivak (Baltimore, MD: Johns Hopkins University Press, 1976).

Derrida, Jacques, *Writing and Difference* [1967], trans. Alan Bass (Chicago: University of Chicago Press, 1978).

Derrida, Jacques, *Margins of Philosophy* [1972], trans. Alan Bass (Brighton: Harvester, 1982).

Derrida, Jacques, *The Post Card: From Socrates to Freud and Beyond* [1980], trans. Alan Bass (Chicago: University of Chicago Press, 1987).

Derrida, Jacques, *The Monolingualism of the Other, or, The Prosthesis of Origin*, trans. Patrick Mensah (Stanford, CA: Stanford University Press, 1998).

Derrida, Jacques, 'Et Cetera ...', trans. Geoff Bennington, in Nicholas Royle, ed., *Deconstructions: A User's Guide* (London: Macmillan, 2000), pp. 282–305.

Diderot, Denis, *Rameau's Nephew* [1761], trans. Leonard Tancock (Harmondsworth: Penguin, 1976).

Dilthey, Wilhelm, *Selected Works, Volume I: Introduction to the Human Sciences*, eds Rudolf A. Makkreel and Frithjof Rodi (Princeton, NJ: Princeton University Press, 1991).

Dispenza, Vincenzo, 'Encountering Management', in David Golding and David Currie, eds, *Thinking About Management: A Reflective Practice Approach* (London: Routledge, 2000), pp. 17–33.

Di Stefano, Christine, 'Dilemmas of Difference: Feminism, Modernity, and Postmodernism', in L. J. Nicholson, ed., *Feminism/Postmodernism* (London: Routledge, 1990), pp. 63–82.

Docherty, Thomas, ed., *Postmodernism: A Reader* (Hemel Hempstead: Harvester, 1993).

Doctorow, E. L., *Ragtime* (London: Macmillan, 1975).

Dolan, Jill, 'Geographies of Learning: Theatre Studies, Performance and the Performative', *Theatre Journal*, 45:4 (1993), pp. 417–41.

Dougherty, Deborah J., Borrelli, Leslie, Munir, Kamal and O'Sullivan, Allan, 'Systems of Organizational Sensemaking for Sustained Product Innovation', *Journal of Engineering and Technology Management*, 17 (2000), pp. 321–55.

Druckman, James, 'The Power of Television Images: The First Kennedy–Nixon Debate Revisited', *The Journal of Politics*, 65:2 (2003), pp. 559–71.

du Toit, Angélique, *Corporate Strategy: A Feminist Perspective* (London: Routledge, 2006).

Eco, Umberto, *The Name of the Rose*, trans. William Weaver (New York: Harcourt Brace Jovanovich, 1983).

Eco, Umberto, *Foucault's Pendulum*, trans. William Weaver (New York: Harcourt Brace Jovanovich, 1988).

Eliot, T. S., *The Complete Poems and Plays of T. S. Eliot* (London: Faber & Faber, 1969).

Elliott, Emory, ed., *Columbia History of the United States* (New York: Columbia University Press, 1988).

Enwezor, Okwui, 'Modernity and Postcolonial Ambivalence', in Nicolas Bourriaud, ed., *Altermodern: Tate Triennial* (London: Tate Publishing, 2009), pp. 25–40.

Federman, Raymond, *Double or Nothing* (Chicago: Swallow, 1971).

Federman, Raymond, ed., *Surfiction: Fiction Now … and Tomorrow* (Chicago: Swallow Press, 1975).

Federman, Raymond, *Take It or Leave It* (New York: Fiction Collective, 1976).

Federman, Raymond, 'Self-Reflexive Fiction', in Emory Elliott, ed., *Columbia History of the United States* (New York: Columbia University Press, 1988), pp. 1142–57.

Fekete, John, ed., *Life after Postmodernism: Essays on Value and Culture* (London: Macmillan, 1987).

Feuer, Jane, 'Genre Study and Television', in Robert C. Allen, ed., *Channels of Discourse, Reassembled: Television and Contemporary Criticism*, 2nd edn (London: Routledge, 1992), pp. 138–60.

Filipczak, Dorota, 'Autonomy and Female Spirituality in a Polish Context: Divining a Self', in Pamela Sue Anderson and Beverley Clack, eds, *Feminist Philosophy of Religion: Critical Readings* (London: Routledge, 2004), pp. 210–20.

Filler, Martin, 'Building in the Past Tense', *The Times Literary Supplement*, 24 March 1989, pp. 295–6.

Firestone, Shulamith, *The Dialectic of Sex: The Case for Feminist Revolution* [1970] (London: The Women's Press, 1979).

Fisher, Mark, *Capitalist Realism: Is There No Alternative?* (Ropley: O Books, 2009).

Fisher, Mark, 'They Killed Their Mother: *Avatar* as Ideological Symptom', *k-punk*, 6 January 2010, http://k-punk.abstractdynamics.org/archives/011437.html (accessed 8 February 2011).

Fiske, John, *Media Matters* (Minneapolis, MN: University of Minnesota Press, 1994).

Flandrin, J. L., *Families in Former Times: Kinship, Household and Sexuality* (New York: Cambridge University Press, 1979).

Flax, Jane, 'Gender as a Social Problem: In and for Feminist Theory', *Amerikastudien/American Studies*, 31 (1986), pp. 193–213.

Flax, Jane, 'Postmodernism and Gender Relations in Feminist Theory', in L. J. Nicholson, ed., *Feminism/Postmodernism* (London: 1990), pp. 39–62.

Forster, E. M., *Howards End* [1910], ed. Oliver Stallybrass (Harmondsworth: Penguin, 1989).

Foster, Hal, ed., *Postmodern Culture* (London: Pluto Press, 1985); originally published as *The Anti-Aesthetic: Essays on Postmodern Culture* (Port Townsend, WA: Bay Press, 1983).

Foster, Hal, *The Return of the Real: The Avant-garde at the End of the Century* (Cambridge, MA: MIT Press, 1996).

Foucault, Michel, *Madness and Civilization: A History of Insanity in the Age of Reason*, trans. Richard Howard (London: Tavistock, 1967).

Foucault, Michel, *The Order of Things: An Archaeology of the Human Sciences* [1966], trans. Alan Sheridan-Smith (New York: Random House, 1970).

Foucault, Michel, 'Power and Strategies', in *Power/Knowledge: Selected Interviews and other Writings, 1972–1977*, ed. Colin Gordon (New York: Pantheon Books, 1980).

Foucault, Michel, *The History of Sexuality*, vols I–III. vol. I: *The History of Sexuality: An Introduction* [1976], trans. Robert Hurley (Harmondsworth: Penguin, 1981); vol. II: *The Use of Pleasure* [1984], trans. Robert Hurley (Harmondsworth: Penguin, 1987); vol. III: *The Care of the Self* [1984], trans. Robert Hurley (Harmondsworth: Penguin, 1988).

Foucault, Michel, *Ethics: Subjectivity and Truth*, trans. Robert Hurley, ed. Paul Rabinow (New York: New Press, 1997).

Fowles, John, *The French Lieutenant's Woman* (London: Jonathan Cape, 1969).

Frampton, Kenneth, 'Towards a Critical Regionalism', in Hal Foster, ed., *Postmodern Culture* (London: Pluto Press, 1985), pp. 16–30.

Fraser, Nancy and Nicholson, Linda J., 'Social Criticism without Philosophy: An Encounter between Feminism and Postmodernism', in L. J. Nicholson, ed., *Feminism/ Postmodernism* (London: Routledge, 1990), pp. 19–38.

French, Philip, *Westerns* (London: Secker & Warburg, 1973).

Fried, Michael, *Three American Painters* (Cambridge, MA: Fogg Museum of Art, 1965).

Fukuyama, Francis, *The End of History and the Last Man* (London: Hamish Hamilton, 1992).

Fuller, Richard Buckminster, 'Tensegrity', *Portfolio and Art News Annual*, 4 (1961), pp. 112–27.

Fuss, D., ed., *Inside/Out: Lesbian Theories, Gay Theories* (London: Routledge, 1991).

Gass, William, *Willie Masters' Lonesome Wife* (Evanston, IL: Northwestern University Press, 1967).

Gauntlet, David, *Moving Experiences – Second Edition: Media Effects and Beyond* (London: John Libbey, 2005).

Gellner, Ernest, *Postmodernism, Reason and Religion* (London: Routledge, 1992).

Genosko, Gary, ed., *The Guattari Reader* (Oxford: Blackwell, 1996).

Gergen, Kenneth J., 'Organization Theory in the Postmodern Era', in Mike Reed and Michael D. Hughes, eds, *Rethinking Organization: New Directions in Organization Theory and Analysis* (London: Sage, 1992), pp. 207–26.

Gergen, Kenneth J., *Toward Transformation in Social Knowledge*, 2nd edn (London: Sage, 1994).

Gergen, Kenneth J., *Social Construction in Context* (London: Sage, 2001).

Gergen, Kenneth J., and Gergen, Mary M., 'Social Construction and Research as Action', in P. Reason and H. Bradbury, eds, *The SAGE Handbook of Action Research: Participative Inquiry and Practice*, 2nd edn (London: Sage, 2008).

Giedion, Sigfried, *Building in France: Building in Iron, Building in Ferro-Concrete* [1928], trans. J. Duncan Berry (Santa Monica, CA: Getty Center, 1995).

Gilligan, Carol, *In a Different Voice: Psychological Theory and Women's Development* (Cambridge, MA: Harvard University Press, 1983).

Glasgow Media Group, www.glasgowmediagroup.org/ (accessed 23 February 2011).

Goffman, Erving, *The Presentation of Self in Everyday Life* [1959] (Harmondsworth: Penguin, 1990).

Golding, David and Currie, David, eds, *Thinking About Management: A Reflective Practice Approach* (London: Routledge, 2000).

Goodchild, Philip, ed., *Rethinking Philosophy of Religion: Approaches from Continental Philosophy* (New York: Fordham University Press, 2002).

Goodwin, Andrew, 'Popular Music and Postmodern Theory', *Cultural Studies*, 5:2 (1991), pp. 174–90.

Greenberg, Clement, *Clement Greenberg: The Collected Essays and Criticism*, vols 1–4, ed. John O'Brian (Chicago: Chicago University Press, 1986–93).

Greer, Chris, *Sex Crime and the Media: Sex Offending and the Press in a Divided Society* (Cullompton: Willan, 2003).

Gripsrud, Jostein, *The Dynasty Years: Hollywood Television and Critical Media Studies* (London: Routledge, 1995).

Gripsrud, Jostein, *Understanding Media Culture* (London: Hodder Education, 2002).

Guattari, Félix, *Chaosmosis: An Ethicoaesthetic Paradigm*, trans. Paul Bains and Julian Pefanis (Bloomington, IN: Indiana University Press, 1995).

Guha, Ranajit, *Dominance without Hegemony: History and Power in Colonial India* (Cambridge, MA: Harvard University Press, 1997).

Guy-Sheftall, B., ed., *Words of Fire: An Anthology of African-American Thought* (New York: New Press, 1995).

Habermas, Jürgen, 'Modernity versus Postmodernity', *New German Critique*, 22 (1981), pp. 3–14.

Habermas, Jürgen, 'Modernity – An Incomplete Project', in Hal Foster, ed., *Postmodern Culture* (London and Concord, MA: Pluto, 1985), pp. 3–15.

Habermas, Jürgen, *The Philosophical Discourse of Modernity* [1985], trans. Frederick Lawrence (Cambridge: Polity Press, 1987).

Habermas, Jürgen, *The Structural Transformation of the Public Sphere: An Inquiry into a Category of Bourgeois Society* [1962], trans. Thomas Burger (Cambridge, MA: MIT Press, 1989).

Hall, Stuart, 'Encoding and Decoding in the Television Discourse', Occasional Paper no. 7 (Birmingham: CCCS, 1973).

Hall, Stuart, 'Television as a Medium and its Relation to Culture', Occasional Paper no. 34 (Birmingham: CCCS, 1975).

Halley, Peter, *Collected Essays 1981–1987* (Zurich and New York: Bruno Bischofberger Gallery and Sonnabend Gallery, 1987).

Halperin, David M., *Saint Foucault: Towards a Gay Hagiography* (Oxford: Oxford University Press, 1997).

Haraway, Donna, *Primate Visions: Gender, Race and Nature in the World of Modern Science* (London: Routledge, 1989).

Haraway, Donna, 'A Manifesto for Cyborgs: Science, Technology, and Socialist Feminism in the 1980s' [1985], in L. J. Nicholson, ed., *Feminism/Postmodernism* (London: Routledge, 1990), pp. 190–233.

Haraway, Donna, *Simians, Cyborgs, and Women* (London: Free Association Books, 1991).

Harding, Sandra, 'The Instability of the Analytical Categories of Feminist Theory' [1986], in H. Crowley and S. Himmelweit, eds, *Knowing Women: Feminism and Knowledge* (Cambridge: Polity Press, 1992), pp. 338–54.

Harding, Sandra, *Science and Social Inequality: Feminist and Postcolonial Issues* (Champaign, IL: University of Illinois Press, 2006).

Hartsock, Nancy, 'Foucault on Power: A Theory for Women' [1987], in L. J. Nicholson, ed., *Feminism/Postmodernism* (London: Routledge, 1990), pp. 157–75.

Hawkes, John, 'John Hawkes: An Interview', *Wisconsin Studies in Contemporary Literature*, 6 (1964), p. 149.

Hayles, N. Katharine, *How We Became Posthuman: Virtual Bodies in Cybernetics, Literature, and Informatics* (Chicago: University of Chicago Press, 1999).

Heath, Stephen, 'Representing Television', in P. Mellencamp, ed., *Logics of Television* (London: BFI, 1990), pp. 267–302.

Heidegger, Martin, *On the Way to Language* [1959], trans. Peter D. Herz (New York: Harper & Row, 1971).

Heidegger, Martin, *Poetry, Language, Thought*, trans. Alan Hofstadter (New York: Harper & Row, 1971).

Heller, Joseph, *Catch-22* (London: Jonathan Cape, 1962).

Hennessy, Rosemary, *Profit and Pleasure: Sexual Identities in Late Capitalism* (London: Routledge, 2000).

Higgins, Dick, *A Dialectic of Centuries* (New York: Printed Editions, 1978).

Hitchcock, Henry-Russell and Johnson, Philip, *The International Style*, 2nd edn (New York: W. W. Norton, 1966).

Hoggart, Richard, *The Uses of Literacy: Aspects of Working Class Life* (London: Chatto & Windus, 1957).

Hollywood, Amy, 'Practice, Belief and Feminist Philosophy of Religion,' in Pamela Sue Anderson and Beverley Clack, eds, *Feminist Philosophy of Religion: Critical Readings* (London: Routledge, 2004), pp. 225–40.

Hubbard, Phil, 'Sex Zones: Intimacy, Citizenship and Public Space', *Sexualities*, 4:1 (2001), pp. 51–71.

Hudnut, Joseph, *Architecture and the Spirit of Man* (Cambridge, MA: Harvard University Press, 1949).

Humm, Maggie, ed., *Feminisms: A Reader* (Hemel Hempstead: Harvester Wheatsheaf, 1992).

Hutcheon, Linda, *A Poetics of Postmodernism: History, Theory, Fiction* (London: Routledge, 1988).

Hutcheon, Linda, *The Politics of Postmodernism* (London: Routledge, 1989).

Huyssen, Andreas, *After the Great Divide: Modernism, Mass Culture, Postmodernism* (Bloomington, IN: Indiana University Press, 1986).

Irigaray, Luce, *This Sex Which is Not One* [1985], trans. Catherine Porter (Ithaca, NY: Cornell University Press, 1985).

Jameson, Fredric, 'Postmodernism, or, The Cultural Logic of Late Capitalism', *New Left Review*, 146 (1984), pp. 53–92.

Jameson, Fredric, 'Postmodernism and Consumer Society', in Hal Foster, ed., *Postmodern Culture* (London: Pluto, 1985), pp. 111–25.

Jameson, Fredric, 'Third World Literature in the Age of Multinational Capitalism', *Social Text* (Fall, 1986), pp. 65–88.

Jameson, Fredric, *The Ideologies of Theory: Essays 1971–1986. Vol. 2. The Syntax of History* (Minneapolis, MN: University of Minnesota Press, 1988).

Jameson, Fredric, *Postmodernism, or, The Cultural Logic of Late Capitalism* (London: Verso, 1991).

Jameson, Fredric, *The Cultural Turn: Selected Writings on the Postmodern 1983–1998* (London: Verso, 1998).

Janicaud, Dominique, 'The Theological Turn of French Phenomenology', in *Phenomenology and the "Theological Turn": The French Debate*, trans. Bernard G. Prusak (New York: Fordham University Press, 2000), pp. 3–103.

Janis, Irving L., *Victims of Groupthink* (Boston, MA: Houghton Mifflin, 1972).

Jencks, Charles, *What is Post-modernism?*, 3rd edn (London: Art and Design, 1989).

Jencks, Charles, *The Language of Post-Modern Architecture* [1975], 6th edn (London: Academy Editions, 1991).

Jenkins, Henry, 'Avatar Activism', *Le Monde Diplomatique*, September 2009, http://mondediplo.com/2010/09/15avatar (accessed 8 February 2011).

Jenks, Chris, *Childhood* (London: Routledge, 1996).

Johnson, B. S., *The Unfortunates* (London: Panther, 1969).

Jordanova, Ludmilla, *Images of Gender in Science and Medicine Between the Eighteenth and Twentieth Centuries* (Madison, WI: University of Wisconsin Press, 1989).

Joyce, James, *A Portrait of the Artist as a Young Man* [1916], ed. Chester G. Anderson (Harmondsworth: Penguin, 1977).

Joyrich, Lynn, *Re-viewing Reception: Television, Gender and Postmodern Culture* (Bloomington, IN: Indiana University Press, 1996).

Kant, Immanuel, *Critique of the Power of Judgment* [1790], trans. Paul Guyer and Eric Matthews (Cambridge: Cambridge University Press, 2000).

Kellner, Douglas, *Jean Baudrillard: From Marxism to Postmodernism and Beyond* (Cambridge: Polity Press, 1989).

Kellner, Douglas, 'Boundaries and Borderlines: Reflections on Jean Baudrillard and Critical Theory', *Illuminations: The Critical Theory Web Site*, www.uta.edu/huma/illuminations/kell2.htm (accessed 8 February 2011).

Kesey, Ken, *One Flew Over the Cuckoo's Nest* (New York: Viking, 1962).

King, Richard, *Orientalism and Religion: Postcolonial Theory, India and 'The Mystic East'* (London: Routledge, 1999).

King, Richard, 'Philosophy of Religion as Border Control: Globalization and the Decolonization of "the Love of Wisdom"', in Purushottama Bilimoria and Andrew B. Irvine, eds, *Postcolonial Philosophy of Religion* (Dordrecht: Springer, 2009), pp. 35–53.

Kirby, Alan, 'The Death of Postmodernism and Beyond', *Philosophy Now*, 58 (November/December, 2006), pp. 34–7.

Kirby, Alan, *Digimodernism: How New Technologies Dismantle the Postmodern and Reconfigure our Culture* (London: Continuum, 2009).

Kirby, Alan, 'Successor States to an Empire in Free Fall', *Times Higher Education*, 27 May 2010, www.timeshighereducation.co.uk/story.asp?storycode=411731 (accessed 8 February 2011).

Klein, Naomi, *No Logo* (London: Flamingo, 2001).

Kuhn, Annette, *The Power of the Image: Essays on Representation and Sexuality* (London: Routledge and Kegan Paul, 1985).

Kuhn, Annette, ed., *Alien Zone: Cultural Theory and Contemporary Science Fiction Cinema* (London: Verso, 1990)

Kuhn, Thomas, *The Structure of Scientific Revolutions* (Chicago: University of Chicago Press, 1962).

Laclau, Ernesto and Mouffe, Chantal, *Hegemony and Socialist Strategy: Towards a Radical Democratic Politics* (London: Verso, 1985).

Latour, Bruno, *We Have Never Been Modern*, trans. Catherine Porter (Cambridge: Cambridge University Press, 1993).

Latour, Bruno, *Reassembling the Social: An Introduction to Actor-Network-Theory* (Oxford: Oxford University Press, 2005).

Le Corbusier, *Towards a New Architecture* [1923], trans. Frederick Etchells (New York: Dover, 1986).

Le Corbusier, *The Decorative Art of Today* [1925], trans. James I. Dunnett (London: Architectural Press, 1987).

Le Doeuff, Michèle, *The Sex of Knowing*, trans. Kathryn Hamer and Lorraine Code (London: Routledge, 2003).

Leavis, F. R. and Thompson, Denys, *Culture and Environment: The Training of Critical Awareness* (London: Chatto & Windus, 1933).

Lehmann, Hans-Thies, *Postdramatic Theatre* [1999], trans. Karen Jürs-Munby (London: Routledge, 2006).

Lem, Stanislaw, *Solaris*, trans. Joanna Kilmartin and Steve Cox (London: Faber & Faber, 1961).

Lévi-Strauss, Claude, *Structural Anthropology*, vol. 1, trans. Claire Jacobson and Brooke Grundfest Shoepf (New York: Basic Books, 1963).

Lihotzky, Grete, 'Rationalization in the Household', in Anton Kaes, Martin Jay and Edward Dimendberg, eds, *The Weimar Republic Sourcebook* (Berkeley, CA: University of California Press, 1995), pp. 462–4.

Livingstone, Ira, *Between Science and Literature: An Introduction to Autopoetics* (Champaign, IL: University of Illinois Press, 2005).

Lovibond, Sabina, 'Feminism and Postmodernism', in T. Docherty, ed., *Postmodernism: A Reader* (Hemel Hempstead: Harvester Wheatsheaf, 1993), pp. 390–414.

Lull, James and Hinerman, Stephen, 'The Search for Scandal', in James Lull and Stephen Hinerman, eds, *Media Scandals: Morality and Desire in the Popular Culture Marketplace* (Cambridge: Polity Press, 1997), pp. 1–33.

Lyotard, Jean-François, *The Postmodern Condition: A Report on Knowledge* [1979], trans. Geoffrey Bennington and Brian Massumi (Manchester: Manchester University Press, 1984).

Lyotard, Jean-François (with Jean-Loup Thébaud), *Just Gaming* [1979], trans. Wlad Godzich (Manchester: Manchester University Press, 1985).

Lyotard, Jean-François, *The Differend: Phrases in Dispute* [1983], trans. George Van Den Abbeele (Manchester: Manchester University Press, 1988).

Lyotard, Jean-François, *Pacific Wall* [1975], trans. Bruce Boone (Venice, CA: Lapis Press, 1990).

Lyotard, Jean-François, *The Inhuman: Reflections on Time* [1988], trans. Geoffrey Bennington and Rachel Bowlby (Oxford: Blackwell, 1991).

Lyotard, Jean-François, *The Postmodern Explained to Children: Correspondence 1982–1985*, trans. Don Barry *et al.*, eds Julian Pefanis and Morgan Thomas (Minneapolis, MN: University of Minnesota Press, 1992).

Lyotard, Jean-François, *Libidinal Economy* [1974], trans. Iain Hamilton Grant (London: Athlone Press, 1993).

Lyotard, Jean-François, *Political Writings*, trans. Bill Readings and Kevin Paul Geiman (London: UCL Press, 1993).

Lyotard, Jean-François, *Lessons on the Analytic of the Sublime* [1991], trans. Elizabeth Rottenberg (Berkeley, CA: Stanford University Press, 1994).

Lyotard, Jean-François, *Postmodern Fables* [1993], trans. Georges Van Den Abbeele (Minneapolis, MN: University of Minnesota Press, 1997).

Lyotard, Jean-François, *Enthusiasm: The Kantian Critique of History* [1986], trans. Georges Van Den Abbeele (Stanford, CA: Stanford University Press, 2009).

McCaffery, Larry, *Postmodern Fiction: A Bio-Biographical Guide* (Westport, CT: Greenwood, 1986).

McHale, Brian, *Postmodernist Fiction* (London: Methuen, 1987).

McIntosh, Mary, 'Queer Theory and the War of the Sexes', in Joseph Bristow and Angie Wilson, eds, *Activating Theory: Lesbian, Gay, Bisexual Politics* (London: Lawrence & Wishart, 1993), pp. 30–52.

McKenzie, Jon, *Perform or Else: From Discipline to Performance* (London: Routledge, 2001).

McNair, Brian, *Striptease Culture* (London: Routledge, 2002).

McQuail, D. and Siune, K., eds, *Media Policy: Convergence, Concentration, Commerce* (London: Sage, 1998).

McRobbie, Angela, *Postmodernism and Popular Culture* (London: Routledge, 1994).

McRobbie, Angela, *The Aftermath of Feminism: Gender, Culture and Social Change* (London: Sage, 2009).

Mandel, Ernest, *Late Capitalism* (London: New Left Books, 1975).

Mandelbrot, Benoit, *The Fractal Geometry of Nature* (New York: Freeman, 1977).

Marx, Karl and Engels, Frederick, *The German Ideology* [1845] (London: Lawrence & Wishart, 1965).

Massumi, Brian, *Parables for the Virtual: Movement, Affect, Sensation* (Durham, NC: Duke University Press, 2002).

Mellencamp, P., ed., *Logics of Television* (London: BFI, 1990).

Mercer, Kobena, *Welcome to the Jungle* (London: Routledge, 1994).

Merton, Thomas, *Faith and Violence* (Notre Dame, IN: University of Notre Dame Press, 1968).

Milbank, John, *Theology and Social Theory: Beyond Secular Reason* (Oxford: Blackwell, 1990).

Milbank, John, 'Problematizing the Secular: the Post-Postmodern Agenda', in Philippa Berry and Andrew Wernick, eds, *Shadow of Spirit: Postmodernism and Religion* (London: Routledge, 1992).

Milbank, John, Pickstock, Catherine and Ward, Graham, eds, *Radical Orthodoxy: A New Theology* (London: Routledge, 1999).

Millett, Kate, *Sexual Politics* [1970] (London: Virago, 1977).

Mitchell, J. and Oakley, A., eds, *What is Feminism?* (Oxford: Blackwell, 1986).

Modleski, Tania, *Feminism without Women: Culture and Criticism in a 'Postfeminist' Age* (London: Routledge, 1991).

Morgan, Robert P., 'Rewriting Music History – Second Thoughts on Ives and Varèse', *Musical Newsletter*, 111:1 (1973), pp. 3–12.

Morley, David, *Television, Audiences and Cultural Studies* (London: Routledge, 1992).

Morris, Meaghan, *The Pirate's Fiancée: Feminism, Reading, Postmodernism* (London: Verso, 1988).

Nicholson, L. J., ed., *Feminism/Postmodernism* (London: Routledge, 1990).

Nicol, Brian, *The Cambridge Introduction to Postmodernist Fiction* (Cambridge: Cambridge University Press, 2009).

Nietzsche, Friedrich, *The Will to Power* [1901], trans. Walter Kaufmann and R. J. Hollingdale, ed. Walter Kaufmann (New York: Vintage, 1968).

Norfolk, Lawrence, *Lemprière's Dictionary* (London: Sinclair-Stevenson, 1991).

Norfolk, Lawrence, *The Pope's Rhinoceros* (London: Sinclair-Stevenson, 1996).

Norris, Christopher, *The Truth about Postmodernism* (Oxford: Blackwell, 1993).

O'Callaghan, Marion, 'Continuities in Imagination', in Jan P. Nederveen Pieterse and Bhikhu Parekh, eds, *The Decolonization of Imagination: Culture, Knowledge and Power* (London: Zed Books, 1995), pp. 22–42.

Oakley, Judith G., 'Gender-Based Barriers to Senior Management Positions: Understanding the Scarcity of Female CEOs', *Journal of Business Ethics*, 27 (2000), pp. 321–34.

Ohi, Kevin, 'Molestation 101: Child Abuse, Homophobia, and The Boys of St. Vincent', *GLQ: A Journal of Lesbian and Gay Studies*, 6:2 (2000), pp. 195–248.

Oliva, Achille Bonito, 'The International Trans-Avantgarde', *Flash Art*, 104 (1982), pp. 36–43.

Omnès, Roland, *Quantum Philosophy: Understanding and Interpreting Contemporary Science* [1994], trans. Arturo Sangalli (Princeton, NJ: Princeton University Press, 1999).

'On the Gift: A Discussion between Jacques Derrida and Jean-Luc Marion, Moderated by Richard Kearney', in John D. Caputo and Michael J. Scanlon, *God, the Gift and Postmodernism* (Bloomington, IN: Indiana University Press, 1999), pp. 54–78.

Osborne, Peter, *Philosophy in Cultural Theory* (London: Routledge, 2000).

Owens, Craig, 'The Discourse of Others: Feminists and Postmodernism', in H. Foster, ed., *Postmodern Culture* [1983] (London: Pluto, 1985), pp. 57–82.

Parker, A., Russo, M., Sommer, D. and Yeager, P., eds, *Nationalism & Sexualities* (London: Routledge, 1992).

Parker, Martin and Hassard, John, *Postmodernism and Organizations* (London: Sage, 1993).

Parry, Benita, 'Problems in Current Theories of Colonial Discourse', *Oxford Literary Review*, 9:1–2 (1987), pp. 27–58.

Participations (journal of audience and reception studies), www.participations.org/index.htm (accessed 23 February 2011)

Penley, Constance, 'Time Travel, Primal Scene and the Critical Dystopia', in Annette Kuhn, ed., *Alien Zone: Cultural Theory and Contemporary Science Fiction Cinema* (London: Verso, 1990), pp. 116–27.

Perec, Georges, *Life: A User's Manual*, trans. David Bellos (London: Collins Harvill, 1978).

Peterson, Richard A., 'The Rise and Fall of Highbrow Snobbery as a Status Marker', *Poetics*, 25 (1977), pp. 75–92.

Pieterse, Jan P. Nederveen and Parekh, Bhikhu, eds, *The Decolonization of Imagination: Culture, Knowledge and Power* (London: Zed Books, 1995).

Plantinga, Alvin, *Warranted Christian Belief* (New York: Oxford University Press, 2000).

Potter, James W., *On Media Violence* (Thousand Oaks, CA: Sage, 1999).

Prigogine, Ilya and Stengers, Isabelle, *Order Out of Chaos: Man's New Dialogue with Nature* (London: Heinemann, 1984).

Pynchon, Thomas, *V.* (London: Jonathan Cape, 1963).

Pynchon, Thomas, *The Crying of Lot 49* (Philadelphia: Lippincott, 1966).

Pynchon, Thomas, *Gravity's Rainbow* (London: Jonathan Cape, 1973).

Pynchon, Thomas, *Vineland* (London: Secker & Warburg, 1990).

Pynchon, Thomas, *Mason & Dixon* (London: Jonathan Cape, 1997).

Quaife, G. R., *Wanton Wenches and Wayward Wives: Peasants and Illicit Sex in Early Seventeenth Century England* (London: Croom Helm, 1979).

Quine, Willard van Orman, *Word and Object* (Cambridge, MA: MIT Press, 1964).

Rand, Ayn, *The Fountainhead* [1943] (London: HarperCollins, 1994).

Ray, Thomas S., 'An Evolutionary Approach to Synthetic Biology: Zen and the Art of Creating Life', *Artificial Life*, 1:1/2 (1994), pp. 195–226.

Reason, P., and Bradbury, H., eds, *The SAGE Handbook of Action Research: Participative Inquiry and Practice*, 2nd edn (London: Sage, 2008).

Reed, Ishmael, *Yellow Back Radio Broke-Down* (New York: Doubleday, 1969).

Reed, Ishmael, *Flight to Canada* (New York: Random House, 1976).

Reed, Mike, and Hughes, Michael D., eds, *Rethinking Organization: New Directions in Organization Theory and Analysis* (London: Sage, 1992).

Rich, Adrienne, *Blood, Bread, and Poetry: Selected Prose 1979–85* (New York: Norton, 1986).

Rorty, Richard, *Consequences of Pragmatism (Essays: 1972–1980)* (Brighton: Harvester, 1982).

Rorty, Richard, 'Habermas and Lyotard on Postmodernity', in Richard J. Bernstein, ed., *Habermas and Modernity* (Cambridge: Polity Press, 1985), pp. 161–75.

Royle, Nicholas, ed., *Deconstructions: A Users' Guide* (London: Macmillan, 2000).

Said, Edward, *Orientalism: Western Conceptions of the Orient*, 2nd edn (Harmondsworth: Penguin, 1995).

Salecl, Renata, *Choice* (London: Profile, 2010).

Sartre, Jean-Paul, *Search for a Method* [1957], trans. Hazel E. Barnes (New York: Vintage Books, 1968).

Saussure, Ferdinand de, *Course in General Linguistics* [1916], ed. C. Bally, A. Sechehaye and A. Reidlinger, trans. Wade Baskin (London: Peter Owen, 1960).

Schechner, Richard, *Performance Theory* (New York: Taylor & Francis, 1988).

Schoenberg, Arnold, *Letters*, trans. Ethne Wilkins and Ernst Kaiser, ed. Edwin Stein (London: Faber & Faber, 1964).

Scott, Derek B., *From the Erotic to the Demonic: On Critical Musicology* (New York: Oxford University Press, 2003).

Seamon, David, *A Geography of the Lifeworld* (New York: St. Martin's Press, 1979).

Serres, Michel and Latour, Bruno, *Conversations on Science, Culture and Time* [1990], trans. Roxanne Lapidus (Ann Arbor, MI: University of Michigan Press, 1995).

Sim, Stuart, *Irony and Crisis: A Critical History of Postmodern Culture* (Cambridge: Icon Press, 2002).

Sim, Stuart, *Fundamentalist World: The New Dark Age of Dogma* (Cambridge: Icon, 2004).

Simon, David, speaking to *Salon*, 'Everything you were afraid to ask about *The Wire*', http://dir.salon.com/ent/feature/2004/10/01/the_wire/index.html (accessed 23 February 2011).

Simon, Herbert, *Sciences of the Artificial*, 3rd edn (Cambridge, MA: MIT Press, 1996).

Simon, William, *Postmodern Sexualities* (London: Routledge, 1996).

Siune, Karen and Hultén, Olof, 'Does Public Broadcasting have a Future?', in D. McQuail and K. Siune, eds, *Media Policy: Convergence, Concentration, Commerce* (London: Sage, 1998), pp. 23–37.

Sloan, De Villo, 'The Decline of American Postmodernism', *SubStance*, 16:3 (1987), pp. 29–43.

Smith, Anthony Paul and Whistler, Daniel, eds, *After the Postsecular and the Postmodern: New Essays in Continental Philosophy of Religion* (Newcastle upon Tyne: Cambridge Scholars Publishing, 2010).

Sokal, Alan, 'Transgressing the Boundaries: Towards a Transformative Hermeneutics of Quantum Gravity', *Social Text*, 46/47 (1996), pp. 217–52.

Sontag, Susan, *Against Interpretation, and Other Essays* (New York: Dell, 1966).

Soros, George, *The Crisis of Global Capitalism: Open Society Endangered* (New York: BBS/Public Affairs, 1998).

Spencer, Herbert, *Political Writings*, ed. John Offer (Cambridge: Cambridge University Press, 1994).

Spivak, Gayatri Chakravorty, *The Post-Colonial Critic: Interviews, Strategies, Dialogues*, ed. Sarah Harasym (London: Routledge, 1990).

Steinbach, Heim, *et al.*, 'From Criticism to Complicity', *Flash Art*, 129 (1986), pp. 46–9.

Stelarc, 'Towards the Post-human: From Psycho-Body to Cyber-system', *Architectural Design [Profile 118]*, 65:11–12 (1995), pp. 90–6.

Sterling, Bruce, 'Cyberpunk in the Nineties', *Interzone*, 23 May 1998, lib.ru/STERLINGB/interzone.txt (accessed 8 February 2011).

Storey, John, *Cultural Theory and Popular Culture: An Introduction*, 5th edn (London: Pearson, 2009).

Storey, John, ed., *Cultural Theory and Popular Culture: A Reader*, 4th edn (London: Pearson, 2009).

Storey, John, *Culture and Power in Cultural Studies: The Politics of Signification* (Edinburgh: Edinburgh University Press, 2010).

Stravinsky, Igor, *Poetics of Music in the Form of Six Lessons* [1942] (Cambridge, MA: Harvard University Press, 1974).

Strinati, Dominic and Wagg, Steven, *Come On Down?: Popular Media Culture in Post-War Britain* (London: Routledge, 1992).

Sukenick, Ronald, *The Death of the Novel and Other Stories* (New York: Dial, 1969).

Sukenick, Ronald, *Out* (Chicago: Swallow, 1973).

Swift, Graham, *Waterland* (London: William Heinemann, 1983).

Tanner, Tony, *City of Words: American Fiction, 1950–1970* (London: Jonathan Cape, 1971).

Taut, Bruno, 'The New Dwelling: The Woman as Creator', in Anton Kaes, Martin Jay and Edward Dimendberg, eds, *The Weimar Republic Sourcebook* (Berkeley, CA: University of California Press, 1995), pp. 461–2.

Taylor, Frederick, *Principles of Scientific Management* (New York: Harper, 1911).

Taylor, Jeremy G., *Television Style* (London: Routledge, 2009).

Taylor, Paul and Harris, Jan, *Critical Theories of Mass Media: Then and Now* (Basingstoke: Open University Press, 2008).

Thom, René, *Structural Stability and Morphogenesis: An Outline of a General Theory of Models* [1972], trans. D. H. Fowler (Reading, MA: W. A. Benjamin, 1975).

The Times, '"Mickey Mouse" studies are no longer a laughing stock', 18 December 2008, www.timesonline.co.uk/tol/life_and_style/education/article5361672.ece (accessed 8 February 2011).

Toulmin, Stephen, *The Return to Cosmology: Postmodern Science and the Theology of Nature* (Berkeley, CA: University of California Press, 1982).

Touraine, Alain, *The Post-Industrial Society. Tomorrow's Social History: Classes, Conflicts and Culture in a Programmed Society* [1969], trans. Leonard F. X. Mayhew (New York: Random House, 1971).

Toynbee, Arnold, *A Study of History*, vols I–IX, abridged by D. C. Somervell (New York: Oxford University Press, 1947–54).

Turner, Graeme and Tay, Jinna, eds, *Television Studies after TV: Understanding Television in the Post-Broadcast Era* (London: Routledge, 2009).

Ulmer, Gregory, *Applied Grammatology: Post(e)-Pedagogy from Jacques Derrida to Joseph Beuys* (Baltimore, MD: Johns Hopkins University Press, 1985).

UNEF Strasbourg, 'On the Poverty of Student Life' (AFGES: Strasbourg, 1966), library.nothingness.org/articles/SI/en/display/4 (accessed 8 February 2011).

Vardy, Peter, *Being Human: Fulfilling Genetic and Spiritual Potential* (London: Darton, Longman and Todd, 2003).

Venturi, Robert, *Complexity and Contradiction in Architecture* (New York: Museum of Modern Architecture, 1968).

Venturi, Robert, Izenour, Steven and Brown, Denise Scott, *Learning from Las Vegas: The Forgotten Symbolism of Architectural Form*, 2nd edn (Cambridge, MA: MIT Press, 1977).

Vice, Sue, *Introducing Bakhtin* (Manchester: Manchester University Press, 1998).

Virilio, Paul, *Desert Screen: War at the Speed of Light* [1991], trans. Michael Degener (London: Continuum, 2002).

Vonnegut, Kurt, *Slaughterhouse-Five* (New York: Dial, 1969).

Waugh, Patricia, *Metafiction: The Theory and Practice of Self-Conscious Fiction* (London: Methuen, 1984).

Weick, Karl E., *Sensemaking in Organizations* (London: Sage, 1995).

Williams, Raymond, *The Long Revolution* (Harmondsworth: Penguin, 1961).

Williams, Raymond, *Television: Technology and Cultural Form* (London: Routledge, 1990).

Wilson, Elizabeth, 'Fashion and Postmodernism', in John Storey, ed., *Cultural Theory and Popular Culture: A Reader* (London: Pearson, 2009), pp. 444–53.

Winkler, Karen J., 'After Postmodernism: A Historian Reflects on Where the Field is Going', *Chronicle of Higher Education*, January 2009, http://chronicle.com/article/After-Postmodernism-A/42181 (accessed 8 February 2011).

Wollstonecraft, Mary, *A Vindication of the Rights of Woman* [1792] (Harmondsworth: Penguin, 1992).

Wood, Michael, 'At the Movies', *London Review of Books*, 14 August 2008, p. 32.

Wood, William, 'On the New Analytic Theology; or, the Road Less Traveled,' *Journal of the American Academy of Religion*, 77:4 (December 2009), pp. 941–60.

Wrigley, E. A., 'Growth of Population in Eighteenth-Century England: A Conundrum Resolved', *Past and Present*, 98 (1983), pp. 121–50.

Young, Robert, *White Mythologies: Writing History and the West* (London: Routledge, 1990).

Young, Robert, 'Deconstruction and the Postcolonial', in Nicholas Royle, ed., *Deconstruction: A User's Guide* (London: Macmillan, 2000), pp. 187–210.

Ziman, John, ed., *Technological Innovation as an Evolutionary Process* (Cambridge: Cambridge University Press, 2000).

Žižek, Slavoj, *The Sublime Object of Ideology* (London: Verso, 1989).

Žižek, Slavoj, 'Class Struggle or Postmodernism? Yes, Please!', in Judith Butler, Ernesto Laclau and Slavoj Žižek, eds, *Contingency, Hegemony, Universality: Contemporary Dialogues on the Left* (London: Verso, 2000), pp. 90–135.

Žižek, Slavoj, *Welcome to the Desert of the Real* (London: Verso, 2002).

Žižek, Slavoj, *Violence: Six Sideways Reflections* (London: Profile, 2008).

Žižek, Slavoj, 'Return of the Natives', *New Statesman*, 4 March 2010, www.newstatesman.com/film/2010/03/avatar-reality-love-couple-sex (accessed 8 February 2011).

INDEX

The index covers the Preface and Part I. Any critical terms that subsequently appear in Part II are given in **bold** type. Readers are encouraged to consult both the index and the alphabetically-listed entries in Part II when searching for other terms.

www.routledge.com/literature

The Ideal Companion to
The Routledge Companion to Postmodernism

The Routledge Companion to Critical Theory

Edited by **Paul Wake, Simon Malpas**

The Routledge Companion to Critical Theory is an indispensable aid for anyone approaching this exciting field of study for the first time.

By exploring ideas from a diverse range of disciplines, 'theory' encourages us to develop a deeper understanding of how we approach the written word. This book defines what is generically referred to as 'critical theory', and guides readers through some of the most complex and fundamental concepts in the field, ranging from Historicism to Postmodernism, from Psychoanalytic Criticism to Race and Postcoloniality.

Fully cross referenced throughout, the book encompasses manageable introductions to important ideas followed by a dictionary of terms and thinkers which students are likely to encounter. Further reading is offered to guide students to crucial primary essays and introductory chapters on each concept.

Pb: 978-0-415-33296-5
Hb: 978-0-415-33295-8
eBook: 978-0-203-41268-8

For more information and to order a copy visit
www.routledge.com/9780415332965

Available from all good bookshops